STRIVE FOR A

STRIVE FOR A 5

Preparing for the AP® European History Exam

Louise Forsyth
Poly Prep Country Day School

A HISTORY OF WESTERN SOCIETY
Eleventh Edition

John P. McKay
Merry E. Wiesner-Hanks
Clare Haru Crowston
Joe Perry

Bedford/St. Martin's   Boston ◆ New York

Manufactured in the United States of America.

e   8   7   6

For information, write: Bedford/St. Martin's, 75 Arlington Street, Boston, MA 02116 (617-399-4000)

ISBN 978-1-4576-5268-4

AP is a trademark registered by the College Board, which was not involved in the production of, and does not endorse, this product.

Brief Contents

SECTION 1
Strategies for the AP Exam   1

Preparing for the AP European History Exam   3

Taking the AP European History Exam   9

SECTION 2
A Review of AP European History   31

Part 1: The Fourteenth Through Sixteenth Centuries   33
Practice Exam 1   54
Answer Key for Practice Exam 1   76

Part 2: The Seventeenth and Eighteenth Centuries   97
Practice Exam 2   117
Answer Key for Practice Exam 2   141

Part 3: The Long Nineteenth Century   161
Practice Exam 3   195
Answer Key for Practice Exam 3   224

Part 4: The Twentieth Century to the Present   243
Practice Exam 4   276
Answer Key for Practice Exam 4   302

Contents

Preface for Teachers   ix
About the Author   x

SECTION 1
Strategies for the AP Exam   1

Preparing for the AP European History Exam   **3**
What's in This Book?   3
Registering for the Exam   4
Familiarizing Yourself with the Exam   5
Setting Up a Review Schedule   5
How the Exams Are Scored   6

Taking the AP European History Exam   **9**
Types of Multiple-Choice Questions   9
Strategies for the Multiple-Choice Section   15
Strategies for the Free-Response Questions   15
The Document-Based Question Essay   17
The Thematic Essay Questions   20
Calculating Your Score on a Practice Exam   26

SECTION 2
A Review of AP European History   31

Part 1: The Fourteenth Through Sixteenth Centuries   **33**
Chapter 11: The Later Middle Ages, 1300–1450   37
Chapter 12: European Society in the Age of the Renaissance,
          1350–1550   41
Chapter 13: Reformations and Religious Wars, 1500–1600   46
Chapter 14: European Exploration and Conquest, 1450–1650   50
Practice Exam 1   **54**
Answer Key for Practice Exam 1   **76**

Part 2: The Seventeenth and Eighteenth Centuries   97

Chapter 15: Absolutism and Constitutionalism, ca. 1589–1725   101
Chapter 16: Toward a New Worldview, 1540–1789   106
Chapter 17: The Expansion of Europe, 1650–1800   110
Chapter 18: Life in the Era of Expansion, 1650–1800   114
Practice Exam 2   117
Answer Key for Practice Exam 2   141

Part 3: The Long Nineteenth Century   161

Chapter 19: Revolutions in Politics, 1775–1815   165
Chapter 20: The Revolution in Energy and Industry,
      ca. 1780–1850   171
Chapter 21: Ideologies and Upheavals, 1815–1850   175
Chapter 22: Life in the Emerging Urban Society, 1840–1914   180
Chapter 23: The Age of Nationalism, 1850–1914   185
Chapter 24: The West and the World, 1815–1914   190
Practice Exam 3   195
Answer Key for Practice Exam 3   224

Part 4: The Twentieth Century to the Present   243

Chapter 25: War and Revolution, 1914–1919   247
Chapter 26: The Age of Anxiety, 1880–1940   251
Chapter 27: Dictatorships and the Second World War,
      1919–1945   257
Chapter 28: Cold War Conflict and Consensus, 1945–1965   262
Chapter 29: Challenging the Postwar Order, 1960–1991   267
Chapter 30: Life in an Age of Globalization, 1990 to the Present   271
Practice Exam 4   276
Answer Key for Practice Exam 4   302

Preface for Teachers

Strive for a 5: Preparing for the AP European History Exam is a student prep guide, designed to provide your students with a thorough review of the course material while teaching AP test-taking skills that will stand them in good stead for the AP European History (APEH) Exam.

Designed to pair seamlessly with *A History of Western Society*, Eleventh Edition, by John P. McKay et al., *Strive for a 5* applies a strong AP-specific framework to the text's narrative and offers extended attention to the College Board exam format and test-taking strategies. Either assigned as a core component of your test preparation coursework or recommended to students as an independently navigable review and practice tool, *Strive for a 5* is designed to familiarize students with the APEH Exam format, thematically organize and review the key concepts, and provide level-appropriate practice exams. For students who are striving for a 5, there is no better preparation guide.

Features of This Prep Guide

The **Strategies for the AP Exam** section serves as an introduction to the College Board's AP European History Exam, complete with a breakdown of the scoring system, an overview of the different question forms, and essay-writing instruction.

Period overviews anticipate upcoming revisions to the APEH program and group the course material into four broad chronological periods, each with its own narrative summary. Within each period, **thematic chapter reviews** organize and summarize the major developments of each era using six thematic categories with the acronym "PERSIA"—politics, economy, religion, society and culture, ideas and literature, and the arts. The PERSIA categories organize the material for students, reveal thematic threads from chapter to chapter, and allow students to review in the categories that are often used in APEH Exam questions. **AP Tips** scattered throughout the thematic reviews make strategic connections between the material and the College Board exam.

Full-length AP-style practice exams conclude each of the four chronological periods. Each with eighty multiple-choice questions, a document-based essay, and six thematic essay questions, the practice exams can be assigned as a meaningful assessment at the end of each major unit, or students can independently measure their progress and areas in need of further review with level-appropriate practice tests four times before the College Board exam. Each practice exam comes with model answers and rationales keyed to *A History of Western Society,* Eleventh Edition. Students will become increasingly comfortable with the AP style while completing a comprehensive review of the textbook material.

About the Author

Louise Forsyth holds a B.A. and an M.A. in European history and has been teaching AP European History at Poly Prep Country Day School in Brooklyn, New York, for more than twenty-five years, including one year teaching the course via Skype from London. She has been an AP European History Exam reader and table leader for nearly as long, and she served as question leader for the document-based essay when core scoring was introduced. In addition to publishing several scholarly articles and several other textbook manuals, she has made numerous presentations on European and world history at the AHA and NCSS, as well as other conferences here and abroad. She teaches AP Comparative Government and Politics as well as AP European History and served as head of the history department at Poly Prep for seven years. Most recently she was the curriculum specialist for the NEH Summer Institutes on Bach in 2008, 2010, and 2012, and she also recently participated in a Fulbright-Hays seminar abroad in Turkey and the Balkans.

SECTION 1
Strategies for the AP⁺ Exam

Preparing for the AP European History Exam

By the time you open this book to help prepare you for the AP Exam, you are fully immersed in the study of European history, either in an AP course or studying independently on your own. AP European History (APEH) courses are typically deep and rich experiences, demanding a high level of understanding and sophisticated analysis from you not only of textbook material but also of a variety of primary and secondary sources. Such an experience has great value beyond the AP Exam. By studying thoroughly for one of these courses, you gain the intellectual tools to wrestle with complex ideas, to see connections between the past and the present, to write cogently and thoughtfully, and to make meaningful political choices in your adult life. We teachers also hope that you come away with a richer understanding of yourself and of the extraordinary vitality and variety of human beings.

This book is designed to ease your way into a high score on the AP Exam. Many students feel overwhelmed by the amount of material that the exam covers—six centuries of the history of a dozen or so European countries and many, many complex ideas and developments. But do not be daunted; you *can* master it and walk into the exam confident that you have the knowledge and skills to do well and strive for a 5.

What's in This Book?

This study guide is designed to go with John P. McKay's *A History of Western Society,* Eleventh Edition, and follows the organization of that text, but it can be used with almost any European history text. In addition, the study guide is divided into four chronological periods—the fourteenth through sixteenth centuries, the seventeenth and eighteenth centuries, the nineteenth century, and the twentieth century. For each period, there is an overview of the main developments of that period, followed by a succinct summary of each McKay chapter.

These chapter summaries are organized thematically rather than chronologically, using the acronym PERSIA. PERSIA stands for politics (which includes wars and diplomacy), economy, religion, society and culture (how people lived and understood their own times), ideas and literature, and the arts. Following the PERSIA summaries for each period, there is a two-section practice exam in AP format and style. Section I contains eighty multiple-choice questions; Section II has a document-based question essay (Part A) and six thematic essay questions divided into two groups of three (Parts B and C).

Certified AP Exams cover, of course, the whole time frame of the AP European History course, from about 1400 to the present. Conversely, each of our practice exams covers only the material you're likely to have covered through that period. By using the practice test after each one of the four chronological periods instead of at the end of your course of study, you will be able to get valuable practice in the AP Exam format—multiple-choice questions, document-based questions, and thematic essays—and meaningful assessment of your mastery of course content as you progress through the course. If you can do well on these practice tests, we are confident you will do well on the AP Exam in May.

The division of the content of this guide into four chronological periods helps structure the learning of the main themes of the course and put the details of events and ideas into an overall context. All of the AP History Examinations are moving toward a thematic focus, as does our Strive for a 5. Our four practice tests are in fact congruent with the distribution of multiple-choice questions by time period on the AP Exam: one-half of the questions cover from about 1450 through the French Revolution and Napoleon era, one-fourth cover the nineteenth century, and the remaining quarter cover the twentieth century. In addition, the PERSIA summaries will help you get ready for the weighted focus of the multiple-choice questions: one-third address cultural and intellectual issues, one-third are on political and diplomatic material, and one-third cover social and economic themes. If you work through all four practice tests and the PERSIA summaries, you will be in good shape for the breadth and type of multiple-choice questions on May's AP Examination.

There are two good ways to use the practice tests. First, you can use them to review for the AP Examination; as you review each chronological period, test yourself on that period and then read the answers and rationales in the corresponding Answer Key section to deepen your knowledge. Second, if you acquire this book before review begins, we urge you to take the tests as you complete the relevant unit in your AP course, score them yourself, and evaluate your weaknesses and strengths. With either approach, do not just get your score and leave it at that. Take the time to look over each question carefully and read the explanations for the correct answers. Make a list of the themes and content of the questions you got wrong. Are there areas where you were particularly weak, as indicated by a high proportion of wrong answers? Are there types of questions that you often got wrong, for example, factual recall, interpretation of visual documents like cartoons or art, comparative questions, or "EXCEPT" questions? Did you struggle with your essays? You probably already have a sense of your test-taking skills from your assessments in class; are those confirmed or challenged by your scores on the tests in this book? Once you have a better sense of what you need to work on, you can organize your exam preparation better. Do not be shy about asking your teacher, too; he or she is likely to be able to make recommendations about where to focus your energies and attention.

Registering for the Exam

Most likely your school will be taking care of this for you, but if not, make sure that you register in time, sometime during the month of February. If you are homeschooled, you need to contact AP Services at the College Board by March 1 to find out the name of an AP coordinator near you; you will have until March 15 to contact a school near you where you can take the examination. If you qualify for extra time or are a student with a disability, make sure that all your paperwork is in order and that the AP coordinator at your school is aware of your special needs. The coordinator will have to submit a Student Eligibility Form by mid-February if documentation is needed or early March if it is not. Check the AP Web site early for exact dates.

If your family is struggling to pay the examination fee of $89 ($117 if outside the U.S. except for Department of Defense Dependents Schools), it can be reduced by $28 by the College Board through your school, so look into this early on. Your school would then waive another $8, so your total cost would be $53. In addition, most states subsidize the cost of the exams for those with financial needs; this information is available on the College Board Web site in the spring before the exam. You want to make sure all your paperwork is in order long before the exam. For all these issues, go to https://apstudent.collegeboard.org/exploreap and navigate until you get to the pages with information on registration, fees, and other issues. If you have questions, e-mail apexams@info.collegeboard.org or call AP Services at 888-225-5427.

Familiarizing Yourself with the Exam

If your teacher has not given you AP Exam questions or old AP Exams as practice, then you should examine closely the four practice tests in this book. You can also go to the AP Web site (**http://apstudent.collegeboard.org**). Once there, search for information on the AP European History Exam. You will be able to download a booklet that contains the College Board's course description, information about the exam, and sample questions.

The AP European History Exam is three hours and five minutes long; it consists of two parts. The first part of the exam is the multiple-choice (MC) section, which is fifty-five minutes long. It contains eighty multiple-choice questions, varying in degree of difficulty, with five answer options for each question. The second part of the exam consists of three free-response questions (FRQs). You will have fifteen minutes of mandatory reading time at the beginning of the second part of the exam to read each essay question and the documents provided as the basis for one of them. You will then have one hour and fifty-five minutes of writing time total. The first essay in this section is a document-based question (DBQ). The DBQ is a specific question to be answered only on the basis of the provided documents—usually between ten and twelve documents total—and a brief paragraph of historical background included before the documents. You have forty-five minutes to write the DBQ essay. After the DBQ, you will write answers to two thematic essay questions. You will be able to choose one thematic essay question from each of two groups of three. For this part of the exam, you'll have seventy minutes of planning and writing time. The College Board recommends that you divide the time equally between the two questions, using about five minutes for planning and thirty minutes to write. The two sets of thematic essay questions may be organized chronologically or thematically. For example, in Practice Exam 1 in this book, the first group of essays all require you to write on one aspect or another of the Renaissance; the second group is more eclectic, with a social history question, a political question, and an evaluative question.

Setting Up a Review Schedule

Your teacher will almost certainly organize review sessions or review in class, but students often want to do more to feel really ready for the exam. Some students like to reread the textbook to prepare, but for most students, that's impossible because of time constraints. A study guide like this one is an excellent way to prepare, as it crystallizes the information in a textbook and allows you to hear a fresh voice.

The ideal time to allot for review would probably be three weeks or so, but in most cases, your teacher will still be trying to complete the curriculum—which goes up to the present—in April. Therefore, you have to begin reviewing while you are still learning new material. How to do this?

Ideally, take the three weeks leading up to the exam and read one chapter of the study guide a night, which, if you focus your attention, should be about a half hour's work. Since there are twenty chapters, this works out to about three weeks of review. If this plan doesn't work for you, try to set up a schedule before the end of April in which you complete two or three chapters a night. Remember that on the exam half of the multiple-choice questions cover material from about 1450–1800 and half from 1800–2000, so you can't afford to neglect any part of the year's curriculum to be ready for the examination.

The time before the AP Exams is often very hectic for students. If you are on an athletic team, you may have playoffs or championship games, and the workload from the rest of your classes may be getting intense as the year is coming to its conclusion as well. You do not want to let your other responsibilities get in the way of earning a 5 on the exam, so an absolute key to success is time management. While time management is always useful, it is crucial in the period before AP Exams. Otherwise, you will not prepare much and have to rely on your innate abilities and your memory. In most cases, such "preparation" will not bring you to a score higher than 3. If you want the 5, you need to spend the three weeks or so before the AP Exams preparing for the test instead of socializing or focusing on your other activities. Is it worth it? Absolutely! In almost every college, a score of 5, and in some places a 4, will bring you three or four credits, and if not credit, then placement in an advanced-level history course, which can be a phenomenally exciting experience for a first-year student. It was for me!

The AP Exam is physically grueling—an hour's worth of multiple-choice questions and two hours of writing. If you are not used to writing by hand, be sure to practice in the weeks before the exam; otherwise your hand might cramp up or get tired. Be sure to eat well, stay away from junk food, and get enough sleep the night before so that your body will be an ally and not a detriment. And be sure to have a good and healthy lunch before the exam so your energies will not flag in the last hour or so. Do not drink too many liquids; you don't want to lose valuable exam time making frequent bathroom visits. Take a snack in with you to the exam for the break if that's allowed, wear comfortable clothes and shoes, and bring a sweater or jacket in case the room is too cold. You do not want anything to interfere with your ability to concentrate on the exam. Most importantly, bring a watch! You will not be able to use your cell phone to help you with timing. You need a good reliable timepiece that will accurately tell you how much time is left. Do not assume there will be a clock in the room.

Your examination proctor will remind you of this, but leave all cell phones and other electronic devices outside the examination room. If you are involved in a breach of security, your examination will likely be canceled, and there could be other consequences at your school. It's simply not worth it to take such a chance.

Lastly, make a couple of mantras to help you remember what to do on the exam. For example, my students chant "T, 3G, 3P" as they walk in to remember to include a thesis, three groups, and three POV analyses in their answer to the DBQ. The PERSIA format used for the chapter summaries will help you remember what topics to include in a comprehensive free-response essay.

How the Exams Are Scored

It helps to know how the exams are scored so that you can understand how to earn a 5. The multiple-choice question answers are scored electronically, but the essays are read by people. Your score on the multiple-choice section counts for half of your exam score. The other half is a combination of your scores on the FRQs, with the DBQ weighted at 45 percent of that composite and the two thematic essay responses combined to provide the other 55 percent.

In June, some 400 readers—university professors and high school teachers of AP European History—meet for a week in a central location to read and score the three FRQ responses. Readers are organized into groups of six to eight at a table, chaired by a table leader who is responsible for quality control. A question leader meets with a small group before the reading begins to create a specific scoring rubric for each FRQ. The question leader trains the table leaders, who then train the readers; the table leaders check that the rubric is being applied competently and fairly. Everything possible is done to ensure that the scoring rubrics and their application by readers are fair and consistent. To see the scoring guidelines for AP Exams from 2004 to 2010, see the European History course description at **http://apcentral.collegeboard.com/apc/public/repository/ap-european-history-course -description.pdf**. After the reading, the raw scores are evaluated by statisticians at

Educational Testing Services in Princeton, and with the chief faculty consultant (always a university professor) the cutoffs for the 5, 4, 3, 2, and 1 final scores are set.

Scores are sent out to students in July. As of 2013, scores will be available online in July. Check the College Board Web site for details on how to obtain scores in this manner. You need a College Board account to obtain the scores online. If you took the SAT, you probably have such an account.

Scores are released to the colleges and universities of your choice at the same time they are released to students and their schools. While it is unlikely to happen if you prepare correctly, if you know coming out of the exam that it was a disaster, you can cancel the score and withhold notification of colleges by contacting AP Services by June 15, before you get your score. To contact AP Services, e-mail apexams@info.collegeboard.org, call 877-274-6474, or write to this address:

AP Services
P.O. Box 6671
Princeton, NJ 08541-6671

Taking the AP European History Exam

If you are well prepared, you will be successful on the AP Exam. However, there are key test-taking skills that will all but guarantee that you get the score that your level of mastery should bring you.

The most common problems are *not reading the question carefully or ignoring parts of a question*. For the essays, read the question carefully, think about what the question is asking, and answer it in all its parts. Students sometimes answer the question they know or the one they wished had been asked, rather than the one that has been asked; this is particularly true on the essays but can be happen with multiple-choice questions too. Do not rush and assume you understand the question before you read it carefully.

Types of Multiple-Choice Questions

There are seven types of multiple-choice questions that appear on the AP Exam.

1. Factual Recall

There are relatively few of these on the exam, but with them it is a matter of knowing the answer or not, as the correct answer is not open to interpretation.

Example:

1. The king of England replaced by the Glorious Revolution of 1688 was
   - (A) James I
   - (B) Charles I
   - (C) James II
   - (D) Charles II
   - (E) William III

Answer: (C) James II. William, husband of Mary, the Protestant daughter of James II, became king of England in 1688.

2. Best Answer

Here you are to select the best option of five. One or two of the choices will be nearly right, so you need to evaluate the options carefully.

Example:

2. The Thirty Years' War began when
   (A) a Holy Roman emperor began persecuting Protestants for the first time
   (B) the nobles of Bohemia rejected the Holy Roman emperor as their new king
   (C) the Protestants of Bohemia, mostly of bourgeois origin, attacked the nobility of Bohemia, who were mostly Catholic
   (D) Cardinal Richelieu of France sent troops against the Habsburgs
   (E) the nobles of Bohemia tried to appoint one of their own to be their king

Answer: (B)   Option D is clearly wrong, as Richelieu sent troops against the Habsburgs only after the war had started. It is also the only option that refers to something outside the Holy Roman Empire. Option A is also out of the question if you remember that Charles V, the Holy Roman emperor, fought against Protestants during his entire reign, so the beginning of persecution of Protestants by the Holy Roman emperor was much earlier than 1618. Assuming you remember that the war began with the defenestration of Prague in 1618, you will know that it cannot be C. It was the nobles of Bohemia, largely Calvinists, who rejected the Holy Roman emperor Ferdinand and asked the Protestant king of the Palatinate, Frederick IV, to be their king, not one from their own group. The bourgeoisie or middle classes of Bohemia (option D) were hardly involved in starting the war. If you read the answers too quickly, you might have selected C or E.

3. "EXCEPT" Questions

In these questions, all options but one are correct. Often, if you detect a consistent element among four options but not the fifth, you should choose the distinct one—even if you do not know the answer—as it is likely the correct answer. Careful reading here can usually bring good results. Remember that in these questions, four choices are right and only one is wrong; that is the one you need to find.

Example:

3. The results of the Thirty Years' War included all of the following EXCEPT
   (A) economic dislocation in the Germanic states
   (B) weakening of the Holy Roman Empire
   (C) loss of population within the Holy Roman Empire
   (D) enhancement of the personal prestige of the Holy Roman emperor
   (E) France and Denmark acquiring territories formerly within the Holy Roman Empire

Answer: (D)   It is the only one that shows the Holy Roman Empire to have had a gain. Even if you do not know the answer, you can guess this one correctly by seeing the inherent connections between the four other answers.

4. Graphs and Charts

Sometimes, these questions ask you to interpret the results of information, rather than calling on what you know. Other times, they will ask you to use your knowledge to interpret the results of a graph or chart.

Example of the first type:

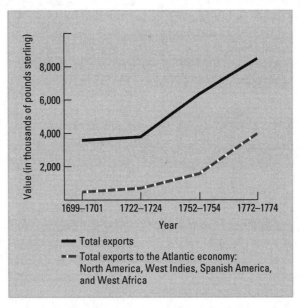

Exports of English Manufactured Goods 1700–1774

4. Which of the following statements is best supported by the graph above?
    (A) English exports to the Atlantic economy declined as a percentage of its total trade from 1699 to 1752 but increased after that.
    (B) English exports to the Atlantic economy and its total exports both grew at their highest rate between 1724 and 1754.
    (C) After the 1750s, English total exports grew less rapidly than did their exports to the Atlantic economy.
    (D) English exports to Europe remained constant as a percentage of their total exports.
    (E) The main reason for the growth of English exports in the eighteenth century was the dramatic increase in their exports to the Atlantic economy.

Answer: (C)   From 1754 to 1774, English exports to the Atlantic economy more than doubled while their total exports increased by only a quarter.

5. Cartoons

Similar to graphs and charts. These typically relate to content from the eighteenth through the twentieth centuries rather than earlier.

Example:

www.CartoonStock.com

5. The cartoon above refers to the

   (A)   threat of extremism
   (B)   struggles Turkey faces in joining the European Union
   (C)   problems within Turkey's government
   (D)   struggles between the Turkish government and Turkish Kurds
   (E)   strength of the Turkish people

Answer: (B)   The general population of Turkey wants to "join Europe," but the road to membership in the European Union (EU) is proving difficult. The EU has requested many changes of Turkey's government. Some Turks now believe that the real roadblock is anti-Muslim sentiment in Europe.

6. Map Questions

Usually these are designed to test your knowledge of the changing borders of European states. Make sure you look carefully at the borders and the dates on the map.

Example:

6. This map describes the Balkans in

   (A)   1673 after the Turkish siege of Vienna
   (B)   1815 after the Congress of Vienna
   (C)   1853 after the Crimean War
   (D)   1878 after the Congress of Berlin
   (E)   1919 after the Paris Peace Conference

Answer: (D)   How can you tell? The Ottoman Empire still has part of the Balkans, but Romania, Bulgaria, and Serbia are independent and Austria has occupied Bosnia-Herzegovina; this happened in 1878. By 1919, the Ottoman Empire had lost all its European territories except the part of the city of Istanbul on the European side of the Bosporus.

7. Reproductions of Art

Usually these questions ask you to identify either the school of art that the image represents or the time period in which it was likely to have been made. To prepare for these questions, make sure you have looked at the artworks in your textbook and know the major schools of art: Renaissance (fifteenth and sixteenth centuries); mannerism (sixteenth century); Baroque (sixteenth and seventeenth centuries); classicism (eighteenth century); realism, romanticism, and Impressionism (nineteenth century); and Expressionism, surrealism, and abstract art (twentieth century). In other cases, as in the example below, you'll be asked to put the painting in historical context.

Example:

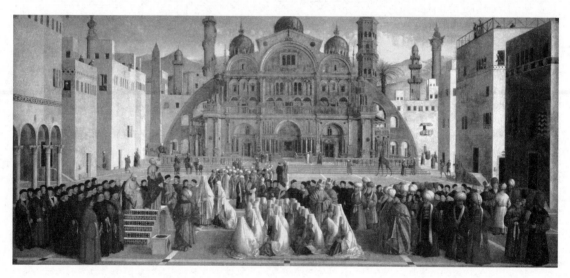

Erich Lessing/Art Resource, NY.

7. This painting by the Italian Bellini, "Saint Mark Preaching in Alexandria" (1504–1507), most likely reflects

(A) Renaissance fascination with Greek culture
(B) European support for Greek independence
(C) fears of Muslim conquests in Europe
(D) respect and fascination with the Ottoman Empire
(E) European glee over their naval victory over the Ottomans at Lepanto

Answer (D) Europeans grew increasingly impressed by the city of Istanbul and with the Ottoman Empire as a whole. Contacts, both political and economic, grew in the sixteenth century. Alexandria is in Egypt, not Greece, and was part of the Ottoman Empire. The Greek War of Independence took place in the nineteenth century. The Battle of Lepanto in 1571 was more than sixty years later than the painting.

Strategies for the Multiple-Choice Section

1. *Pace yourself.* You are expected to answer the questions in an average of three-quarters of a minute per question, so do not spend a long time on any one question. If you are struggling to select the correct answer, leave it and move on to the next question. You can always return to skipped questions if you have time left at the end of the allotted time.

2. Make sure that you *key in your answers accurately.* If you skip a question to come back to it later, be sure that you skip that question number on the answer sheet. Periodically, check that you are filling in the circles on the correct line. You do not want to find at the end of the exam that you have recorded your answers out of order, as you may not have time to correct the errors. If you like working questions in your test booklet and *then* bubbling in the answers, make sure you leave plenty of time to do so. Once time is called, you will not be able to bubble answers. Anything in your multiple-choice test booklet but not on the answer sheet will not be scored.

3. About guessing: go ahead and do it. Until 2011, there was a penalty of one-quarter of a point off for each wrong answer, but this policy was eliminated for the 2011 AP Examinations and all subsequent exams in all subjects. As there is no longer a guessing penalty, answer every question, even with a wild guess; you have nothing to lose and a 20 percent chance of getting the answer right.

4. Some questions will be quite straightforward and easy for you, so *don't assume that such questions are trying to trick you.* The eighty questions offer an array of difficulty, and a number of them in each exam are answered correctly by the vast majority of students. Similarly, there will be a few multiple-choice questions that are really difficult, and only a small percentage of students will get them right.

5. In order to earn a 3 or higher, you need to answer about half the multiple-choice questions correctly. The higher you score on the MC section, the greater the likelihood of a high score on the exam. Remember, the MC section counts for half of your final score.

6. *Read the questions and the answer choices carefully* and be sure to notice if the question is an EXCEPT question. Use the *process of elimination* method as you read the choices (you can write on the exam booklet), crossing out the choices that you know for sure are wrong. Keep in mind that absolute answers (such as all or none) are usually wrong. Remember, the correct answer for a multiple-choice question should be the *best* answer of the five options. Typically one answer will be clearly and definitively wrong, three might be correct or partially true, but one is the most accurate or complete answer to the question.

Strategies for the Free-Response Questions

As explained before, you will prepare and write three essays in two hours and ten minutes. You will have fifteen minutes of mandatory reading and preparation time, which students generally use for the document-based question. It is also a good idea to use this time to pick out the two thematic essay questions that you will answer. As with the multiple-choice questions, the free-response questions will address content from European history from 1450 and after. While there may be some multiple-choice questions on individuals, events, or trends that have taken place since 2001, that is not the case with the free-response questions. The FRQs will only cover material from 1450 to 2001.

The scoring scale for each essay is 0 to 9. Zero is a real score and is reserved for those essays that make some sort of effort to answer the question, perhaps just by restating it, but get almost nothing right in the process. Skipping an essay question entirely (or writing something completely irrelevant) will not even earn a zero. If you want a score of 5 on the exam, you want to make sure that you get a 7, 8, or 9 on the DBQ and at least a 5 or 6 on each of the two thematic essays. This means that you have to stay focused, concentrate well, and work assiduously for those two hours and ten minutes.

The AP European History Exam essays are scored according to two different methods as of this writing. The DBQ essay is scored according to a core scoring method, which assigns one point to each of six core historical skills to be applied in the analysis of documents. The first six points are awarded for the completion of these specific skills. You must earn all six points to score higher. If you do earn all six core points, you have the opportunity to receive up to three additional points based on the quality of your essay. (The core points are discussed in more detail below.) The thematic essay questions are scored in a more holistic way in order to accommodate the great variety of student responses. We will discuss the key elements for a competent thematic essay in a later section.

Both types of essays require a thesis statement. A thesis statement can often seem intimidating or difficult to write, so be sure you understand what it is and what it is not. Too often an essay that displays a student's substantial knowledge will fail to get a high score because it lacks a clear thesis. Without one, an essay reads more like a report. A thesis statement is a short, one- or two-sentence articulation of what the essay will argue—the points you will try to prove in the essay. It is not a description or a rewording of the question. A good thesis statement is often strengthened by a thesis paragraph in which the student lays out some of the key points of the arguments to be made in the essay. While it is acceptable for a thesis statement to be found in the conclusion, you do not want the essay readers to have to search for it, so starting out the essay with a strong thesis statement is the best idea. Below are three possible thesis statements in response to the following question:

Example:

Analyze the political, economic, and religious factors that stimulated European exploration and conquest in the fifteenth and sixteenth centuries.

Answer A

There were many political, economic, and religious factors that stimulated Spain and Portugal to explore and conquer in the New World and Asia in the fifteenth and sixteenth centuries.

✦ Is this a thesis statement? No! Mostly, it is a rewording of the question, with the addition of naming the European countries mostly involved in the exploration and conquest in the time period.

Answer B

Although there were many factors that stimulated exploration and conquest in the fifteenth and sixteenth centuries, it was economic motives that were more important in leading Spain and Portugal in that direction.

✦ Is this a thesis statement? Yes! The student tells the reader what he or she will try to prove in the course of the essay. The essay can be evaluated on the degree to which it proves the thesis. This is a basic thesis statement but perfectly acceptable.

Answer C

> Although the drive to spread Christianity was highly important to the kings of Spain and Portugal who began the period of European exploration and conquest in the fifteenth century, and certainly it was relevant to the desire to outmaneuver the Muslims who controlled the spice trade in Asia, ultimately it was economic issues that led Spain and Portugal to seek new routes to Asia. The need to find new sources for gold and cheaper access to spices and other valuable goods from Asia spurred Henry the Navigator's push down the coast of Africa and Ferdinand and Isabella's sponsorship of the voyages of Columbus.

+ Is this a thesis statement? Yes. It has the same thesis as Answer B above, but it is more detailed, more fleshed out, and more nuanced. This is a strong thesis statement.

The Document-Based Question Essay

The DBQ in each of the three AP History Examinations is different, so if you have already taken AP World History or AP U.S. History, you have to retrain for the AP European History DBQ. The AP U.S. History DBQ expects you to answer the question with the documents *and* bring in outside knowledge, while the AP World History DBQ asks you to come up with one additional document that would help answer the question. In AP European History, however, *no* outside knowledge is required or expected in your answer and you *do not* have to come up with any additional documents.

Sometimes the European History DBQ is on a topic about which you may have substantial knowledge, but quite often it deals with relatively obscure issues, such as nineteenth-century Pan-Slavism or the treatment of juvenile delinquents in England in the seventeenth and eighteenth centuries. So *don't worry at all* if you know nothing at all about the subject; you need not bring in one iota of outside knowledge. Everything you need to write an excellent DBQ essay can be found in the documents themselves.

Core Scoring

As stated earlier, in the AP European History case, the DBQ essay is scored according to core scoring. The basic premise of core scoring is that there are specific and identifiable skills that can be articulated as demonstrations of competence in DBQ essay writing. These six core points, listed individually, are worth one point each. If you earn *all* six points, then can you earn up to three additional points, giving you a score of 7, 8, or 9. If you miss a core point, it does not matter how good your essay is; the maximum score you can get on the DBQ is 5. In order to maximize your potential score, *learn the core points, internalize each point, and be sure to demonstrate each skill in the core points.*

These are the six core points, as of the May 2011 exams:

1. **The thesis statement is appropriate, explicit, and addresses all parts of the question.** A thesis statement that is general does *not* earn a point for the thesis statement. *Do not simply repeat the question. A thesis statement that addresses some aspects of the question but not all of them does not earn a point.* It is best to derive your thesis statement in some manner or other from the documents themselves.

2. **The answer uses a majority of the documents, individually and specifically.** This is an easy point to get. Divide the number of documents in half and add one; that's the

minimum number to use. What does it mean to use a document? It means you must refer to the document by name or by reference to its content and discuss that content. It will *not* count if you make a list of documents that support a point, for example, "documents 3, 5, and 7." You must make individual use of each of the majority of documents to earn this point.

3. **The answer demonstrates understanding of the basic meaning of most of the documents.** You are allowed one and only one major error in your analysis of the documents to earn this point. What is a major error? It is an error that leads you to group a document inappropriately or to draw an erroneous conclusion from it. Minor errors, such as misstating the name of the author of a document or writing a date incorrectly, are tolerated.

4. **The answer supports the thesis using a majority of the documents with appropriate interpretations.** If you do not get point one, you cannot get this point.

5. **The answer analyzes at least three documents using point-of-view analysis.** The next subsection has a detailed discussion of this type of analysis.

6. **The answer analyzes the documents by explicitly organizing them into three or more appropriate groups.** A group is a minimum of two documents. How do you group documents? You can group them by the identity of the author (for example, Germans, socialists, peasants, aristocrats, Protestants, or government officials), by the type of document (letters, diary entries, government reports, cartoons, or speeches), by the views expressed or similarity of positions taken (opponents of the Nazis or advocates of imperialism), by the time period they were written in, or by issues they address.

Point-of-View (POV) Analysis

One of the most common reasons that students do not earn a 6 on the DBQ is the failure to properly analyze the documents using point-of-view analysis. For this reason, POV analysis is an important skill to learn and practice in advance of the exam.

Point-of-view analysis is different from point of view. The point of view of a document is the opinion expressed by the author, in other words, his or her viewpoint. Point-of-view *analysis* either questions the reliability of the document—that is, the degree of bias it reflects—or evaluates the degree to which the views expressed in the document reflect or contradict the likely views of similar authors. Every document in the DBQ will be identified by author, name, type of document, and date and include some information about the author. Your task is to connect something within the document with something in the identification. The information given about the author and about the document will offer many opportunities for POV analysis.

In order to base your point-of-view analysis on the reliability of a document, you should try to determine how *who* the author is might affect the *way* he or she explains or describes the ideas or events in the document. For example, if an aristocrat or merchant is describing the life of peasants, you can ask whether his or her views are accurate because the author probably had little direct experience of peasant life. Similarly, if a tract written during a peasants' revolt vilifies aristocrats as greedy, you can suggest that the depiction of aristocrats is biased because of strong animosities stirred up during the revolt. Another very useful way of doing POV analysis for reliability is to consider the type of document. For example, if the document is a diary entry, you can argue that it is likely to reflect the true views of the author as he or she would not have expected it to be read by anyone else. If it is a diary entry written by a political leader, you can suggest that it might not reflect the full truth because a politician could reasonably expect that his or her diary might be part of the public record or read by biographers. A government document might reflect the particular interests of government officials seeking to either protect or enhance their positions. A speech or a newspaper article has an intended audience, but it might be heard or read by others—the unintended audience—who might understand the intent differently.

Sometimes a document clearly reflects the class or nationalist position of its author. A letter written by someone identified as a humanist might reflect humanist values through references to ancient authors or an enthusiasm for education. An aristocrat would express typical views of his class if he wrote disdainfully of peasants or described merchants as upstarts. A landowner typically defends agricultural interests over mercantile ones. A Calvinist would typically be appalled by dancing or displays of Catholic devotion. Statements that contradict the typical views of a group of people—say, an aristocrat who lauds peasants or merchants—provide notable counterexamples. Similar analysis could be easily applied to national identity or political affiliation.

What is *not* acceptable as POV analysis? You might think that just saying the author is biased is sufficient, but I can assure you that you will not earn POV credit for something this simplistic. If you write "the author is biased because he's a lawyer" or "there's obvious bias in this document about women's suffrage because the author is a woman and women were in favor of it" without any further explanation, the reader will recognize that you made an attempt at POV analysis but judge that you failed to do it. You need to explain why this specific author is biased in saying what he or she said in the document. For example, look at the second case. Remembering that some women did oppose women's suffrage, you need to explain what factors might explain why this particular woman advocates it. Some students think bias is a dirty word, that it implies something immoral. Historians aren't making moral judgments when they use this word; in the study of history, bias means that every actor on the historical stage presents a view or plays a role based on identity, position, and experiences. POV analysis, like any good historical analysis, depends on careful examination of the details to identify the biases that are relevant to a particular document.

What is the point of asking students to do POV analysis? Historians do research by finding and examining documents, and in each case, they too have to evaluate the reliability of documents and consider how much those documents represent the views of various subgroups in society. Teachers of history want to know that students have learned to think like historians. A document is not the whole historical truth; it is a particular document written at a particular time by a particular person or persons for a particular purpose in a particular manner.

For many examples of POV analysis, look at the explanations for the DBQs in the answer keys for each of the four practice tests in this guide.

Other DBQ Essay-Writing Tips

1. *Pay attention to the wording of the question.* It's crucial that you focus your essay to answer the prompt. Pay particular attention if the question asks you to analyze change over time. Even if the question doesn't but the documents are from various periods, try to include a few sentences about changes over time. It's a sign of sophisticated historical thinking.

2. *Do not repeat the historical background.* Each DBQ begins with a question, followed by a paragraph of historical background, which is designed to give you key information you need to understand and analyze the documents. Do not repeat the historical background. You may use or refer to it, of course, but do not waste your time repeating it. The readers already know it.

3. *Do not refer to documents by number.* Always, always, always, refer to documents by name, author, or content, never by number alone. It is all right for you to use the numbers if it will help you keep count—put them in parentheses—but be sure to have some specific identification, typically the author or the title. Never say "Document 1 says." It is not the document that speaks; the author of the document speaks.

4. *Do not be colloquial.* If the author of a document has a common nickname, do not use it and do not refer to historic figures by their first names alone. For example, it is Queen Elizabeth not Elizabeth, it is Lenin not Vladimir, it is Churchill not Winnie.

5. *Do not feel compelled to use every document.* If there is a document you cannot figure out, skip it. An essay can earn a 9 using most but not all of the documents. But remember: *There are no intentionally misleading or trick documents;* every document *can* be used.

6. *Do not simply paraphrase or summarize a document.* While this counts for document usage, it doesn't show analysis, even minimally. Always try to have something to say about the documents you use.

In summation, what you need to do minimally in your DBQ essay is have a thesis statement, use a majority of the documents, discuss them individually, make few errors of interpretation, show that you have divided the documents into three groups, and give three POV analyses. Set the chant "T, 3G, 3P" in your mind to help you remember—thesis, three groups, three POV analyses. As you read the documents for the first time during the AP Exam, mark up the examination booklet, making notes that suggest possible groupings and POV analyses, and begin to formulate your thesis. If you do all this, you are likely to earn at least a 6 on the DBQ essay.

But you shouldn't aim just for a score of 6. If you want an AP Exam score of 5, then you must work to go beyond the core. You can do this by composing a stronger and more comprehensive thesis, using more documents (even all of them), forming more groups, or making more POV analyses (try for four or five). If you do this you will earn a high score of 7, 8, or 9. As mentioned before, you need not bring in one iota of outside information to earn a 9, but if you have some accurate and relevant knowledge that can enrich your analysis, by all means include it; it can only strengthen your essay.

The Thematic Essay Questions

Answering the thematic essay questions demands some similar skills to answering the DBQs but also some different ones. The answers to these questions reflect your knowledge and understanding in addition to your skills. Be sure to select the question in each group that involves content you know best. And remember to select one question from each group; if you select two from the same group, the second essay will not count at all.

To write a good essay:

1. *Formulate a clear thesis statement.* Take a position on the question and express it in the thesis statement. Many questions are worded in such a way as to encourage a thesis with prompt instructions like *evaluate* or *analyze*, but you should have a thesis statement even if the question does not seem to ask for one, as when the question asks you to *explain* or *discuss*, for example.

2. *Answer all parts of the question.* Most questions have at least two elements, referring, for example, to political and economic issues, or Spain and France, or seventeenth and nineteenth centuries. It may be that you know more about one part of the question than about another, but *be sure to discuss all parts of the question, even if you devote more time and space to addressing select parts.*

3. If you are working with a comparative question, remember to identify *both* similarities and differences, even if you stress one more than the other.

4. Develop several arguments, usually although not necessarily in separate paragraphs, and *use specific evidence* to support them. Vague generalizations or broad statements on their own will not do you much good; try to provide at least one but preferably several specific facts, dates, or individuals for each argument. The best essays are filled with lots and lots of evidence, accompanied by good analysis.

5. *Be well organized.* Although essays are not scored on their writing per se, a good essay is typically a well-organized one. If you know the five-paragraph essay format, use it: an introductory paragraph with thesis statement, argument one with supporting evidence in paragraph two, argument two with supporting evidence in paragraph three, argument three with supporting evidence in paragraph four, and a conclusion in paragraph five. The very best essays will acknowledge a counterargument to the thesis and give reasons why that position is less valid than yours.

6. *Avoid making major errors.* Small mistakes of dates or people's names are not taken all that seriously, and even an essay earning a 9 need not be perfect, but many, many small errors will keep your score down and including major errors leading to erroneous conclusions will keep your score down.

7. *Watch your time.* If you have written the DBQ in forty-five minutes, you will have seventy minutes left for the two thematic essay questions. You want to be sure to write both essays, even if they are unbalanced in length or detail. Try to use only thirty minutes for the first thematic essay so you will have time to write the second. Remember to allocate some time—about five minutes per question is recommended—to planning each essay.

Sample Essays

Question (from the 1997 AP exam):

> *Focusing on the period before 1600, describe and analyze the cultural and economic interactions between Europe and the Western Hemisphere as a result of the Spanish and Portuguese exploration and settlement.*

Actual Student Answer

Before the turn of the sixteenth century, Europe, especially Spain and Portugal, had already left its mark on the Western Hemisphere. And, the New World had left its mark on Europe as well. The interaction that is known as the Columbian Exchange had a dramatic effect on both Europe and the Western Hemisphere. However, the drastic cultural changes affected the Western Hemisphere more, while Europe experienced more of the economic changes.

In Latin America, after much of the conquest by the Europeans was finished by the mid-sixteenth century, religious missionaries attempted to convert the locals. The missionaries succeeded because of the "opportunities" that were given to the natives. The natives were taught how to read, write, and speak Spanish, and they were given residence in towns created for the sake of the missionaries.

Also, when the use of Native Americans as slaves began to become obsolete due to the deaths of many natives, the Spanish and Portuguese began to import Africans to the New World. Culturally, this affected Latin Americans because of the mix of Europeans, Native Americans, Africans, and mestizos. This mix of different peoples gave Latin Americans a less rigid attitude concerning race and racial differences. In Europe, cultural change occurred somewhat in the exchange of goods back to Europe. For example, the potato became a staple crop for the poor in Europe and eventually led to cultures that revolved very much around the harvesting and use of potatoes such as in Ireland and Germany.

In Europe, the economic gains during this period were tremendous. The harvesting of sugar by Native Americans at first and then by Africans in Brazil and the Caribbean led to astounding profits for Portugal and Spain. Going back to potatoes and the poor, potatoes had a big effect on economics in Europe as well. Since potatoes grew easily and grew well in cold climates, poor people lived longer. When more people live, there are more people who work and more people to sell goods to. Also, the silver and gold mines that were found not only had the obvious effect of making European countries richer, but in the case of trading with China, silver became more valuable than ever. And with the silver in Bolivian and Peruvian mines plentiful, Spain was able to prosper greatly. In Latin America, the obvious change in economic interaction was the use of slavery, which put wealth in the hands of Europeans who lived in Latin America. Also, wives of colonists in Latin America had a chance to get lucky if their rich husbands died unexpectedly in the unpredictable violent world in the Western Hemisphere.

The cultural effects of Spanish and Portuguese exploration were greater in Latin America, while the economic effects were greater in Europe. There were more than a few exceptions, such as the reaffirmation of European attitudes of superiority and ranching in South America, but in the sixteenth century and before, this was the extent of cultural and economic change in Europe and the Western Hemisphere.

This essay has several strengths:

1. A clear thesis in the opening paragraph, repeated in the final paragraph

2. Well-organized

3. Use of some specific evidence

This essay also has several weaknesses:

1. It leaves out some of the crucial developments in both Europe and Latin America, especially the *encomienda* system in the colonies and the price revolution in Europe. Spain's *siglo d'oro* is hinted at but not mentioned specifically. Only one element of the Columbian exchange—the potato—is discussed; what is left out is the importation into Latin America of animals like horses, pigs, and sheep from Europe and discussion of other crops, such as maize (corn) brought into Europe and those, such as wheat and sugar, that went to Latin America. Many aspects of cultural impact are also ignored.

2. Much of the analysis refers to developments after 1600, particularly the racial mixing in Latin America and attitudes of greater tolerance, and the impact of the potato on Germany and Ireland.

SCORE: 5 This essay has some good points but too little that addresses the period under question. Let us rewrite this same essay to turn it into an essay earning an 8 or 9. In boldface, you will find corrections and additions.

Revised Answer

Before the **end** of the sixteenth century, Europe, especially Spain and Portugal, had already left its mark on the Western Hemisphere. And the New World had left its mark on Europe as well. The interaction, which is known as the Columbian Exchange, had a dramatic effect on both Europe and the Western Hemisphere. However, the drastic cultural changes affected the Western Hemisphere more, while Europe experienced more of the economic changes.

In Latin America, **soon after** the conquest by the Europeans **began in the late fifteenth and early** sixteenth centur**ies,** religious missionaries attempted to convert the locals. The missionaries succeeded because of the "opportunities" that were given to the natives. The natives were taught how to read, write, and speak Spanish, and they were given residence in towns created for the sake of the missionaries. **Christianity replaced the indigenous religions, although over time a syncretism of the two was forged. The conversion en masse to Christianity brought the entire apparatus of the church structure to the New World, from cathedrals to charitable institutions and schools to the Inquisition.**

Also, when the use of Native Americans as slaves began to become obsolete due to the deaths of many natives, the Spanish and Portuguese began to import Africans to the New World. Culturally, this affected Latin Americans because of the mix of Europeans, Native Americans, Africans, mestizos **(the offspring of Europeans and natives), and mulattoes (the offspring of Africans and whites).** This mix of different peoples **would give** Latin America a less rigid attitude concerning race and racial differences.

In Europe, cultural change occurred somewhat in the exchange of goods back to Europe. For example, the potato **later** became a staple crop for the poor in Europe and eventually led to cultures that revolved very much around the harvesting and use of potatoes such as Ireland and Germany. **Europeans had many reactions to the encounter with the natives in the New World; some, perhaps most, took the primitive lifestyle of the natives as confirmation of their own superiority, while others were impressed by the dignity and high state of civilization of the natives. Bartolomé de Las Casas, the Dominican missionary who came to the New World in the early sixteenth century, praised the Indians he met and argued that they could be converted to Christianity but that they were too superior to be forced into slavery. He lamented the brutal treatment of the natives by the Spaniards. European intellectuals such as Thomas More** wondered if the New World offered examples of earthly paradises; it is no accident that he placed his Utopia there. The discovery of the New World created a new cosmology for Europeans.

In Europe, the economic gains during this period were tremendous. The harvesting of sugar by Native Americans at first and then by Africans in Brazil and the Caribbean led to astounding profits for Portugal and Spain. Going back to potatoes and the poor, potatoes had a big effect on economics in Europe as well, **beginning well after 1600 in the mid-eighteenth century. Other crops also transformed the European diet, such as maize and later on chocolate and tobacco.**

A much bigger impact came from the massive importation of silver and gold. Silver and gold mines that were found not only had the obvious effect of making European countries richer, but in the case of trading with China, silver became more valuable than ever. **Silver was how the Chinese wanted to be paid, so the increased amount available encouraged trade with China. Originally** the silver in Bolivian and Peruvian mines was plentiful, and Spain was able to prosper greatly. **The crown particularly benefited because of the** *quinto*, **but most of the gold and silver went out of Spain to various parts of Europe. The sudden wealth of Spain produced what it not accidentally called its siglo d'oro, its golden age. But Spain made inefficient use of its new wealth in terms of building or supporting native industries; this led to serious financial difficulties, so much so that the king, Philip II, repudiated the royal debt in 1596. Nevertheless, the new mining industries prompted technological improvements and the growth of the shipbuilding industries.**

A second and more widespread impact of the silver and gold rush was the price revolution. After centuries of more or less stable prices, prices in Europe began to inflate, only a few percentage points a year but enough to have significant impact. Merchants benefited, but the standard of living of workers and peasants went down. The price revolution helped fuel the growth of commercial capitalism.

In Latin America, **the first change in the economic situation as a result of the Spanish conquest was the encomienda system, a type of forced labor placed on the Native Americans, which ended their traditional economic arrangements and put them in the all-too-often rough hands of the Spaniards. The brutality of this system, combined with the awful impact of diseases previously unknown to the natives, led to a horrific loss of life, 30 to 40 percent in general and in some places even more.** An obvious change in economic interaction was the use of slavery that put wealth in the hands of Europeans who lived in Latin America.

New crops introduced from Europe transformed the economies of the Spanish and Portuguese colonies, none more so than sugar, which the Portuguese had first cultivated in the Azores. They quickly established large-scale sugar cane plantations and sugar-producing factories in Brazil. The

Portuguese first brought slaves to the New World from Africa in 1518 to use on such plantations. Other new crops included wheat and rice. A third impact on the Spanish and Portuguese colonies came from the introduction of animals hitherto unknown in the New World, particularly horses, swine, and cattle. The latter would become the basis of the Argentinean beef industry.

While the economic consequences of the Columbian Exchange were great in both Europe and the Western Hemisphere, the cultural impact of the Spanish and Portuguese were greater in Latin America than the other way around. There were more than a few exceptions, such as the reaffirmation of European attitudes of superiority, and over time the cultural impact of the Americas on Europe would be great. However, in the sixteenth century and before, this was still somewhat limited, especially in contrast to the great economic changes in both Europe and the Western Hemisphere.

Calculating Your Score on a Practice Exam

The following is based on the 2009 AP European History Exam as well as the new College Board guidelines for the 2010 exam.

Scoring the Multiple-Choice Section

Remember that the two parts of the exam—Section I, multiple-choice, and Section II, three essays—are equally weighted at 50 percent each in determining your final score. Of the three essays, the DBQ essay counts for 45 percent of the Section II score, and the thematic essays together counts for 55 percent.

Use the following formula to calculate your raw score on the multiple-choice section of the exam:

$$\underline{\hspace{4cm}} \times 1.125 = \underline{\hspace{4cm}}$$

    number correct   **weighted Section I score**
    (out of 80)

The highest possible score for the multiple-choice section is 80 correct answers, for a score of 90.

Scoring the Document-Based Essay: The Core-Scoring Standards

1. Do you have a thesis that derives from the documents, and does it do more than restate the question?

2. Have you used more than half the documents?

3. Have you made no more than one major error in your analysis of the documents?

4. Have you supported your thesis with evidence from the documents?

5. Have you grouped the documents in at least three ways?

6. Have you analyzed POV in at least three documents?

Give yourself one point for each affirmative answer. If you have earned the six core points, evaluate how much better than the minimum you have done and give yourself an additional one, two, or three additional points. If you missed a core point, go back over the DBQ to see what you could have done differently.

Part A Score: _____ **(out of 9)**

Scoring the Thematic Essay Section

The essays are scored on a scale of 0 to 9, with 0 being a real score. A response that is completely off topic does not even earn a zero. Here are generic scoring guidelines for the essays in Parts B and C.

9–8

Has a clear, well-developed thesis
Is well organized
Addresses the terms of the question
Supports the thesis with substantial specific evidence
Has sophisticated analysis
May contain minor errors; even a 9 need not be flawless

7–6

Has a clear thesis
Addresses all parts of the question but discussion is uneven
Has competent analysis, but it may be superficial
Supports the thesis with some specific evidence

5–4

Contains a thesis, perhaps superficial or simplistic
Has uneven responses to the question's terms
May contain errors, factual or interpretative
Addresses the question with generally accurate discussion but without specific
    evidence; analysis is implicit or superficial
May contain major errors within a generally accurate and appropriate discussion
Is descriptive rather than analytical

3–2

Has weak or muddled thesis, perhaps suggesting false or inappropriate dichotomies
    or connections
Contains significant errors of chronology or fact
Has minimal discussion
Offers limited evidence

1–0

Has confused or absent thesis or merely restates the question
Misconstrues the question or omits major tasks
May contain major errors or irrelevant historical information
Addresses only one part of the question
Offers minimal or no evidence

Section II, Part B Score: _____ **(out of 9)**

Section II, Part C Score: _____ **(out of 9)**

Use the following formula to calculate your raw score on the thematic essay section of the exam:

Part A _____ × **4.5** = _____
        (out of 9)   **(do not round)**

Part B _____ × 2.75 = _____
        (out of 9)   (do not round)

Part C _____ × 2.75 = _____
        (out of 9)   (do not round)

Sum = _____ weighted Section II score
      (do not round)

Your Composite Score

_____ + _____ = _____
  Section I score   Section II score   composite score
                             (round to nearest whole number)

Once you have calculated your composite score, see where it falls in the Composite Score Range below. *Remember that your composite score is only an estimate of your performance on the College Board exam.*

Composite Score Range AP Grade

Composite Score Range	AP Grade
119–180	5
100–118	4
71–99	3
60–70	2
0–59	1

In May 2012, the score distributions of the more than 100,000 students who took the exam broke down as such: 10.5 percent earned 5s and 19.2 percent earned 4s (a little less than a third of all students earned either a 4 or 5). More than a third of students (36.0 percent) scored a 3. Overall, then, two-thirds of students scored a 3 or higher. If you prepare well for the examination and thoroughly use this guide, you can reasonably expect to earn a 4 or 5.

How to Interpret Your Practice Test Results

1. First, look at the multiple-choice score. It is a fair indicator of what your overall score will be. How many questions out of 80 did you get right?

2. According to College Board statistics for the 2009 Released Exam, most students who got a score of 5 on the examination earned a weighted score of 79 to 90 (or 71 to 80 questions answered correctly) on the multiple-choice section. More than one-third earning a 4 had weighted multiple-choice scores of 66 to 78 (61 to 70 correct answers); about 42 percent had a weighted score of 53 to 65 (46 to 60 correct answers). The vast majority of students earning a 3 on the exam had a weighted score of 40 to 65 (36 to 60 correct answers). Nearly 70 percent of students with a weighted score of 28 to 39 (25 to 35 correct answers) earned an exam score of 1 or 2. Students with a weighted score below 27 (24 correct answers) were mostly likely to get a 1 on the exam.

This demonstrates very clearly that if you want a 3, you must work to get at least half of the multiple-choice questions right; if you want a 4, you need to aim for two-thirds right; if you want a 5, you're aiming to get about 90 percent right.

3. Check to see if you got too many wrong answers for the goal you have set for yourself. Examine the ones you got wrong to see if you got them wrong because you did not know the answer or because you guessed poorly. Look at those questions closely to see what you might have missed that would have helped you make a better choice.

4. Examine your essay scores. What strengths and weaknesses do you find? If you did not do as well as you would have liked, try to focus on whatever problems you had in writing the essays. Was it your thesis statement, use of evidence, errors, or lack of organization? Once you identify your difficulties, you can focus your attention on addressing them.

5. Set a realistic goal for yourself. If you want a score of 4, for example, then your goal should be 55 out of 80 multiple-choice answers correct, a 6 or 7 on the document-based question, and a 5 or 6 on each thematic essay question. For an exam score of 5, raise the ante to 70 multiple-choice answers correct and essay scores of 8 (DBQ), 7, and 7 (thematic essays). If you have used this book and prepared well for the examination, you have every right to expect a score of 4 or 5.

6. Make it happen!

SECTION 2
A Review of
AP⋄ European History

PART 1
The Fourteenth Through Sixteenth Centuries

This part covers the following chapters in *A History of Western Society,* Eleventh Edition:

Chapter 11: The Later Middle Ages, 1300–1450

Chapter 12: European Society in the Age of the Renaissance, 1350–1550

Chapter 13: Reformations and Religious Wars, 1500–1600

Chapter 14: European Exploration and Conquest, 1450–1650

Although historians may disagree about a specific chronology or the lasting impact of the previous medieval period, most would agree that the fifteenth and sixteenth centuries were pivotal in creating the fundamental patterns and ideas that define modern Europe. The Renaissance, which began in Italy and slowly spread throughout Europe, empowered the individual, transformed both the arts and education, and sparked new interest in travel. This led to the "encounter" between the Old World and the New as well as European colonization of coastal regions of Asia and Africa. New religious movements fissured Catholic Europe. Serfdom virtually disappeared and the commercial middle classes became an increasingly powerful economic and political force in western Europe. This was less true in central Europe and hardly at all in eastern Europe, creating profound regional differences still apparent to this day.

One major transformation of this period was the movement of the dynamic center of Europe's economy from the Mediterranean to the Atlantic states—France, England, and Spain. While profitable commerce and thriving manufacturing provided the disposable wealth that funded Renaissance culture, the Ottoman conquest of Constantinople in 1453 and the economic disruptions caused by the Hundred Years' War between England and France (which ended that same year) began an economic decline of Italy that lasted until the industrialization of the Italian north 450 years later. The exploration of the New World, while often undertaken by Italians, was accomplished under the aegis of the Atlantic states—all of which began to prosper from ever-increasing trade with their American colonies. England and France underwent a commercial revolution in which newly formed mercantile elites, usually called the bourgeoisie, became increasingly powerful and a public force. The rise of this social class would have enormous political consequences in the seventeenth and eighteenth centuries. Europe's economy was transformed in other ways by the encounter with the New World. New crops, particularly the potato and maize (corn), provided more plentiful and healthier food for humans and animals alike. The influx of gold and silver drove up the prices of goods, which made the cost of living much higher for some, but also encouraged capitalistic production and the adoption of mercantilist policies by governments in order to retain that wealth.

Spain, England, and France became nation-states in this period, meaning that most people who spoke their language and shared their culture were united into one state under one ruler. The combined kingdom of Castile and Aragon conquered the last Muslim kingdom and opted for a monoreligious state, expelling its large and prosperous Jewish population in 1492 and forcibly converting Muslims. These changes reduced the viability of the bourgeoisie in Spain. The combined kingdom of Castile and Aragon was inherited by Charles V, whose empire included Austria, Spain, and the Netherlands. England and France developed nationalistic identities during their intermittent 100-year-long war. Due to England's early traditions of limitations on the power of the king, enshrined in the Magna Carta in 1215, England's Parliament formed its current bicameral structure and met regularly to approve new taxes to finance the war. When that war ended (1453), a civil war between rival factions erupted, resulting in a reduction of the aristocracy in size and the Tudor ascension to the throne. Two Tudors, Henry VIII and Elizabeth I, were remarkably able rulers. While manipulating the extant parliamentary structures, they expanded both the powers of the monarch and the wealth and prestige of the state as a whole by adopting Protestantism and competing fiercely with other Atlantic states. France too had strong monarchs, the Valois, who engaged in regular and persistent struggles with the Habsburg rulers of Austria and the Holy Roman emperors.

In central Europe, the Germanic and the Italian areas remained divided into many states until the nineteenth century rather than forging centralized nation-states. It was in the virtually independent city-states of Italy, and particularly in the republic of Florence, that the Renaissance was born. In the fifteenth century, the Florentines embraced new political and social values for which they found validation in classical antiquity, particularly the literature of the republic of Rome, whose eloquent defender Cicero was especially beloved by Renaissance humanists. These intellectuals sought to restore the study of classical literature and languages and created schools to encourage the study of letters, which they believed fostered both morality and the "universal man"—one competent in a wide variety of human pursuits from the arts to scholarship. Artists also turned to antiquity to find new aesthetic principles, new subjects, and new or rediscovered techniques, and in the 1420s made breathtaking innovations using mathematical perspective to create three-dimensional depth in painting (Masaccio), sculpting the first nudes since antiquity (Donatello), and designing the first dome in Europe in 900 years (Brunelleschi). Renaissance art reached its high point at the beginning of the sixteenth century with the extraordinary sculptures by Michelangelo and paintings by Leonardo da Vinci. Renaissance culture glorified the nobility and potential of humans, encouraging the growth of individualism, secularism, intellectual independence, and materialism.

Northern humanists were less attached to the Romans and Greeks and more involved in religious questions and texts. This study helped spark the Reformation, a religious movement that created the third major division within Christianity. Protestant churches rejected the primacy of the pope, the validity of most of the seven Catholic sacraments, and the role of priests and good works in winning salvation on the basis that such principles could not be found in Scripture. Martin Luther began this movement in 1517. Luther was protected by some German princes who sought to break out from the domination of the Holy Roman Empire and of the Catholic Church. Charles V, the Holy Roman emperor, defended Catholicism for the next thirty years after attempts to force Luther to recant failed. The Peace of Augsburg (1555), which ended this long struggle, gave each prince within the Holy Roman Empire the right to choose Lutheranism or Catholicism as the religion for his subjects. This enhancement of the power of local princes prevented the development of centralized monarchy within the empire. The Lutheran churches became national churches, elevating the language of the people to the language of liturgy and Scripture, and enhancing the power and wealth of rulers who confiscated Catholic lands and properties. Luther translated the Bible into German and urged his followers to read it. Protestantism spread widely throughout western and central Europe, with variations reflecting theological and national differences. Generally, Protestants rejected transubstantiation (the doctrine that the bread and wine of the Eucharist became the actual body and blood of Christ), monasticism, highly decorated churches, and priestly celibacy.

The most influential of the other Protestant sects was Calvinism, which emphasized the doctrine of predestination and demanded a puritanical, sober practice. Calvinism became popular in the commercial centers of the Netherlands and in Scotland, England, and western France. France's religious division was resolved by the victory of the Bourbons. When Henry IV of Navarre became king of France after a fractious religious war, he accepted Catholicism but issued the Edict of Nantes granting religious toleration to the Protestants in certain cities. In England, Henry VIII established the Anglican Church with the king as its titular head. The Catholic Church reorganized itself in the face of the Protestant challenge. The Council of Trent in the mid-sixteenth century reconfirmed Catholic doctrine but imposed some reforms. The pope created the Jesuits as a new order loyal to him to proselytize the faith at home and abroad and to create educational institutions for the Catholic elite. The Counter-Reformation, or the Catholic Reformation as it is also called, was successful in limiting the spread of Protestantism to parts of northern and western Europe.

By the sixteenth century, the population of Europe was restored to the level it had reached before 1347, when the Black Death—the bubonic plague—arrived and killed off about a third of the population as a whole and more than 60 percent of the residents in cities like Florence. Those who had survived were able to negotiate higher wages in the cities and a reduction in manorial obligations in the countryside. Although governments attempted to restrict wages and brutally repressed the French and English peasant revolts of the fourteenth century, this loosening of medieval restrictions became permanent in western Europe.

Technology also had a huge impact on the lives of people in this period. The mid-fifteenth-century printing press spread ideas (such as Protestantism) quickly, encouraged literacy, and benefited women, who now had the means for self-education. Maritime technological improvements made possible exploration, conquest, and transatlantic trade. The introduction of new foods and animals from the New World transformed agriculture.

Eastern Europe saw few of these changes. Orthodoxy was already a form of national church, and Protestantism made few inroads. Lacking access to the sea or the unity that promoted colonization, eastern European states remained almost entirely agricultural and feudal with small bourgeois classes. Muscovy began to organize the Russian state under the leadership of the Romanov dynasty. In Poland and Lithuania, the Jagellonian dynasty ruled a large state but did not develop a strong monarchy. Most of the Balkans was under the rule of the Ottoman Empire, which had conquered the region under the military skill of Sultan Suleiman the Magnificent.

Put broadly, the developments of the fourteenth, fifteenth, and sixteenth centuries created the foundations for later history: nation-states in western Europe; religious innovations and tensions; commercial capitalism; growing literacy; new values such as materialism, secularism, and individualism; decentralization in central Europe; and the retention of feudalism in eastern Europe.

CHAPTER 11
The Later Middle Ages, 1300–1450

Areas of focus: England, France, Italy, and Holland/Flanders

Main events: the Black Death, Hundred Years' War, the Babylonian Captivity/ Great Schism, and peasant revolts/urban uprisings

---

The following is a thematic summary of the material covered in Chapter 11 of *A History of Western Society:*

Politics

+ England and France became more nationalistic during the intermittently fought Hundred Years' War (1337–1453), which began as a feudal war over disputed claims of kingship and vassalage. The English won most of the important battles due to their use of new technologies like the longbow and cannon, but lost the crucial siege of Orléans because of the extraordinary political and military leadership of the young Joan d'Arc, later captured, tried, and executed as a witch. In the end, England had to give up most of its territorial gains.

+ In England (but not in France) the war led to the strengthening of Parliament, the national representative body. Kings called Parliament into session many times to get funds for the war. In France there were many provincial assemblies, not one.

✦ **AP Tip**   Typically, the AP Exam has few multiple-choice questions on specific battles; its focus is on the causes and consequences of war. It is wise not to skim over wars. If England had won the Hundred Years' War and held onto its French territories, its development as a nation-state would have been hindered. As it was, by losing everything in France except Calais, English nationalism was much enhanced.

Economy

+ The "Little Ice Age" (1300–1450) brought wetter and colder climates, severely reducing agricultural output. A terrible famine across Europe (1315–1322) increased vulnerability to diseases.

+ As a result of the massive population loss from the plague known as the Black Death (first reported in mainland Europe in 1347), urban craft guilds opened their doors to "new men" and tried efficient methods of production. Due to the scarcity of able-bodied workers, laborers could demand higher wages and the prices of goods rose.

✦ The Hundred Years' War devastated France's lands and disrupted its trade; high taxes to finance the war angered the peasants who bore their brunt. The war was also very costly for England.

✦ These economic dislocations led to the decline of serfdom in western Europe as landlords switched to cash rents and payments.

✦ **AP Tip** Pilgrimages and the veneration of saints continued to be an important part of the urban economy, since pilgrimages fostered trade and the founding of towns along their routes. The economic was tied to the religious. A question along those lines could potentially appear on the exam.

Religion

✦ Many people were convinced that the Black Death was a punishment from God; flagellants went from town to town whipping themselves in repentance.

✦ The papacy became subject to the French kings when it moved to Avignon in 1309. The sixty-seven years of the Avignon residency known as the Babylonian Captivity (1309–1376) were famously extravagant and hurt the prestige of the Catholic Church.

✦ John Wyclif denied a Scriptural basis for the church's secular powers and insisted that Scripture alone should be the basis of Christian belief and practice. He also insisted that it should be read by the laity. He was the first person to translate the Bible into English. Wyclif's followers, known as Lollards, allowed women to preach.

✦ Jan Hus brought Wyclif's ideas to Bohemia around 1400, where they were extremely popular among nationalistic Czechs. Hus was condemned as a heretic by the Council of Constance and burned at the stake. The Hussite Wars that followed (1419–1430s) were caused by a fusion of Czech nationalism and Hus's religious ideas. In the 1430s the emperor recognized the Hussite church in Bohemia.

✦ When the papacy returned to Rome in 1377, political disputes divided Europe into factions supporting one of the two, and later three, popes in what became known as the Great Schism. In 1417 the schism ended with the selection of a new pope at the Council of Constance.

✦ Popular Christianity expressed itself in confraternities, voluntary associations of men devoted to particular Christian tasks, and in the spread of lay mysticism, inspired by such figures as Meister Eckhart and Bridget of Sweden. The Brethren and Sisters of the Common Life, founded in Holland in the late fourteenth century, lived simple lives devoted to Christian charity. Their ideas were developed by Thomas à Kempis in his hugely popular work, *The Imitation of Christ*.

Society and Culture

✦ The event with the greatest impact on every aspect of society in the fourteenth century was the Black Death, the epidemic of bubonic plague that killed at least one-third of the population of Europe and upwards of 60 percent of the population in cities like Florence. Cities were crowded, filthy, and filled with rats bearing the disease; medical science was limited in its ability to cure the plague. Wealthier people fled the cities but remained vulnerable to the plague, which returned with increasingly less effect until 1721.

✦ The clergy generally tended the sick and dying at great risk. Contemporaries like the Florentine Boccaccio described a decline in moral standards and family feelings.

✦ The plague loosened social class strictures and briefly allowed greater social mobility.

✦ Economic hardship and then the plague increased ethnic group tensions, leading to violence against outsiders like Jews and lepers. Minorities were increasingly excluded from positions in church or government, and laws against intermarriage were instituted. New ideas about the importance of "blood" were particularly strong in Spain where "purity of blood"—meaning no Jewish or Muslim ancestors—became a national obsession. In Ireland, the English issued statutes denying the Irish the same rights as Englishmen.

✦ Peasants, angered by high taxes and their poor quality of life and resenting the privileges and demands of nobility and church, rose up in several rebellions, first in Flanders in the 1320s, then in a large-scale uprising in France—the Jacquerie—in 1358. In 1381, the English Peasants' Revolt exploded from resentment over the replacement of labor services by cash rents and a statute freezing wages and binding workers to their manors. Manors were attacked, nobles killed or attacked, manorial records destroyed. The rebellions were brutally suppressed.

✦ Demands for greater opportunity for journeymen in the guild system generally failed.

✦ Men and women married later, usually in their twenties, or even older for wealthier men. To deal with the problem of unwed young men, city governments in various parts of Europe set up brothels and regulated the women workers. Young men also took sex by force. Some engaged in same-sex relations, usually called "sodomy," which by the end of the fourteenth century had become a capital crime in most of Europe.

✦ Suffering from inflation and reduced income, some nobles became bandits and demanded protection money. This "fur-collar crime" aggravated peasants' lives.

Ideas and Literature

✦ New colleges and universities were established that, unlike their early medieval counterparts, tended to be more national (rather than international) in focus. Schools also spread, as did literacy.

✦ Several intellectuals and philosophers in the first half of the fourteenth century challenged the legitimacy of the papacy as an institution. William of Occam argued for separation of church and state and that governments must be limited and accountable to those they govern. Marsiglio of Padua argued that the church ought to be subordinate to the state and that the church should be run not by the pope and a hierarchical structure subservient to him but by a council of laymen and priests. The Catholic Church declared both men's works heretical, but a movement arose in support of their ideas.

✦ The fourteenth century saw the growth of vernacular literature, with two literary masterpieces bracketing the century. Dante's *Divine Comedy* described in poetic cantos the author's journey through Hell, Purgatory, and Heaven; in Hell, the great Roman poet Virgil accompanied him. Dante is considered a pivotal figure between the medieval and Renaissance periods, and due to his work, the Florentine vernacular became the basis of modern Italian. Geoffrey Chaucer's *Canterbury Tales* related ribald stories told by a group of pilgrims, reflecting the secularism and materialism of late medieval England.

Arts

✦ The Dance of Death became a common artistic motif, reflecting the impact of the plague.

CHAPTER 12
European Society in the Age of the Renaissance, 1350–1550

Areas of focus: England, France, Italy, and Spain

Main events: the Renaissance; nation-state development in France and England

---

The following is a thematic summary of the material covered in Chapter 12 of *A History of Western Society:*

Politics

+ The Italian peninsula was divided into numerous city-states that asserted their sovereignty even though they were technically under the rule of the Holy Roman Empire, the papacy, or local nobles. North of Rome, these city-states were organized into self-governing communes, either republics (such as Florence) or one-man dynasties known as *signori* (such as Milan). Most were dominated by oligarchies of merchants and wealthy guildsmen who repressed the political aspirations of the *popolo* (common people) and created courts as centers of culture.

+ The Medici banking family came to dominate Florence and later became hereditary dukes. Other important families were the Sforza in Milan and the Borgias, including Pope Alexander VI and his notorious son Cesare Borgia.

+ Italian city-states were constantly at war with each other, which left them vulnerable to the ambitions of France and the Holy Roman Empire. Periodically, they would form an alliance to prevent any one state from domination and to restore a balance of power.

+ In France, the Hundred Years' War (1337–1453) ended with the expulsion of the British (except from Calais). Charles VII strengthened the royal treasury with two new taxes, the *gabelle* on salt and the *taille* on land. His son Louis XI (the "Spider King") conquered Burgundy and brought other provinces into the kingdom through marriage, war, and inheritance.

+ In England, the Hundred Years' War was followed by civil war among the nobles known as the War of the Roses (1455–1471). It was won by the Tudor family, who set about enhancing royal power and prestige by dominating the nobles. Parliament continued to meet, but the royal council held the real power. Troublesome aristocrats were tortured and secretly tried in the Star Chamber. The Tudors restored domestic stability, encouraged economic growth, and empowered the monarchy.

+ Spain became a territorially unified state. The *reconquista,* the 700-year-old struggle to regain Spain as a Christian state from Muslim rule, was completed in 1492 with the conquest of Granada by Ferdinand of Aragon and Isabella of Castile. Ferdinand and

Isabella followed a common policy of dominating the aristocrats and enhancing their political authority, but they did not unite their states. Their grandson, the Holy Roman emperor Charles V, was the last great dynastic ruler of large areas of western and central Europe, including Spain, the Netherlands, and Austria.

✦ **AP Tip** Advances in military technology such as artillery and the longbow enabled common men to wield weapons. First used by the English in the Hundred Years' War, these weapons put noblemen out of work as knights.

Economy

+ Prosperous trade and thriving manufacture created a great deal of disposable wealth in the northern Italian communes. The wealthy medieval ports of Venice and Genoa were soon rivaled by Florence, whose merchants traded a great variety of goods and whose bankers dominated investments and loans throughout Europe. Florence also generated wealth through its high-quality silk and wool manufacturing.

+ City economic life was dominated by trade guilds, which acted to guarantee profit for all guild masters with controls over quality of materials, hours of operation, and wages. The leaders of the major guilds (such as wool or silk manufacturers) became wealthy and powerful and often patrons of the arts.

Religion

+ Both France and Spain developed national churches under the effective authority of the king by the early sixteenth century. François I negotiated the Concordat of Bologna with the papacy, giving the French monarch virtual control of church officials in France. Ferdinand and Isabella won from the papacy the right to appoint bishops in Spain. Later in the century, these concessions made it easier for the monarchs to resist Protestantism.

+ In Spain, the royal goal of uniformity in religion led to the 1492 expulsion of those Jews who would not convert (about 150,000 people) and the forced conversion of Muslims. An all-Spain Inquisition was established in 1478 to ferret out false *conversos* or New Christians, and stress was placed on "purity of blood," implying Jewishness was a hereditary condition.

Society and Culture

+ The terms *race, people,* and *nation* were used interchangeably during this period.

+ While the word *class* itself was not in use, social gradations based on wealth were widely acknowledged, particularly in towns where wealthy merchants gained much political power. Nevertheless, the basic medieval social order (those who fight, those who pray, those who work) retained influence, with nobles holding onto prestige and power.

+ By the end of the fourteenth century, *les querelles des femmes* (debates about women)— their characters, intellectual abilities, and natures, and what type of education they should receive—were avidly discussed, mostly by learned men and some women, particularly writers like Christine de Pizan and women humanists like Laura Cereta. Though much of this discourse touted the virtuous wife and the domestic ideal, many women worked (at one-half to two-thirds the wages of men). The debate intensified when such powerful rulers as Elizabeth I of England or Isabella of Castile challenged gender stereotypes.

✦ The printing press using movable type was developed in Germany, especially by Johann Gutenberg, in the mid-fifteenth century. The press and the increasing availability of inexpensive paper sparked an exponential growth in the output of printed books (somewhere between 8 and 20 million within a half century of the publication of Gutenberg's Bible in 1456) and in the number of printers. The printing press transformed the lives of ordinary people as well as intellectuals, reducing the gap between the illiterate who relied on oral culture and the literate. Printed books encouraged communication among readers and served to unite people who read and discussed ideas. Governments and churches feared the new technology and censored books but used the printing press for their own purposes as well.

✦ A good number of black slaves came to Europe in the fifteenth century; by 1530, the Portuguese sold about 4,000–5,000 each year to the markets of Seville, Barcelona, Marseilles, and Genoa. In some Portuguese cities, the slaves and free blacks comprised about 10 percent of the population. In western Europe, free blacks worked in virtually all occupations and, on the Iberian Peninsula, sometimes intermarried with locals.

✦ **AP Tip**   Keep in mind the way the cultural movement of the Renaissance and the new values it spawned intersected with changes in political, social, and religious ideas in the next centuries and the ways the Renaissance changed as it moved from country to country. Many free-response questions on the AP Exams have asked students to answer questions using their knowledge of the Renaissance as a starting point.

Ideas and Literature

✦ The Renaissance is defined in part by the development of a new intellectual movement called humanism, which rejected the scholasticism of medieval universities. Instead, humanists called for a rediscovery of classical antiquity, at first Roman, and then, beginning in the fifteenth century, Greek. In classical literature, humanists found models of excellent Latin (Cicero); information on science, medicine, and the arts (Galen, Vitruvius, and Plato); justification for republican values and even regicide (again Cicero); and guidance for the ideal man who had *virtú* (the ability to shape the world around oneself) and sought excellence in every human endeavor.

✦ Humanism began in the fourteenth century, first as a literary movement with the writings of Dante; the poetry of Petrarch; and the work of Florentines Boccaccio, Bruni, and Alberti, who all articulated humanist ideals and expressed their great love of antiquity. Later humanists became Neoplatonists and established schools for the education of young men according to the new principles.

✦ Under the patronage of Cosimo de Medici (1389–1464), the scholar Marsilio Ficino (1433–1499) established the Platonic Academy, an informal group of Florence's cultural elite.

✦ Florentine humanist Niccolò Machiavelli (1469–1527) created the first modern analysis of political science in writing *The Prince* (1513), which uses the examples of classical and contemporary rulers to argue that the function of a ruler (or any government) is to preserve order and security. Whereas medieval political philosophers regarded the standards by which all governments were to be judged as emanating from moral principles established by God, Machiavelli argued that governments should instead be judged by how well they provided security, order, and safety to their populace.

✦ In the late fifteenth century, northern humanists synthesized the Christian and classical traditions, seeing humanist learning as a way to bring about reform of the church and deepen people's spiritual lives. Christian humanists like Desiderius Erasmus (1466?–1536) of Rotterdam and Thomas More (1478–1535), sought to combine classical ideals of calmness, stoical patience, and broad-mindedness with the Christian virtues of love, faith, and hope.

✦ **AP Tip** Renaissance individualism is easily seen in the new literary genre of autobiography or the new artistic genre of the portrait—a useful point to make in essays.

Arts

✦ Perhaps the most noted achievements of the Renaissance were in the visual arts: painting, sculpture, and architecture.

✦ At the beginning of the fourteenth century, Giotto had added monumentality and emotionality to painting. In 1420s Florence, Renaissance artists such as Masaccio discovered the potential of mathematical perspective and proportionality in bringing their paintings to life.

✦ Donatello sculpted the first nude since antiquity, the Old Testament figure of David. Sculptors aimed to represent the realities and the glories of the human body as they had in ancient times.

✦ In architecture, Brunelleschi designed the Foundling Hospital—the first contemporary building to use rounded Roman arches instead of pointed Gothic arches, and he designed and built the first dome in 900 years in Europe.

✦ Artists increasingly turned to classical antiquity for subjects, depicting pagan gods, goddesses, and heroes, as seen in Botticelli's *The Birth of Venus*, although religious scenes remained popular subjects.

✦ In Florence, most of the commissions in the early Renaissance came from the commune (city government), guilds, or wealthy merchants. Later in the Renaissance, princely courts (such as the Duke of Ferrara and the Medicis of Florence), churches, and the Vatican itself became major patrons of the arts. The Vatican commissioned both Raphael's *School of Athens* and Michelangelo's Sistine Chapel frescos. Venice, too, became an important artistic center with such noteworthy artists as Titian.

✦ Two new art forms developed during the Renaissance, landscape painting and portraiture. The latter reflected the dramatic individualism of the day.

✦ In northern Europe, great Flemish artists like Jan van Eyck and Rogier van der Weyden made technological innovations such as the use of oil-based paint (instead of fresco) and striking attention to detail and realism.

✦ The social status of artists increased enormously during the Renaissance, as they moved from being viewed as artisans to "men of genius"—wealthy, adored, and sought after. Young artists trained at the workshops of well-established artists, and by the mid-sixteenth century artistic academies were established.

✦ Women were generally excluded from this new artistic world; there were no women architects and only one sculptress. There were a number of painters, but most women involved in artistic activity worked as embroiderers or painted on porcelain. Women were excluded from the art academies and usually trained with artists, often their fathers.

✦ **AP Tip** The most famous female artist was painter Artemisia Gentileschi, whose life and work illustrate the intersection of gender issues and art particularly well.

CHAPTER 13
Reformations and Religious Wars, 1500–1600

Areas of focus: Germanic states, England, France, Switzerland, the Netherlands

Main events: the development of Lutheranism, Calvinism, and other forms of Protestantism; the Catholic Reformation; religious violence

---

The following is a thematic summary of the material covered in Chapter 13 of *A History of Western Society:*

Politics

+ Political developments and wars of this period were intimately connected with religious movements and challenges to the Catholic Church and its supporters. In every country in western and central Europe, religion and politics intersected.

+ Protestantism in most places enhanced the power of the monarch or prince. Protestant churches were national churches whose liturgy was spoken and written in the vernacular, and typically Protestant churches were under the authority of the ruler in one way or another.

+ Many rulers in the Germanic states around 1300, under the titular authority of the Holy Roman emperor, saw Protestantism as a way to break free of the emperor, enhance their own authority, and fill the coffers of the state with confiscated church properties like monasteries. The support of these princes was crucial for the success of the Protestant reformers. The political and military effort led by Holy Roman Emperor Charles V to stop Protestantism ultimately failed.

+ The Peace of Augsburg in 1555 granted each prince or ruler within the empire the right to choose Catholicism or Lutheranism, to which all his subjects were to adhere or move. With this division, the possibility of the Germanic states unifying under a centralized state dimmed.

+ In England, the Tudor king Henry VIII, unable to win a marriage annulment from the pope (desired because he lacked a male heir), with parliamentary support established a national Church of England with himself as the head. There was substantial opposition from those loyal to the Catholic Church, such as Sir Thomas More (author of *Utopia*), who was executed, and Henry's daughter Mary Tudor, whose five-year reign (1553–1558) temporarily restored Catholicism in England.

+ Under Elizabeth I (r. 1558–1603) an uneasy compromise was reached in doctrine and practice in England, although fundamental religious differences between the official

Church of England and Puritans flared up again with great intensity in the seventeenth century.

✦ In France, the struggle over religion led to civil war and violent outbursts such as the notorious St. Bartholomew's Day massacre of the Huguenots (Calvinists) on August 24, 1572. Henry of Navarre, leader of the Protestant forces, ultimately won the war but converted back to Catholicism to achieve domestic peace. In 1598, he issued the Edict of Nantes granting religious liberty to the Huguenots in 150 towns. His practical political compromise identifies him as a *politique*.

Economy

✦ In the Germanic states, peasants latched onto the new Protestant ideas, while in France, England, and Scotland, the urban middle classes were drawn toward Calvinism. The commercial classes found the Calvinist emphasis on labor and hard work especially appealing. This phenomenon led to impassioned debate among historians about the intersection of capitalism and Calvinism.

✦ In early-sixteenth-century Germany, the economic condition of the peasantry was generally worse than it had been in the previous century and was deteriorating. Crop failures in 1523 and 1524 aggravated religious tensions.

Religion

✦ There were long-standing criticisms of the church prior to the Reformation, aimed at church practices—simony (the selling of offices); nepotism; pluralism (the holding of more than one office by a church official) and its accompaniment, absenteeism; and the luxury and wealth of the papacy. Anticlericalism—the disparaging of priests for drunkenness, cupidity, and sexual immorality—was also widespread.

✦ Martin Luther, an Augustinian monk and professor at the University of Wittenberg, was consumed by religious doubts. When the church authorized the selling of indulgences (deeds promising forgiveness of sins and reduction of time in purgatory), Luther responded with his famous *Ninety-five Theses* (1517), which challenged the theological justification for indulgences. When Charles V called upon Luther to recant at the Diet of Worms in 1521 or face excommunication, Luther refused and, protected by the Elector of Saxony, escaped persecution. Luther married, wrote voluminously (both prose and hymns), translated the Bible into German, and formed a new church. Lutheranism spread in north Germany and to Scandinavia.

✦ Ulrich Zwingli, who disagreed with Luther about the nature of the Eucharist, believed that the Scriptures were the words of God. He devoted his life to reforming the church in Zurich, and he established the Swiss Reformation.

✦ John Calvin stressed predestination, the belief that God had decided at the beginning of time who would be saved and who damned. In Geneva, Calvin established a theocratic state in which city laws were determined by religious values. Gambling, the theater, dancing, prostitution, and the like were all banned. Calvinism's sober, strict vision became the most widespread variety of Protestantism. John Knox brought it to Scotland, and it also spread to the Netherlands, England (the Puritans), and France (the Huguenots).

✦ There was great variety among radical Protestants. Some sought to establish a new society with communal values and eschewed private property. Some, such as Michael Servetus, who was executed in Geneva for heresy, denied the Scriptural basis of the Trinity. The Anabaptists denied the validity of infant baptism. Most radical Protestants rejected the notion of an established church and were persecuted by other Protestants and Catholics alike.

✦ In response to the Protestant threat, the Catholic Church initiated internal reforms, ended abuses like simony, improved the education of priests, and initiated new orders. The Ursulines, founded by Angela Merici, focused on the education of women, while the Jesuits, founded by Ignatius Loyola, saw themselves as soldiers of Christ. They took a special oath to the pope, proselytized in the New World and Asia, and created educational institutions for the Catholic elite. At the same time, the church at the Council of Trent in the mid-sixteenth century refused to modify its theological doctrines. By and large, the Catholic Reformation proved successful in preventing the further spread of Protestantism after the sixteenth century.

✦ **AP Tip** In 1500 there was one Christian church in western Europe to which all Christians at least nominally belonged. One hundred years later there were many. Below is a chart highlighting differences among the different religious groups. Note that for the Calvinists and radicals, only their differences with the Lutherans are listed, as they are all Protestant divisions.

	DENOMINATION			
THEOLOGICAL POINT	**Catholic**	**Lutheran**	**Calvinist**	**Radicals: Anabaptist**
Afterlife	Heaven, Hell, purgatory	Heaven, Hell (no purgatory)		
Role of Church	crucial for salvation hierarchy	justification by faith alone	salvation predestined	
Role of Priests	perform miracle of the Mass; hear confession; offer penance	priesthood of believers; ministers as teachers/leaders	ministers as moral arbiters	ministers as community leaders
Eucharist	transubstantiation	real presence		
Baptism	infant	infant		adult
Church/State Relations	universal church; church above state	state above church	state and church together	religious conscience outweighs state law
Language of Liturgy	Latin	vernacular		
Church Decoration	elaborate, showing the glory of God	simple	austere; no images	

Society and Culture

✦ In the Germanic states, peasants flocked to Lutheranism, seeing the principle of social equality in its doctrine of a "priesthood of all believers." In 1525, the peasants rose up in rebellion. The German Peasants' War was triggered by crop failures, noble seizure of common lands that had been traditionally farmed by peasants, and unjust rents and taxes. The peasants believed that their demands conformed to the Scriptures and sought support from Luther. Although initially sympathetic, Luther soon decried the lawlessness of the peasants and wrote a tract urging the nobles to suppress and if necessary kill the marauding hordes. The peasants were brutally suppressed, with about 75,000 killed.

✦ Protestantism is often associated with growing individualism, as each individual was to meet his God directly, and with secularism, as nearly all Protestants rejected the monastic ideal. On the whole, though, Protestantism was neither secular nor tolerant of individualism.

✦ Women's roles were enhanced by Protestant notions of marriage as the bedrock of Christian communities. While women were not allowed to preach in Protestant churches, they were encouraged to read the Bible and take charge of the religious education of their young. Marriage in this period began to be seen as a partnership.

✦ The period 1550–1650 was the height of the witchcraft craze, when hundreds of thousands of people, mostly women, were accused of witchcraft. Those accused of acting on behalf of Satan were interrogated, tried, and often tortured. Some 40,000–60,000 were put to death. Surprisingly, few people were executed for witchcraft in strongly Catholic states like Italy and Spain; the greatest numbers of victims were in the areas of greatest religious conflict. In countries like England, where the legal rights of the accused were protected, relatively few "witches" perished.

Ideas and Literature

✦ The Reformation spawned much furious intellectual discourse over religion.

✦ Protestantism encouraged literacy. Initially, the spread of Luther's ideas was made possible by illustrated broadsides, often with anti-papal cartoons. With Luther's translation of the Bible into German and similar translations made into the vernacular by Protestants elsewhere (including the King James Bible in early-seventeenth-century Britain), as well as the theological emphasis given to Scripture, ordinary people were increasingly taught to read.

Arts

✦ Calvinists were iconoclasts, that is, destroyers of religious images. Believing that such images broke the Ten Commandments, they frequently destroyed the art in ornate Catholic churches. Calvinist churches by contrast were austere, with little or no decoration.

CHAPTER 14
European Exploration and Conquest, 1450–1650

> **Areas of focus:** Europe, the New World, Asia, Africa
>
> **Main events:** exploration and colonization of Asia, Africa, and the New World; the Columbian Exchange

The following is a thematic summary of the material covered in Chapter 14 of *A History of Western Society:*

Politics

✦ **AP Tip** This chapter is rich with detail regarding global trade. Pay particular attention to those sections that deal with Europe. The chapter also provides important background to the long-term legacy of colonialism.

✦ European exploration was made possible by the growth of government power. The reassertion of monarchical authority and state centralization in the fifteenth century enabled rulers to provide the massive funds needed for exploration.

✦ Portugal led the way in empire expansion, starting in 1415 with the conquest of Ceuta in Northern Africa, and then the exploration of the entire African coast. After a route to India via the Cape of Good Hope was discovered in 1497, Lisbon became the entrance port for Asian goods into Europe. In 1500 a Portuguese fleet claimed Brazil for the Crown.

✦ Spain, newly unified as a territorial state after the defeat of the last Moorish kingdom in 1492 (also the year of Columbus's first journey), became a hugely powerful state in the next century and competed with the Dutch, the English, and the French both abroad and within Europe. The two most famous Spanish conquistadors were soldier-explorers Hernando Cortés and Francisco Pizarro, who defeated the Aztecs and Incas respectively.

✦ Among the most famous explorers were Columbus (a Genoese); Vasco da Gama (Portuguese), the first explorer to round the coast of Africa (1498); and Ferdinand Magellan (Portuguese), who first circumnavigated the globe (1522). The Florentine Amerigo Vespucci's name was given to the New World. While many explorers were Italian, the Italian city-states did not participate in colonization.

✦ The Dutch, although still officially under Spanish rule until 1609, became an international power, with valuable colonies in Indonesia (the Spice Islands), western South Africa, and the Americas (parts of Brazil and New Amsterdam, taken by the British and renamed New York in 1664).

✦ Spain and France introduced European political concepts into its colonies in the New World. *Intendants* were royal officials possessing broad political, military, and financial powers. Portugal used similar officials called *corregidores*.

✦ The colonization of the New World accelerated the economic and political ascendancy of the Atlantic states over the Mediterranean and central European states.

Economy

✦ A new global economy emerged in this period, with Europeans bringing goods from the New World to Europe and Asia and buying Asian goods with New World silver to take back to Europe, Africa, and the New World for sale. This trade included the import and sale of African slaves in the New World, where they were put to work producing sugar and other commodities of high value in the world market.

✦ Spain had a huge surge in national wealth as a result of the gold and silver mined in its colonies in the New World, especially after the 1545 discovery of silver mines in Potosi (modern Bolivia), leading to its *siglo d'oro,* or Golden Age. As China demanded payment for its goods in silver, silver was a key element in global trade.

✦ Europeans experienced a price revolution exacerbated by the infusion of gold and silver from the New World into Spain, resulting in inflation that spread throughout the continent. Inflation strained government budgets, and prices doubled or even quadrupled in much of Europe. Inflation also put a squeeze on those with fixed incomes, particularly aristocrats whose income was limited by customary rents on their lands.

✦ New crops from the New World—particularly corn and the potato, and later the tomato—transformed the European economy and diet. In turn, the economy and diet of the New World was transformed by the introduction of European crops and livestock, especially sugar and wheat, sheep, horses, pigs, and chickens. This system is commonly known as the Columbian Exchange. Its darker side was the exchange of disease, with European diseases like smallpox causing unprecedented death tolls among the natives of the Americas.

✦ The slave trade was lucrative for European capitalists. Slaves remained relatively rare on the continent, but the importation of black slaves from Africa to European colonies in the New World, probably some 10 million in all, made the slave trade a greatly valued component in the expanding commercial economy.

✦ Spain introduced the encomienda system to its New World colonies to manage its many plantations and the treatment of the Native Americans. Conquerors were given the right to demand forced labor from the Indians, though officially enslaving them was banned.

Religion

✦ Religious motivations for exploration were galvanized by Spain's successful reconquista, by legends like that of Prester John, widely believed to have established a Christian kingdom somewhere in Africa, and by the expansion of Islam into Europe following the Ottoman conquest of Constantinople in 1453.

✦ Religious motives were important factors of the European colonization. In the New World, missionaries—mostly Franciscans, Dominicans, and Jesuits—spread not only Christianity but also European methods of agriculture and the idea of loyalty to the Crown. Huge numbers of Indians were converted, although their new faith was often based on cultural misunderstandings and imbued with elements of their original faiths.

✦ In the English colonies on the Atlantic coast of North America, various groups of religious dissidents founded colonies, including Puritans in Massachusetts, Catholics in Maryland, and Quakers in Pennsylvania.

Society and Culture

✦ The consequences of the European conquest and colonization were devastating for the native peoples of the New World. Disease to which indigenous people had no immunity claimed the lives of millions. Estimated death tolls vary, but they go as high as 95 percent of the pre-conquest population. Overwork, malnutrition, and hunger from forced labor killed many more.

✦ Europeans interbred with the native populations and imported slaves, creating new populations and ethnicities. In Spanish America the complex feelings of self-identity gave rise to a new vocabulary that sought to define racial mixing. In the Portuguese, Spanish, and French colonies, substantial populations of free blacks descended from the freed children of these unions. In English colonies, masters were less likely to free children they fathered with female slaves.

✦ Exploration and colonization offered opportunities of adventure and wealth for ambitious young European men and havens for religions dissidents.

✦ Where English and Spanish women accompanied the men as colonial settlers, European languages and culture took root; where women did not, as in European colonies in West Africa and Asia, indigenous peoples retained their own languages and religion.

✦ The English maintained an attitude of cultural superiority toward the natives of the New World and segregated them both physically and socially, while in the French colonies, settlers were encouraged to develop relationships with local people.

Ideas and Literature

✦ Exploration was made possible by numerous technological innovations, many from Asia, such as the magnetic compass, the lateen sail, and gunpowder. The Portuguese development of the caravel, replacing the galley ship, enabled larger cargos to be carried. Great advances in mapmaking were also made in this period. Ptolemy's *Geography,* introduced by Arab scholars in 1410, vastly improved geographical knowledge over medieval texts. Invented by the ancient Greeks and perfected in the Islamic world, the astrolabe allowed mariners to plot their latitude.

✦ Encounters with the "primitive" natives of the New World stirred the imagination of European intellectuals, most notably the French writer Michel de Montaigne. In the sixteenth century he created a new form of writing, the personal essay. One of these essays, "On Cannibals," challenged the labeling of New World natives as savages or barbarians. He argued that such terms reflected discomfort with new ideas and experiences rather than a rational understanding of them.

✦ William Shakespeare's work reveals the impact of the new discoveries and contacts of his day. In his play *The Tempest,* Shakespeare explored race relations with the encounter of Europeans and natives on an unnamed island, and in *Othello* the title character is a Moor, a Muslim of North African origin.

✦ Cosmography, natural history, and geography aroused enormous interest among educated people in the fifteenth and sixteenth centuries. One of the most popular books of the time was the fourteenth-century text *The Travels of Sir John Mandeville,* which purported to be a firsthand account of the author's travels.

✦ As Europeans' involvement in the slave trade grew, they drew on and developed ideas about Africans' primitiveness and barbarity to defend slavery and even argue that enslavement benefited Africans by bringing Christianity to pagan peoples. Slavery became identified with blackness as the African slave trade fostered such racist ideas.

Arts

✦ European artists were fascinated with images of "the other"—the natives of Asia, Africa, and particularly the Americas.

✦ In the Spanish-controlled areas of the New World a popular genre of paintings known as *castas* depicted couples composed of individuals of different ethnic origin and their children.

PRACTICE EXAM 1

EUROPEAN HISTORY
SECTION I

Multiple-Choice Questions
(Time—55 minutes)
Number of questions—80

Directions: Each of the questions or incomplete statements below is followed by five suggested answers or completions. For each question, select the best response.

1. Among the consequences of European involvement in the African slave trade was
   (A) a decrease in anti-Semitism
   (B) the development of new racist ideas
   (C) greater respect for the idea that all men are equal before God
   (D) the association of blackness with vigor and strength
   (E) greater tolerance of Islam

2. Until the beginning of the sixteenth century, criticism of the Catholic Church was focused primarily on
   (A) relics and transubstantiation
   (B) the church's refusal to allow priests to marry
   (C) immorality and ignorance among the clergy
   (D) overly spiritual bishops who devoted themselves to religious studies
   (E) the refusal of the church to allow divorce

3. The impact of the Protestant Reformation included all of the following EXCEPT
   (A) reform of practices within the Catholic Church
   (B) division among Protestants
   (C) religious wars
   (D) religious fragmentation of the Holy Roman Empire
   (E) improved social conditions for the peasants

4. Henry VIII broke from the Catholic Church because of
   (A) his serious doubts about Catholic theology
   (B) his concerns about succession
   (C) his desire to protect Protestants in England
   (D) the influence of his first wife
   (E) his political conflicts with Spain

GO ON TO THE NEXT PAGE.

5. The Council of Trent

   (A) affirmed Catholic theology
   (B) offered reconciliation with the Protestants
   (C) limited the number of saints to be honored
   (D) separated the papacy from its role as temporal ruler
   (E) allowed couples to exchange marriage vows without witnesses

6. The series of civil wars in France during the sixteenth century ended because of

   (A) success by the Catholics
   (B) a moderate policy by King Henry IV
   (C) the expulsion of the Huguenots
   (D) invasion by the Spanish Habsburgs
   (E) peacemaking efforts by the pope

7. The importation of massive amounts of gold and silver into Spain ultimately damaged Spain by

   (A) creating a huge crime wave
   (B) personally corrupting the monarchs such as Philip II
   (C) fostering inflation, which increased the royal debt
   (D) allowing Spain to engage in war after war
   (E) dividing Spain from Portugal

8. What most contributed to Europeans' susceptibility to the Black Death in the fourteenth and fifteenth centuries?

   (A) Outbreaks of smallpox occurring at the same time
   (B) Superstition and fear
   (C) Famine and malnutrition
   (D) Dependence on herbal remedies
   (E) Most people living in the countryside

9. The Renaissance was able to begin in Italy primarily because of

   (A) Italy's culturally sophisticated monasteries
   (B) the dominance of the Catholic Church in Italy
   (C) strong alliances between Italian city-states
   (D) wealth created from Italy's extensive trade network
   (E) Italy's strong sense of nationalism

10. An educated woman during the Renaissance

   (A) was expected to bring honor and order to her husband and household
   (B) was allowed to teach a limited number of courses at local universities
   (C) was no better educated than an educated woman from the medieval era
   (D) had to publish any writings under the name of a man
   (E) could run for political office in the smaller republics

11. Florentine humanists were particularly drawn to Cicero because of his eloquence and his

   (A) eulogies for Caesar Augustus, the first Roman emperor
   (B) moral philosophy
   (C) historical writings
   (D) defense of the Roman Republic
   (E) defense of Christianity in its early days

GO ON TO THE NEXT PAGE.

12. The Inquisition in Spain was spurred by

  (A) rising unrest among the peasants as famine struck the countryside
  (B) Ferdinand and Isabella's unification of their two states into one
  (C) resentment toward wealthy New Christians
  (D) Spain's desire for French lands on the continent
  (E) the intellectual curiosity promoted during the Renaissance

13. Which of the following statements could be made by a Protestant but not by a Catholic?

  (A) Salvation comes through faith alone.
  (B) Indulgences demonstrate one's sincerity of repentance.
  (C) Only clergy should interpret Scriptures.
  (D) There are seven sacraments.
  (E) In the process of transubstantiation, the bread and wine become the actual body and blood of Christ.

14. Which of the following was NOT an outcome of the Catholic Reformation?

  (A) The establishment of new religious orders
  (B) Modification of the doctrine of penance
  (C) Greater clerical discipline
  (D) A strong Roman Inquisition to destroy heresy
  (E) Spiritual renewal within the church

15. France experienced riots and civil wars during the sixteenth century because of

  (A) religious conflicts between Catholics and Huguenots
  (B) religious conflicts between Protestants and Huguenots
  (C) class conflicts between the aristocracy and the peasants
  (D) political conflicts between politiques and monarchists
  (E) political conflicts between republicans and politiques

16. The initial leader in Europe's exploration of the world during the fifteenth century was

  (A) France
  (B) England
  (C) Spain
  (D) Portugal
  (E) The Netherlands

17. Which of the following was NOT a motive for European exploration during the fifteenth and sixteenth centuries?

  (A) Widespread desire for greater economic opportunities
  (B) Curiosity during the Renaissance about the physical world and its peoples
  (C) Italians hoping to find land that emigrants from their overpopulated states could settle
  (D) An increased desire for spices and luxury goods
  (E) A fervent desire to spread Christianity to other lands

GO ON TO THE NEXT PAGE.

18. The results of the Hundred Years' War included all of the following EXCEPT

    (A) losses in the number of knights, which led to a decline in the number of local magistrates and an increase in disorder
    (B) a significant decline in English wool exports
    (C) the House of Commons in England won the right to approve all royal taxes
    (D) France established a powerful single national assembly from its many provincial assemblies
    (E) nationalistic feelings rose in Britain and France

19. Which is true about literature before the Renaissance?

    (A) Vernacular poetry and stories were the dominant literary forms.
    (B) Only the clergy were allowed to read literature.
    (C) Virtually all works of literature were written in Latin.
    (D) Major works of literature were written but banned by the Catholic Church.
    (E) Literacy rates remained low, so few people were reading in the fifteenth century.

20. In his writings, Erasmus of Rotterdam advocated

    (A) a utopian society
    (B) the importance of civic virtue
    (C) the importance of simplicity and education in religion
    (D) an end to gender inequality in education
    (E) the end of the papacy as a temporal power after the discovery that the Donation of Constantine was a forgery

21. Henry VII of England instituted the Court of Star Chamber as a method of

    (A) implementing the beginning stages of democracy
    (B) intimidating aristocrats who might compete for his power
    (C) punishing rebellious peasants
    (D) support for the Inquisition
    (E) the initial foundation of a judicial system

22. "I cannot and will not recant anything for it is neither safe nor right to go against conscience. God help me." Which critic of the Catholic Church made the statement?

    (A) Jan Hus
    (B) John Wyclif
    (C) Erasmus of Rotterdam
    (D) Martin Luther
    (E) John Calvin

23. Elizabeth I resolved the religious issue in sixteenth-century England by

    (A) eliminating all Catholic elements in the Church of England
    (B) requiring all subjects to attend church but not caring what they believed
    (C) returning England to its Catholic roots
    (D) converting to Catholicism for the sake of peace in her country
    (E) remaining Protestant but marrying a Catholic

GO ON TO THE NEXT PAGE.

24. Calvin's followers

    (A) were held to a high standard of morality
    (B) believed that baptism should be granted only to adults
    (C) objected to the English Puritans
    (D) were granted freedom of religion with the Peace of Augsburg
    (E) were most known for their missionary work

25. Calvinists attracted large numbers of converts in all of the following countries EXCEPT

    (A) Scotland
    (B) The Netherlands
    (C) Switzerland
    (D) Austria
    (E) France

26. Which group on the continent did NOT benefit economically from the Black Death?

    (A) Men seeking admission to guilds
    (B) Rich farmers who could buy out their poorer neighbors
    (C) Speculators
    (D) Aristocratic landowners dependent on rents
    (E) Wage earners

27. Joan of Arc became and remains an important symbolic figure in France because she

    (A) was a martyr for the Christian faith
    (B) saved the French monarchy
    (C) was an early advocate of equality for women
    (D) was tried and executed for heresy and witchcraft by the Burgundians
    (E) had been publicly thanked by Charles VII

28. The impact of the Hundred Years' War on representative assemblies was that

    (A) both French and English assemblies were strengthened
    (B) neither French nor English assemblies were strengthened
    (C) the French but not the English assembly was strengthened
    (D) the English but not the French assembly was strengthened
    (E) representative assemblies everywhere in Europe were getting stronger, so that the Hundred Years' War's impact was relatively small

29. John Wyclif's and Marsiglio of Padua's criticisms of the church

    (A) were similar in that both advocated that the authority of the church should lie in church councils
    (B) differed in that Marsiglio focused on theological issues while Wyclif focused on church abuses
    (C) led to both men's excommunication
    (D) had little immediate impact
    (E) differed in that Marsiglio focused on political and administrative issues while Wyclif focused on theological issues

GO ON TO THE NEXT PAGE.

30. Thomas à Kempis, author of the *Imitation of Christ*, and Bridget of Sweden are both representative of

    (A) the conciliar movement
    (B) the growth of lay piety and mysticism in the fourteenth and fifteenth centuries
    (C) disillusionment with Christianity as a religion
    (D) the impact of religious figures on the Hundred Years' War
    (E) the impact of the Black Death in the fourteenth century

31. The English Peasants' Revolt of 1381 reflected the

    (A) deteriorating conditions of the peasants
    (B) overwhelming success of the Statute of Laborers of 1351
    (C) rising expectations of the peasants
    (D) widespread support for the head tax
    (E) lack of common interests between urban workers and peasants

32. How did practices surrounding sex and gender change in the fourteenth and fifteenth centuries?

    (A) Women were granted membership in the guilds for the first time.
    (B) Women typically married late in their twenties in northwestern Europe.
    (C) Prostitution was outlawed and severely punished.
    (D) There were many prosecutions and severe punishment for rape.
    (E) Homosexuality rarely came to the attention of public authorities.

33. Jan Hus, Dante Alighieri, and Geoffrey Chaucer were all

    (A) religious reformers
    (B) advocates for the Catholic Church
    (C) well-known poets
    (D) residents of England
    (E) forgers of national identity

34. In the typical northern Italian commune during the Renaissance

    (A) people owned property in common
    (B) the entire male adult population had the franchise; women did not
    (C) nobles ruled as princes
    (D) the ruling families had similar interests and rarely fought each other
    (E) merchant oligarchies held power

35. Renaissance humanists were different from their medieval counterparts in that

    (A) medieval humanists did not read the classics
    (B) Renaissance humanists did not read Christian texts from antiquity
    (C) Renaissance humanists exalted the dignity of man, while medieval humanists exalted the dignity of God
    (D) Renaissance humanists rejected Christianity in favor of paganism, while medieval humanists rejected paganism in favor of Christianity
    (E) Renaissance humanists rarely wrote about political matters, while medieval humanists were focused on political issues

GO ON TO THE NEXT PAGE.

36. Which would be least likely to be studied in a humanist school?

    (A) History
    (B) Philosophy
    (C) Grammar
    (D) Rhetoric
    (E) Theology

37. Which Renaissance text best exemplifies the Renaissance ideal of the multitalented, well-trained individual?

    (A) Castiglione's *The Courtier*
    (B) More's *Utopia*
    (C) Machiavelli's *The Prince*
    (D) Erasmus's *In Praise of Folly*
    (E) Boccaccio's *Decameron*

38. Machiavelli differed from medieval political theorists in that he wrote about

    (A) the morality of the prince
    (B) the importance for a prince to win over the masses
    (C) how political life operates, not how it should be
    (D) the importance for the prince to come to terms with the church
    (E) how the prince ought to engage in immoral behavior

39. The Christian humanism of Erasmus led him to

    (A) reject the idea that the Bible should be translated into the vernacular
    (B) translate a new edition of the Greek New Testament
    (C) call for strict adherence to the rules of the church
    (D) reject the Catholic Church wholeheartedly
    (E) insist that the Latin Bible was the only legitimate one

40. Which statement is most accurate about the invention of the modern printing press?

    (A) It created a demand for books that had not existed before.
    (B) The European discovery of paper proved Europeans' technological superiority.
    (C) It spread slowly and had no real impact until the sixteenth century.
    (D) It led to government censorship and often to the arrest of printers.
    (E) The gap between oral and written cultures grew.

41. Over the course of the fifteenth century, artistic patronage

    (A) came mostly from private wealthy patrons
    (B) came mostly from corporate bodies like guilds and governments
    (C) shifted from private patronage to corporate bodies
    (D) shifted from corporate bodies to private patronage
    (E) came almost entirely from the popes

42. The admiration given to artists that developed in the Renaissance reflected all of the following social trends EXCEPT

    (A) the growing stress on individualism
    (B) new ways of earning social prestige
    (C) the hierarchy of wealth created in Renaissance cities
    (D) humanistic respect for human potential
    (E) the voluntary withdrawal of artists from public life and political activity

GO ON TO THE NEXT PAGE.

43. Northern Renaissance art differed from its Italian counterpart in that

    (A) it was less religious
    (B) it was mostly landscape paintings
    (C) it was less detailed
    (D) it was more religious
    (E) its paintings rarely used perspective

44. In late-fifteenth-century Florence, Girolamo Savonarola

    (A) became pope after having served as archbishop
    (B) called for "the bonfire of the vanities"
    (C) was an important member of the Platonic Academy
    (D) died a martyr's death at the hand of the Ottoman Turks
    (E) wrote secular love poetry

45. Blacks in Renaissance Europe

    (A) were extremely rare
    (B) were used for both slave and wage labor
    (C) had been imported into Portugal from Africa but were isolated there
    (D) were employed exclusively as entertainers
    (E) were vilified since black was always seen as a negative color

46. The monarchs of England, France, and Spain all used which of the following in their efforts to centralize power and forge national unity?

    (A) The Inquisition
    (B) Royal councils with many middle-class members
    (C) Parliaments, or representative bodies
    (D) Citizens' councils empowered to curtail the nobility
    (E) Encouragement of warfare among nobles

47. Pluralism and absenteeism led to major criticisms of the church because they

    (A) caused parishioners to be deprived of receiving the sacraments
    (B) resulted from so many bishops having concubines
    (C) caused nationalistic resentments
    (D) resulted in the widespread illiteracy of the priesthood
    (E) were part of church doctrine as well as practice

48. Martin Luther demonstrated Protestant attitudes in his personal life when he

    (A) remained committed to the monastic life
    (B) became a minister but remained celibate
    (C) insisted on the right to be a professor without being a monk
    (D) married a woman who had also taken religious vows
    (E) raised his daughter to become a Lutheran minister

49. The selling of indulgences bothered Luther so much because

    (A) it was another example of corruption in the church
    (B) Tetzel had no legal authority in the church
    (C) Tetzel was charging too much money
    (D) he believed that there was no need to raise money for St. Peter's Basilica in Rome
    (E) it undermined the sacrament of penance

GO ON TO THE NEXT PAGE.

50. At the Diet of Worms, Martin Luther

    (A) refused to speak
    (B) recanted to save his life
    (C) was treated the same way Jan Hus had been at the Council of Constance
    (D) asserted that he was bound only by the Scriptures and conscience
    (E) attacked Calvinist ideas

51. The most significant disagreement between Zwingli and Luther was about

    (A) the nature of the Eucharist
    (B) justification by faith alone
    (C) the importance of the Scriptures
    (D) clerical marriage
    (E) collaborating with political authorities

52. Ultimately the factor that *most* determined the spread of Lutheranism was

    (A) Luther's translation of the Bible
    (B) the popularity of anti-papal broadsides
    (C) Luther's gift for writing, including hymns like "A Mighty Fortress Is Our God"
    (D) the Council of Trent
    (E) the decisions made by princes or rulers to adopt or reject Protestantism

53. Protestant radicals like the Anabaptists were

    (A) protected by Luther but attacked by Zwingli
    (B) attacked by both Protestants and Catholics
    (C) protected by Protestants but attacked by Catholics
    (D) attacked by Protestants but given safe haven by Catholics
    (E) generally ignored and left alone

54. The long-lasting significance of the German Peasants' War of 1525 was that it

    (A) was prompted by a drop in prices due to overproduction
    (B) led Luther to call for absolute obedience to the state
    (C) was inspired by Anabaptist ideas
    (D) alienated the nobles from the Lutherans
    (E) ended with the peasantry becoming conservative

55. As a result of the Reformation and the Counter-Reformation,

    (A) clandestine unions became less acceptable
    (B) convents for women were abolished in both Catholic and Protestant states
    (C) brothels were closed in Catholic cities but tolerated in Protestant cities
    (D) witches ceased to be tried and executed
    (E) women came to be considered the equals of men

56. Which territory did Charles V NOT rule?

    (A) Burgundy
    (B) Spain
    (C) The Netherlands
    (D) Hungary
    (E) Sicily

GO ON TO THE NEXT PAGE.

57. The Peace of Augsburg
    - (A) was a victory for Charles V
    - (B) gave rulers of member states of the Holy Roman Empire the right to choose whichever religion they wanted
    - (C) gave rulers of member states of the Holy Roman Empire the right to choose Catholicism or Lutheranism as their state religion
    - (D) gave religious toleration to Lutherans but not to Anabaptists
    - (E) led to a new war over religion within a decade

58. Women artists during the Renaissance
    - (A) are known to have painted works, but their names are unknown
    - (B) generally had fathers who were painters or patrons
    - (C) were active in the visual arts but harshly opposed humanism
    - (D) were most known for their frescoes
    - (E) generally were married and began to paint after their children were grown

59. Which factor best explains why Calvinism had greater international impact than Lutheranism did?
    - (A) It spread to Scotland.
    - (B) The concept of the "calling" proved to be dynamic.
    - (C) The Geneva Consistory was noted for its fairness and moderation.
    - (D) The doctrine of predestination created a deep sense of pessimism.
    - (E) Lutheranism spread only in the Germanic states of the Holy Roman Empire.

60. Which major change in the world economy prompted European exploration in the late fifteenth century?
    - (A) A decline in the Chinese population led to a shrinking market in Asia for European goods.
    - (B) The Mongols discouraged trade between China and the West.
    - (C) The Genoese took over the spice trade from Venice.
    - (D) Profits in the African slave trade went down over the course of the century.
    - (E) The Ottomans expanded territorially and dominated trade routes.

61. What was the common thread between the religious wars in France (which resulted in it remaining Catholic) and those in the Netherlands (which led it to become Protestant)?
    - (A) England's involvement
    - (B) The military victories of the Catholic and Protestant sides, respectively
    - (C) The decisions made by politiques
    - (D) Spain's involvement
    - (E) National interests

62. What impact did the reconquista have on Spain's exploration and conquest?
    - (A) It encouraged the Spaniards to immediately attack the Ottoman Empire.
    - (B) It meant that there were fewer opportunities for ambitious young men within Spain.
    - (C) The conquest of Granada was accompanied by anti-Muslim riots.
    - (D) Spain acquired huge sums of money to fund Columbus's voyages.
    - (E) Many of the conquered Spanish Muslims acted as navigators and pilots.

GO ON TO THE NEXT PAGE.

63. How did technology and better scientific information fuel the explorations?

    (A) Ptolemy's *Geography* gave a reasonably accurate estimate of the distance from Europe to Asia.
    (B) The recent European invention of the astrolabe made sea navigation possible.
    (C) Caravels with lateen sails were more maneuverable and could carry more than previous ships.
    (D) The magnetic compass allowed sailors to calculate their longitude.
    (E) Cannons proved useful in almost every climate and condition.

64. Which is NOT true about Columbus's voyages of exploration?

    (A) His decision not to sail north to look for the Great Khan was based on his interest in finding gold.
    (B) He believed the Indians would convert easily to Christianity.
    (C) He established permanent control as the governor of Hispaniola.
    (D) He traveled with letters to the Great Khan from Ferdinand and Isabella.
    (E) He enslaved the Indians under his control.

65. Which factor *best* explains the Spanish conquest of the Incan and Aztec Empires?

    (A) The fierceness and military expertise of the Spanish soldiers
    (B) The internal dissensions within each of the empires
    (C) The auguries and religious legends that led the rulers to see the Spaniards as possible gods
    (D) The effectiveness of cannons and muskets
    (E) The cultural values and attitudes of the Mexicans and Peruvians

66. For Spain, the most important consequence of Magellan's voyage was that

    (A) it led to the immediate conquest and colonization of the Philippines
    (B) Spain became discouraged from competing with Portugal for the Asian spice trade
    (C) Spain focused more on the Asian trade rather than on the New World for the next half century
    (D) Magellan returned to the strait south of Chile that bears his name to improve the passage to Asia via the Atlantic
    (E) Portugal ceded Goa to Spain

67. The importance of the defeat of the Spanish Armada in 1588 was that

    (A) Spain's navy never recuperated
    (B) England invaded the northern Spanish coast
    (C) Mary Queen of Scots was executed for treason
    (D) ultimately the Dutch won their independence from Spain
    (E) Philip abdicated in favor of his son Don Carlos

68. The Spanish set up the encomienda system in the New World to create

    (A) a system of forced labor for the Amerindians
    (B) the sugar plantation system in the Caribbean islands
    (C) the outright enslavement of the Amerindians
    (D) the establishment of churches for the Amerindians with services in their languages
    (E) the use of African slaves as laborers

GO ON TO THE NEXT PAGE.

69. The one social group who were clearly beneficiaries of the sixteenth-century price revolution were the

    (A) poor
    (B) merchants
    (C) monarchs
    (D) clergy
    (E) landlords

70. Which did NOT travel from the Old World to the New?

    (A) Horses
    (B) Pigs
    (C) Wheat
    (D) Corn
    (E) Dogs

71. The importance of sugar for the world economy was its

    (A) impact on agriculture in Spain
    (B) transformation of the economy of Mexico
    (C) role in encouraging the African slave trade
    (D) role in the increase in the demand for silver
    (E) usefulness in direct exchange for Chinese silks

72. The essayist Michel de Montaigne was noted for expressing

    (A) religious zeal
    (B) nationalism in France
    (C) a new reason for supporting the monarchy
    (D) skepticism
    (E) racist views of the native populations of the New World

73. The Babylonian Captivity and the Great Schism both demonstrate the

    (A) vulnerability of the papacy to increasingly powerful monarchies
    (B) spread of heretical ideas
    (C) growth of lay piety
    (D) success of the conciliar movement
    (E) influence of the Roman elites on the selection of the popes

74. A major cause of the Hundred Years' War for the French was that

    (A) the nobles were divided in their support for Philip VI
    (B) a woman had become ruler of France for the first time
    (C) the French were urged to go to war by wealthy Flemish merchants
    (D) the King of France claimed the throne of England
    (E) the Capetian dynasty ended and the Valois dynasty began

GO ON TO THE NEXT PAGE.

Image copyright © The Metropolitan Museum of Art. Image source: Art Resource, NY.

75. The life story of the painter and slave Juan de Pareja, shown here in a painting by his master, Diego Velázquez, reveals

(A) how brutal European slavery was
(B) how race was the ultimate determinant of his destiny
(C) that in the seventeenth century Europeans owned slaves born in Europe
(D) that black painters had a very difficult time
(E) that slavery was illegal within Spain by the seventeenth century

76. Uprisings such as the Jacquerie that occurred in the fourteenth century were *least* caused by

(A) tensions between social classes
(B) taxation
(C) religious differences
(D) frustration with the nobility
(E) defeat in war

77. Which is true about the Protestant Reformation in eastern Europe?

(A) The Ottoman Empire persecuted Protestants in its European areas of control.
(B) Protestantism found few supporters there in the sixteenth century.
(C) Lutheranism was much preferred to Calvinism in Poland.
(D) The Protestants won a great victory at the Battle of Mohács in 1526.
(E) The majority of Hungarians were Protestant until the seventeenth century.

GO ON TO THE NEXT PAGE.

78. Which idea was *least* expressed or promoted by the Italian Renaissance humanists?

    (A) Individualism
    (B) Nationalism
    (C) Humanism
    (D) Secularism
    (E) Aestheticism

Erich Lessing/Art Resource, NY.

79. Which would NOT define Bennozzo Gozzoli's *Procession of the Magi*, above, as a Renaissance painting?

    (A) Its portrayal of contemporary Italians
    (B) Its realistic depiction of the human body
    (C) It was probably commissioned by the church or a religious organization.
    (D) The landscape was painted using perspective.
    (E) It conveys energy and movement.

GO ON TO THE NEXT PAGE.

80. China helped bring about inflation in sixteenth-century Europe by
    (A) flooding Europe with inexpensive manufactured goods
    (B) radically reducing the price of silk
    (C) demanding silver as payment for its goods
    (D) taking over the Philippines where Spanish traders bought Asian goods
    (E) importing gold from Japan and using it to buy European goods

STOP

END OF SECTION I

EUROPEAN HISTORY
SECTION II

Part A
(Suggested writing time—45 minutes)
Percent of Section II score—45

Directions: The following question is based on the accompanying Documents 1–13. The documents have been edited for the purpose of this exercise.

This question is designed to test your ability to work with and understand historical documents. Write an essay that:

+ Provides an appropriate, explicitly stated thesis that directly addresses all parts of the question and does NOT simply restate the question.

+ Discusses a majority of the documents individually and specifically.

+ Demonstrates understanding of the basic meaning of a majority of the documents.

+ Supports the thesis with appropriate interpretation of a majority of the documents.

+ Analyzes the documents by explicitly grouping them in at least three appropriate ways.

+ Takes into account both the sources of the documents and the authors' points of view.

You may refer to relevant historical information not mentioned in the documents.

1. Describe and analyze the various political, religious, and social views about Savonarola, the dominant figure in the Florentine Republic from 1494 to 1498.

Historical background: Girolamo Savonarola (born in Ferrara 1452, died in Florence 1498) was a Dominican monk, an impassioned and hugely popular preacher in Florence, and prior of the Monastery of San Marco. He preached against sexual sins, blasphemy, and gambling, against the "vanities" or material possessions, and against political tyranny. He criticized the papacy for corruption and decadence, made striking prophecies (many of which came true), and asserted that Scripture was the best source of religious knowledge.

Florence, although nominally a republic, had been dominated by Lorenzo de' Medici, who ruled from behind the scenes. He was a great patron of the arts and scholarship through his Platonic Academy. When Lorenzo died in 1492, his son's incompetence and the invasion of French troops in Italy led to the re-establishment of the republic. From 1494 to 1498, Savonarola was its dominant figure. In 1497, he staged a "bonfire of the vanities" in which Florentine citizens threw books, jewelry, and art into the flames. Later that year, Pope Alexander VI excommunicated Savonarola. In May of 1498, Savonarola was tried for heresy, hanged, and burned at the stake by the Signoria, Florence's eight-man government council. In 1512, the Medici were restored to power and the republic ended.

GO ON TO THE NEXT PAGE.

Document 1

Source: Pico della Mirandola (1463–1494), widely admired humanist, Neoplatonist, and protégé of Lorenzo de' Medici, after hearing Savonarola speak at a Dominican chapter meeting in 1482.

Here is a man who once known can never be forgotten. . . . [he] has more theological insight and sincerity than a hundred Fra Marianos put together.

Document 2

Source: Piero Capponi (1447–1496), statesman, warrior, Florentine ambassador, and politician, speech made at a meeting of prominent citizens, 1494.

Piero de' Medici is no longer capable of ruling; the Republic must provide for itself; it is time to be done with this government of children . . . do not neglect to send with the other ambassadors [to the French king Charles VIII] Father Girolamo Savonarola, for he has the love of the people.

Document 3

Source: Fra Antonio Benivieni (1443–1502), physician and monk, from a letter to Savonarola.

Reform there must be, reform of Florence, reform of Italy, reform of the Church, all things must be made over. But I warn you the Kingdom of God cannot be forced . . . You are not following Christ when you threaten the whole city with direst punishments. . . . Think deeply, Father Girolamo, before you condemn the harlots in general . . . Awaken them by kindness. Do not scold or threaten them . . . Are you aware that since you began to hurl your imprecations to left and right, men and women run for cover when they see a man in the Dominican habit coming their way?

Document 4

Source: Luca Landucci (1436–1516), Florentine apothecary, diary entry of February 27, 1496.

The children had received such encouragement from Fra Girolamo to reprove unbecoming modes of dress and the vice of gambling, that when the people said, "Here come the prior's children" every gambler, however bold he might be would take himself off and women attired and conducted themselves with all modesty. The children were held in such reverence that every one abstained from scandalous vice.

GO ON TO THE NEXT PAGE.

Document 5

Source: Bartolomeo Redditi, lawyer, notary, and ambassador to the Papal Court (1489–1490), in a letter regarding Savonarola, published in *Breve Compedio*, 1501.

I believed and I believe because his preaching made Florence a paradise on earth.

Document 6

Source: Mariano da Genazzano, Augustinian friar and popular Florentine preacher who had engaged in a preaching competition with Savonarola at the behest of Lorenzo de' Medici in 1491, from a sermon before the pope and cardinals, 1497.

Savonarola, that braying ass who has thrown so much discredit on the fair city of Florence, is chiefly responsible for keeping the Florentines from joining the Holy League . . . the monkish ignoramus preaches against the Pope. Inspired by the most ignoble ambition, one of them being to ascend the throne of St. Peter himself, this monstrous half-breed drives the people of Florence to distraction with his insanities that pass for sermons . . . these sermons, it should be known by all present here, are infected with the vilest blasphemies. Savonarola blasphemes against Christ and the mother of God.

Document 7

Source: The prior of San Marco in response to Pope Alexander VI's ordered transfer of the Monastery of San Marco out of Savonarola's control, letter, 1497.

Fra Girolamo is a holy man whose prayers and admonitions have saved the Republic from great peril. He has made Christ the King of our City. He spends his time in prayer and meditation. He is disinterested, and asks for no reward for himself.

Document 8

Source: Signoria of Florence, petition to Pope Alexander VI, May 1, 1497, signed by more than two hundred prominent citizens, including Machiavelli.

Most Holy Father, we are deeply afflicted to have incurred the ban of the Church, not only because of the respect always entertained by our Republic for the Holy Keys but because we see that a most innocent man has been wrongfully and maliciously accused to Your Holiness. He has labored for many years for the welfare of our people and no fault has ever been detected either in his life or his doctrine. But as virtue is never free from the attacks of envy, so there be many of our people who invert the name of honesty and think to rise to greatness by attacking the good.

GO ON TO THE NEXT PAGE.

Document 9

Source: Statement by one of the Arrabiati, a political party opposed to Savonarola and tied to the Duke of Milan and the pope, 1498.

At last we can all see plainly how the Friar has deceived us. This is the happiness he predicted for Florence: enemy armies are bearing down on Florence, the plague is snatching more victims every day, the scarcity of food is robbing us of our strength to perform our everyday duties!

Document 10

Source: Giuliano de Gondi (1421–1501), Florentine banker and politician, at a consultation of leading citizens called by the Signoria, March 1498.

[Savonarola] is creating a sect of Fraticelli* like the one that once existed in this city, and this is a sect of heresy that you are making in this land.

*Fourteenth- and fifteenth-century dissident Franciscan groups.

Document 11

Source: Pope Alexander VI (Rodrigo Borgia, 1431–1503), letter to the Signoria of Florence after they excommunicated Savonarola and banned his preaching, 1497.

Your conduct has profoundly incensed us. You have not only encouraged the disobedience of this Friar; but by preventing all others from preaching, you have made him almost your oracle of Apollo. And we shall never relent . . . for only as you show yourselves ready to obey will we concede your requests for the material welfare of your Republic. In any event, reply with no more letters but with acts; for we are firmly resolved to tolerate your disobedience no longer and we will place the interdict* on your city, to last as long as you continue to favor this monstrous idol of yours.

*An interdict is a papal decree forbidding any sacrament to be performed in a city.

Document 12

Source: Niccolò Machiavelli, humanist and author of The Prince, chancellor of the republic until 1512, in a letter to a friend in Rome after hearing Savonarola's sermon in 1498.

Whereas formerly he attempted to unite his own party in the hatred of their enemies and to frighten them with the prospect of a tyrant, now he changes his tune, and exhorting them all to union and making no more mention of tyrant or wickedness, seeks to incite them all against the Pope, and turning them against him and his curbs, speaks of him as the most vicious man you can conceive, and thus in my opinion, he follows the time and colors his lies accordingly.

GO ON TO THE NEXT PAGE.

Document 13

Source: Raffaello da Volterra (1451–1522), humanist, theologian, and philosopher, founder of an educational academy and a monastery at Volterra, in a statement made after Savonarola's fall.

He used to say that everyone ought to abandon and not even go near the City of Rome, which all Christians venerate and which is the very source of religion. And with such arguments and promptings, he would have founded a new heretical sect, if divine providence had not intervened.

GO ON TO THE NEXT PAGE.

EUROPEAN HISTORY
SECTION II

Part B
(Suggested planning and writing time—35 minutes)
Percent of Section II score—27.5

Directions: You are to answer ONE question from the three questions below. Make your selection carefully, choosing the question that you are best prepared to answer thoroughly in the time permitted. You should spend 5 minutes organizing or outlining your answer.

Write an essay that:

+ Has a relevant thesis.

+ Addresses all parts of the question.

+ Supports the thesis with specific evidence.

+ Is well organized.

2. To what degree and in what ways was the Reformation an outgrowth of the Italian Renaissance?

3. What characteristics of Italian cities in the fifteenth century created an environment that fostered the development of Renaissance culture?

4. In what ways did developments during the Renaissance help bring about the Age of Exploration?

STOP

EUROPEAN HISTORY
SECTION II

Part C
(Suggested planning and writing time—35 minutes)
Percent of Section II score—27.5

Directions: You are to answer ONE question from the three questions below. Make your selection carefully, choosing the question that you are best prepared to answer thoroughly in the time permitted. You should spend 5 minutes organizing or outlining your answer.

Write an essay that:

- Has a relevant thesis.

- Addresses all parts of the question.

- Supports the thesis with specific evidence.

- Is well organized.

5. What are the differing views concerning the roles of women held by Catholics and Protestants? What do these views reveal about the impact of theology on gender roles?

6. Select two states in which there was substantial conflict between Protestants and Catholics in sixteenth-century Europe, and analyze the role national politics played in those domestic struggles.

7. Discuss the various motives that prompted the exploration and colonization of the New World and evaluate their relative importance.

STOP

END OF EXAM

Answer Key for Practice Exam 1

Answers for Section I: Multiple-Choice Questions

1. B	21. B	41. D	61. E
2. C	22. D	42. E	62. B
3. E	23. B	43. D	63. C
4. B	24. A	44. B	64. C
5. A	25. D	45. B	65. B
6. B	26. D	46. B	66. B
7. C	27. B	47. C	67. D
8. C	28. D	48. D	68. A
9. D	29. E	49. E	69. B
10. A	30. B	50. D	70. D
11. D	31. C	51. A	71. C
12. C	32. B	52. E	72. D
13. A	33. E	53. B	73. A
14. B	34. E	54. B	74. E
15. A	35. C	55. A	75. C
16. D	36. E	56. D	76. C
17. C	37. A	57. C	77. E
18. D	38. C	58. B	78. B
19. A	39. B	59. B	79. C
20. C	40. D	60. E	80. C

Scoring the Multiple-Choice Section

Use the following formula to calculate your raw score on the multiple-choice section of the exam:

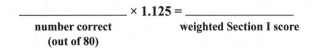

$$\underline{\hspace{3cm}} \times 1.125 = \underline{\hspace{3cm}}$$

number correct   **weighted Section I score**
(out of 80)

Rationales

1. **Answer: (B)**   Over time European participation in the slave trade led to new ideas about race. While previously Africans were seen as pagan heathens or Muslim infidels, they began to be seen as a distinct and inferior race. Using Aristotle and the

Bible, Europeans were able to justify their enslavement of Africans. (McKay, *A History of Western Society*, Eleventh Edition, pp. 379–380)

2. **Answer: (C)** Criticism of the Catholic Church did not begin with Martin Luther. Anticlericalism was often based on the ignorance and immorality of the local priests. (McKay, *A History of Western Society*, Eleventh Edition, p. 392)

3. **Answer: (E)** The peasants originally took Lutheran doctrine to mean that they could legitimately demand greater rights and improve their social conditions. Luther initially sympathized with the plight of the peasants, but he was dismayed at the Peasants' Revolt in 1525, chiding the peasants for using Scripture to support their claims to earthly rewards. Therefore, the Protestant Reformation did not in itself promote social mobility for the peasants. The Treaty of Augsburg in 1555 resulted in a lack of religious uniformity within the Holy Roman Empire. (McKay, *A History of Western Society*, Eleventh Edition, pp. 417–419, 400–402, 405–407, 414–416)

4. **Answer: (B)** Like many monarchs, Henry VIII was very concerned about having a son to continue the dynasty. Since the pope would not grant him a divorce, he broke with the church and created the Anglican Church so that he could divorce and marry Anne Boleyn. (McKay, *A History of Western Society*, Eleventh Edition, pp. 407–409)

5. **Answer: (A)** The Catholics reconsidered both theology and practice in a series of meetings entitled the Council of Trent. Although the Council of Trent bolstered the discipline of the clergy, the church maintained all of its former theological doctrines. (McKay, *A History of Western Society*, Eleventh Edition, pp. 414–416)

6. **Answer: (B)** Henry IV, a politique, was willing to forgo his Protestant faith and become Catholic in order to spare France further religious war. He issued the Edict of Nantes, giving Protestants freedom to worship. (McKay, *A History of Western Society*, Eleventh Edition, pp. 417–419)

7. **Answer: (C)** Due to the easy wealth generated by the importation of silver and gold from the New World, inflation in Spain skyrocketed, which increased the royal debt. Philip II repudiated the debt several times. Spain overall was less motivated than the other Atlantic states in developing strong industries to create export goods. Philip II was strongly moral and deeply religious and certainly not personally corrupt. (McKay, *A History of Western Society*, Eleventh Edition, pp. 454–455)

8. **Answer: (C)** Famine and malnutrition, prevalent during this time, weakened peoples' immune systems so they were more susceptible to disease. (McKay, *A History of Western Society*, Eleventh Edition, pp. 324–325)

9. **Answer: (D)** The enormous wealth of the Italian cities, such as Venice and Florence, allowed merchants and others who benefited from trade to patronize artists and intellectuals. This led to a cultural renaissance in Italy, which slowly spread throughout Europe. (McKay, *A History of Western Society*, Eleventh Edition, pp. 357–360, 373–375)

10. **Answer: (A)** Although Renaissance women were better educated than women in the past, they still had limited outlets for their intellect. For the most part, women were expected to grace the home with their learning but not to reach too far beyond that. (McKay, *A History of Western Society*, Eleventh Edition, pp. 365–366)

11. **Answer: (D)** Cicero was widely admired by humanists for the beauty of his Latin prose, but particularly in the republics like Florence. His writings in defense of the Roman Republic against the imperial system created by Caesar Augustus were used by the Florentine humanists to defend the assertion of sovereignty and the rejection of monarchy by city-states. (McKay, *A History of Western Society*, Eleventh Edition, p. 363)

12. **Answer: (C)**   Ferdinand responded to the rising anti-Semitic feelings in Spain by asking the pope for permission to launch the Inquisition. In theory, this would punish any New Christians who still clung to their Jewish practices and beliefs. The Inquisition allowed Spaniards to persecute and drive out Jews and Christian converts in the years following the reconquista. (McKay, *A History of Western Society*, Eleventh Edition, pp. 386–387)

13. **Answer: (A)**   Protestants such as Martin Luther disputed the Catholic Church's teaching that salvation comes from both faith and good works. They maintained that faith alone was enough to merit salvation; they also believed that good works would be an inevitable result of gratitude for God's love. (McKay, *A History of Western Society*, Eleventh Edition, pp. 397–399)

14. **Answer: (B)**   The Catholic Reformation came about in response to the Protestant Reformation. In the Council of Trent, Catholic leaders sought to reconcile Catholic and Protestant doctrines, while maintaining the theological backbone of the Catholic Church. While the Catholics did succeed in strengthening and renewing their church, they never achieved reconciliation with Protestants, nor did they alter their existing doctrines. (McKay, *A History of Western Society*, Eleventh Edition, pp. 414–416)

15. **Answer: (A)**   Fighting between Catholics and Huguenots resulted in violent attacks such as the Saint Bartholomew's Day massacre. Huguenots are Calvinists, the popular form of Protestantism in France. Social class tensions had dominated in the fourteenth century, not the sixteenth. (McKay, *A History of Western Society*, Eleventh Edition, pp. 417–419)

16. **Answer: (D)**   Portugal was not a significant European power, but in the fifteenth century sought greater prestige through its commitment to overseas exploration. Prince Henry the Navigator, Bartholomew Diaz, and Vasco da Gama, all from Portugal, were among the earliest European explorers of this time. (McKay, *A History of Western Society*, Eleventh Edition, p. 435)

17. **Answer: (C)**   The European exploration of other lands was primarily fueled by self-serving motives, including the drive for profits and spices. While some European explorers did express an interest in converting other peoples to Christianity, no one was motivated by a desire to educate other people in the Renaissance ideals. Italians played important roles as explorers and writers but had little interest in leaving Italy for the New World. Overpopulation was not a problem anywhere in Europe in the century or two after the Black Death. (McKay, *A History of Western Society*, Eleventh Edition, pp. 432–433)

18. **Answer: (D)**   France was not able to create a central representative body; instead it had many provincial assemblies. (McKay, *A History of Western Society*, Eleventh Edition, p. 338)

19. **Answer: (A)**   Vernacular poems like Dante's *Divine Comedy* and Chaucer's *Canterbury Tales* dominated literature in the fourteenth century. Literacy rates rose in the course of the fifteenth century. The Index of Prohibited Books was issued by the Catholic Church after the Reformation. (McKay, *A History of Western Society*, Eleventh Edition, pp. 351–353)

20. **Answer: (C)**   *In Praise of Folly* was a critique of the Catholic Church in favor of simplicity of faith. It was Erasmus's friend, Thomas More, who wrote *Utopia*. (McKay, *A History of Western Society*, Eleventh Edition, pp. 370–371)

21. **Answer: (B)**   Henry VII used the court to punish any nobles who seemed to threaten his power. (McKay, *A History of Western Society*, Eleventh Edition, p. 384)

22. **Answer: (D)**   Luther was brought before a diet and expected to recant, which he refused to do. Luther's statement is famous. Jan Hus was tried and executed in 1415 at the Council of Constance. (McKay, *A History of Western Society*, Eleventh Edition, p. 395)

23. **Answer: (B)**   Those who did not attend church were subject to a fine. In general Elizabeth chose a middle ground between Protestants and Catholics, while glorifying England and her own position. (McKay, *A History of Western Society*, Eleventh Edition, p. 409)

24. **Answer: (A)**   Calvin believed that the purity of Christians would draw others to become believers and even promoted theocracy based on the idea of a city on a hill. (McKay, *A History of Western Society*, Eleventh Edition, pp. 410–412)

25. **Answer: (D)**   Austria remained staunchly Catholic. Scotland became Calvinist under the leadership of John Knox. (McKay, *A History of Western Society*, Eleventh Edition, pp. 410–413, 417–420)

26. **Answer: (D)**   Wage earners and guild members had more bargaining power because of the decimation of guild membership. Aristocrats faced inflation, had lost much of their workforce, and could not increase rents. (McKay, *A History of Western Society*, Eleventh Edition, p. 330)

27. **Answer: (B)**   Through the intensity of her convictions and her inspiring leadership, Joan was able to rally the French troops to force the British to retreat from Orléans; this allowed Charles VII to be crowned king and restored French morale and pride. The war would probably have ended quite differently without her role. Although she was, of course, intensely religious and from peasant stock, it was her patriotism that mattered to nationalists. Charles VII ungratefully did not protest her trial by English ecclesiastical authorities. (McKay, *A History of Western Society*, Eleventh Edition, pp. 335–337)

28. **Answer: (D)**   Throughout Europe, representative assemblies were getting weaker as monarchs became stronger, and that was true for France. But in England, which was unusual in that it had only one national assembly (not the plethora of provincial assemblies that existed throughout the European continent), the king was forced to call the assembly, Parliament, into session often in order to obtain increased funding for the war effort, and Parliament became well established. (McKay, *A History of Western Society*, Eleventh Edition, pp. 338–339)

29. **Answer: (E)**   Marsiglio was mostly concerned about the church's relationship with society, arguing that the church should be under the authority of the state, while Wyclif argued that Christian practice and theology should be determined by the Scriptures. Marsiglio was excommunicated, but Wyclif was protected by the isolation of England. Wyclif's ideas had a huge impact, particularly in Bohemia where they were spread by Jan Hus. (McKay, *A History of Western Society*, Eleventh Edition, pp. 340–341)

30. **Answer: (B)**   Bridget of Sweden was a fourteenth-century mystic, and Thomas à Kempis was the most prominent fifteenth-century author of texts expressing lay piety, particularly the ideas of the Brethren and Sisters of the Common Life. (McKay, *A History of Western Society*, Eleventh Edition, p. 343)

31. **Answer: (C)**   Most historians argue that peasants were better off for the century after the Black Death than ever before. Since the Statute of Laborers had failed to uniformly roll back wages or limit social mobility, peasants expected a better future and were angry at attempts like the head tax to increase their taxes. Protests by urban workers over similar issues merged with the peasants' unrest. (McKay, *A History of Western Society*, Eleventh Edition, pp. 343–346)

32. **Answer: (B)** There were important changes in the late medieval period in gender roles. Women who had played important roles in the guild system in the Middle Ages became excluded in the fourteenth century. Women married later in northwestern Europe. Since men too were marrying later, towns provided brothels and supervised prostitutes. The penalties for rape were usually lighter than those for theft, and there were few prosecutions for this crime. Homosexuality was a matter of concern to city governments, some of which set up commissions to investigate and prosecute cases of sodomy. (McKay, *A History of Western Society*, Eleventh Edition, pp. 346–350)

33. **Answer: (E)** Jan Hus's promotion of Wyclif's ideas found a welcome reception among nationalistic Bohemians, while Dante's and Chaucer's literary works were crucial for establishing the forms of their respective national languages and for helping create a sense of national identity. Dante and Chaucer held positions in government, but neither was directly engaged in church reform movements; Hus was a professor of theology. (McKay, *A History of Western Society*, Eleventh Edition, pp. 340–341, 351–352)

34. **Answer: (E)** Most of the city-states were ruled by merchant oligarchies, although some were ruled by one man who came from a powerful family. Most such families competed furiously with each other. The nobles generally played a secondary role in these communes. In no commune did more than a small percentage of the men have political rights; most ordinary people were completely excluded from power. Option A is a twentieth-century definition of commune, not the one used in the Italian Renaissance. (McKay, *A History of Western Society*, Eleventh Edition, pp. 358–360)

35. **Answer: (C)** A humanist by Renaissance definition is someone who reads the classics. Scholars did so in the medieval period as well, but in the Renaissance, new stress was placed on human achievement, dignity, and individualism. Renaissance humanists were Christians who sought to reconcile pagan learning with Christian faith and with their contemporary world. They wrote a great deal about political matters. (McKay, *A History of Western Society*, Eleventh Edition, pp. 362–365)

36. **Answer: (E)** Greek and Latin grammar, rhetoric, history, and philosophy were the fundamentals of humanist education. Theology itself was of little interest to most humanists. (McKay, *A History of Western Society*, Eleventh Edition, p. 365)

37. **Answer: (A)** Castiglione's book became like a bible in the training of the ideal gentleman, who could write and recite poetry, fight well, dance, play music, and speak eloquently. *Utopia* imagined a semisocialistic ideal state; *The Prince* focused almost exclusively on the political talents needed by a prince; *In Praise of Folly* satirized human pretensions; and *The Decameron* was a fourteenth-century book of tales revealing the hearty sensuality and acquisitiveness of ordinary life. (McKay, *A History of Western Society*, Eleventh Edition, pp. 329, 366–371)

38. **Answer: (C)** Machiavelli argued not for immorality or morality in the behavior of the prince but for a realistic assessment of human fickleness and self-interest and a consequent focus on what works, not what ought to work. It is his lack of concern for the moral standing of the prince that led to accusations of amorality or immorality in his work. (McKay, *A History of Western Society*, Eleventh Edition, pp. 367–369)

39. **Answer: (B)** Erasmus, the most renowned of the northern European intellectuals in the sixteenth century, used his humanistic knowledge of Latin and Greek to create a new, critical edition of the New Testament. At the same time, he called for the widespread reading of the Bible by ordinary people and therefore its translation into many languages. While he focused on inner spirituality, he never rejected the Catholic Church outright. (McKay, *A History of Western Society*, Eleventh Edition, p. 371)

40. **Answer: (D)** The printing press, which included a whole variety of inventions and technologies, spread quickly throughout Europe, as it was better able to meet the

growing demand for books than earlier techniques such as hand copying and block printing. Books were printed on paper, a discovery the Chinese brought to Europe. Governments and churches quickly made up lists of prohibited books and often attacked printers and their presses. As books and broadsides were read to illiterate listeners, the gap between written and oral cultures shrank. (McKay, *A History of Western Society*, Eleventh Edition, pp. 371–373)

41. **Answer: (D)**   The early Renaissance artistic masterpieces, such as Brunelleschi's dome for the Florentine cathedral, were commissioned by guilds or oligarchic governments. After the middle of the century, private patrons such as the Medicis played more and more of a prominent role. The popes became prominent patrons in the sixteenth century. (McKay, *A History of Western Society*, Eleventh Edition, pp. 373–375)

42. **Answer: (E)**   Renaissance artists had high prestige and were often very well paid, even wealthy, so their rise in social status reflects the social mobility in Renaissance cities created by wealth as well as the articulation of human potentiality by humanists. (McKay, *A History of Western Society*, Eleventh Edition, p. 377)

43. **Answer: (D)**   Northern art during the Renaissance tended to be more religious and more detailed. Artists used the innovations from Italy of perspective in painting but not its new architectural principles. (McKay, *A History of Western Society*, Eleventh Edition, pp. 375–376)

44. **Answer: (B)**   Savonarola was a Dominican monk who dominated Florentine politics for a few years in the 1490s. He denounced materialism and secularism and urged the Florentines to destroy their frivolous material goods in public "bonfires of the vanities." He was tried and executed by the Florentine government in 1498. (McKay, *A History of Western Society*, Eleventh Edition, pp. 360–362)

45. **Answer: (B)**   Beginning in the fifteenth century, there were substantial numbers of African blacks in European cities and courts, both slave and free. Some worked as entertainers, and others were treasured servants, craftsmen, and sailors. Europeans had ambivalent notions about blackness: it was the color of demons but also the color worn by monks and mourners. (McKay, *A History of Western Society*, Eleventh Edition, pp. 379–380)

46. **Answer: (B)**   Royal councils with middle-class members were effective tools for dominating the aristocracies. The Inquisition and citizens' councils were used only in Spain in the fifteenth century. All the monarchs tried to avoid calling representative bodies as they were strongholds of aristocratic power. The monarchs sought to curb aristocratic violence and become guarantors of law and order. (McKay, *A History of Western Society*, Eleventh Edition, pp. 383–387)

47. **Answer: (C)**   Concubinage and illiteracy were all too common, but they were not directly related to the fact that so many high churchmen held more than one position, usually in different cities or even countries, which led them to be absent most of the time from their duties in each of them. When these churchmen were part of the papal curia and held positions abroad, resentment included nationalistic sentiments as well. Usually, low-level priests fulfilled the spiritual duties of those positions. (McKay, *A History of Western Society*, Eleventh Edition, p. 392)

48. **Answer: (D)**   Both Luther and his wife had taken religious vows and left their orders to marry. (McKay, *A History of Western Society*, Eleventh Edition, p. 402)

49. **Answer: (E)**   The issue of indulgences was primarily theological, in that Luther could find no justification for it in Scripture, and it implied that humans, rather than God, could determine their own destinies. Indulgences would lead people to thinking they didn't need to repent. The notion that one could buy time off one's penitential

service in purgatory was also challenged because there is no mention of purgatory in Scripture, only Heaven and Hell. (McKay, *A History of Western Society*, Eleventh Edition, pp. 393–394)

50. **Answer: (D)**   Luther was ordered to recant, but refused, saying that he was bound only by the Scriptures and conscience. Unlike Jan Hus, he escaped punishment. Calvin was still a child in 1521. (McKay, *A History of Western Society*, Eleventh Edition, p. 395)

51. **Answer: (A)**   Protestants generally agreed on most issues, but they did disagree about the meaning of the Eucharist. Luther argued for the Real Presence of Jesus during communion, while Zwingli asserted it was only a memorial. They also disagreed about the legitimacy of having artistic representations in the church, with Luther seeing their value and Zwingli insisting on relying solely on God's words. (McKay, *A History of Western Society*, Eleventh Edition, pp. 397–399)

52. **Answer: (E)**   Although A, B, and C all helped spread Protestant ideas, it was only when rulers decided to adopt Protestantism that it was accepted and territories became Protestant. The Council of Trent was where the Catholic Reformation was formed, confirming Catholic doctrine but making important reforms. (McKay, *A History of Western Society*, Eleventh Edition, pp. 399–400)

53. **Answer: (B)**   Protestants and Catholics alike thought the radicals would bring dangerous secularization because they advocated separation of church and state; on this issue, they held common views. (McKay, *A History of Western Society*, Eleventh Edition, p. 400)

54. **Answer: (B)**   Although initially supportive of the peasants who adopted his religious ideas to protest their social and economic grievances, Luther quickly turned against them, saying that freedom was in the realm of faith, not disobedience to the state. This pleased the nobles and the rulers, of course. The revolt was prompted by several years of crop failures, not by Anabaptism, which was just being developed. Many peasants turned to the radical sects after the failure of the revolt. (McKay, *A History of Western Society*, Eleventh Edition, pp. 400–402)

55. **Answer: (A)**   As part of the Catholic Reformation, marriage rules were tightened and secret marriages discouraged. Protestants closed brothels. Protestants avidly persecuted witches after the 1560s; Catholics were less likely to do so. Neither saw women as equal. (McKay, *A History of Western Society*, Eleventh Edition, pp. 402–404, 414, 420–422)

56. **Answer: (D)**   Charles V inherited all of those territories except Hungary, which was lost to the Ottomans in 1526 at the Battle of Mohács and retaken by the Habsburgs only in 1699. (McKay, *A History of Western Society*, Eleventh Edition, pp. 404–405)

57. **Answer: (C)**   The Peace of Augsburg gave Germanic rulers the right to choose Lutheranism or Catholicism for their states. No religious toleration was given to any group. Charles V abdicated after the treaty was signed, his dream lost. A new religious war was fought but only in the seventeenth century. (McKay, *A History of Western Society*, Eleventh Edition, pp. 406–407)

58. **Answer: (B)**   Most women artists were daughters of painters or patrons, and they generally painted before but not after their marriages. We know the names of several, such as Artemisia Gentileschi. They may not have been involved in humanistic studies, but they didn't oppose it. They weren't allowed to learn fresco techniques. (McKay, *A History of Western Society*, Eleventh Edition, pp. 377–378)

59. **Answer: (B)**   The concept of the "calling" sanctified work and attracted the hard-working bourgeoisie of France, England, and the American colonies, as well as else-

where in Europe. Lutheranism spread to Scandinavia as well as within the Holy Roman Empire. Calvinists believed that they were predestined for salvation, so they were, generally speaking, personally optimistic. Calvinism did spread to Scotland, but it was more important that it spread to Holland. (McKay, *A History of Western Society*, Eleventh Edition, pp. 412–413)

60. **Answer: (E)** The major change in the world economy in the early modern period is Ottoman expansion, capturing Constantinople, and domination of trade routes in the eastern Mediterranean. China's population in fact increased substantially. The Mongols fostered international trade. Venice, not Genoa, dominated the spice trade. (McKay, *A History of Western Society*, Eleventh Edition, pp. 430–431)

61. **Answer: (E)** Dutch nationalism was a strong element in the Protestant cause there. French national interest ultimately led the Protestant victor in France, Henry of Navarre, to change to Catholicism; he was a politique. But the Dutch leaders were not so indifferent concerning matters of religion. Neither England nor Spain was involved in the French civil war in a major way. (McKay, *A History of Western Society*, Eleventh Edition, pp. 417–420)

62. **Answer: (B)** The reconquista was a period of movement and opportunity for Spanish Christians. After their victory, the social structure solidified and became more restrictive. None of the other options are accurate. (McKay, *A History of Western Society*, Eleventh Edition, p. 432)

63. **Answer: (C)** Ptolemy was wrong in his estimates of the distance to Asia. The ancient Greeks invented the astrolabe, which could be used to estimate latitude. Cannons were unreliable in the tropics. (McKay, *A History of Western Society*, Eleventh Edition, pp. 433–434)

64. **Answer: (C)** Columbus was a poor ruler; there was a revolt on the island, and Columbus and his brother were brought back to Spain in chains. (McKay, *A History of Western Society*, Eleventh Edition, pp. 435–439)

65. **Answer: (B)** All the factors are valid, but as the number of Spanish soldiers was small, they could have been easily overcome if they had not had help from some unhappy subjects of the Aztec and Incan Empires. (McKay, *A History of Western Society*, Eleventh Edition, pp. 441–443)

66. **Answer: (B)** The Philippines were indeed colonized by Spain but not until the 1560s. Magellan died there. Portugal kept hold of Goa through most of the twentieth century. Spain recognized that, with the size of the Pacific, they could not compete with the well-established Portuguese. (McKay, *A History of Western Society*, Eleventh Edition, p. 440)

67. **Answer: (D)** The English, having defeated the Armada, continued to aid the Dutch, who won their independence in 1609. Mary Queen of Scots was executed before the invasion. Don Carlos died while Philip was king. Spain quickly rebuilt its navy. (McKay, *A History of Western Society*, Eleventh Edition, pp. 409–410, 419)

68. **Answer: (A)** The encomienda system was the first system of forced labor in the New World, a legalized form of enslavement of the native population, many of whom died from overwork and brutal treatment. (McKay, *A History of Western Society*, Eleventh Edition, p. 446)

69. **Answer: (B)** During periods of inflation, the people who benefit are those who are in debt, which in this case would be merchants who often borrow money to conduct business. Those who suffer are those on a fixed income, like the clergy and the landlords.

The monarchs had to pay more for services and soldiers, and the poor had to pay more for food; neither had an easy time increasing their income to pay for these increases in necessary costs. (McKay, *A History of Western Society*, Eleventh Edition, pp. 454–455)

70. **Answer: (D)**   Corn was one of the most important gifts of the New World to the Old in the Columbian exchange. (McKay, *A History of Western Society*, Eleventh Edition, pp. 448–450)

71. **Answer: (C)**   Sugar plantations required a substantial labor force, which could not be filled by the decimated Native American populations; African slaves were imported to fill that need. Sugar was not planted in most of Mexico or in Spain. (McKay, *A History of Western Society*, Eleventh Edition, pp. 449–454)

72. **Answer: (D)**   Montaigne is noted for his skepticism, personal contemplation, and rationalism. He wrote an expressly nonracist essay and espoused religious toleration. Generally, he stayed away from politics. (McKay, *A History of Western Society*, Eleventh Edition, pp. 457–458)

73. **Answer: (A)**   During the Babylonian Captivity and the Great Schism, the French monarchs exerted substantial control over the papacy. The conciliar movement was an unsuccessful effort to reform church administration. Lay piety did grow in this period but as a result of the decline in the prestige of the church, not as its cause. The Roman elites, but not the Italian people, did have a great say in the selection of the pope in 1378. (McKay, *A History of Western Society*, Eleventh Edition, pp. 339–343)

74. **Answer: (E)**   The end of the Capetian dynasty in 1328 was the immediate cause of the war, in that the French nobility refused to give the crown to the sister of the last Capetian king or to her son, Edward III of England, who later claimed the throne of France. Many French nobles did not support the French king but instead supported Edward III during the war because of their resistance to royal centralization; this prolonged the war but was not its immediate cause. The Flemish merchants supported the English because of their need for English wool. (McKay, *A History of Western Society*, Eleventh Edition, pp. 332–333)

75. **Answer: (C)**   The subject of this portrait is dignified and prosperous. C and E contradict each other, and so one of these must be wrong. Slavery was not abolished in Europe until the nineteenth century, although it played a small role in the economy for centuries. Although most slaves were imported, some were born in Europe. Race was generally not a major factor in slavery in Europe, since traditionally most slaves there were white. (McKay, *A History of Western Society*, Eleventh Edition, pp. 449–450)

76. **Answer: (C)**   Peasants blamed the nobility for their miserable lives, including taxation, chaos in the countryside, and defeat in war. Although they sometimes resented church taxes, they did not revolt for religious reasons. (McKay, *A History of Western Society*, Eleventh Edition, pp. 343–346)

77. **Answer: (E)**   Protestantism made strong inroads in eastern Europe in the sixteenth and seventeenth centuries, but the Catholic Church was generally able to wrest back control. Poles preferred Calvinism to the German Lutheranism. The Battle of Mohács was an Ottoman victory. (McKay, *A History of Western Society*, Eleventh Edition, pp. 413–414)

78. **Answer: (B)**   Nationalism was a concept that did not fully develop in Europe until well into the eighteenth century. Though nationalism was present in countries such as England on a limited basis during this time, it was not a significant part of the Renaissance, which tended toward internationalism in its creation of a cultural movement

open to any European in that it was Latin-based. (McKay, *A History of Western Society*, Eleventh Edition, pp. 362–365, 373–379)

79. **Answer: (C)**   Although the title of the painting is religious, it is less about a religious theme than a glorification of the Medicis, who commissioned the painting. The figures are painted realistically but they are contemporary Italians in ordinary dress. The landscape uses perspective to great depth. The Magi are key components of the story of the birth of Jesus and were commonly painted in medieval religious paintings. Unlike medieval paintings that tended to be static, Renaissance artists wanted to convey movement. (McKay, *A History of Western Society*, Eleventh Edition, pp. 375–377)

80. **Answer: (C)**   China was the largest single buyer of the world's silver, which it got from New Spain and Japan. It demanded payment for its goods in silver, and to feed that demand, Spain increased production from its silver mines. The infusion of silver from the New World fed the inflation in sixteenth-century Europe known as the price revolution. Most of China's exports to Europe were silk fabrics. The Philippines remained a Spanish colony until 1898. (McKay, *A History of Western Society*, Eleventh Edition, pp. 455–456)

Answers for Section II: Part A

Remember that the two parts of the exam—Section I (multiple-choice) and Section II (three essays)—are equally weighted at 50 percent each in determining the final score. Of the three essays, the document-based question essay counts for 45 percent of the Section II score, and the two thematic question essays together count for 55 percent of the Section II score.

As these are not official AP Exam questions, we don't have official AP scoring standards for them. But you can use the following general guidelines to score your own essays.

AP European History DBQ essays are scored on the core-scoring method. Each specific instruction before the DBQ question itself refers to a core point. Once you earn all core points, you can earn additional points for doing those tasks well or for effectively bringing in outside information.

The following guidelines will be useful:

Include a thesis.   To earn a point for your thesis it must be specific, refer to documents, and not just repeat the question. If you don't earn a point for the thesis, you can't earn the point for supporting the thesis with an appropriate number of documents.

The following examples are of thesis statements that would not earn a point:

There were many positive and negative views about Savonarola.

Why is this not acceptable? It doesn't refer to the documents in any specific way, nor does it address the specific terms of the questions. Here's another poor example:

Savonarola was very controversial, and people differed about his impact on social, political, and religious aspects of life in Florence.

This is better, but it doesn't show you've done much more than read the question. Here is an example of a thesis statement that would earn a point:

While some people in Renaissance Florence praised Savonarola for his holiness and the good he was doing for both the political and social life of the city, others saw him as a dangerous fanatic.

This thesis refers to specific positive and negative aspects of Savonarola's impact in the political, social, and religious arenas, therefore addressing the question.

Use a majority of the documents.   You must use at least half of the documents to earn this point. In the case of this practice exam, that means seven documents. Using a document means discussing something in the box specifically. You can still earn this point even if you make mistakes on one or two documents.

Interpret documents correctly.   You are allowed to make only one major error, which is defined as an interpretation that leads you to an erroneous conclusion or to an erroneous grouping. A major error, for example, would be if you described the Arrabiati (Document 9) as supporters of Savonarola.

Group the documents.   You must have three groups of documents. A group must have at least two documents in it, discussed specifically and together. Be specific when describing each group; that is, don't merely list documents together by number (for example, Documents 4, 5, and 7), but explain what the documents in a group have in common. Typical ways of making groups include: by opinion of author, by identity of author (nationality, political party or orientation, gender, age, position, and so on), by type of document (speech, government documents), or by time period.

Possible groups in this DBQ include:

Political concerns: [2] Capponi, [6] Genazzano

Religious concerns: [1] Pico, [3] Benivieni, [6] Genazzano or [7] prior of San Marco, [10] de Gondi, [13] da Volterra

Clergymen authors: [3] Benivieni, [6] Genazzano, [7] prior of San Marco, [11] Pope Alexander VI

Political leader authors: [2] Capponi, [5] Redditi, [8] Signoria, [9] Arrabiati, [10] de Gondi, [12] Machiavelli

Humanist authors: [1] Pico, [12] Machiavelli, [13] da Volterra

Businessmen authors: [4] Landucci, [10] de Gondi

Allies and opponents of the Medici authors: [1] Pico, [2] Capponi

Include point-of-view analysis.   This is a crucial core point, one that some students don't do or do poorly. POV analysis shows that you understand that a particular person wrote a document at a particular time and place for a particular purpose and that it may not present the whole truth. It's important to think about the reliability of the document. For example, how accurate can an engraving or a commentary be if it was made by someone who was not an eyewitness of the scene depicted or, even if he or she was an eyewitness, may not have understood what he or she saw? Another way to do POV analysis is to connect the author's position in society or anything given in the source identification with the views the author expresses. The document summaries that follow show examples of the POV analysis you might make for each document.

Analyze individual documents.

Document 1   Pico della Mirandola is impressed by Savonarola after hearing him speak, particularly by his theological knowledge. The Fra Mariano he compares Savonarola to is the author of Document 6. POV: Pico was a humanist and Neoplatonist and would therefore not be very interested in theology, which was typically identified with medieval Scholasticism, but in this document we see that Pico was interested enough to go hear Savonarola and praise him. Neoplatonists emphasized the glories of the individual, secular man (Pico was the author of *On the Dignity of Man*), yet Pico was impressed by someone who represented very strict Catholic views about the sinfulness of man.

Document 2   Capponi criticizes Piero de' Medici and calls for Savonarola to be sent to negotiate with the French king Charles VIII, whose armies are invading Italy. He states that Savonarola is beloved by the people. POV: Capponi was in the midst of challenging the legitimate ruler of Florence and wanted to use Savonarola to give himself legitimacy with the people. He probably wanted to send Savonarola as one of the negotiators not because he was so beloved by the people but because he was a respected clergyman, which would have given him a better chance of getting good terms from the French king.

Document 3   Benivieni criticizes Savonarola for overzealousness and harshness in his language. POV: A monk of the Dominican order, Benivieni was trying to protect the reputation of that order. As a physician, he may have treated some of these fallen women and developed sympathies for their plight.

Document 4   Landucci praises the effect of the children inspired by Savonarola on the moral behavior of the Florentines. POV: As an apothecary, Landucci was probably more aware than most observers of the debilitating effects of gambling and other vices. While a diary entry would make this document seem reliable, it seems unlikely that what he described could be fully true, in view of the fact that Savonarola is executed just two years later. Perhaps Landucci's own children or children he knew were some of the "prior's children" and he was defending their participation.

Document 5   Redditi says Savonarola's preaching made Florence a heavenly city. POV: Redditi had been ambassador to the Holy See under Lorenzo the Magnificent (de' Medici), yet he shows here his admiration for someone who had taken over from the Medici and who criticized their values. As he wrote after the execution of Savonarola, he was probably trying to explain why he had been one of his supporters.

Document 6   Mariano de Genazzano viciously attacks Savonarola as a dangerous heretic. POV: Genazzano used strong language to urge the pope to act. He had lost to Savonarola in the preaching competition in 1491, and his vehemence here may derive from anger and jealousy over that loss. Despite the language of the document, his concerns may have been political rather than religious, as he was upset that Florence had not joined the Holy League under the pope.

Document 7   The prior of San Marco writes to defend Savonarola. POV: As head of the monastery made popular by Savonarola, the prior defended the preacher from accusations and may have exaggerated his purity in order to protect the monastery's reputation.

Document 8   The Signoria writes in defense of Savonarola to the pope. POV: The Signoria and the prominent citizens who signed the petition may have been trying to prevent the pope from imposing an interdict on the city that would harm its economy as well as people's abilities to get married and the like. They impugned the motives of Savonarola'a accusers as masking naked ambition (which might be seen in Fra Mariano's accusation against Savonarola in Document 6) in order to discredit them.

Document 9   The political party opposed to Savonarola mocks his prophecies, saying the results have been famine, plague, and invasion. POV: As Savonarola's popularity grew because of his prophecies, it was important to dispute them to win away his supporters. They probably exaggerated how badly things had gone under Savonarola's leadership.

Document 10   Giuliano de Gondi accuses Savonarola not only of heresy but also of creating heretical sects. POV: As a banker, de Gondi may have opposed Savonarola not because of religious concerns but because of Savonarola's attacks on ill-gotten gains, which would presumably include banking profits. As a political leader of the city, he may have exaggerated Savonarola's heretical influence as a way of trying to get rid of the friar since he was causing the city so much difficulty with the pope (see Document 11).

Document 11   Pope Alexander VI harshly criticizes the Signoria for letting Savonarola continue to preach after his excommunication, and he threatens the use of the interdict unless his orders are obeyed. POV: The pope used the Signoria's request for some help on behalf of the Florentines as leverage to force the Signoria to act against Savonarola. By calling Savonarola the "oracle of Apollo," the pope showed that he had humanist inclinations to win the support of a Renaissance Signoria.

Document 12   Machiavelli describes Savonarola as two-faced and changing his tune to suit the political situation. POV: Machiavelli was a supporter of the republic and would have been distressed to see Savonarola move away from his staunch republicanism. Machiavelli was cynical in his views of people, and thus he saw Savonarola as yet another leader who courted favor.

Document 13   Da Volterra says Savonarola was founding heretical sects and urging his followers to stay away from Rome, and that only divine intervention prevented them from following suit. POV: Da Volterra may have criticized Savonarola because he was trying to protect his reputation with the Medici (who were restored to power in 1512) and, due to his relationship with his brother, would have been seen as an enemy by them. As the founder of a monastery himself, he might have been trying to curry favor with the pope in Rome.

Answers for Section II: Parts B and C

General AP Scoring Standards for Free-Response Questions

The essays are scored on a scale of 0 to 9, with 0 being a real score. A response that is completely off topic does not even earn a zero. Here are generic scoring guidelines for the essays in Parts B and C.

9–8

Has a clear, well-developed thesis
Is well organized
Addresses the terms of the question
Supports the thesis with substantial specific evidence
Has sophisticated analysis
May contain minor errors; even a 9 need not be flawless

7–6

Has a clear thesis
Addresses all parts of the question but discussion is uneven
Shows competent analysis, but it may be superficial
Supports the thesis with some specific evidence

5–4

Contains a thesis, perhaps superficial or simplistic
Has uneven responses to the question's terms
May contain errors, factual or interpretative
Addresses the question with generally accurate discussion but without specific evidence; analysis is implicit or superficial
May contain major errors within a generally accurate and appropriate discussion
Is descriptive rather than analytical

3–2

Has weak or muddled thesis, perhaps suggesting false or inappropriate dichotomies or connections
Contains significant errors of chronology or fact
Has minimal discussion
Offers limited evidence

1–0

Has confused or absent thesis or merely restates the question
Misconstrues the question or omits major tasks
May contain major errors or irrelevant historical information
Addresses only one part of the question
Offers minimal or no evidence

Reread your essay and ask yourself the following questions—or if you can work with a fellow student in AP European History (APEH), read each other's essays and ask these questions:

1. How well organized is the essay? Is it clearly divided into distinct paragraphs? Is there an introduction and a conclusion?

2. How clear is the thesis? Is the thesis statement at the beginning of the essay or in the conclusion?

3. How many arguments support the thesis?

4. How much evidence is used to support the thesis? How specific was it?

5. Were all parts of the question addressed? Was the discussion of the different parts more or less balanced?

6. How many of the points noted in the explanations of the answer were made in the essay?

7. Were there major factual, chronological, or interpretative errors? Or minor errors?

8. Was the analysis explicit or implicit? Was it sophisticated or minimal?

Now reread the Scoring Guidelines and give yourself a score.

In general, the scores on the document-based questions average higher than those of the thematic essay questions, because the DBQ is a skill-based question that uses evidence, while the thematic essays are content-based and require recall of information. The median score on the DBQ is 5 (usually because of lack of POV analysis), while the median scores on the thematic essays are typically 4 to 5 on the first and approximately 3 to 4 on the second group, often because students run out of time.

Part B Responses

2. **To what degree and in what ways was the Reformation an outgrowth of the Italian Renaissance?**

To address this essay, you need to think about which elements the Renaissance and the Reformation share and in which they differ. The question asks you to make an evaluation in addition to demonstrating your knowledge of the two periods.

Ways the Renaissance influenced the Reformation: Secularism fostered by the Renaissance was reinforced by Protestantism. The Protestants argued that one must do God's work in this world rather than abandon material life. They rejected celibacy in favor of marriage and family and accepted worldly work as a calling from God. The individualistic spirit of the Renaissance was acknowledged by the Reformation's insistence on each individual's ability to read and interpret Scripture. Renaissance humanism made the work of Christian textual analysis and editing possible. The nationalism spawned in the Renaissance period was acknowledged by the establishment of national churches.

Ways in which the Renaissance did not foster the Reformation: The Renaissance was profoundly interested in antiquity (which the Reformation ignored except for Scripture), including the republican and homoerotic values of ancient Greece and Rome. The Italian humanists explored various aspects of paganism (Pico), while northern humanists (More and Erasmus), although critical of the church, remained faithful to the notion of a universal church. The Renaissance exalted the arts, and the graphic arts conveyed the values of proportion, realism, and imitation of nature, including the nude body. The Protestants generally rejected visual representation or elaborate architecture, seeing art as potentially dangerous or distracting rather than fundamental and liberating.

3. **What characteristics of Italian cities in the fifteenth century created an environment that fostered the development of Renaissance culture?**

To answer this essay well, you must first articulate defining aspects of Renaissance culture—humanism, new artistic styles and values, and new educational systems—and then connect it to the Italian cities.

Possible thesis: It was the unique nature of Italian cities in the fourteenth and fifteenth centuries that allowed for the development of Renaissance culture. Among the specific characteristics of Italian cities like Florence were strength of republican political life and a thriving commercial culture, which fostered secularism and the search for justification of new values and lifestyles.

Communal governments and powerful guilds were important patrons of early Renaissance architects, painters, and sculptors, from Masaccio to Michelangelo. They commissioned most of the major works of the early Renaissance using the new artistic techniques of perspective and classical motifs, such as the Foundling Hospital or the Cathedral Dome (both designed by Brunelleschi). The David, probably the most famous masterpiece of the Renaissance, was commissioned by the city of Florence when it had expelled the Medici and restored the republic.

Merchants and bankers became wealthy from wool and silk manufacturing and trade, and they developed a new hierarchy of wealth for social status, thus fostering secularism and individualism. They had disposable income to spend, which they used for patronage of the arts and humanities, particularly those pursuits that glorified the values of classical antiquity. Paintings and sculptures became prestige markers for this upwardly mobile class. The opportunities for individuals to become wealthy and to rise in social standing paralleled the humanistic sense of man's potentiality and were reflected in the noticeable rise in the status of artists. Political thinkers used examples from ancient Greece and Rome to justify and explore their republican city-states, which required an educated political class.

4. **In what ways did developments during the Renaissance help bring about the Age of Exploration?**

In this question, you are asked to discuss not the Italian Renaissance per se but what aspects of it promoted the Age of Exploration. You do not need to spend time explaining what the Renaissance was, unless doing so is relevant to your thesis. For example, you could safely ignore the role the Medicis and other wealthy individuals played as patrons of the arts.

Possible thesis: The intellectual curiosity and general prosperity fostered by the Renaissance provided crucial foundations for the Age of Exploration but were not itself its direct cause.

The Renaissance passion for antiquity brought into the public eye ancient geographic texts, the most important of which was Ptolemy's *Geography*. This confirmed notions of the roundness of the earth and implied a relatively short distance from Asia if one went west from Europe. Renaissance Neoplatonism stressed mathematical thinking, which allowed explorers to believe that they could rely on their computations (even if, in fact, these were often wrong), and encouraged notions of the enormous potential of human achievement. The Renaissance was marked by intense curiosity about not only the world of the past but also about the physical universe, promoting exploration.

Italian Renaissance cities thrived on international trade with the East. They encouraged the importation of products, technologies, and ideas from what remained of the Byzantine Empire, as well as Asia and the Middle East. They stimulated demand for such goods. Northern Renaissance cities—such as Amsterdam or Rotterdam—had a thriving trade with the East and created a relatively tolerant international culture that brought a wide variety of peoples into contact with each other. Dutch innovations encouraged exploration.

Renaissance Italians, particularly Florentines, played a crucial role in the exploration of the New World. Many of the earliest explorers—for example, Columbus, John Cabot, and Vespucci—were Italians. The lack of a unified Italian state meant that the Italians were explorers, not conquerors. They worked on behalf of nation-states like Spain and England.

The printing press made possible the dissemination of relatively inexpensive books, which spread new ideas and encouraged new ways of thinking. Such popular works as the stories of Prester John or *The Travels of John Mandeville* did a great deal to spark curiosity and a thirst for travel.

Counterargument: On the other hand, there were many motivations for the explorations that contradicted the Renaissance spirit, particularly the religious, missionizing fervor. On balance, the Renaissance may have been a precondition of the explorations rather than the cause of the explorations.

Part C Responses

5. **What are the differing views concerning the roles of women held by Catholics and Protestants? What do these views reveal about the impact of theology on gender roles?**

This is a typical social history question. It asks you to discuss a mainstream topic from the point of view of a particular side. It's important to address the question as asked; this is not a place to discuss the general differences between Catholicism and Protestantism, unless you're relating them to the gender issue. In your thesis, you can stress the similarities or the differences.

Possible thesis: Both Protestants and Catholics saw women as subservient to men and limited their scope of influence to the household. Neither gave women an official role within the structure or administration of the church or in the Mass.

Catholic women could achieve important positions as the heads of convents or founders of monastic orders. Angela Merici, founder of the Ursuline Order during the Counter-Reformation, played a significant role in the education of women. Catholic women also achieved renown and status for their religiosity. Joan of Arc was allowed to inspire the French army to victory over the English because of her religious convictions; she later became patron saint of France. Teresa of Avila was famous for her mystical visions as well as for her writings, whose importance were acknowledged when she was made a Doctor of the Church. The ideal life for a Catholic was a monastic one, away from the world, celibate, and devoted to religious work, so unmarried women would often be highly regarded as long as they were cloistered.

Protestant women had different status issues. Protestants (except in the Church of England) banned monasticism because it is not found in the Scriptures; instead they argued that to do God's work, one must live in this world, in secular society. Women lost opportunities for status and power when convents disappeared; unmarried women lost a place to live as well as a career path. Protestants also removed the special status of priests by denying transubstantiation. All believers were equal. The minister's role was to lead the congregation, not to act as an intermediary between man and God. This meant that ministers married and had children. Women gained new importance in their particular roles as wives of pastors and in general for management of their households. They were encouraged to become literate so they could read the Bible and properly raise their children. Marriage began to be seen as more of an equal partnership. Martin Luther and his wife, like many other Protestant couples, had double portraits commissioned, reflecting this new spirit. Marriage was not a sacrament to Protestants, so divorce was permitted. This meant that an unpleasant or abusive relationship could be ended, thus providing greater protection for women.

6. **Select two states in which there was substantial conflict between Protestants and Catholics in sixteenth-century Europe, and analyze the role national politics played in those domestic struggles.**

Although the question does not ask you to make direct comparisons, a superior essay will draw conclusions that show similarities and differences between the two states.

England: The need for a male heir led Henry VIII of England to ask the pope for an annulment; when the pope denied it in obedience to Charles V (Henry's wife's nephew), Henry used the Protestant movement to break away from Rome, establishing the Church of England under royal control. As a Protestant, Henry was able to obtain legal divorce; Henry used this right twice. Henry used wealth confiscated from monasteries to gain strong support for the Tudor dynasty. Mary Tudor's attempts to restore Catholicism were compromised by her marriage to Philip II of Spain, which sparked nationalistic as well as religious resentment. Elizabeth I acted as a politique to settle the religious matters, restore stability, and encourage national economic development. England defended the Protestant cause as part of its great competition with Habsburg Spain, helping the Dutch to become independent of Spain.

France: The French kings had won control over the church in France in the Pragmatic Sanction of Bourges and the Concordat of Bologna. Because the kings appointed their own bishops, they had no great need to break away from Rome; Catholicism had already become a national church in practice. Protestantism appealed to all classes in France, particularly the nobles who sought relief from the centralizing Valois kings and the middle classes who sought to reduce their taxes and control their economic decisions in the towns where they lived. Both groups saw Protestantism as a way to resist the monarchy. The war between Protestants and Catholics ended when the politique Henry of Navarre, the leader of the Protestant forces, converted to Catholicism in order to win acceptance by still-Catholic Paris, and he issued the Edict of Nantes that gave Protestants freedom of worship and rights in their towns.

Holy Roman Empire: This decentralized conglomeration of more than 300 states was loosely ruled by the emperor, always a Habsburg. Many princes sought more independence from him, and Protestantism gave them a way. Luther's survival after the Diet of Worms was dependent on the protection he got from the Elector of Saxony. Protestantism allowed princes to establish national churches over which they were the ultimate authority in their states. It also allowed them to benefit economically from expropriated church lands and monasteries. Charles V fought to hold his empire together and to keep it Catholic; the Peace of Augsburg, settling the religious war of the sixteenth century, allowed each prince to choose either Catholicism or Lutheranism for his state, thus enhancing their power and weakening that of the emperor.

7. **Discuss the various motives that prompted the exploration and colonization of the New World and evaluate their relative importance.**

This is a very typical question, and similar questions appear frequently on the exam; the key to a successful answer is the evaluation of the various motives. "Gold, God, and Glory" summarizes the motivations of the New World colonizers. Because the question asks for relative importance, you need to argue for one being more important than the other two. Gold was the primary motivator in the Age of Exploration, and the sample response is structured accordingly.

Gold: Columbus was promised 10 percent of all material wealth he took for Spain. Columbus changed route on his voyage, from going north to the expected court of Genghis Khan to a southern route where gold was promised. The chief reason for the voyage was to search for new trading routes after trade was cut off with the East, including trade in slaves after the Ottoman conquest of Constantinople. Native populations were treated with disdain and brutality. For example, Cortés deceived and murdered an Aztec ruler to obtain huge stores of Mexican gold; the encomienda system was established to turn Amerindians into forced laborers, who were made to pan for gold or mine silver and were cruelly treated. The African slave trade began soon after the first contact with the New World and provided huge profits for European traders, as did the sugar plantations where the slaves worked.

God: Columbus was a deeply religious man who believed God promoted his voyages, and he delighted in the possible conversion of natives. Missionaries were among the earliest settlers of the New World. Most native populations converted to Christianity. Muslim dominance of world trade was a major reason for the search for new trading routes. However, these motives were as much (if not more) commercial than religious.

Glory: This motive reflected Renaissance values of individualism and fame seeking. Europeans were willing to do something that they had not done before, to sail without sight of land. Renaissance humanism and interest in technology and geography, combined with individual egoism, encouraged men to become explorers, conquerors, and settlers. After the Age of Exploration began, a desire for national glory, prestige, and power fueled further explorations and expansion of empires. However, the desire for glory was also intertwined with and promoted by commercial interests.

PART 2
The Seventeenth and Eighteenth Centuries

This part covers the following chapters in *A History of Western Society*, Eleventh Edition:

Chapter 15: Absolutism and Constitutionalism, ca. 1589–1725

Chapter 16: Toward a New Worldview, 1540–1789

Chapter 17: The Expansion of Europe, 1650–1800

Chapter 18: Life in the Era of Expansion, 1650–1800

The developments of the seventeenth and eighteenth centuries were in almost every way the foundation of modern Europe—intellectually, politically, economically, and socially. They jointly fueled the two great revolutions of the long nineteenth century, the French Revolution and the Industrial Revolution. They also established the basis for European domination among world powers.

Politically, the English created Europe's first constitutional monarchy via revolution, war, much political infighting, and religious turmoil. The primary dispute was between the Stuart monarchs attempting to impose absolutism based on the divine right of kings on Parliament, whose constitutional rights in the Magna Carta of 1215 had been enhanced by rights won during the Hundred Years' War (1337–1453). The most notable religious dispute was between Anglicans, who tended to support the monarchy, and Puritans, Calvinist Protestants who had a strong voice in Parliament. The Stuart kings who took the crown after Queen Elizabeth's death in 1603 tried to rule without Parliament; in 1642 things came to a head with the outbreak of war between the royalists and the parliamentary forces, under the leadership of Oliver Cromwell, who captured the king. In 1649 Cromwell maneuvered the Parliament into voting for the execution of the king, sending shockwaves across Europe.

After a period of rule by Cromwell, the Stuarts were restored to the monarchy in 1660. The Catholicism of James II alarmed the Protestant-dominated Parliament, however, which offered the crown to the king's Protestant daughter, Mary, and her husband, William of Orange, the Stadholder of Holland. Their accession to the English throne in 1688 and the Bill of Rights issued the following year acknowledged the civil liberties of the people and the ultimate sovereignty of Parliament.

The seven provinces of the Netherlands were each a republic with a common body for foreign policy decisions. These republics were unique in Europe, as the Italian city-states had long since become despotisms or dukedoms. In the eighteenth century, the Netherlands became a constitutional monarchy, but it retained its tradition of relative religious toleration.

On the continent, absolutism, based on the theory of the divine right of kings, was the order of the day. France's absolutist government, created by Louis XIII and his shrewd adviser, Richelieu, and then cleverly developed by Louis XIV, set the standard. The French kings used intendants (administrative officials often of bourgeois origin) to enforce royal will in the provinces and spy on the nobility. They also attacked religious centers of possible opposition to the monarchs—Protestants (expelled by Louis XIV in 1685) and Jansenists (a Catholic movement condemned as heresy in the mid-seventeenth century). Louis XIV, the self-proclaimed "Sun King," manipulated the nobility by requiring their residence at least part of the year at his splendid, impressive new palace at Versailles, outside of Paris. There the nobles were entertained and participated in elaborate court rituals through which the king managed and controlled them. The splendor and high fashion of Versailles and the many ballets, operas, and plays commissioned by Louis made France the cultural center of Europe and French the international language for the next two centuries. Maintaining the court at Versailles was hugely expensive. At the same time, Louis built up the largest army in Europe and engaged in warfare for a good part of his reign, adding small but valuable territories to France. As a result, the tax burden on the people grew, with that burden falling on the peasants and bourgeoisie, as the nobles were exempt from property taxes.

In the Germanic states, the Thirty Years' War (1618–1648), the last major religious war in Europe, ravaged the lands and reduced the population. The Peace of Westphalia that concluded the war ended any remaining possibility that the Holy Roman Empire could become a functioning state. In this vacuum grew two powerful German-speaking absolutist states: Austria, under Habsburg rule, and Prussia, under the Hohenzollerns. In Austria, the Habsburgs succeeded in lifting the Ottoman siege of Vienna in 1683 and made the city into a cultural as well as administrative capital. The Habsburgs took Hungary and Transylvania from the Ottomans and were able to tame the Bohemian but not the Hungarian aristocratic elites. In Prussia, Frederick William, the "Great Elector," convinced the nobles to give up their right to approve new taxes in exchange for greater control over their serfs and the creation of a strong Prussian army. His successors, Frederick I (first king of Prussia) and Frederick William I, created an effective bureaucracy; a highly disciplined army with a Junker (Prussian noble) officer corps; and a society based on the values of duty, discipline, and obedience.

In Russia, Tsar Peter the Great sought to modernize his state by forced westernization of dress, cultural habits, and education of the nobles. He defeated Sweden in the Great War and built a new capital on the Baltic—St. Petersburg, which was a gorgeous city modeled on a European city. As Louis XIV had done at Versailles, Peter required his nobles and merchants to live there for most of the year. He controlled the Russian Orthodox Church, created a new noble hierarchy based on service to the state, acquired new territories for Russia, and set the stage for Russian emergence as a great power.

While these transformations were occurring within the political world, even more profound changes were under way in the intellectual world. In the seventeenth century, the astronomers and physicists Galileo Galilei (using the telescope) and Johannes Kepler (using mathematics) proved the validity of the Copernican heliocentric theory of the solar system that had been first proposed the previous century. This overturned the Aristotelian and Ptolemaic models that had held sway for 1,600 years. Isaac Newton discovered the idea of gravity, providing for the first time a scientific law of universal gravitation that operated both in the heavens and on earth. This idea, combined with his laws of motion, offered a model of a mechanistic universe.

In medicine, chemistry, botany, and biology, scientists grasped and applied the empirical methods advocated by English scientist Francis Bacon and the mathematics advocated by French philosopher René Descartes. This combination created the scientific method still used today. Cartesian dualism philosophically separated mind from matter, thereby freeing the study of matter or the body from issues of religion. In spite of much resistance toward these new ideas, symbolized by the church's prosecution of Galileo and his forced recantation of Copernican ideas, they were well established by the end of the century.

Over the course of the eighteenth century, scholars and writers applied the scientific method to the study of human life, thereby creating the social sciences. The Age of Reason, or the Enlightenment, asserted the profound vision of man's fundamental rationality and the ability of humans to use their God-given reason to understand and solve society's problems.

In political theory, John Locke asserted that the social contract requires governments to protect life, liberty, and property, and that the people have the right to overturn their governments if they do not. Montesquieu advocated checks and balances and the separation of power. Voltaire, the prolific and popular French philosophe and writer, condemned organized religion for its oppression and superstitions. The German philosopher Immanuel Kant advocated complete intellectual freedom while his French contemporary, Denis Diderot, co-edited the information-rich, seventeen-volume *Encyclopedia*, the first book of its kind. Adam Smith, a Scottish professor and moral philosopher, discovered the law of supply and demand. He argued against mercantilism and for capitalism. In the late eighteenth century, Jean-Jacques Rousseau challenged the idea of representative government by arguing for a radical democracy in which the people held sovereignty but the government was run by those few who knew the general will or what's best for the people.

The Enlightenment—articulated in France through salons organized by upper-class women and promoted by books—presented a vision of human progress and optimism. A number of monarchs—Joseph II of Austria, Frederick the Great of Prussia, and Catherine the Great of Russia—were enthusiasts of the Enlightenment. They implemented reforms suggested by the philosophes. These included abolishing torture, rationalizing the laws, granting limited religious freedom, encouraging education, and streamlining government structures. Those reforms were curtailed, however, when monarchical authority and aristocratic privilege were challenged.

As a result of this entrenchment, eastern Europe experienced a resurgence of serfdom, while in the west, conditions for peasants improved. In western Europe, merchant classes enriched by the overseas trade (including the slave trade) created a new system of manufacturing. This was called in turns the domestic system, cottage industry, or the putting-out system. In this system, the manufacture of goods, mostly textiles, was done in rural households far away from guild control. Agriculturalists applied experimental methods to increase the fertility of the soil, discovering new crops along the way. The new scientific approach encouraged the enclosure of common fields, which concentrated land ownership in a few hands, particularly in England. This process increased agricultural output but also created many landless peasants, primed to become a desperate and mobile labor force.

Such large-scale economic changes had great consequences. Populations grew significantly as the plague finally disappeared and the death rate fell. A good third of the babies born were illegitimate as community controls weakened. A consumer culture took root not only in the upper classes but in the lower classes as well. The consumption of sugar and tea exploded while cheaper clothing and other goods from the New World became more readily available.

Toward the end of the eighteenth century, England was poised for its industrial revolution, France for its political revolution, western Europe for mass politics, central Europe for political unifications under the domination of economically advanced states, and Russia for great-power status.

CHAPTER 15
Absolutism and Constitutionalism,
ca. 1589–1725

> **Areas of focus:** France, Spain, Austria, Prussia, Russia, the Ottoman Empire, England, and the Netherlands
>
> **Main events:** absolutism; the Thirty Years' War; the English Civil War and constitutionalism

The following is a thematic summary of the material covered in Chapter 15 of *A History of Western Society:*

Politics

✦ **AP Tip** Absolutism and constitutionalism shaped Europe's political destiny and are often subjects of comparative questions on how politics intersected with class, economy, and religion.

✦ England became Europe's first constitutional monarchy but only after war, revolution, and the execution of the king. It developed a strong Parliament with power of the purse and other rights granted in the Magna Carta of 1215. In 1603 the Protestant queen Elizabeth I was succeeded by the Stuarts—Scots, absolutists, and Anglicans with sympathies for Catholicism. Many of their subjects, conversely, had become Puritans (Calvinists).

✦ Charles I (r. 1625–1629) came into conflict with Parliament first politically then militarily. After defeat by the New Model Army under Oliver Cromwell, Charles I was executed in 1649. England became a commonwealth or republic in name but a military dictatorship in practice.

✦ The monarchy was temporarily restored in 1660, but when James II (r. 1685–1688) actively promoted the Catholic cause, Parliament offered the crown to James's Protestant daughter, Mary, and her husband, William, the Stadholder of Holland. This Glorious Revolution of 1688 permanently established constitutionalism, and the Bill of Rights in 1689 guaranteed civil liberties.

✦ The English Cabinet system enhanced Parliament's power as its members (MPs) began to formulate policy and execute programs when the new royal dynasty had little interest in governing. Robert Walpole was the first prime minister.

✦ **AP Tip** Some historians have used the English Revolution to create a model of revolutions, beginning with (1) a reform stage in which most people see the need for political change; followed by (2) civil war (and often foreign wars as well); (3) radicalization of the revolution with major divisions among the revolutionaries over values and class interests, leading to violence and repression; followed by (4) one-man rule; and, ultimately, by (5) restoration. This pattern fits the French and Russian Revolutions as well. It can be useful to distill the narrative of extremely complex revolutions along these lines.

✦ In France, Austria, Prussia, and Russia, traditional limitations on the power of the monarch disappeared as the monarchs established themselves as absolute rulers. In absolutism, sovereignty was held by the king who ruled with divine right and without limitation from church, tradition, or nobles—the dominant social class, who had to be forced or enticed to give up their traditional political rights.

✦ **AP Tip**   Students sometimes see "absolutism" as synonymous with "dictatorship." No seventeenth- or eighteenth-century monarch, however absolute, could be called a dictator by today's standard. Hereditary monarchs ruled without institutional constraints and established power that was later inherited by their heirs; twentieth- and twenty-first-century dictatorships rarely outlived their founders. They are fundamentally different forms of power and control. At the same time, modern dictatorships often extended the impact of their rule into social, economic, and cultural realms to a far greater extent than absolute monarchs.

✦ The absolute monarchs shared a number of traits and policies: long reigns; standing armies composed primarily of infantry employed, trained, and outfitted by the state; higher state costs; the maneuvering of religious and cultural life for political purposes; and transformed royal relationships with the nobles.

✦ In France, the rich bourgeoisie became allies of the kings against the nobles. In central and eastern Europe, nobles were given greater control over their serfs but lost political power. The French monarchs used royal officials, known as intendants, to execute royal policies in the provinces and spy on local nobles. Louis XIV required the nobles to reside at Versailles for at least part of the year, where they participated in elaborate court rituals. Frederick William I convinced his nobles to give up their right to approve new taxes in exchange for economic security and positions as officers in a strong Prussian army. Russia's Peter the Great created a new ranking system for nobles based on service to the state. The Habsburgs tamed the Bohemian nobility but struggled to subjugate the Hungarians.

✦ The Thirty Years' War began in 1618 when Bohemian nobles attempted to assert their independence from the Holy Roman emperor and win the right to practice Protestantism. The belligerents were divided into the Catholic League (the Habsburgs) against the Protestant Union (Denmark, Prussia, and Sweden). France, though Catholic, supported the Protestants to weaken the Habsburgs. The Peace of Westphalia of 1648 permanently crippled the Holy Roman Empire by recognizing the independent authority of hundreds of German princes and added valuable territories to Prussia.

✦ Spain declined in the seventeenth century for economic, religious, and political reasons. These included the expulsion of the Moriscos (Muslim converts to Christianity) and weak kings who left the administration of the state in the hands of ministers.

✦ The Peace of Utrecht ended the War of the Spanish Succession (1701–1714) between Louis XIV and the Grand Alliance of other European powers. It also redrew the boundaries of French, Spanish, English, Dutch, Austrian, and Prussian control. This marked the end of French expansion.

✦ The Ottoman Empire was also an absolutist state in that the sultan had sole political power and owned all agricultural lands. There was no hereditary nobility. Its highly effective army, the janissary corps, was made up of former Christian boys taken from the Balkans; some became high administrators. Religious and ethnic communities called millets were given autonomous self-government, the right to practice their religion, and the right to use their own languages.

✦ The two most developed capitalistic states in Europe in the seventeenth century—England and the United Provinces (the Netherlands)—established constitutional governments. In these governments, sovereignty lay with the people, and the powers of the monarchs were limited by a constitution, either written or unwritten.

✦ The Netherlands became a republic. Each of its seven provinces had their own Estate (assembly) but all shared a common executive officer, the Stadholder, and a federal assembly for foreign affairs. The Dutch were highly prosperous and by far the most tolerant state in Europe at the time, particularly for Jews.

	FRANCE	AUSTRIA	PRUSSIA	RUSSIA
DYNASTY	**Bourbon**	**Habsburg**	**Hohenzollern**	**Romanov**
Most Important King / Years Ruled	Louis XIV 1643/1661–1715 (54 years)	Leopold I 1658–1705 (47 years)	Fredrick William, the "Great Elector" 1640–1689 (48 years)	Peter the Great 1682–1725 (36 years)
Conquests / Wars	Franche-Comté; Alsace-Lorraine; lost War of the Spanish Succession 1714; largest army in Europe	Hungary; Transylvania; defeated Ottoman siege of Vienna 1683	Built militaristic state with small but well-trained army; best army in Europe	Defeated Sweden in the Great Northern War; acquired Baltic states
Use of the Arts / Culture	The splendor and function of the Versailles palace as a center for government set the standard for other absolutist monarchs	Vienna was center for arts and music; Baroque art and music flourished; German language dominant over the many ethnicities		St. Petersburg built as new capital city; westernized nobles' education, attire, social life
Allied Class	Wealthy bourgeoisie	Nobility	Nobility (Junkers)	Nobility (boyars)
Religious Issues	Revoked Edict of Nantes 1685; 200,000 Huguenots leave	Catholicism used to create national identity and forge loyalty to the Crown	Religiously tolerant; welcomed Huguenots from France	Holy Synod run by government official appointed by the tsar

Economy

- ✦ Mercantilism was the dominant economic policy in this period. It was characterized by the active intervention of the state to increase its power and its supply of gold and silver by promoting exports and reducing imports. In France, Jean-Baptiste Colbert, Louis XIV's finance minister (1665–1683), subsidized local manufacturing, imposed protectionist tariffs and abolished domestic tariffs, created new textile industries, invited foreign craftsmen to France, and promoted colonial growth. In England, Oliver Cromwell also enacted mercantilist legislation, such as the Navigation Act of 1651.

- ✦ Russia's Ivan the Terrible (r. 1533–1584) attempted to make commoners servants of the tsar, binding them to their towns and jobs so he could tax them. Many fled the country and joined Cossack armies.

- ✦ The population and economy of central Europe was devastated by the Thirty Years' War; it would take two centuries to rebound.

- ✦ Spain's economy declined partially because of the competition of the Dutch and the English, who built up their shipbuilding industries and established hugely successful trading companies in the East and West Indies. Spain also suffered from declining manufacturing, a small middle class, the continuing effects of inflation, and the exhaustion of its mines in the New World.

- ✦ The Dutch merchant marine was the largest in Europe, and trade and commerce brought the Dutch the highest standard of living in Europe, perhaps in the world.

Religion

- ✦ The Thirty Years' War (1618–1648) was the last of the great religious wars in Europe; the concluding Peace of Westphalia guaranteed the more than 300 princes within the Holy Roman Empire the right to choose Catholicism, Lutheranism, or Calvinism as their state religion.

- ✦ Charles I of England, backing the Catholic supporters of his throne during a period of Puritan unrest, summoned Parliament to create an army to suppress Presbyterian Scots. The unforeseen consequence was the English Civil War (1642–1649) and Charles's execution.

- ✦ Oliver Cromwell's Protectorate (1653–1658) repressed Catholicism in Ireland but allowed the Jews to return to England.

- ✦ James II (r. 1685–1688) granted religious freedom to all during the English Restoration but ultimately lost his throne.

- ✦ With the millet system in the Ottoman Empire, which granted religious freedom to non-Muslims in exchange for the payment of taxes, there was almost no compulsion for conversion, unlike in most other absolutist states.

Society and Culture

✦ As the feudal lords of seventeenth-century central and eastern Europe gained authority and the cultural gap between lords and peasants grew, the lives of peasants worsened considerably.

✦ While few feudal obligations remained for the peasants of western Europe, most lived at subsistence level, with bread as the primary element in their diet. While some small peasant landowners lived better, the majority were vulnerable to famine, and there were numerous riots over the high prices of bread in bad times. French peasants opposed to financing the monarchy's wars and government policies rioted in a series of uprisings known as the Fronde (1648–1653), but the rebellions died out and reinforced the desire for a strong monarchy.

✦ Peter the Great instigated the westernization of Russian dress, cultural habits, and educational systems. He also built up the city of St. Petersburg.

✦ Under Suleiman the Magnificent, Istanbul became a great center of culture and commerce.

✦ Aristocratic women played important roles in absolutist courts not only as wives and mistresses, but also as power brokers. In the Ottoman Empire, the sultan's concubines lived in the harem in the palace and vied to produce the next sultan.

Ideas and Literature

✦ Both constitutionalism and absolutism had major theorists in England. Thomas Hobbes argued in his 1651 treatise Leviathan that in the state of nature, man's life was "nasty, brutish and short." Men should join in a social contract and install themselves under an absolute government to prevent the war of "all against all."

✦ John Locke argued in his *Second Treatise of Civil Government* (1690) that men have natural rights to life, liberty, and property, and that governments are instituted to protect those rights. If the government does not do so and becomes a tyranny, men have the right to revolt. Locke advocated constitutional governments in which the people (men with property) have a say in their governments.

Arts

✦ Baroque art, with its dramatic and elaborate decorations and sensuous colors, was defined in Italy after 1600 and used in the Counter-Reformation to inspire religiosity among Catholics and by absolute monarchs to inspire awe. The Baroque style in the arts flourished especially in Catholic regions: Spain and its Latin American colonies, Austria, southern Germany, and Poland. The greatest Baroque painter was Peter Paul Rubens (1577–1640).

✦ Baroque music reached its apogee with Johann Sebastian Bach (1685–1750), a Lutheran from Saxony in Germany, and an extraordinarily talented composer of religious and secular music.

✦ French classicism, the imitation by artists and writers of classical antiquity, dominated the court at Versailles.

CHAPTER 16
Toward a New Worldview, 1540–1789

> **Areas of focus:** England, France, Italy, Austria, Prussia, Russia
>
> **Main events:** the Scientific Revolution; the Enlightenment; enlightened absolutism

The following is a thematic summary of the material covered in Chapter 16 of *A History of Western Society:*

Politics

✦ **AP Tip** This chapter describes the scientific and intellectual movements that formed the foundation of modern Western civilization, and it goes some way toward explaining how the West came to dominate the world in the next century. Virtually every AP examination has an essay question related to the ideas of the Scientific Revolution and the Enlightenment, their implementation by absolute monarchs, or their impact on society.

✦ In the eighteenth century, absolute monarchs in Austria, Prussia, and Russia adopted some Enlightenment ideas, reforming legal and educational systems and improving agriculture. The most radical enlightened monarch was Joseph II of Austria (r. 1780–1790), famous as Mozart's patron, who abolished serfdom and instituted religious toleration—reforms nullified by his successors. Frederick II of Prussia ("Frederick the Great," r. 1740–1786) called himself the "first servant of the state" and made significant administrative and legal reforms, improved education, and abolished torture. At the same time, he maintained serfdom and extended the privileges of the nobility, on whom he depended to serve as officers in his army. Catherine the Great of Russia (r. 1762–1796), a financial supporter of Diderot's Encyclopedia after the French government banned it, restricted the use of torture and improved education and government. But after relying on nobles to suppress a peasant uprising, she gave them more control than ever over their serfs.

✦ In the War of the Austrian Succession (1740–1748), Frederick the Great expanded Prussia by taking Silesia and its valuable resources from Maria Theresa of Austria.

✦ The Russian, Austrian, and Prussian rulers dismembered Poland, where the monarchy was weak, in the late eighteenth century. Each took a share of its former territories.

Economy

✦ Within the "public sphere," intellectuals came together to discuss important issues relating to the intersection of society, the economy, and politics. However, the major advances of the Scientific Revolution had relatively few practical economic applications in the eighteenth century.

106

Religion

✦ Before the Enlightenment, the accepted theories of natural philosophy—such as Ptolemy's and Aristotle's geocentric models of the universe—reinforced religious thought. This approach to the natural world was later supplanted by the Enlightenment concept of secular "rationalism."

✦ Both Protestant and Catholic churches grew more hostile toward science and Protestant countries (such as the Netherlands, Denmark, and England) less so.

✦ In the eighteenth century, Enlightenment philosophes, most notably Voltaire, attacked organized religion as oppressive, superstitious, and inimical to free thought. Many philosophes were deists, believing in God as creator but not redeemer, who gave man reason to understand his universe. Deists supported separation of church and state.

✦ Pierre Bayle (French, 1647–1706) was a famous skeptic who demonstrated that human beliefs were historically varied and often mistaken, and that nothing, not even God's existence, could be known beyond all doubt.

✦ Most enlightened monarchs took some steps toward religious toleration.

✦ Led by Prussian philosopher Moses Mendelssohn (1729–1786), a Jewish Enlightenment movement (called the Haskalah) fostered greater contact with the Christian community and urged states to give Jews civil rights. Only Austria's Joseph II did so. Catherine the Great established the Pale of Settlement (1791) where Russian Jews were required to live.

Society and Culture

✦ Most royal or ducal families founded scientific societies and promoted research.

✦ An international community of scholars developed, linked by journals and the scientific societies or academies founded in most major cities. Lending libraries and coffeehouses offered commoners public spaces for debate.

✦ Scientific societies excluded women, but women were very much involved in informal scientific communities, such as salons. Women interested in science were illustrators, model makers, and astronomers, and a few did experiments or wrote on science. The important translation of Newton's major (Latin) work, the Principia Mathematica, into French was made by a woman, Madame du Châtelet.

✦ The philosophes met at salons—uncensored evenings of discussion on literature, science, and philosophy held in the private homes of sophisticated and wealthy women.

✦ During the Enlightenment, European notions of racial and ethnic superiority began to morph into racism. Hume and Kant wrote classifications of humans by race following botanical and biological models, although Diderot and the Scottish philosopher James Beattie argued that no culture was intrinsically more worthy than any other.

Ideas and Literature

✦ The Scientific Revolution, a transformation over a century that drew on long-term developments in European culture rather than a sudden change in attitudes, was a profound revision in the methods of ascertaining truth and knowledge of the physical world. Before the seventeenth century, disciples of "natural philosophy" found answers to scientific questions in classical authorities like Aristotle, Ptolemy, or Galen, but afterward they used the experimental method, observation, and mathematical analysis.

SCIENTIFIC FIELD	MAJOR FIGURES	THEORIES AND DISCOVERIES
Astronomy	Nicolaus Copernicus (Polish), 1473–1543	Copernican hypothesis; heliocentric theory, spherical planetary orbits
	Tycho Brahe (Dutch), 1546–1601	Improved planetary observational charts
	Johannes Kepler (German), 1571–1630	Three laws of planetary motion; elliptical orbits proved mathematically
	Galileo Galilei (Florentine), 1564–1642	Used telescope to observe the moons of Jupiter, sunspots, the moon's craters
	Isaac Newton (English), 1642–1727	Unified theory of the universe, same laws operate on earth and in the heavens; law of universal gravitation
Chemistry	Robert Boyle (Irish), 1493–1541	First to create vacuum tube; Boyle's law
Physics	Galileo Galilei (see Astronomy)	Conducted experiments on motion; proved the law of acceleration of falling objects
Medicine	Andrea Vesalius (Flemish), 1514–1564	Dissected human bodies; wrote important book on anatomy
	William Harvey (English), 1578–1657	Discovered circulation of the blood, function of the heart
	Paracelsus (Swiss), 1627–1691	Pioneered the use of medicinal drugs
Scientific Method and Philosophy of Science	Francis Bacon (English), 1561–1626	Promoted science as socially useful and advocated empiricism and inductive reasoning, asserting that knowledge comes from the senses and experiments
	René Descartes (French), 1596–1650	Creator of analytical geometry; argued that sensory knowledge was unreliable. Scientific truth needed deductive reasoning and mathematics. All substances could be divided into "matter" or "mind," the physical or spiritual, and one had little to do with the other.
	Isaac Newton (see Astronomy)	Combined mathematics and empiricism

✦ The use of reason to ascertain of the workings of the physical world ("rationalism") inspired a new generation of philosophers, commonly known by the French term philosophes, who used reason to understand the human world, or the social sciences. The Age of Reason held the optimistic premise that society could be improved by the use of reason and observation freed from religious and classical authorities.

✦ The Enlightenment, while forged in France, was an international movement.

✦ John Locke (English, 1632–1704), in addition to asserting the legitimacy of republicanism and the right of revolution, articulated the concept of tabula rasa, that man is born a blank slate with no innate ideas or original sin, thus creating modern psychology and the powerful political notion that humanity can be remade (*Essay Concerning Human Understanding,* 1690).

✦ Baron de Montesquieu (1689–1755) and Voltaire (1694–1778) both used satire to criticize their native France. Montesquieu's *The Spirit of Laws* developed the idea of separation of powers and a system of checks and balances to protect liberty. Voltaire relentlessly criticized the hypocrisy and intolerance of organized religion. His bestselling novel, *Candide,* lampooned virtually every aspect of society and the philosophy known as optimism.

✦ The Enlightenment saw a publishing explosion and a "reading revolution," with an expanded community of readers who read more on the arts and sciences than on religion.

✦ Philosophes wrote dictionaries and encyclopedias to enlighten the common man. Pierre Bayle's popular *Historical and Critical Dictionary* (1697) fostered skepticism. Denis Diderot and Jean le Rond d'Alembert filled their hugely influential seventeen-volume *Encyclopedia* (1765) with technical and scientific knowledge and denunciations of intolerance, repression, immorality, and legal injustice.

✦ The most influential of the later philosophes was Jean-Jacques Rousseau (1712–1778) who denied the primacy of reason (thereby fostering early-nineteenth-century Romanticism) and articulated a radical republican vision by which the people have sole sovereignty but are to be led by those few who know the "general will," the common interests of all the people, a doctrine that would underlie twentieth-century totalitarianism.

Arts

✦ Artists participated in the Scientific Revolution and the Enlightenment, painting experiments, scientific illustrations, medical school classes, and salon scenes.

✦ Women artists were important illustrators, noted for botanical paintings. Illustrated texts popularized the new science.

✦ Neoclassicism, an art style based on a selection (canon) of work from classical antiquity and the Renaissance, was the dominant style.

✦ Rococo, with its soft pastels, ornate interiors, and sentimental portraits and lush paintings with cupids, was popular throughout Europe.

The Expansion of Europe, 1650–1800

Areas of focus: western Europe, Atlantic states and their colonies

Main events: the Agricultural Revolution; rural industry; population growth; mercantilism and colonial wars; the Atlantic slave trade

---

The following is a thematic summary of the material covered in Chapter 17 of *A History of Western Society:*

Politics

+ In the age of the Atlantic economy (1650–1790), governments inextricably intertwined politics and economics in their mercantilist policies.

+ Great Britain, formed in 1707 by the union of England and Scotland, strengthened its shipbuilding industry and gained a virtual monopoly on trade with its American colonies through its Navigation Acts (1651–1663), which disallowed importing goods on the ships of its foreign competition.

+ Economic (and maritime) advantage was the main issue in the eighteenth-century English-French mercantilist wars (1701–1763).

+ The Atlantic states—France, England, and Holland—eclipsed Portugal and Spain and fiercely competed with each other for trade in Asia and Africa. The Dutch East India Company (established 1602), took over the spice trade from Portugal in Indonesia and Ceylon, only to face competition from the British East India Company (established 1600).

+ The British took over French concessions in India as a result of the War of the Spanish Succession (1701–1714) and in 1764 defeated the Mughal emperor. By the early 1800s the British had gained economic and political dominance over much of India.

+ In the New World, where the Dutch had already lost most of their colonies, France and England competed with each other and with Spain. England's mercantilist policies were highly successful. France and England fought several wars for colonial domination. After the last, the Seven Years' War, the 1763 Treaty of Paris ratified British victory on all colonial fronts; they won formerly French holdings in the Mississippi and Ohio River Valleys, Canada, and most of India.

+ France derived great wealth from its remaining colony of Haiti, a slave-based plantation economy producing sugar and coffee.

+ Spain acquired Louisiana and expanded its empire in western North America. Spanish landowners used debt peonage to keep indigenous workers bound to them.

110

✦ In 1807, the slave trade in the British Empire was banned by Parliament, largely due to a political mass movement in which women played an important role.

Economy

✦ The discipline of economics was founded during this period. Adam Smith, a Scot, discovered the law of supply and demand as the basis of economic life. His seminal work—*Inquiry into the Nature and Causes of the Wealth of Nations* (1776)—criticized mercantilism and argued for capitalism, with a limited government role to allow for the free operation of the economy, which would benefit consumers and nations alike. His theories formed a classic argument for economic liberalism.

✦ The domestic system of manufacturing and the Agricultural Revolution (1650–1850) developed to the greatest degree in England and to a lesser degree in the Low Countries.

✦ The domestic or "putting-out" system, also known as the cottage industry, involved a merchant capitalist who would bring materials to peasants, such as raw wool to be spun into thread, or thread to weavers to be woven into cloth. The merchant controlled the entire process, avoided guild regulations, paid low wages, and produced textile and household goods inexpensively. In this way rural families could earn cash and supplement their incomes, but relations between the merchant capitalists and the rural laborers were often contentious.

✦ The Agricultural Revolution led to a huge increase in the amount and variety of food-stuffs. Its goal was to increase agricultural yield by using new methods of revitalizing the soil, which had been planted in the open-field system for centuries. Instead of failed harvests every eight or nine years, "crop rotation" and planting novel crops restored fertility. It provided new foods for humans and animals: potatoes, turnips, peas, beans, and clovers and grasses. This led to an increase in the number of cattle and sheep, which in turn meant more high-protein food for consumers and more fertilizer for the soil.

✦ To implement improvements and allow for greater experimentation, some landowners joined together to enclose the common fields that had been used for grazing, firewood, foraging, and gleaning as part of the open-field system. Elsewhere, peasants held onto their traditional rights and prevented enclosure.

✦ England led in enclosing land; half was already enclosed by 1700. Most of the rest of the land was enclosed by parliamentary legislation in the eighteenth century. The enclosure movement was a huge transformation of village life. In effect, most of the land in England was held by a few landowners as the majority of small landowners became rural wage earners in a process called proletarization.

✦ The landowners of large estates used new equipment like the seed drill promoted by English innovator Jethro Tull (1674–1741). They learned drainage and water control from the Dutch and cultivated marginal lands. Agriculture became a capitalistic, market-oriented business.

✦ After 1700 Britain became the undisputed leader in the Atlantic slave trade. London was the wealthiest and largest city in Europe. Relying on African merchants and rulers to provide slaves, this trade was a major source of wealth until the slave trade was banned in the British Empire in 1807.

✦ Population growth increased the market for manufactured goods and dampened the wages of workers.

Religion

- ✦ The conversion of native peoples of the New World remained a key goal for Europeans. The Spanish sent many missionaries who built missions and acted as agents of cultural exchange, so that Catholicism in its colonies in Central and South America was syncretic, filled with elements of native religious practice.

- ✦ Conversion of the natives in North America was less successful.

- ✦ Jews, as white Europeans, were ineligible for enslavement, but they were discriminated against in European colonies.

Society and Culture

- ✦ **AP Tip** This chapter focuses mostly on social history, that is, changes in the lives of ordinary people. AP History curricula and exams have increasingly focused on social history. It is now seen as important as the deeds and thoughts of great men and women, wars, and governments.

- ✦ Women entered the paid labor force in hitherto unknown numbers, which gave them greater authority in the household.

- ✦ Leisure time was reduced in this "industrious revolution" as people worked harder.

- ✦ As the traditional rights of peasants and rural laborers were lost, many former small landowners moved to cities, which grew in size.

- ✦ With expanding armies, many men were conscripted or joined the military.

- ✦ Population growth had been slow until 1700, when it began to skyrocket, reaching a growth rate of 1 percent per year. The cause was more a reduction of the death rate than an increase in the birthrate. In England, inoculations against smallpox began to reduce deaths there. In the 1720s, the periodic recurrences of plague ended. Better public health, better methods of safeguarding food supplies, more building of canals and roads, and less destructive wars all helped reduce death rates.

- ✦ Wealthy Creoles (American-born people of Spanish ancestry) and their counterparts throughout the Atlantic colonies—the colonial elite—took pride in assimilating fine European ways of life.

- ✦ Atlantic cultural identities and race relations throughout the colonies were complex. Some mixed-race populations (such as those in the Spanish and French Caribbean) were embraced, while others were kept in slavery.

Ideas and Literature

- ✦ Adam Smith's *Inquiry into the Nature and Causes of the Wealth of Nations* (1776) catapulted his ideas regarding capitalism into the public sphere.

- ✦ There was much discussion about the proper role of guilds, which had grown dramatically in the seventeenth century. Smith opposed them for their interference with the natural operation of the law of supply and demand, and he spurred support for their abolition.

Arts

- ✦ Eighteenth-century painters portrayed the newly grown, bustling, cosmopolitan cities, scenes of rural life, the exotic peoples of the colonies, and the hard work of slaves.

- ✦ Skilled artisans across Europe espoused the values of hand craftsmanship and limited competition as opposed to the mechanized production system, which devalued the worker.

CHAPTER 18
Life in the Era of Expansion, 1650–1800

Area of focus: western Europe

Main events: illegitimacy explosion; more widespread education; consumer revolution; Methodism

---

The following is a thematic summary of the material covered in Chapter 18 of *A History of Western Society:*

Politics

+ Several monarchs expanded the educational opportunities of their subjects; Prussian king Frederick I made elementary education mandatory in 1717.

+ The Jesuits, seen as politically dangerous, were expelled from France by Louis XV in 1763. The order was dissolved by the pope ten years later (and restored in 1814).

+ The Jansenists, dissident Catholics in France, were strong in their opposition to Bourbon absolutism and were persecuted by the French monarchs.

Economy

+ A burgeoning consumer culture emerged in the elite and among people of modest means who could buy cheap reproductions of luxury goods and affordable clothes made out of new fabrics like cotton.

+ The consumer revolution was aided by marketing campaigns as fashion merchants took over from courtiers. Homes too changed as privacy and individual household goods became seen as necessary.

+ Peasants, landless laborers, and urban workers believed in the idea of a fair "just price" that could be imposed by government decree if necessary. When prices rose above acceptable levels, they often rioted.

Religion

+ The parish church remained central to the community, but it was subject to greater state control.

✦ Methodism was a widely popular movement in eighteenth-century England, created by the energetic preacher John Wesley (1703–1791). He wanted to restore emotionality to individual religious faith and offer the assurance of salvation to all by rejecting predestination.

✦ Pietism also stressed emotional religiosity and inspired a strong Protestant revival spreading outward from Germany.

✦ In Catholic communities, the church retained its vibrancy due to the exuberance of Baroque art and the close connections between parish priests and the laity.

✦ Jansenists in the Spanish Netherlands and France called for a return to austere Christianity. Much of France's urban elite became Jansenists.

✦ Popular beliefs were increasingly under attack by the critical rationalism of the enlightened elite as well as by secular authorities.

Society and Culture

✦ **AP Tip** Numerous AP European History Exam document-based questions have focused on the social history of the early modern period; for example, the 2000 DBQ addressed peasant rituals and the 2007 DBQ was about attitudes toward children. They are available on the College Board Web site. The documents in these DBQs are worthwhile reading, and they make great practice exercises.

✦ Nuclear families were the norm in Europe at this time, which was unusual in world history. Most people married in their twenties, waiting until they had the means to establish independent households.

✦ Young people often worked away from home, boys as apprentices or day laborers and girls as domestic servants or employees hired by guilds. Such work was unregulated and many youths were abused at work.

✦ Prostitution was less and less tolerated. More repressive laws were passed, but the practice continued to flourish because of the irregular employment of young women.

✦ Homosexuality was roundly condemned, but homosexual and even lesbian subcultures began to emerge in Paris, Amsterdam, and London.

✦ Premarital intercourse was common but generally led to marriage in cases of pregnancy in the first half of the century, mostly due to strong community controls. As these controls weakened, illegitimate births became much more common; about one-third of all births were illegitimate in the late eighteenth century. Condoms made from sheep intestines became available, but as they were expensive, they were rarely used by commoners, who relied on coitus interruptus.

✦ As abortion was illegal, women with unwanted babies had few choices. Some committed infanticide while others left their babies in urban foundling hospitals, favorite charities of the rich but with horrific mortality rates.

✦ Poor women nursed their babies and often served as wet nurses to the children of the well-to-do. Rural wet-nursing was a widespread business, particularly in northern France, and it was linked with high infant mortality rates.

✦ Historians long thought that high childhood mortalities (typically two or three out of every five babies died) may have led parents to limit their emotional attachments to children. Ample documentary evidence, however, shows great emotional attachments to infants, even those who died at very young ages. With Enlightenment philosophes rethinking the use of strict and severe discipline, as in Rousseau's popular work *Emile* (1762), the educated elite began to give their children freedom of movement in their dress, to nurse them themselves, and to educate both sons and daughters.

✦ In Catholic areas, the education of the children of the elite was managed by the Jesuits, and for the poor, by parish schools. Education in Prussia was at mandatory state schools, in Scotland under the Presbyterians, and in England in religious-based "charity schools." The result was a surge in literacy and a growth in reading.

✦ People spent their leisure time enjoying blood sports like cockfighting and boxing, going to urban pleasure gardens, theater, or commercial spectator sports. Both urban and rural Catholics delighted in the often ribald carnival festivities before Lent.

✦ The diet of Europeans noticeably improved in the eighteenth century, with a greater variety of vegetables and the consumption of sugar and tea. Upper-class people enjoyed formal teas, while ordinary people drank tea to provide energy for work.

✦ Medical care was typically given by apothecaries, faith healers using herbal medicines, midwives (all women), and physicians and surgeons (all men). Army surgeons made some improvements in field amputations. When forceps were invented, physician-surgeons attacked the qualifications of midwives. An important text written by Madame du Coudray in 1757 did much to improve midwifery practice.

✦ Vaccination against smallpox began when Lady Mary Wortley Montagu brought back Ottoman inoculation practices to England, and it improved when Edward Jenner discovered the efficacy of using cowpox (1796).

Ideas and Literature

✦ The expansion of the size of the reading public allowed for the proliferation of published materials such as cheap broadsheets, and it set the stage for the popularity of the novel in the nineteenth century.

✦ Books, printed on cheap paper, were mostly religious texts, stories, practical guides, almanacs, or pamphlets simplifying Enlightenment ideas.

Arts

✦ Artists portrayed the lives of ordinary people both in cities and villages, with images such as market scenes, weddings, and family scenes, often showing the interactions among people of different social classes.

✦ Caricaturists like James Gillray and satirical artists like William Hogarth were popular in eighteenth-century England.

PRACTICE EXAM 2

EUROPEAN HISTORY
SECTION I

Multiple-Choice Questions
(Time—55 minutes)
Number of questions—80

Directions: Each of the questions or incomplete statements below is followed by five suggested answers or completions. For each question, select the best response.

1. In which region were there no significant popular revolts in the seventeenth century?

   (A) France
   (B) Spain
   (C) Holland
   (D) England
   (E) The Italian states

2. Which attitude toward religion did Louis XIV adopt from Spain?

   (A) Toleration for all religions
   (B) Uniformity and conformity
   (C) Toleration for Lutherans but not Calvinists
   (D) Toleration for Protestants but not Jews
   (E) Widespread use of the Inquisition

3. Spain's economic troubles in the seventeenth and eighteenth centuries came about primarily when

   (A) it lost Gibraltar
   (B) the colonies in the New World revolted
   (C) it lost control of the slave trade to the French
   (D) the Dutch began to raid Spain's northern coasts
   (E) the gold and silver mines in the Americas began to run dry

4. The execution of Charles I

   (A) ended the Stuart line
   (B) was voted for by a large majority of the Long Parliament
   (C) led Louis XIV of France to send troops to defend his son, Charles II
   (D) was approved by a Parliament purged of moderates
   (E) was opposed by Oliver Cromwell, who argued that exile was sufficient

GO ON TO THE NEXT PAGE.

5. Mercantilist policies established in France during the seventeenth century involved all of the following EXCEPT

(A) government subsidies for textile manufacturing
(B) a strong interest in colonies
(C) reductions in domestic tariffs
(D) abolition of guilds
(E) inviting foreign workers to France to improve the quality of goods

6. The response of the Spanish kings to their economic difficulties in the seventeenth century was

(A) generally passive and uninspired
(B) to reorganize the administrative structure of Spain
(C) to adopt mercantilist policies similar to France
(D) to insist on paying their debts, thus adding to their financial problems
(E) energetic and forward thinking, although ultimately unsuccessful

7. The Peace of Utrecht

(A) put a Habsburg on the throne of Spain
(B) was a victory for Louis XIV in his claim to the throne of Spain
(C) gave France control over the former Spanish Netherlands
(D) ended French ambitions to combine the crowns of France and Spain
(E) upset the balance of power in Europe

8. Not a supporter of the divine right of kings, Thomas Hobbes advocated strong governments, basing his views on

(A) man's selfish and aggressive nature
(B) Machiavellian ideas about the need for a prince to unify the nation
(C) More's ideal community in which the government carefully supervised the population
(D) reference to the endurance of the Roman Empire
(E) the analogy of the brain's role in the body

9. The English civil war was fundamentally fought over

(A) Catholic demands for the right to freely practice their religion
(B) Puritan demands for the right to freely practice their religion
(C) whether Parliament or the king has the power to levy taxes
(D) whether the House of Lords or the House of Commons should have ultimate authority
(E) whether Parliament or the king would appoint the head of the Anglican Church

10. Which event most directly prompted the Glorious Revolution?

(A) Charles II's treaty with Louis XIV
(B) Publication of John Locke's Second Treatise of Civil Government
(C) The death of Oliver Cromwell
(D) James II's violations of the Test Act
(E) The marriage of James II to a French princess

GO ON TO THE NEXT PAGE.

11. The most important factor in creating Dutch prosperity in the seventeenth century was

    (A)   their political unity
    (B)   their alliance with the British
    (C)   the size of their merchant marine
    (D)   their important colonies in the New World
    (E)   the establishment of constitutional monarchy

12. Two great Baroque masters, Peter Paul Rubens and Johann Sebastian Bach, show that the Baroque style was

    (A)   popular exclusively in Catholic countries
    (B)   popular exclusively in Protestant countries
    (C)   popular with absolute monarchs
    (D)   popular in the constitutional states like England and France
    (E)   a Europe-wide phenomenon

13. With regard to the nobles of France, Louis XIV

    (A)   emasculated them
    (B)   severely diminished their wealth
    (C)   collaborated with them
    (D)   successfully replaced them with the bourgeoisie as the dominant political class
    (E)   ignored them

14. Armies changed in the seventeenth century in all of the following ways EXCEPT that

    (A)   they became larger
    (B)   they became more professional
    (C)   most soldiers were mercenaries, as few countries had standing armies
    (D)   the death toll was high, particularly for officers
    (E)   they became more expensive for kings to maintain

15. A comparison of serfdom in western Europe and eastern Europe would best be summarized as

    (A)   in both regions, serfdom disappeared by 1500
    (B)   in both regions, serfdom remained in 1500
    (C)   in eastern, but not in western Europe, serfdom was reinstated after 1500
    (D)   in western, but not in eastern Europe, serfdom was reinstated after 1500
    (E)   in both, serfdom had disappeared by 1300 but was reinstated after 1500

16. Which was NOT a consequence of the Thirty Years' War in the Germanic states?

    (A)   Steep decline in trade
    (B)   High death tolls of both civilians and soldiers
    (C)   Devastation of agriculture
    (D)   Disintegration of large noble estates
    (E)   Long-term economic stagnation

GO ON TO THE NEXT PAGE.

17. Eastern European towns in the seventeenth century

    (A) were dominated by a growing merchant class
    (B) grew in population
    (C) retained their medieval privileges
    (D) were bypassed by landlords who sold their goods directly to foreign merchants
    (E) protected runaways from the great estates

18. After the Peace of Westphalia in 1648, the Habsburgs

    (A) turned their attention eastward
    (B) competed furiously with the Bavarian rulers for dominance in the Holy Roman Empire
    (C) began to allow religious toleration in Bohemia and Hungary
    (D) moved the capital from Vienna to Budapest
    (E) crushed the Hungarian nobility

19. Frederick William, the "Great Elector," was able to build up the Prussian army by

    (A) calling the diet into sessions annually to approve funds
    (B) hiring well-trained foreign mercenaries
    (C) expanding the army to become larger than France's
    (D) opening the officer corps to men of talent, regardless of social class
    (E) levying taxes without approval by the Prussian Diet

20. Frederick William I, the "Soldiers' King," of Prussia

    (A) thought only soldiers could have militaristic values
    (B) created an efficient and honest bureaucracy
    (C) joined Russia in the Great Northern War
    (D) built a lavish palace outside of Berlin
    (E) was the first king of Prussia

21. The princes of Moscow were able to make it the central state of Russia

    (A) after having been the servants of the Mongols
    (B) because they had refused for two centuries to serve the Mongols
    (C) after Ivan the Terrible killed off his opponents
    (D) because they were blessed by the patriarch of Kiev
    (E) after its princes moved there from St. Petersburg

22. Peter the Great's primary motive for westernizing Russia was

    (A) political
    (B) economic
    (C) military
    (D) cultural
    (E) architectural

23. Which was NOT a reform Peter the Great enacted to change society?

    (A) Allowing daughters to inherit lands along with their brothers
    (B) Establishing schools and universities
    (C) Insisting that social events of the nobles include both men and women
    (D) Requiring nobles to become educated
    (E) Bringing in Western ideas about clothes and beards

GO ON TO THE NEXT PAGE.

24. The discontent of Russian peasants under the tsars
    (A) prompted the reforms of Peter the Great
    (B) increased because of expectations of continuing improvement
    (C) broke out in a revolt led by Stenka Razin
    (D) was usually expressed by organized protests in the capital
    (E) brought them into alliance with urban workers

25. The janissaries, or slave corps, of the Ottoman Empire
    (A) were horribly treated because they were Christians
    (B) were able to rise to important positions of power in the top ranks of the bureaucracy
    (C) mostly came from Anatolia (now Turkey)
    (D) were employed as eunuchs in the harems
    (E) were not allowed to convert to Islam

26. What feature did the Prussian state NOT share with the Ottoman, Russian, and Austrian Empires?
    (A) Absolute monarchs
    (B) Repressed peasantry
    (C) Territorial integrity
    (D) Territorially expansionist regimes
    (E) Great capital cities

27. Eighteenth-century Methodists and Pietists both
    (A) advocated that religion must incorporate new scientific ideas
    (B) stressed an emotional commitment to Christianity
    (C) based their ideas on deism
    (D) fought for religious toleration of Jews and Catholics
    (E) centralized their religious bureaucracies

28. Before the Scientific Revolution, people seeking scientific information generally found it in
    (A) the Bible
    (B) statements issued by the church
    (C) the writings of Aristotle and Ptolemy
    (D) the writings of Marsiglio of Padua
    (E) Chinese texts

29. Johannes Kepler's relationship to the Copernican thesis was to
    (A) prove it by using the telescope
    (B) reject it, as had his mentor Tycho Brahe
    (C) challenge it because it did not include the harmony of the spheres
    (D) provide mathematical proof for it
    (E) denounce Galileo's support of it

30. Newton provided the theory to explain which of Galileo's observations?
    (A) That Jupiter has moons as Earth does
    (B) That the moon's surface is uneven and rough
    (C) That the Milky Way is filled with stars
    (D) That the moon is not perfectly spherical
    (E) That bodies have a uniform rate of acceleration

GO ON TO THE NEXT PAGE.

31. Cartesian dualism can best be described as the division between
    (A) truth and untruth
    (B) science and humanities
    (C) mind and matter
    (D) right and wrong
    (E) the heavens and the earth

32. Which was NOT a cause of the Scientific Revolution?
    (A) The recovery of ancient mathematical texts during the Renaissance
    (B) The search for the physical location of the soul within the body
    (C) The patronage of princes and kings
    (D) New technology
    (E) The establishment of new professorships in physics and mathematics at universities

33. Who first formally articulated the value of the empirical method?
    (A) Galileo Galilei
    (B) Francis Bacon
    (C) Johannes Kepler
    (D) Isaac Newton
    (E) Margaret Cavendish

34. The chief difference between the Scientific Revolution and the Enlightenment is
    (A) the gender of the scientists, all male, and the philosophes, many female
    (B) the country in which each began
    (C) the focus on the natural world or the human world
    (D) the religions of the scientists and philosophes
    (E) the attitude of the church

35. Which philosophe wrote in support of popular sovereignty?
    (A) Voltaire
    (B) Montesquieu
    (C) Jean-Jacques Rousseau
    (D) David Hume
    (E) Immanuel Kant

36. René Descartes and Pierre Bayle would agree on the importance of
    (A) mathematics
    (B) doubt
    (C) empirical research
    (D) believing in God
    (E) constitutional monarchy

37. John Locke's concept of the tabula rasa was taken in the eighteenth century to mean that
    (A) knowledge comes from perception
    (B) public education ought to be established for all children
    (C) enlightened monarchy was the best form of government
    (D) rebellion was a natural right
    (E) parents could have little influence over their children

GO ON TO THE NEXT PAGE.

38. Madame du Châtelet's importance in the Enlightenment was due to her role as

    (A) an important salon hostess
    (B) a correspondent of Catherine the Great
    (C) mistress of Voltaire
    (D) adviser to Peter the Great
    (E) translator of Newton's Principia

39. The enlightened monarchs Catherine the Great and Frederick the Great both

    (A) abolished serfdom
    (B) granted religious toleration to the Jews
    (C) established public education for young children
    (D) abolished or restricted the use of torture
    (E) re-established legislative assemblies

40. Catherine the Great's effort at reforms came to a virtual end when

    (A) the nobles of Russia resisted
    (B) Voltaire publicly criticized her, thus humiliating her
    (C) the peasants rose in the Pugachev revolt
    (D) Prussia declared war on Russia
    (E) she was assassinated by a former lover

41. Denis Diderot's Encyclopedia

    (A) was published in its entirety in France
    (B) democratized knowledge
    (C) was read by only a small number of people because it was so expensive
    (D) had little technical information
    (E) was published in part with funds from Frederick the Great

42. The term *reading revolution* refers to the

    (A) nearly universal literacy in the eighteenth century
    (B) new literacy of women
    (C) way reading became private and silent
    (D) great expansion in the number and variety of newspapers during the Enlightenment
    (E) the public reading of the texts of the philosophes

43. The term *industrious revolution* refers to

    (A) the industrial revolution in the countryside rather than in the cities
    (B) the shift from laboring to produce goods for household consumption to laboring to earn wages
    (C) men working harder to support their households so that wives and children did not work
    (D) the use of new tools in agricultural work
    (E) the cottage industry in southern and southeastern Europe

GO ON TO THE NEXT PAGE.

44. What is the correct order in which these states became dominant in trade with Asia from the sixteenth to the eighteenth centuries?
    I. Britain   II. France   III. Holland   IV. Portugal
    - (A) III, IV, II, and I
    - (B) I, III, IV, and II
    - (C) IV, III, II, and I
    - (D) II, IV, III, and I
    - (E) IV, II, III, and I

45. The theory of economic liberalism, first articulated by Adam Smith, is concerned mostly with the needs of
    - (A) manufacturers
    - (B) governments
    - (C) merchants
    - (D) consumers
    - (E) landlords

46. The Navigation Acts helped Britain to become a great naval power by
    - (A) requiring that foreign goods be brought into Britain on British ships
    - (B) requiring that all slaves going to the Americas be transported on British ships
    - (C) creating Europe's first naval academy for the training of officers
    - (D) requiring the use of sailors from the American colonies
    - (E) arming British ships with the newest military technology

47. Which was NOT an advantage of the cottage, or putting-out, system?
    - (A) It allowed merchant capitalists to evade guild regulations.
    - (B) It allowed households to increase their incomes.
    - (C) It gave women greater say in household decisions.
    - (D) Women began to earn almost the same as men.
    - (E) It kept the family together as an economic unit.

48. The guild system in the seventeenth and eighteenth centuries
    - (A) went into serious decline, never to recuperate
    - (B) expanded its control over manufacturing into the countryside
    - (C) flourished as never before
    - (D) was too rigid to adapt to new methods of production and new technology
    - (E) remained closed to women

49. Which was the least popular leisure activity in the eighteenth century?
    - (A) Blood sports like cockfighting
    - (B) Spectator sports like horseracing
    - (C) Urban fairs
    - (D) Reading novels
    - (E) Annual festivities like carnival

50. Spain's New World colonies were different from Britain's in that
    - (A) few Europeans settled there
    - (B) the economy was city based, not land based
    - (C) mixed-race children were typically freed from slavery
    - (D) the British were not allowed to trade there
    - (E) African slavery was relatively uncommon

GO ON TO THE NEXT PAGE.

51. The single most important component of the Agricultural Revolution was the

    (A) progressive elimination of the fallow
    (B) animal breeding
    (C) use of the potato
    (D) use of root crops
    (E) enclosure movement

52. The chief reason for the rise in population in the eighteenth century was the

    (A) rise in birthrates
    (B) rise in illegitimacy
    (C) decline in death rates
    (D) improvements in medicine
    (E) widespread use of the smallpox vaccine

53. The most remarkable dietary change in the eighteenth century was the dramatic increase in consumption of

    (A) meat
    (B) dairy products
    (C) tea and sugar
    (D) beer
    (E) semitropical fruits

54. The time span between when Britain took over the slave trade and when Parliament abolished it was about

    (A) 30 years
    (B) 50 years
    (C) 100 years
    (D) 10 years
    (E) 125 years

55. The impact of the slave trade on African states was

    (A) uniformly disastrous
    (B) uniformly beneficial
    (C) negligible, as slaving was mostly a coastal matter
    (D) to increase local populations with European traders
    (E) to encourage warfare among Africans

56. By the terms of the Treaty of Paris in 1763

    (A) England won the asiento (control over the slave trade)
    (B) France took possession of Louisiana from Spain
    (C) Spain gave England its colonies in the Caribbean
    (D) France ceded its territories in India to Britain
    (E) France ceded Nova Scotia and Newfoundland to Britain

57. By the end of the eighteenth century, London

    (A) had become the second-largest city in Europe, behind Paris
    (B) had expanded with new townhouses surrounding squares in the West End
    (C) had abandoned its location on the Thames after the Great Fire
    (D) had become more industrial than commercial
    (E) had been rebuilt as a series of circular rings

GO ON TO THE NEXT PAGE.

58. Louis XIV would best be described as

  (A) the founder of French cultural pre-eminence
  (B) a politique
  (C) the main victor in the Thirty Years' War
  (D) a leader who accomplished a lot during his short reign
  (E) a monarch who made peace with the Protestants in his country

59. The works of Enlightenment philosophes

  (A) appealed to peasants and the urban poor as well as to intellectuals
  (B) criticized the scientific method as too mechanical
  (C) were profoundly secular
  (D) aimed to reform the church
  (E) were known mostly in the universities of France

60. All of the following were true about eighteenth-century medical practice EXCEPT

  (A) physicians used bloodletting and purging to cure illness
  (B) midwives lost more patients than medical doctors did in childbirth
  (C) most surgeries were performed without painkillers
  (D) surgeons learned to cauterize wounds
  (E) smallpox inoculations eradicated much of the disease

61. The enclosure movement contributed to the Agricultural Revolution because

  (A) the peasants supported it
  (B) it consolidated land
  (C) it allowed the government to control more land
  (D) it preserved the monasteries
  (E) it led to the end of tariffs

62. Which of the following factors did NOT contribute to Europe's population growth in the early eighteenth century?

  (A) High rates of illegitimate birth
  (B) More scientific farming methods
  (C) The introduction of the potato
  (D) Lower death rates for soldiers in war
  (E) Better systems for transporting foods during famines

63. The Atlantic slave trade

  (A) reached its height in the 1750s before the American Revolution
  (B) brought more slaves to Brazil than any other single country
  (C) was supported by freed slaves like Olaudah Equiano who became slave owners themselves
  (D) was not formally opposed in Europe until the U.S. Civil War
  (E) brought more slaves to the American colonies than to the Caribbean

GO ON TO THE NEXT PAGE.

64. Until the late eighteenth century, women

   (A) married late and immediately began bearing children
   (B) married early but waited to begin bearing children
   (C) married when the family could provide a sufficient dowry
   (D) lived with their extended families, even after marriage
   (E) were encouraged to date before settling into an arranged marriage

65. Which of the following was true about the poor in the eighteenth century?

   (A) Peasants ate less meat in 1700 than in 1500.
   (B) Small traders and master craftsmen had a less varied diet than peasants.
   (C) Very few goods from the colonies were available to them.
   (D) The urban poor did not have ready access to vegetables.
   (E) By 1700, bread had become a secondary staple in the diet.

66. The Peace of Westphalia, which marked the end of the Thirty Years' War, was a turning point in Europe because it signified

   (A) an end to the religious wars that began during the Reformation
   (B) a unified Germany, ruled by the king of Prussia
   (C) an end to the Holy Roman Empire
   (D) the dominance of Calvinism throughout Germany
   (E) a German nation on the rise with a strong economy to support it

67. Oliver Cromwell's Protectorate can best be described as a(n)

   (A) Puritan democracy
   (B) military dictatorship
   (C) constitutional monarchy
   (D) absolute monarchy
   (E) Catholic commonwealth

68. The sixteenth-century idea that sparked the Scientific Revolution was the

   (A) geocentric model of the universe
   (B) theory of relativity
   (C) heliocentric model of the universe
   (D) law of universal gravitation
   (E) idea that deductive reasoning is more scientific than empiricism

69. Which of the following statements describes foundling hospitals in Europe in the eighteenth century?

   (A) There were long waiting lists for families to adopt foundlings.
   (B) Foundling hospitals were necessary only in the cities.
   (C) Foundling hospitals provided care that enabled most foundlings to survive.
   (D) Foundling hospitals did not adequately address the problem of abandoned children.
   (E) Foundling hospitals provided simple education for the older children.

GO ON TO THE NEXT PAGE.

70. Place the following British rulers in the correct chronological order:
    I. James I   II. Elizabeth I   III. Charles I   IV. George I

    (A) IV, II, I, and III
    (B) II, III, IV, and I
    (C) I, III, II, and IV
    (D) II, I, III, and IV
    (E) III, I, IV, and II

71. Both absolute and constitutional monarchs in the seventeenth and eighteenth centuries
    focused most of their energies on

    (A) responding to the needs of the people
    (B) developing positive relationships with representative bodies
    (C) strengthening provincial governments
    (D) expanding state control
    (E) developing a single language

72. The War of the Austrian Succession

    (A) began when Prussia insisted that the Pragmatic Sanction be honored
    (B) ended with the independence of Hungary
    (C) ended with Austria's loss of resource-rich Silesia to Prussia
    (D) sent an intimidating message to Peter the Great
    (E) protected central Europe from the Turks

73. Suleiman the Magnificent encouraged all of the following EXCEPT

    (A) religious toleration
    (B) trade
    (C) cultural autonomy for minority groups
    (D) a slave corps in the bureaucracy
    (E) private property

74. During the eighteenth century, Poland

    (A) lost territory on the east but gained on the west
    (B) lost territory on the west but gained on the east
    (C) was dismembered by Austria, Prussia, and Russia
    (D) gained territory from its neighboring absolute monarchs
    (E) emerged as an independent kingdom

75. Moses Mendelssohn

    (A) fostered the Jewish Enlightenment
    (B) led the Polish uprising against partitioning of the country
    (C) converted to Christianity to advance his career as a philosopher
    (D) persuaded Catherine the Great to become more tolerant
    (E) argued against the immortality of the soul

GO ON TO THE NEXT PAGE.

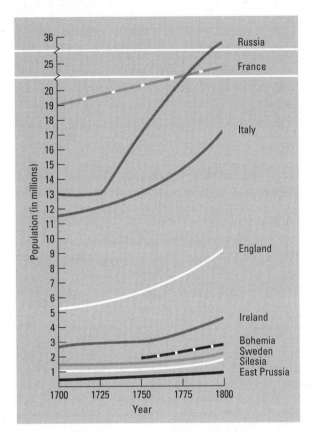

The Increase of Population in Europe in the Eighteenth Century

76. Using the graph, what conclusion can be drawn about the rise in population in Europe during the eighteenth century?

(A) The biggest increases were in industrializing areas.
(B) The biggest increases were in mostly agricultural countries.
(C) Northern Europe had the highest rate of increase.
(D) Southern Europe had the highest rate of increase.
(E) Wars were less destructive in the eighteenth century.

GO ON TO THE NEXT PAGE.

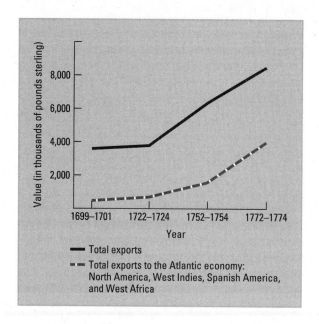

77. According to the graph

 (A) exports to the transatlantic area paralleled the total growth of exports
 (B) exports from England to Europe expanded dramatically after 1700
 (C) slaves were the predominant trading item after 1722
 (D) imports to England surpassed exports
 (E) exports from the Atlantic economy included sugar, tobacco, and cotton

78. In which state did Jews NOT have some measure of religious toleration?

 (A) Prussia under Frederick the Great
 (B) The Austrian Empire under Joseph II
 (C) England under Cromwell
 (D) The Ottoman Empire after 1492
 (E) The Dutch Republic in the seventeenth century

79. Adam Smith

 (A) was critical of mercantilism
 (B) wrote a rationale for having a command economy
 (C) argued that workers should be paid the lowest possible wage to increase profits
 (D) hoped to combine government and business
 (E) advocated social welfare practices

80. During the eighteenth century, attitudes toward children softened as a result of

 (A) government policies
 (B) child-rearing manuals
 (C) the evolution of psychology
 (D) the Enlightenment
 (E) medical improvements

STOP

END OF SECTION I

EUROPEAN HISTORY
SECTION II

Part A
(Suggested writing time—45 minutes)
Percent of Section II score—45

Directions: The following question is based on the accompanying Documents 1–12. The documents have been edited for the purpose of this exercise.

This question is designed to test your ability to work with and understand historical documents. Write an essay that:

✦ Provides an appropriate, explicitly stated thesis that directly addresses all parts of the question and does NOT simply restate the question.

✦ Discusses a majority of the documents individually and specifically.

✦ Demonstrates understanding of the basic meaning of a majority of the documents.

✦ Supports the thesis with appropriate interpretation of a majority of the documents.

✦ Analyzes the documents by explicitly grouping them in at least three appropriate ways.

✦ Takes into account both the sources of the documents and the authors' points of view.

You may refer to relevant historical information not mentioned in the documents.

1. Analyze the various reactions to and views about the execution of Charles I.

Historical background: The Stuarts, who took over the throne of England upon the death of Elizabeth I in 1603, believed in the divine right of kings and were sympathetic to Catholicism. Charles I ruled without Parliament from 1629 to 1640, but a Scottish threat forced him to call it into session. Many parliamentarians had become radical Protestants who sought to "purify" the Church of England created by the English Reformation. Civil war broke out between the supporters of the king and the supporters of Parliament. Parliament's forces, led by Oliver Cromwell, won. Parliament appointed a court that put the captured king on trial for treason and ordered his execution on January 30, 1649. A commonwealth (or republic) was declared, but in 1660 the monarchy was restored. Charles II, son of the executed king Charles I, ascended the throne. In 1688, the more liberal members of Parliament, the Whigs, joined with the conservatives, the Tories, to exclude his son James II from the throne and offer it to William of Orange and his wife Mary jointly. This peaceful Glorious Revolution established the sovereignty of Parliament.

GO ON TO THE NEXT PAGE.

Document 1

Source: Various eyewitnesses to the conclusion of the trial of Charles I, published 1650.

Now . . . this court is in judgment and conscience satisfied that he (the said Charles Stuart) is guilty of levying war against the said Parliament and people, and [of] maintaining and continuing the same, for which . . . he stands accused. . . . This court is fully satisfied in their judgments and consciences that he hath been and is guilty of the wicked designs and endeavors in the said charge set forth; and that the said war hath been levied, maintained, and continued by him as aforesaid . . . and that he hath been and is the occasioner, author, and continuer of the said unnatural, cruel, and bloody wars, and therein guilty of High Treason and of the murders, rapines, burnings, spoils, desolations, damage, and mischief to this nation acted and committed in the said war and occasioned thereby. For all which treasons and crimes this court doth adjudge that he, the said Charles Stuart, as a tyrant, traitor, murderer, and public enemy to the good people of this nation, shall be put to death by the severing of his head from his body.

Document 2

Source: Anonymous, "KING CHARLS, HIS SPEECH Made upon the SCAFFOLD At Whitehall-Gate Immediately before his Execution On Tuesday the 30 of Jan. 1649 With a Relation of the maner of his going to Execution Published by Special Authority." Printed by Peter Cole, London, 1649.

[As for the people,] truly I desire their liberty and freedom as much as anybody whomsoever; but I must tell you that their liberty and freedom consist in having of government. . . . It is not for having share in government, sirs; that is nothing pertaining to them; a subject and a sovereign are clear different things. . . . I tell you (and I pray God it be not laid to your charge) that I am the martyr of the people. . . . And to the executioner he said, 'I shall say but very short prayers, and when I thrust out my hands. . . .' The bishop: 'You are exchanged from a temporal to an eternal crown,—a good exchange.' After a very short pause, his Majesty stretching forth his hands, the executioner at one blow severed his head from his body; which, being held up and showed to the people, was with his body put into a coffin covered with black velvet and carried into his lodging. His blood was taken up by divers persons for different ends: by some as trophies of their villainy; by others as relics of a martyr; and in some had had the same effect, by the blessing of God, which was often found in his sacred touch when living.

GO ON TO THE NEXT PAGE.

Document 3

Source: Unknown artist, German engraving of the execution of Charles I, 1649.

© The British Library Board, Crach.1.Tab.4.c.1.(18.).

Document 4

Source: John Milton, poet and Puritan pamphleteer, title page of *The Tenure of Kings and Magistrates*, 1650.

PROVING THAT IT IS LAWFUL, AND HATH BEEN HELD SO THROUGH ALL AGES, FOR ANY, WHO HAVE THE POWER, TO CALL TO ACCOUNT A TYRANT, OR WICKED KING; AND, AFTER DUE CONVICTION, TO DEPOSE, AND PUT HIM TO DEATH; IF THE ORDINARY MAGISTRATE HAVE NEGLECTED, OR DENIED TO DO IT. AND THAT THEY, WHO OF LATE SO MUCH BLAME DEPOSING, ARE THE MEN THAT DID IT THEMSELVES.

GO ON TO THE NEXT PAGE.

Document 5

Source: Mary Bayly, "A Letter Sent into France to the Lord Duke of Buckingham His Grace: of a Great Miracle wrought by a piece of a Handkerchief dipped in His Majesty's Blood. The Truth whereof, he himself saw, and is ready to depose it, and doth believe will be attested by 500 others, if occasion requires," 1649.

This my Daughter about a year and a half after her birth was troubled with a swelling under her Chin . . . both her eyes and lips were extremely ill, the swelling in her neck still continuing, and at last she was absolutely blind in her right eye for twelve months . . . that she could scarce discern the light of a Candle; some telling me that it was the King's Evil, others doubting of it; I never sought for remedy by a touch from the hand of His Sacred Majesty while He was living; the Saturday after his death, [a] Journey-man gave me a little piece of a Handkerchief that was dipped in the King's blood, and then returning home . . . whereupon I stroked my Daughters eyes, and the swelling under her chin with it . . . whereupon . . . it hath helped her, and she is now perfectly recovered, as you see, in her eyes, and the swelling under her chin is almost gone, the color of her flesh is recovered, and the pain totally gone: with this [s]mall piece of a Handkerchief was all this done, which many have desired of me; but, although I am but a poor woman, and of mean condition, I protest I will not sell it for forty pounds.

Document 6

Source: Louis XIII (for Louis XIV), King of France and Navarre, declaration of 1649.

At length, with kisses and greetings beginning their betrayal, they invited his Majesty to a personal treaty. To show his passionate desire for peace, he bent over backwards, going beyond all former rulers in generous concessions [giving in and making promises]. Yet even when he had given in beyond their hope and expectation, and surrendered his most unquestionable rights and privileges into their hands, with hate as relentless as the grave, deep and bottomless as hell, they abruptly broke off. By force of arms they dragged him to court. Subordinates took it upon themselves to judge their king. They called him to an account, he who owed an account to none but God alone. They disrespectfully criticized him with the unjust shame of tyrant, traitor and murderer. Having behaved with scorn and contempt, after a short time, in triumph they took him to the scaffold. Making his sorrow worse, they had prepared the scaffold at the entrance to his royal palace. In the sight of his subjects they committed a most brutal murder upon his sacred person, by severing his royal head from his body, by the hands of the common hangman.

GO ON TO THE NEXT PAGE.

Document 7

Source: Abraham Bosse, French Huguenot engraver and artist, frontispiece to *Leviathan* by Thomas Hobbes, as designed in consultation with the author, a mathematician, philosopher, and tutor to Charles II in France, 1651.

Private Collection/The Bridgeman Art Library.

GO ON TO THE NEXT PAGE.

Document 8

Source: Diary of Samuel Pepys, Member of Parliament and naval administrator under King James II and a member of the Royal Society. He attended and supported the execution of Charles I.

Thursday 30 January 1661/62

Fast-day for the murdering of the late King. I went to church, and Mr. Mills made a good sermon upon David's words, "Who can lay his hands upon the Lord's Anointed and be guiltless?" So home and to dinner, and employed all the afternoon in my chamber, setting things and papers to rights, which pleased me very well, and I think I shall begin to take pleasure in being at home and minding my business. I pray God I may.

Document 9

Source: Lucy Hutchinson, Puritan poet and translator and wife of John Hutchinson, close adviser to Oliver Cromwell and signer of the king's death warrant. *Memoirs of the Life of Colonel Hutchinson*, 1664.

So this king was a worse encroacher upon the civil and spiritual liberties of his people by far than his father. He married a papist, a French lady, of a haughty spirit, and a great wit and beauty. . . . By this means the court was replenished with papists, and many who hoped to advance themselves by the change, turned to that religion. All the papists in the kingdom were favored, and . . . the puritans were more than ever discountenanced and persecuted, insomuch that many of them chose to abandon their native country, and leave their dearest relations, to retire into any foreign soil or plantation, where they might, amidst all outward inconveniences, enjoy the free exercise of God's worship. Such as could not flee were tormented in the bishops' courts, fined, whipped, pilloried, imprisoned, and suffered to enjoy no rest, so that death was better than life to them . . . yet was not the king satisfied till the whole land was reduced to perfect slavery.

The example of the French king was propounded to him, and he thought himself no monarch so long as his will was confined to the bounds of any law; but knowing that the people of England were not pliable to an arbitrary rule, he plotted to subdue them to his yoke. . . . He was the most obstinate person in his self-will that ever was, and so bent upon being an absolute, uncontrollable sovereign, that he was resolved either to be such a king or none. . . . But above all these the king had another instigator of his own violent purpose, more powerful than all the rest, and that was the queen . . . let them remember that the felicity of [Queen Elizabeth]'s reign was the effect of her submission to her masculine and wise counselors.

GO ON TO THE NEXT PAGE.

Document 10

Source: Anonymous engraving of the hanging, drawing and quartering of regicides Francis Hacker and Daniel Axtell, October 19, 1660.

Hulton Archive/Getty Images.

GO ON TO THE NEXT PAGE.

Document 11

Source: White Kennet, Bishop of Peterborough, England, *A Complete History of England,* 1719.

It must be dreadfully remembered, that the cruel Powers did suspect that the King would not submit his Head to the Block; and therefore to bring him down by Violence to it; they had prepared Hooks and Staples . . . to haul him as a Victim to the Slaughter . . . by the Example of his Savior, he resisted not, he disappointed their Wit, and yielded to their Malice.

Document 12

Source: Laurence Echard, Whig historian, *The History of England,* 1720.

His head was at one blow severed from his Body. . . . None of the kings of England ever left the world with more open marks of sorrow and affection. The venerable Archbishop Usher, from a Window, swooned at the sight of the fatal blow, as at a prodigy too great for Heaven to permit, or the Earth to behold: And as the rumor of his death spread throughout the Kingdom, women miscarried, many of both sexes fell into palpitations, swoonings and melancholy, and some, with sudden consternations, expired.

GO ON TO THE NEXT PAGE.

EUROPEAN HISTORY
SECTION II

Part B
(Suggested planning and writing time—35 minutes)
Percent of Section II score—27.5

Directions: You are to answer ONE question from the three questions below. Make your selection carefully, choosing the question that you are best prepared to answer thoroughly in the time permitted. You should spend 5 minutes organizing or outlining your answer.

Write an essay that:

+ Has a relevant thesis.

+ Addresses all parts of the question.

+ Supports thesis with specific evidence.

+ Is well organized.

2. Evaluate the degree to which the political ideas of Rousseau and Montesquieu are representative of the main thrusts of Enlightenment thought.

3. "In the seventeenth century, the French kings tamed the aristocracy, while in England, the aristocracy tamed the king." Evaluate the historical accuracy of this statement.

4. Discuss the differences between the empirical and the mathematical approaches to science during the seventeenth century, and analyze how Copernicus, Galileo, Kepler, and Newton used these different approaches.

GO ON TO THE NEXT PAGE.

EUROPEAN HISTORY
SECTION II

Part C
(Suggested planning and writing time—35 minutes)
Percent of Section II score—27.5

Directions: You are to answer ONE question from the three questions below. Make your selection carefully, choosing the question that you are best prepared to answer thoroughly in the time permitted. You should spend 5 minutes organizing or outlining your answer.

Write an essay that:

+ Has a relevant thesis.

+ Addresses all parts of the question.

+ Supports the thesis with specific evidence.

+ Is well organized.

5. Analyze the factors that contributed to the rapid rise of population in much of Europe in the eighteenth century.

6. In what ways did Britain use war and aggression to achieve great-power status by 1763?

7. To what degree and for what reasons did the social gulf between the upper and lower classes widen in the eighteenth century?

STOP

END OF EXAM

Answer Key for Practice Exam 2

Answers for Section I: Multiple-Choice Questions

1. C	21. A	41. B	61. B
2. B	22. C	42. C	62. A
3. E	23. A	43. B	63. B
4. D	24. C	44. C	64. A
5. D	25. B	45. D	65. A
6. A	26. C	46. A	66. A
7. D	27. B	47. D	67. B
8. A	28. C	48. C	68. C
9. C	29. D	49. D	69. D
10. D	30. E	50. C	70. D
11. C	31. C	51. A	71. D
12. E	32. B	52. C	72. C
13. C	33. B	53. C	73. E
14. C	34. C	54. C	74. C
15. C	35. C	55. E	75. A
16. D	36. B	56. D	76. B
17. D	37. A	57. B	77. A
18. A	38. E	58. A	78. A
19. E	39. D	59. C	79. A
20. B	40. C	60. B	80. D

Scoring the Multiple-Choice Section

Use the following formula to calculate your raw score on the multiple-choice section of the exam:

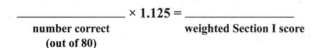

$$\underline{\hspace{3cm}} \times 1.125 = \underline{\hspace{3cm}}$$

number correct   weighted Section I score
(out of 80)

Rationales

1. **Answer: (C)** There were several urban uprisings in France; Spain faced rebellions in Catalonia and Portugal; Palermo and Naples in Italy rose up in rebellion. England experienced the civil war. Only Holland, prosperous and relatively democratic, was safe from popular revolts. (McKay, *A History of Western Society*, Eleventh Edition, p. 469)

GO ON TO THE NEXT PAGE.

2. **Answer: (B)** Louis revoked the Edict of Nantes in 1685, with the aim of creating religious uniformity in France. State power rather than the Inquisition was used to enforce it. (McKay, *A History of Western Society*, Eleventh Edition, pp. 470–472)

3. **Answer: (E)** In the 1713 Peace of Utrecht, Spain gave up the important *asiento,* or the right to supply slaves to its Atlantic colonies, as well as Gibraltar, whose importance was more strategic and symbolic than economic. Spain's colonies did not revolt until the nineteenth century. Spain's supplies of gold and silver, on which the economy was dependent, began to dwindle as the mines ran out. (McKay, *A History of Western Society*, Eleventh Edition, pp. 476–477)

4. **Answer: (D)** Cromwell sought the king's execution and purged Parliament to avoid a negative vote. It was this Rump Parliament that approved the execution. France gave refuge to Charles II but sent no troops. Charles II and James II, both Stuarts, were crowned king in 1660 and 1685, respectively. (McKay, *A History of Western Society*, Eleventh Edition, pp. 492–494)

5. **Answer: (D)** Colbert, Louis XIV's finance minister and great proponent of mercantilism, did everything listed except abolish the guilds, which he empowered to raise quality standards and make French goods more competitive in the export market. (McKay, *A History of Western Society*, Eleventh Edition, pp. 474–476)

6. **Answer: (A)** The kings of Spain in the seventeenth century lacked the will to reform and to lead Spain out of difficulties, and both Philip III and Philip IV essentially handed the reins of government over to advisers rather than taking an active role. They were suspicious of ideas from other countries. They repudiated their debts several times in the late seventeenth and early eighteenth centuries. (McKay, *A History of Western Society*, Eleventh Edition, pp. 476–478)

7. **Answer: (D)** In the Peace of Utrecht, the crown of Spain was given to a Bourbon but with the proviso that it could never be unified with the crown of France. The balance of power was restored when French ambitions were checked. Austria was given the Spanish Netherlands. (McKay, *A History of Western Society*, Eleventh Edition, p. 476)

8. **Answer: (A)** Hobbes argued that men formed governments to protect themselves from their own selfishness and aggression. Without powerful governments, those traits lead society into disorder and chaos. This was an important secular argument for monarchy. While he used the analogy of the monarch as the head and the people of the realm as the body, that was not the basis of his assertion that a strong ruler was needed. (McKay, *A History of Western Society*, Eleventh Edition, p. 492)

9. **Answer: (C)** The English civil war was fundamentally fought over Parliament's assertion of its right to control royal revenues and taxes, that is, its political power against Charles I's attempt to rule without it. Religious issues played a role in alienating Parliament from the king and in sparking revolts in Scotland and Ireland, but the causes of the conflict demonstrate that the political, not the religious, issue was fundamental. (McKay, *A History of Western Society*, Eleventh Edition, pp. 490–492)

10. **Answer: (D)** Although Charles II's treaty with France and James II's Catholic wife and his Declaration of Indulgence rankled most of the English, it was James II's violations of the Test Act that were taken to mean that he hoped to restore absolutism, and which prompted Parliament to offer the crown to Mary, James's Protestant daughter. The death of Oliver Cromwell led to the Restoration of 1660, not the Glorious Revolution. Although it serves a wonderful defense of the Glorious Revolution, Locke's *Second Treatise of Civil Government* was published the year after that event and thus could not have caused it. (McKay, *A History of Western Society*, Eleventh Edition, pp. 493–495)

11. **Answer: (C)** By having the largest merchant marine in Europe, the Dutch dominated shipping; they were also major shipbuilders. There was no unified government of the seven provinces that made up the Netherlands, each of which remained a separate republic, although they pursued a joint foreign policy. They had few important colonies in the New World and in fact lost New Amsterdam in 1664 to the English, with whom they fought several wars in the seventeenth century. (McKay, *A History of Western Society*, Eleventh Edition, pp. 496–497)

12. **Answer: (E)** Johann Sebastian Bach was a Lutheran who worked in Saxony and other Germanic states. Rubens was a Flemish artist who worked for the French royal family, which was Catholic. (McKay, *A History of Western Society*, Eleventh Edition, pp. 498–499)

13. **Answer: (C)** Whereas the older view was that Louis XIV tamed the nobles and weakened both their wealth and their power, the new view is that he cooperated with them as well as co-opted them. Without their cooperation, it would have been impossible to extend his power throughout France or wage his many foreign wars. (McKay, *A History of Western Society*, Eleventh Edition, pp. 470–471)

14. **Answer: (C)** Armies became bigger, more professional, and more expensive. Nobles, who held to traditional ideals of honor, suffered high death tolls. Standing armies—armies that exist in peacetime as well as wartime—were the norm everywhere except in England. (McKay, *A History of Western Society*, Eleventh Edition, p. 468)

15. **Answer: (C)** Western and eastern Europe significantly diverge after 1500 with regard to serfdom, which is reimposed in the east but disappeared in the west. (McKay, *A History of Western Society*, Eleventh Edition, pp. 465, 478)

16. **Answer: (D)** The Thirty Years' War was devastating to the economy and population of the Germanic states. Because of depopulation and agricultural dislocations, the great landlords were able to expand their holdings. It took nearly 200 years for the economy there to rebound. (McKay, *A History of Western Society*, Eleventh Edition, p. 466)

17. **Answer: (D)** Landlords in eastern Europe took control over the distribution of their goods. They sold them directly to foreign merchants, the Dutch for example, bypassing the local towns. The merchant class in eastern Europe and the urban population remained small. Towns also lost medieval privileges, like the right to offer refuge to runaways from estates. (McKay, *A History of Western Society*, Eleventh Edition, p. 479)

18. **Answer: (A)** The Habsburgs conquered Hungary and Transylvania from the Ottomans in the late seventeenth century. There, they made compromises with the Hungarian nobility, allowing them to retain many of their privileges. In Bohemia and Hungary, Protestantism was harshly put down; both states became Catholic. (McKay, *A History of Western Society*, Eleventh Edition, pp. 479–480)

19. **Answer: (E)** Prussia built a relatively small but tightly disciplined army, made up of Prussian subjects. It was over the issue of war funding that Frederick William, the "Great Elector" (1640–1688) was able to convince the Prussian nobility to renounce their rights. They became the officer corps. He did not call the diet into session after 1652. (McKay, *A History of Western Society*, Eleventh Edition, pp. 480–481)

20. **Answer: (B)** Frederick William I, the second king of Prussia (the first was his father, Frederick I), spread militaristic values throughout his state. He built an efficient and honest bureaucracy with similar values of service and honor. Russia would not have wanted nor did it need Prussian help against the Swedes. Frederick William lived an austere soldier's life and disdained luxury. (McKay, *A History of Western Society*, Eleventh Edition, pp. 481–482)

21. **Answer: (A)** The princes of Moscow first served the Mongol overlords; only later did Ivan III refuse to pay obeisance to them. St. Petersburg was built some time after the princes of Moscow centralized rule of Russia in their hands, and Ivan the Terrible inherited the position of prince, although he was the first to take the title of tsar. The important patriarch was in Moscow, not Kiev. (McKay, *A History of Western Society*, Eleventh Edition, p. 482)

22. **Answer: (C)** It was the need to modernize the army so that he could achieve Russia's expansion that primarily motivated Peter. To improve the army, he sought western technology, changed the way noble titles were awarded, and required the nobles to become educated and to symbolize their modernization by cutting off their beards and wearing western dress. For most of his reign, he was at war and substantially expanded the empire. (McKay, *A History of Western Society*, Eleventh Edition, pp. 485–487)

23. **Answer: (A)** Peter the Great changed the practice whereby both sons and daughters inherited estates to one of unigeniture, meaning only one son in each family could inherit. (McKay, *A History of Western Society*, Eleventh Edition, pp. 486–487)

24. **Answer: (C)** Stenka Razin led a widespread revolt, which was ultimately put down; it was one of many. Peter the Great instituted his reforms for his own reasons. The conditions of the Russian peasants were getting worse and worse, so expectations were certainly not rising. There were very few urban workers with whom to make alliances. (McKay, *A History of Western Society*, Eleventh Edition, p. 483)

25. **Answer: (B)** The janissary corps was made up of slaves, which meant they had to be Christians, as Muslims are not allowed to enslave other Muslims. Young men, taken mostly from the Balkans, were brought to Istanbul, raised as Muslims, and trained for government service. Some rose to high positions in the military or civil administration. (McKay, *A History of Western Society*, Eleventh Edition, p. 489)

26. **Answer: (C)** Prussia was the only one of the four states that consisted of territories that were not contiguous, divided as it was into Prussia in the east and Brandenburg to the west. All four monarchs sought to expand their empires and establish firm control over their states, and they all embellished their capital cities. Prussia was also the only one that was not multiethnic. (McKay, *A History of Western Society*, Eleventh Edition, map on p. 480, text on pp. 479–489)

27. **Answer: (B)** Pietists in the Germanic states and Methodists in England focused on the individual's need for emotional connections with their faith. They were little interested in science as part of religion. Their churches tended to be small and individualized. Deists believed in a creator but not redeemer God. (McKay, *A History of Western Society*, Eleventh Edition, pp. 597–600)

28. **Answer: (C)** Aristotle was the main source of information for more than 2,000 years because he had written about virtually every field of science. Ptolemy provided a workable geocentric interpretation of observed data. The Bible was not read very much except by Protestants and not for scientific information. The churches were not focused on science. Chinese texts would have had much scientific information, but they were not available at that time. Marsiglio of Padua wrote about political issues involving the church. (McKay, *A History of Western Society*, Eleventh Edition, pp. 504–505)

29. **Answer: (D)** Although Kepler did have mystical tendencies, it was his three laws of planetary motion expressed mathematically that proved Copernicus's theory. Kepler was already dead when Galileo was tried by the Inquisition. His mentor, Tycho Brahe, never fully accepted Copernican theory, but Kepler did. Galileo used the telescope to study Copernican theory, not Kepler. (McKay, *A History of Western Society*, Eleventh Edition, pp. 507–509)

30. **Answer: (E)**   While the other four observations were crucial for proving Copernican theory, it was Galileo's experiments with falling and moving bodies that could only be explained by Newton's theory of universal gravitation. (McKay, *A History of Western Society*, Eleventh Edition, pp. 509–511)

31. **Answer: (C)**   Cartesian dualism postulates that mind is separate from matter. Man therefore is free to explore the physical world since such exploration cannot affect the spiritual world. (McKay, *A History of Western Society*, Eleventh Edition, p. 512)

32. **Answer: (B)**   When scientists and physicians began to do autopsies, a few did search for the soul, but this was not a major cause of the new science. Kings and princes played an important role by providing funds for observatories, as the king of Denmark did for Tycho Brahe. (McKay, *A History of Western Society*, Eleventh Edition, pp. 505–506)

33. **Answer: (B)**   Bacon's importance lay in his defense of empiricism and the experimental method. He also claimed that science would benefit society and improve people's lives. Galileo, Kepler, and Brahe were more interested in scientific work than in developing a theory of science. Margaret Cavendish wrote about Descartes's mind-body dualism rather than the empirical method. (McKay, *A History of Western Society*, Eleventh Edition, pp. 507–509, 511, 515)

34. **Answer: (C)**   The main difference is that in the seventeenth century, natural philosophers explored the physical world, while in the eighteenth century, they studied the human world. There is no consistent pattern of ethnicity, nationality, or religion; they are similar only in that almost all of the public intellectual work was done by men. (McKay, *A History of Western Society*, Eleventh Edition, p. 516)

35. **Answer: (C)**   Only Rousseau advocated popular sovereignty; Montesquieu and Voltaire supported enlightened monarchy as the best system; Hume and Kant were Enlightenment-era philosophers, not philosophes. (McKay, *A History of Western Society*, Eleventh Edition, p. 520)

36. **Answer: (B)**   Both Descartes and Bayle argued that one must begin an inquiry with doubt. Bayle was the leading skeptic of the Enlightenment. (McKay, *A History of Western Society*, Eleventh Edition, pp. 512, 516)

37. **Answer: (A)**   If children are born blank slates, there can be no inborn knowledge; therefore all knowledge comes from perceptions. It also means that there is no original sin. Parental influences were all-important. Public education would not be a popular idea for another hundred years. (McKay, *A History of Western Society*, Eleventh Edition, p. 517)

38. **Answer: (E)**   By translating Newton, she made his scientific work available to French readers across Europe and thereby encouraged the use of reason and rationalism. (McKay, *A History of Western Society*, Eleventh Edition, p. 518)

39. **Answer: (D)**   All the enlightened monarchs promoted legal reforms, although to varying degrees. Only Joseph II abolished serfdom and instituted religious toleration for Jews. (McKay, *A History of Western Society*, Eleventh Edition, pp. 530–533, 535)

40. **Answer: (C)**   When the peasants rose in rebellion under Pugachev, Catherine abandoned her reform efforts. The nobles' position was strengthened, not weakened, under Catherine. Voltaire never humiliated her in print. Catherine died a natural death. (McKay, *A History of Western Society*, Eleventh Edition, p. 533)

41. **Answer: (B)** Diderot's efforts were underwritten by Catherine the Great, not Frederick. The *Encyclopedia* was a hugely popular work, published mostly abroad because of censorship. It was filled with technical knowledge and helped democratize knowledge, which was its aim. (McKay, *A History of Western Society*, Eleventh Edition, pp. 519–520, 531)

42. **Answer: (C)** A greatly enlarged literate population began to read silently and privately, in contrast to the typical reading aloud by the head of the household in the evenings to his family and guests. As a result, readers also became more likely to question the works they read. (McKay, *A History of Western Society*, Eleventh Edition, p. 522)

43. **Answer: (B)** In rural areas, *industrious revolution* refers to the transformation of household labor, particularly that of women and children, toward production for the market and being paid in wages in the cottage system; in cities, it resulted in more work done outside the home to earn wages. (McKay, *A History of Western Society*, Eleventh Edition, pp. 553–554)

44. **Answer: (C)** The Portuguese were the first to create a commercial empire in Asia. They then lost out to the Dutch, who in turn were replaced by France and then Britain. It is the British who end up on top in Asia at the end of the eighteenth century. (McKay, *A History of Western Society*, Eleventh Edition, pp. 569–570)

45. **Answer: (D)** Mercantilism benefits manufacturers and merchants by protecting them from competition and providing them with guaranteed markets. Consumers, ordinary people who buy goods, would benefit the most from economically liberal policies, as free competition would increase the quality and quantity of goods and reduce their prices. (McKay, *A History of Western Society*, Eleventh Edition, pp. 556–557)

46. **Answer: (A)** With this requirement, the British shipbuilding and shipping industry boomed and outcompeted its nearest rival, the Dutch. (McKay, *A History of Western Society*, Eleventh Edition, p. 558)

47. **Answer: (D)** Women were terribly paid; their wages were a small fraction of what men earned. All the other items listed were advantages of the putting-out system either for the manufacturer or for the households who took part in it. (McKay, *A History of Western Society*, Eleventh Edition, pp. 549–553)

48. **Answer: (C)** The guilds found ways to incorporate new technology and methods of production, and some new guilds were formed, for example, of seamstresses. Historians now say the guilds' high point was the seventeenth and eighteenth centuries, not the High Middle Ages. (McKay, *A History of Western Society*, Eleventh Edition, pp. 554–556)

49. **Answer: (D)** Blood sports, such as bullbaiting and cockfighting, were popular with the masses. Reading novels was relatively rare in the eighteenth century, as the genre was quite new, but became popular in the next century. (McKay, *A History of Western Society*, Eleventh Edition, pp. 586–589)

50. **Answer: (C)** Attitudes about mixed-race children were quite different in Spanish and English colonies. English slave owners in the colonies rarely freed their mixed-race children, unlike Spanish, French, and Portuguese masters. (McKay, *A History of Western Society*, Eleventh Edition, pp. 564–567)

51. **Answer: (A)** By ending the practice of leaving the land fallow, agricultural productivity went up substantially. Although enclosure and the other options also were important and helped make increased productivity possible, crop rotation and planting all fields every year were the definitive elements. (McKay, *A History of Western Society*, Eleventh Edition, pp. 542–543)

52. **Answer: (C)** Only in England was there inoculation against smallpox. There was relatively little rise in birthrates, and illegitimacy was not significant to population growth at that time. (McKay, *A History of Western Society*, Eleventh Edition, pp. 546–547)

53. **Answer: (C)** Slave labor in the colonies, which grew sugar cane and tea, enabled the prices to drop, and they became dietary staples. (McKay, *A History of Western Society*, Eleventh Edition, p. 591)

54. **Answer: (C)** Britain acquired the *asiento*, the control over the New World slave trade, in the 1713 Treaty of Utrecht. The height of the slave trade was the 1780s. Parliament abolished the slave trade in 1807, just shy of 100 years later. (McKay, *A History of Western Society*, Eleventh Edition, pp. 558, 564)

55. **Answer: (E)** The general impact was to increase warfare in the competition to acquire slaves to sell to Europeans. The African population was decimated by the slave trade. (McKay, *A History of Western Society*, Eleventh Edition, pp. 563–564)

56. **Answer: (D)** France gave up its outposts in India in the treaty that ended the Seven Years' War. Spain had ceded the *asiento* and France had ceded Nova Scotia at the Peace of Utrecht in 1713. Spain acquired, not ceded, Louisiana and did not cede its Caribbean colonies at that time. (McKay, *A History of Western Society*, Eleventh Edition, p. 570)

57. **Answer: (B)** London became the largest city in Europe. It was rebuilt after the Great Fire of 1666, expanded westward with townhouses arranged around squares. (McKay, *A History of Western Society*, Eleventh Edition, p. 560)

58. **Answer: (A)** By establishing the court at Versailles and becoming a strong patron of the arts, Louis XIV made French culture dominant on the continent for at least another 100 years. *Politique* is a term used for sixteenth- and early-seventeenth-century monarchs, like Elizabeth I of England and Henry IV of France, who determined religious questions based on political interests. Louis XIV was only five years old when the Thirty Years' War was over, and he then ruled for over fifty years. He expelled the Protestants from France. (McKay, *A History of Western Society*, Eleventh Edition, pp. 470–474)

59. **Answer: (C)** Although many Enlightenment thinkers were deists and believed in God, their philosophies were focused on the nature of man and rationalism. The philosophes were mostly outside of the universities; their setting was the salon. Most philosophes disdained the church but had little interest in reforming it per se. The poor were interested in the ideas but were typically illiterate still; by the end of the eighteenth century, they were reading simplifications of the works of the philosophes published as broadsheets. (McKay, *A History of Western Society*, Eleventh Edition, pp. 517, 522–524)

60. **Answer: (B)** Midwives and physicians had about the same percentage of women who died in their care during childbirth. (McKay, *A History of Western Society*, Eleventh Edition, p. 604)

61. **Answer: (B)** The consolidation of small farms into larger fields was more efficient and allowed for easier introduction of scientific agriculture. It was met with resistance by both poor peasants and noble landowners. (McKay, *A History of Western Society*, Eleventh Edition, pp. 542–543)

62. **Answer: (A)** Illegitimacy rates were still low in the early eighteenth century but began to grow rapidly by around midcentury. (McKay, *A History of Western Society*, Eleventh Edition, pp. 546–547, 578–580)

63. **Answer: (B)** The slave trade reached its heights in the 1780s. It was abolished in the United States during the Civil War (1863) and in other British colonies in 1833. Brazil received almost 4.5 million slaves, while North America took only 3 percent of the African slaves. (McKay, *A History of Western Society*, Eleventh Edition, pp. 562–564)

64. **Answer: (A)** A common misconception is that couples married young, but records confirm that they waited until their late twenties when they could afford to live away from their parents. Europeans lived generally in nuclear families, unlike most of the world. (McKay, *A History of Western Society*, Eleventh Edition, pp. 576–577)

65. **Answer: (A)** As the population grew, so did inflation, which meant that the poorest people could not afford much to eat. Game laws also deprived people of shooting or trapping animals on the land they rented from the nobles. People in towns had a plethora of markets providing fresh produce. (McKay, *A History of Western Society*, Eleventh Edition, pp. 589–592)

66. **Answer: (A)** After a century of religious conflicts in Europe, the Peace of Westphalia marked the end to this fighting. While conflicts remained, there were no major wars fought over them after 1648, when the treaty was signed. The peace treaty doomed efforts of emperors of the Holy Roman Empire to consolidate their power, but the empire lasted until the nineteenth century. (McKay, *A History of Western Society*, Eleventh Edition, p. 466)

67. **Answer: (B)** Although the Protectorate was theoretically a commonwealth, with power divided between Parliament and a council of state, the reality was that the army controlled the government. As head of the army, Oliver Cromwell essentially ruled as a military dictator. (McKay, *A History of Western Society*, Eleventh Edition, p. 492)

68. **Answer: (C)** Copernicus in the mid-sixteenth century advanced the concept of a heliocentric universe, which sparked the search for scientific proof by Galileo, Kepler, and Newton. (McKay, *A History of Western Society*, Eleventh Edition, pp. 506–511)

69. **Answer: (D)** Survival rates for infants and children were low during the eighteenth century. Many infants were abandoned, and other infants and children died due to malnutrition and disease. The foundling hospitals did not provide an answer to the problem of abandoned children, since 50 percent of the foundlings died within the first year, and often as many as 90 percent did not survive. (McKay, *A History of Western Society*, Eleventh Edition, pp. 581–582)

70. **Answer: (D)** Elizabeth I was succeeded by her cousin James I in 1603. His son, Charles I, succeeded him in 1625. Charles I was defeated by Oliver Cromwell's Puritan army and beheaded in 1649. George I in the early eighteenth century was the first monarch of the current dynasty, the Windsor, formerly known as the House of Hanover. (McKay, *A History of Western Society*, Eleventh Edition, pp. 490, 492, 496)

71. **Answer: (D)** Even developing democracies, such as England and the Netherlands, were primarily concerned with establishing a strong central government. (McKay, *A History of Western Society*, Eleventh Edition, pp. 466–468)

72. **Answer: (C)** Frederick the Great, the King of Prussia, broke the Pragmatic Sanction, an agreement signed with the Austrian king, in order to get coal-and-iron-rich Silesia, which he did. Peter the Great was dead by the time of the war (1740), and Hungary didn't become independent until 1918. The Turks had been defeated by the Austrians in the Siege of Vienna in 1683. (McKay, *A History of Western Society*, Eleventh Edition, p. 530)

73. **Answer: (E)** All agricultural property officially belonged to the sultan. This meant there was no hereditary landowning class in the Ottoman Empire. (McKay, *A History of Western Society*, Eleventh Edition, p. 489)

74. **Answer: (C)** Poland was dismembered by Austria, Prussia, and Russia, each taking a share in 1772, 1792, and 1795. (McKay, *A History of Western Society*, Eleventh Edition, map on p. 532)

75. **Answer: (A)** Mendelssohn, well read and a bold thinker, was convinced that Enlightenment ideas could complement religion, including Judaism. He wrote an impressive work on the immortality of the soul. He remained loyal to his Jewish faith. (McKay, *A History of Western Society*, Eleventh Edition, pp. 534–535)

76. **Answer: (B)** The countries with the highest rate of increase were Russia and Italy, both primarily agricultural in the eighteenth century. Northern Europe had the lowest rates of increases, and southern Europe had high rates but not the highest. There's nothing in the graph about war death tolls. (McKay, *A History of Western Society*, Eleventh Edition, p. 547)

77. **Answer: (A)** The graph has information on only exports in general and comparatively between the New World and Africa, and therefore is irrelevant to options B, C, D, and E. (McKay, *A History of Western Society*, Eleventh Edition, pp. 560–562)

78. **Answer: (A)** Frederick the Great refused to emancipate the Jews of Prussia. Cromwell invited the Jews back nearly 400 years after their expulsion from England. The Dutch Republic and the Ottoman Empire welcomed Jewish businessmen and allowed for some freedom of religion. Joseph II of Austria granted religious toleration during his short reign. (McKay, *A History of Western Society*, Eleventh Edition, pp. 487, 489, 492, 497, 533–536)

79. **Answer: (A)** Smith recognized the restrictions of government involvement in the economy as practiced under mercantilism. He was an advocate of relying on the market forces of capitalism and would oppose the command economy or any government intervention in the economy. He advocated that workers be paid decent wages so they could become part of the consumer economy. He wrote before the social welfare reforms of the nineteenth century. (McKay, *A History of Western Society*, Eleventh Edition, pp. 556–557)

80. **Answer: (D)** The Enlightenment emphasized the innate goodness of man and encouraged parents to follow the laws of nature in rearing children. (McKay, *A History of Western Society*, Eleventh Edition, pp. 582–584)

Answers for Section II: Part A

Remember that the two parts of the exam—Section I (multiple-choice) and Section II (three essays) are equally weighted at 50 percent each in determining the final score. Of the three essays, the document-based question essay counts for 45 percent of the Section II score, and the two thematic response essays together count for 55 percent of the Section II score.

As these are not official AP Exam questions, we don't have official AP scoring standards for them. But you can use the following general guidelines to score your own essays.

AP European History DBQ essays are scored using the core-scoring method. Each specific instruction before the DBQ question itself refers to a core point. Once you earn all core points, you can earn additional points for doing those tasks well or for effectively bringing in outside information.

Include a thesis. To earn a point for your thesis, it must be specific, refer to documents, and not just repeat the question. If you don't earn a point for the thesis, you can't earn the point for supporting the thesis with an appropriate number of documents.

The following examples are of thesis statements that would *not* earn a point:

There were many positive and negative views about the execution of Charles I.

Why is this not acceptable? It doesn't refer to the documents in any specific way, nor does it address the specific terms of the questions. Here's another poor example:

The execution of Charles I was very controversial and people had strong religious and political views about it.

This is better, but it doesn't show you've done much more than read the question and the historical background. Here is an example of a thesis statement that would earn a point:

While some people protested the execution of Charles I on moral grounds, others justified it because of his absolutist acts that threatened England's constitutional monarchy.

This thesis refers to both positive and negative views about the execution of Charles I and gives a specific basis for those views, therefore addressing the question. Without those specifics, the thesis statement adds nothing to the question itself and could have been written without reading the documents.

Use a majority of the documents. You must use at least half of the documents to earn this point. In the case of this practice exam, that means seven documents (six would be half; seven constitutes a "majority"). Using a document means discussing something in the box specifically. You can still earn this point even if you make mistakes on one or two documents.

Interpret documents correctly. You are allowed to make only one major error, which is defined as an interpretation that leads you to an erroneous conclusion or to an erroneous grouping. A major error, for example, would be if you described John Milton (Document 4) as a supporter of Charles I.

150

Group the documents. You must have three groups of documents. A group must have at least two documents in it, discussed specifically and together. Be specific when describing each group; that is, don't merely list documents together by number (for example, Documents 4, 5, and 7), but explain what the documents in a group have in common. Typical ways of making groups include: by opinion of author, by identity of author (nationality, political party or orientation, gender, age, position, etc.), by type of document (speeches, government documents, artworks, and so on), or by time period.

Possible groups in this DBQ include:

Supporters of the execution of Charles I: [1] eyewitnesses, [4] Milton, [9] Hutchinson
Opponents of the execution of Charles I: [5] Bayly, [6] Louis XIV, [7] Bosse, [11] Kennet, [12] Echard
Political issues: [1] eyewitnesses, [2] Charles I, [6] Louis XIV, [9] Hutchinson
King is sacred person: [2] Charles I, [5] Bayly, [6] Louis XIV, [8] Pepys
Puritans: [4] Milton, [7] Bosse, [9] Hutchinson
Poets: [4] Milton, [9] Hutchinson
Women: [5] Bayly, [9] Hutchinson
Engravings: [3] German engraving, [7] Bosse, [10] regicide engraving
Opinions written decades after the execution: [8] Pepys, [9] Hutchinson, [10] regicide engraving, [11] Kennet, [12] Echard
Historians: [11] Kennet, [12], Echard

Analyze point of view. This is a crucial core point, one that some students don't do or do poorly. POV analysis shows that you understand that a particular person wrote a document at a particular time and place for a particular purpose and that it may not present the whole truth. It's important to think about the reliability of the document. For example, how accurate can an engraving or a commentary be if it was made by a foreigner who may not have been an eyewitness or may not have understood what he or she witnessed? Another way to do POV analysis is to connect the source's position in society or anything given in the source identification with the views the source expresses. The document summaries that follow show examples of the POV analysis you might make for each document.

Analyze individual documents.

Document 1 The eyewitnesses to the trial of Charles I report that the court found him guilty of going to war against Parliament and the people, which made him a traitor, and that the court was "fully satisfied" of his guilt as a traitor and as a murderer, and of the death penalty it invoked. POV: As there was a great deal of disagreement about the decision to give Charles I the death penalty, as indicated in the historical background, one can question whether this statement is accurate or reliable in describing the full agreement of the court. The document clearly is biased in its use of vilifying words.

Document 2 Charles I, in his speech just before the beheading, says he desires the liberty of the people, but that liberty comes from having a government, and the sovereign and the subjects are different. He calls himself the martyr of the people. There follows a description of the execution itself and how various people took samples of his blood, some because they thought of him as a martyr, others as "trophies" of the people's deed. POV: Charles says he wanted the liberty of the people, but clearly he is justifying himself before the crowd at the execution. By calling himself sovereign, he shows his true colors.

Document 3 German engraving of the execution. Charles I is called Carl Stuart at the top, and his portrait is just below; to the right of that is one of Cromwell. The crowd seems calm, interested, enthusiastic. POV: One can question the reliability of this document. On what would the German engraver have based his engraving? Did he know what the scene actually looked like? Since the source of his information is not given, there's a good chance that this engraving may be based on imagination more than reality. Also, by having Cromwell's portrait at the top, there is an implication that the engraver thought the execution was justified.

Document 4   John Milton, famous Puritan poet, asserts tyrannicide is justified and has always been so, defining a tyrant as a "wicked king." POV: It was the Puritans, of which Milton was one, who were responsible for the death of the king. Milton is justifying it by calling the king wicked and his execution tyrannicide rather than regicide in a pamphlet published the next year.

Document 5   This incident, reported in a letter to an English lord in France, described the miraculous cure of a sick child when the mother stroked her daughter's eyes with a piece of handkerchief soaked with the king's blood. This woman, Mary Bayly, says she will not sell that piece of handkerchief even if offered a large sum. POV: Mary Bayly used the term "His Sacred Majesty," implying belief in the divine right of kings. Her report on the miraculous cure of her daughter is not likely to be objectively true, but reflects her belief in the sacred nature of the king. The source indicates that the author of the letter believes it and can get some 500 people to attest to it; this would imply that the story might not have been seen as credible by most people.

Document 6   This source is a statement of the king of France about the execution. It vilifies those who accused, tried, and executed Charles as hateful betrayers and brutal murderers, while Charles is portrayed as conciliatory and generous. The statement says that kings are accountable only to God and uses the adjective *sacred* to describe the king's person. POV: The French kings were fierce proponents of divine right, as reflected in this document. Louis XIII was its founder in France. (Incidentally, he was dead when this document was dated in 1649 and the new king, Louis XIV, was just ten years old. However, this was how the original document was published, perhaps revealing that some court official rather than either king actually wrote these words.) Therefore, he can see no justification whatsoever in how the king was treated, and portrays Charles (and by implication all kings) as heroic, generous, and noble.

Document 7   In this frontispiece to Thomas Hobbes's *Leviathan*, a king is represented in a very positive light—noble, friendly, protective of farms and towns. Other symbols of strength and power are military and legal. POV: Hobbes defended absolutism on the basis that a strong central government provided safety and security for people. He developed the notion of the social contract between ruler and ruled. Hobbes was also a tutor to the son of the executed king and therefore close to the Stuart monarchs. His book was published only two years after the execution. The artist of the engraving was a Huguenot. French Calvinists, Huguenots, as a group were opposed to the idea of divine right of kings, so while he has produced positive images of the king, there is an absence of religious elements, which may reflect his religious views.

Document 8   Samuel Pepys, famous London diarist and member of Parliament, called the execution of Charles "murdering" and mentions a sermon he heard in church. He says he now wants to mind his own business. POV: Pepys enthusiastically supported the execution of the king in 1649 but eleven years later has changed his mind. As this diary entry is after the Restoration, it's possible that he has changed his mind because the political tide turned against the radicals.

Document 9   Lucy Hutchinson strongly supported the execution of the king for two reasons. One is religious; she identified the king and his French wife as papists who filled the court with people of like mind and disregarded the Puritans. She complained that the king persecuted the Puritans and hoped to reduce them to slavery. The second reason is political; she labeled Charles as an absolutist like the French king. She blamed the queen for Charles's stubbornness and praised Elizabeth I for her submission to her masculine counselors. POV: There are numerous possibilities for POV with this document. As Hutchinson was an important Puritan, she represented in this document the hostility to Catholics (called papists) and to those who supported them. As the wife of someone who signed the king's death warrant, she naturally defended the legitimacy of his actions, portraying Charles as someone who believed in absolute monarchy and therefore threatened the liberties of Englishmen. As a Protestant woman, she accepted that women were to obey their husbands and therefore railed against the queen for her machinations and her influence on Charles.

Document 10   This engraving is of the execution of several regicides in 1660 after the Stuarts had been returned to the throne. There is a large crowd watching the hanging and drawing and quartering of the regicides. POV: It's difficult to do POV analysis for this document, as the identification of the engraver is not given. The fact that they are called "traytors" implies approval of the executions. One can describe it in numerous ways; one example is as the revenge of the restored monarchists in 1660, noting that the regicides were hung, then disembodied, while the king was beheaded (a nobler way to die).

Document 11   White Kennet described the king as acting nobly at his execution while describing his executioners as cruel, malicious, and untrustworthy. This document was published seventy years after the execution. POV: As a bishop, Kennet was an Anglican. Anglicans by and large supported the king in his conflict with Parliament. Kennet reflects the shock and dismay most Anglicans felt at the execution of the king. One can question how reliable the description of the execution would be, seventy years after the fact.

Document 12   In a history of England from 1720, Echard described the execution as cruel and sorrowful, and damaging men and women alike, leading even to a few sudden deaths. POV: Echard is identified as a Whig. The Whigs were the engineers of the Glorious Revolution, which achieved the goals of the English protesters against the Stuarts without shedding a drop of blood. The tone of this description is quite emotional and sentimental and reflects Whig opposition to radicalism. Echard's description of swooning men and women, miscarriages, and sudden deaths is likely to be exaggerated in order to emphasize the Whig interpretation, and because it was written seventy years later, may not have had accurate sources.

Answers for Section II: Parts B and C

General AP Scoring Standards for Thematic Essay Questions

The essays are scored on a scale of 0 to 9, with 0 being a real score. A response that is completely off task does not even earn a zero. Here are generic scoring guidelines for the essays in Parts B and C.

9–8
Has a clear, well-developed thesis
Is well organized
Addresses the terms of the question
Supports the thesis with substantial specific evidence
Has sophisticated analysis
May contain minor errors; even a 9 need not be flawless

7–6
Has a clear thesis
Addresses all parts of the question but discussion is uneven
Has competent analysis, but it may be superficial
Supports the thesis with some specific evidence

5–4
Contains a thesis, perhaps superficial or simplistic
Gives uneven responses to the question's terms
May contain errors, factual or interpretative
Addresses the question with generally accurate discussion but without specific evidence; analysis is implicit or superficial
May contain major errors within a generally accurate and appropriate discussion
Is descriptive rather than analytical

3–2
Has a weak or muddled thesis, perhaps suggesting false or inappropriate dichotomies or connections
Contains significant errors of chronology or fact
Offers minimal discussion
Provides limited evidence

1–0
Has a confused or absent thesis or merely restates the question
Misconstrues the question or omits major tasks
May contain major errors or irrelevant historical information
Addresses only one part of the question
Offers minimal or no evidence

Reread your essay and ask yourself the following questions—or if you can work with a fellow student in AP European History, read each other's essays and ask these questions:

1. How well organized is the essay? Is it clearly divided into distinct paragraphs? Is there an introduction and a conclusion?

2. How clear is the thesis? Is the thesis statement at the beginning of the essay or in the conclusion?

3. How many arguments support the thesis?

4. How much evidence is used to support the thesis? How specific was it?

5. Were all parts of the question addressed? Was the discussion of the different parts more or less balanced?

6. How many of the points noted in the explanations of the answer were made in the essay?

7. Were there major factual, chronological, or interpretative errors? Or minor errors?

8. Was the analysis explicit or implicit? Was it sophisticated or minimal?

Now reread the Scoring Guidelines and give yourself a score.

In general, the scores on the DBQ average higher than those of the thematic essays, because the DBQ is a skill-based question that uses evidence, while the thematic essays are content-based and require recall of information. The median score on the DBQ is 5 (usually because of lack of POV), while the median scores on thematic essays are typically 4 to 5 on the first and approximately 3 to 4 on the second, often because students run out of time.

Part B Responses

2. **Evaluate the degree to which the political ideas of Rousseau and Montesquieu are representative of the main thrusts of Enlightenment thought.**

This is an intellectual history essay. It's crucial that you select this question only if you understand each of these thinkers' ideas and how they fit in with, or differ from, the Enlightenment as a whole. While Montesquieu's ideas were typical of the Enlightenment in many ways, Rousseau's were quite distinct.

Montesquieu: Montesquieu represents the typical philosophe in his scientific examination of political systems. Creating a new social science, he argued that climate, geography, and other nonpolitical elements affect the political system. He was concerned to defend the rights of individuals and argued for a constitutional government to protect them, one in which the legislative, judicial, and executive powers are separated and can check each other. Such a system would prevent abuse of power by any of the branches of the government. Montesquieu was also typical in his belief that a strong aristocracy was necessary to prevent royal despotism. His *Persian Letters* was typical of the Enlightenment in that the philosophes used foreigners as foils to point out the deficiencies of European societies. Like many philosophes, he admired the English political system. Montesquieu was a frequent visitor at the salons in Paris.

Rousseau: Rousseau, on the other hand, used the reasoning methods of the Enlightenment but came to quite different conclusions. He argued that reason was a chain, not a liberator, and that it would be better to trust one's feelings and emotions. Civilization corrupted the innocence and basic goodness of man. Politically, Rousseau was a believer in popular sovereignty and radical democracy, in which a minority might know the long-term interests of the people (the general will) and would therefore have the right to absolute rule. This was the path to individual freedom. Majority rule was not a reliable protector of freedom. Rousseau lived in isolation from the other philosophes and was alienated from the world of the salons. Rousseau rejected the elitist attitudes and the belief in Reason of the Enlightenment.

3. **"In the seventeenth century, the French kings tamed the aristocracy, while in England, the aristocracy tamed the king." Evaluate the historical accuracy of this statement.**

Essentially this question refers to the English Revolution and absolutism in France. Again, you'll need to know both subjects to answer this question well. You should not assume that the statement must be valid if you have evidence to the contrary. A superior essay will answer this not with a yes-or-no response but with a measured answer, carefully delineating the degrees of accuracy and noting, for example, that Louis XIV won the cooperation of the nobility more than he browbeat them into submission.

Possible thesis: Kings Louis XIII and XIV established French absolutism in the seventeenth century. With the guidance of his chief minister, Cardinal Richelieu, Louis XIII attacked the independence of the nobility. Neither king called the Estates General. Intendants were sent to the countryside to impose royal control over local politics. The nobility reacted to Louis XIII's attempts at centralization of power with a revolt called the Fronde. Louis XIV worked assiduously to diminish the power of the nobility. He built the extraordinary palace at Versailles to impress the nobles and turn them into courtiers. He spied on the nobles and used bourgeois men for important positions rather than nobles. He also sold the bourgeoisie titles of nobility, which brought down the prestige of those titles. Although the nobility remained wealthy, they lost prestige and power under Louis XIV.

In England, on the other hand, the lower aristocracy, the gentry, worked with the other classes to insist on their rights when Charles I attempted to rule on his own. They fought and won a civil war with the royalists and executed Charles I, the first monarch to be so treated in Europe. After a complex and convoluted conflict, a short-lived republic, and a period of religious and political turmoil after the Restoration, England became a constitutional monarchy in the Glorious Revolution of 1688. The nobility of England were willing to tax themselves as long as Parliament, in which they sat in great numbers in both houses, had a voice in government expenditures. They retained their political power in Parliament and as advisers to the king in the cabinet system.

4. **Discuss the differences between the empirical and the mathematical approaches to science during the seventeenth century, and analyze how Copernicus, Galileo, Kepler, and Newton used these different approaches.**

This question asks you to specifically discuss two approaches to science developed in the seventeenth century. You need to articulate both, and develop a thesis that either emphasizes the importance of one over the other, or shows the limitations of each approach and how they combine in the modern scientific method.

Possible thesis: Empiricism was developed and defended by Francis Bacon, who argued that only experiments and scientific observations could serve as the basis for scientific truth. He supported the inductive method of reasoning, that is, going from the specific to the general. Galileo was an empiricist who performed many experiments to test Aristotelian physics, which ultimately he disproved. He derived the law of inertia and overturned Aristotle's notions with his experiments. Similarly, with the telescope, he saw sunspots, the craters on the moon, and moons around Jupiter, which provided the observations that helped establish the validity of the Copernican hypothesis. There were many other experiments conducted during the Scientific Revolution (such as those performed by Pascal).

On the other hand, many important figures in the Scientific Revolution were mathematicians who relied on logic and mathematics rather than empirical data to derive their theories or their laws. Copernicus rejected the Ptolemaic system not because of observations that contradicted it but because it didn't make sense mathematically. Descartes rejected empiricism entirely, which he said could provide faulty data, and argued instead for logical and mathematical analysis in the mind. He created analytic geometry when he saw the connections between geometry and algebra. Cartesian dualism separated mind from matter. Kepler used mathematical analysis of data observed by Tycho Brahe (who had rejected Copernicanism) to derive his three laws of planetary motion. Newton used mathematics and logic to derive the theory of universal gravitation, which explained both the mathematical work of Kepler and the observations of Galileo. Copernicus, Kepler, and Newton proved the value of mathematical proof in science, while Galileo demonstrated the value of experiments and observations. The modern scientific method incorporates both approaches, as each has limitations.

Part C Responses

5. **Analyze the factors that contributed to the rapid rise of population across much of Europe in the eighteenth century.**

In this question you are asked to identify the causes of a broad and far-reaching social trend. It is important when responding to address developments in multiple countries and not to focus, for instance, on Britain, even though the early Industrial Revolution and the Agricultural Revolution were major factors in population growth in that country. It is important, also, to limit information and examples to the eighteenth century and not refer to nineteenth-century developments. An effective answer will establish the extent of population growth as well as analyze the causes of that growth.

Possible thesis: Many regions of Europe experienced a substantial boom in population as a result of falling death rates and a mix of other factors, including improvements in public health, transportation, and nutrition.

Extent of population growth: Population surged across Europe in the eighteenth century. While growth was uneven, with England, Italy, and Russia growing more quickly than France and Prussia, all Europe saw a boom in population, with especially dramatic increases after about 1750.

Causes: The chief cause of population growth was declining death rates. Before 1700, populations across Europe had been held down, as periods of steady growth were offset by massive increases in deaths due to war, famine, and disease, the Black Death being the most extreme example. Europeans needed several years of higher than normal population growth to recover from these devastating die-offs. The passing of the plague was a major factor: the plague struck Europe for the last time during the years 1720 to 1722. After that, it never returned to Europe again, though historians are unsure as to why.

Some improvements in public health, particularly improvements in water supply and sewage handling in cities in eastern Europe and adoption of the smallpox vaccine in England, helped cut death rates as well. Improved transportation from roads and along canals allowed societies to transport food faster and more efficiently; as a result, food could be brought more easily to areas experiencing famine. People had access to better nutrition as a result of the spread of New World crops like corn and especially the potato, which provided a much higher caloric yield per acre than grain. The Agricultural Revolution, which pioneered in the

Dutch Republic, moved to Britain, and spread from there to other countries, also played a role. Adoption of crop rotation, the introduction of new equipment like Tull's seed driller, and the use of horses rather than oxen for plowing all improved crop yields. Among the crops used in rotation were hay and clover, which were used to feed animals, with the result that there was more meat in people's diets. The availability of more food and more protein increased health, which also meant people were in better condition to survive famines when they did strike.

6. In what ways did Britain use war and aggression to achieve great-power status by 1763?

This question requires knowledge of British political and military history. Make sure you can discuss at least three wars. You'll need to explain why Britain was able to win these wars (its commercial strength, its well-developed sense of nationalism, its competent leadership) and what its motivations were (commercial, maintaining the balance of power, religious).

Possible thesis: Britain aimed her military might against her chief rivals over the course of three centuries, defeating one enemy and moving on the next one. It forged alliances with other states that also sought to attack its enemies. By the end of the Seven Years' War, Britain was the dominant power in the New World and a great power on the continent, rivaled only by France.

Britain's first competitor was Spain. The tensions between the two states were partially religious, as Spain was the great defender of Catholicism and England had broken away from the Catholic Church. Spain tried to invade England in 1588 with the Armada, only to meet with disastrous defeat. Queen Elizabeth encouraged Sir Walter Raleigh and others to engage in acts of piracy to steal or sink Spanish ships carrying gold and silver back to Spain from the New World. While it was only one reason for the decline of Spain in the seventeenth century, England's hostility to Spain was certainly an important factor.

Britain then turned its attention to Holland, which by the seventeenth century was the dominant force in international trade. Britain went to war with the Dutch three times in the seventeenth century, twice in alliance with France. In 1664, the Dutch ceded their colony of New Amsterdam to the British; it became New York. Dutch trade and finances were seriously affected by these wars; so many Dutch ships were damaged and the wars were so costly that the Dutch ceased to be the dominant economic power in Europe.

Britain and France then became the chief rivals. During the War of the Spanish Succession, Britain, along with Austria, fought against France and prevented the union of the crowns of Spain and France. Britain acquired Gibraltar, Minorca, and the lucrative control of the slave trade. Some thirty years later, Britain aided Maria Theresa during the War of the Austrian Succession, to prevent a power vacuum from developing in the Austrian Empire, which would have removed an effective balance of power to France. Britain and France fought each other in the Seven Years' War. In the New World, Britain won decisively, with France forced to cede its colony in Canada to Britain. On the continent, the settlement ended with modest, but crucial, gains for Britain. The French ceded their trading colony along the Indian coast to Britain; this laid the basis for British domination of India in the next century.

Thus, by the end of the Seven Years' War, Britain had eliminated Spain and Holland as economic and imperial competitors and Britain had prevented French expansion.

7. To what degree and for what reasons did the social gulf between the upper and lower classes widen in the eighteenth century?

This is a social history question. It's important not to wallow in generalities but to provide specific evidence. While wealth had always divided the upper and lower classes, in the eighteenth century new elements were added to their differences, although in some areas, the gap between the classes closed a bit.

Factors dividing the classes: The upper class grew to disdain blood sports, which they had once enjoyed; upper-class women, under the influence of Enlightenment ideas, began to breast-feed their children and to treat them with tenderness, while lower-class women tended to continue to use wet nurses because of their need to work; poor women abandoned babies to foundling hospitals often set up by nobles and gentry as charities; the upper class read Enlightenment texts, whereas the lower classes read chapbooks; the well-to-do drank their tea at home, while the poor drank it at work; the upper classes had a rich diet with plentiful meats, while the diet of the poor remained carbohydrate-based, first bread and later potatoes; prostitutes were divided into two groups—poor women driven to it by lack of employment or marriage and often treated poorly, and the wealthy courtesans who served well-to-do clients and were usually well treated.

Factors lessening the divide between classes: Lower-class women had more possibilities to emulate the fashion of the upper class because of inexpensive imported cotton; both classes enjoyed drinking beer, wine, and hard liquors, which became more available to the poor as prices dropped; lower classes became more literate and increasingly participated in the exchange of ideas in coffeehouses and other public spaces; people of all classes enjoyed urban fairs and commercially produced entertainment; new religious movements like Pietism, Methodism, and Jansenism appealed to people of varied backgrounds.

PART 3
The Long Nineteenth Century

This part covers the following chapters in *A History of Western Society,* Eleventh Edition:

Chapter 19:   Revolutions in Politics, 1775–1815

Chapter 20:   The Revolution in Energy and Industry, ca. 1780–1850

Chapter 21:   Ideologies and Upheavals, 1815–1850

Chapter 22:   Life in the Emerging Urban Society, 1840–1914

Chapter 23:   The Age of Nationalism, 1850–1914

Chapter 24:   The West and the World, 1815–1914

Historians often call the years spanning the French Revolution to the beginning of World War I (1789–1914) the "long nineteenth century." It was the heyday of modern European civilization, a period of extraordinary change and European dominance on the world stage that ended with a catastrophic war that dramatically altered the balance of power in Europe. The two developments that made Europe soar, the French Revolution and the Industrial Revolution, both began in the late eighteenth century as outgrowths of earlier changes but were so remarkable in and of themselves that they changed the course of world history.

The French Revolution fundamentally overturned European absolutism and the social structure that had endured for centuries. The Old (Ancien) Regime involved aristocratic political and social dominance, the exclusion of commoners from both the body politic and society, and reverence for king, church, and tradition. What the French Revolution achieved was to put two previously limited classes—the bourgeoisie and the urban working classes—on the political map. These two classes threw the aristocrats out of power first in France and then, over the next 100 years, throughout the rest of the western world. At the same time, the French Revolution unleashed nationalism, already incipient, but now joined with notions of popular sovereignty and validation of the importance of the lower classes.

France had been the paradigm of the absolutist state, but one limitation of absolutism was that it depended so much on the quality of the monarchs. After Louis XIV's death in 1715, the succeeding Bourbons were not of his mettle and could not manage the increasing problems facing the monarchy. Those problems were fundamentally financial; in a society where the landowners (the nobles) do not pay property taxes, the government is forced to rely on the middle and lower classes for revenues. Essentially, the Revolution began because the French nobles were not willing to pay taxes or relinquish their privileges when the monarchy was desperately in debt. At first, the bourgeoisie—made up of wealthy merchants, manufacturers, judges, and professionals—claimed that political power was their right as the main taxpayers. The first stage of the Revolution established a constitutional monarchy, limiting suffrage to property owners and enacting liberal, laissez-faire policies. But as bourgeois interests contradicted those of the poorer classes (who wanted price controls, government-supplied employment, and political power) as well as those of the upper aristocracy and monarchy (who wanted to maintain the status quo), the Revolution quickly radicalized.

161

The Reign of Terror (1793–1794), led by committed revolutionaries, implemented the urban poor's policies and with brutal force repressed those who opposed them. Napoleon Bonaparte, an extraordinary general, was able to resolve these political and social tensions in his fifteen years in power in France by using his charisma and diplomacy to foster a sense of national unity and stability. He enshrined in his Civil Code many of the common goals that had prompted the 1789 revolution, like equality before the law, the end of feudal rights, and religious liberty. But at the same time, he restored law and order by becoming an authoritarian emperor and ending republican rule. Intellectual and cultural freedom were sacrificed in the name of political unity and military success. By conquering most of continental Europe, Napoleon spread the ideas and ideals of the French Revolution.

The Old Regime of other absolute states—Prussia, Austria, and Russia—and the constitutional monarchy of England, appalled by the excesses in France, defeated Napoleon. The Congress of Vienna restored the Bourbon dynasty to the French throne. But by 1848, when virtually every European city saw its streets barricaded by students, nationalists, and workers, the days of the Old Regime were numbered. Although it would take World War I to end these monarchies permanently, liberal as well as radical ideas were now on the stage along with mass politics.

Perhaps to an even greater degree than the French Revolution transformed the political landscape, the Industrial Revolution revolutionized not only the material conditions of life but also the social fabric in both private and public spheres. Beginning in England around the 1780s and on the continent after 1815, the Industrial Revolution radically improved the standard of living of people of all classes, changed the class structure of society, and radically altered the international balance of power by giving Europeans enormous advantages in warfare and technology. The term *Industrial Revolution* generally refers to the replacement of animal and human power by harnessed forms of natural energy (steam, then later electricity and oil). It encompassed the replacement of hand manufacturing at home or in small shops by the production of goods by machines in factories, the transportation of goods by railroads and steam-powered ships rather than horse-drawn carts and sailing ships, and mass consumption of goods. Industrialization was accompanied by urbanization, the addition of new classes of industrialists and workers to the social structure, and a slow but steady rise in the general standard of living.

At the same time as the Old Regime was challenged in France, England—already a secure constitutional monarchy—developed the world's first industrial economy. In the sixteenth and seventeenth centuries, England—along with some parts of the continent—had modernized medieval economic practices by creating the domestic system of manufacturing to avoid guild restrictions and by revolutionizing agriculture, which greatly increased the yield per acre (see *A History of Western Society,* Chapter 17). In the wake of the Agricultural Revolution and prompted by a growing population's increasing demand for manufactured goods, English manufacturers adopted inventions—such as the spinning jenny, the water frame, the cotton gin, and the power loom—to speed production, eventually creating the factory system of production. The new system demanded that workers come to the factory and work long, highly regimented hours in often brutal conditions The need for more coal to fuel the machinery led to the single most important invention, the steam engine, which also made possible the extraordinary transformation of travel and communication with steamships and railroads. The social and political consequences of this economic change were immense. Initially, the family economic unit remained intact, but working and living conditions were horrid. By 1850, the standard of living of the industrial workers improved, and new legislation restricted the working hours—and also the opportunities—for women and children. Industrialization spread to the continent, first in Belgium by the 1820s and then to the Germanic states, then to France and northern Italy by midcentury.

During the 1848 revolutions, Karl Marx and Friedrich Engels proposed in their *Communist Manifesto* a theory of historical change based on class and economic relationships. They saw the working classes as the vanguard of revolutionaries who could establish socially just societies by taking ownership of the means of production. Workers, they argued, created real value but were exploited by the very nature of the capitalistic system. Within a few decades, their ideas of "scientific socialism" were widely adopted by political organizations and unions of industrial workers. These ideas began to play important political roles in England, Germany, and France. By 1900, the Social Democratic Party was the largest political party in Germany.

Nationalism grew by leaps and bounds in the nineteenth century, coming to rival socialism as the dominant ideology in the twentieth century. People who defined themselves as nations—sharing culture, language, and sometimes religion—who were not already in nation-states, sought to become so. This led to instability in the Balkans and to the unifications of Italy and Germany after nearly a thousand years of division into numerous smaller states. Prussia (led by Otto von Bismarck) and Sardinia-Piedmont (led by Count Camillo Cavour) were the states that dominated the process. Their kings—the Hohenzollerns in Germany and the Savoys in Italy—became the respective ruling families of new nation-states. Italy was a constitutional monarchy, while Germany was created as a federal state, an empire headed by the kaiser. In each case, unification was accompanied by war. Germany, taking quickly to industrialization and soon competing with England, sought to protect the new state with a series of alliances. The unifications of Italy and Germany transformed the balance of power in Europe.

Nationalism was also at the root of the takeover of much of Africa and Asia by the European powers. Imperialism involved the acquisition of colonies with valuable resources for industrial production at home and for military strategy and national prestige. The competition for colonies was intense in the decades just before 1900, when in the Scramble for Africa only two African states remained independent of European control. England held the greatest number of colonies, and France was a close second; Germany and the Netherlands had only a few colonies each. This competition increased tensions among the European powers and was an important cause of World War I.

These economic and political transformations of the nineteenth century also had huge social consequences, transforming the class structure of Europe. Aristocrats who did not participate in the new industrial economy lost political power in the early twentieth century. As a result of the commercial revolution, the middle classes—composed originally of the artisan masters—now became professionals, government officials, and industrial and commercial managers. The peasantry shrank in size. The industrial working classes split into workers with skills who were generally decently paid and saw some upward mobility, and the vast majority of unskilled workers who did not. Workers organized into unions and then into political parties. Urbanization accompanied industrialization; by 1850, half of the people in England lived in cities.

Home and family life changed as well for all classes. "Separate spheres" for men and women, romantic love, and the cult of domesticity were new ideas that took hold in the second half of the nineteenth century. At the same time, life in the crowded cities was rife with crime, prostitution, and poverty. Although some improvements in public health reduced the outbreak of epidemics like cholera and rising wages allowed for improvements in clothes and housing for many workers, class differences in lifestyles became only more apparent in the course of the long nineteenth century.

CHAPTER 19
Revolutions in Politics,
1775–1815

Areas of focus: France, North America, Saint-Domingue (Haiti)

Main events: the American Revolution, the French Revolution, the Reign of Terror, Napoleonic reign and wars, the Haitian war for independence

---

The following is a thematic summary of the material covered in Chapter 19 of *A History of Western Society:*

Politics

✦ **AP Tip** The French Revolution and the reign of Napoleon Bonaparte marked the transition from the feudal to the modern state. Many courses in Modern European History begin there. While some historians find the origins of modern Europe in the Enlightenment or the Industrial Revolution, there is no doubt that the forces of nationalism, the ideologies, and the mass politics that define modern history were given great impetus by the French Revolution. In addition, it set the model for later revolutions, as Napoleon created a new type of popular, progressive, but authoritarian ruler.

✦ The French Revolution of 1789 overthrew the Old (Ancien) Regime, the feudal structure and government of the absolute monarchs. The last two French kings, Louis XV (r. 1715–1774) and Louis XVI (r. 1774–1792), were inadequate leaders, and their libertine behavior led to a desacralization of the monarchy.

✦ The American Revolution against British rule in the colonies and the resulting 1789 United States Constitution inspired reformers in France.

✦ In 1787, facing financial crisis, Louis XVI called an Assembly of Notables to approve a general tax on landed property, but the Assembly insisted that the Estates General — the traditional legislative body — be called to approve such a significant change. When the king tried to impose the tax by decree, it was invalidated by the Parlement of Paris, which had the right to approve royal decrees before they could become law. In 1788, his hand forced, Louis XVI called the Estates General into session for the first time in 175 years. An outburst of discussion everywhere in France accompanied the election of delegates, leading to a general agreement on the desirability of creating a constitutional monarchy and guarantees of individual liberty.

✦ When the Estates General had last met in 1614, each estate met separately and had one vote. In May 1789, the third estate called for the three estates to meet together and vote by delegate, which led to crisis and began the Revolution.

✦ **AP Tip** The revolutionaries had a tripartite slogan—*Liberté, Egalité, Fraternité*—that was shared by all classes in the beginning. But liberty, equality, and fraternity (brotherhood or nationalism) are often contradictory, and the different classes stressed different goals, which destroyed their early unity. A good structure to remember follows the revolutionary slogan: the first stage of the revolution focused on liberty, the "second revolution" on equality, and Napoleon's rule on fraternity.

✦ The following table traces the development and resolution of the French Revolution through the various governmental bodies ruling France:

Political Aspects of the Governments of France, 1789–1815	
THE FIRST STAGE: "LIBERTÉ"	
National Assembly (1789–1791)	✦ The delegates of the third estate declared themselves the National Assembly in June 1789 and swore the Tennis Court Oath not to disband until they had written a constitution for France. This was a radical assertion of sovereignty.
	✦ When the king responded by calling out the troops, angry Parisians (sans-culottes, artisans, and small traders) gathered arms and stormed the Bastille on July 14. The king relented; the National Assembly replaced the Estates General. Bastille Day is now France's national holiday.
	✦ In the summer of 1789, peasants rose up in a spontaneous rebellion against their feudal lords, which perpetuated widespread fear of landlord retaliation (the Great Fear). This fear intensified the rebellions, and on August 4, 1789, the nobles of France voluntarily relinquished their individual feudal privileges. Feudalism was abolished.
	✦ The National Assembly issued the *Declaration of the Rights of Man and of the Citizen* (August 27, 1789), which guaranteed legal equality before the law, representative government, and individual freedoms.
	✦ Seven thousand armed Parisian women marched on Versailles in October to protest high bread prices and brought the royal family back to Paris from Versailles.
	✦ France was reorganized into eighty-three departments, a structure retained to this day.
Constitutional Monarchy and Legislative Assembly (1791–1792)	✦ Louis XVI reluctantly accepted a new constitution that made him a limited monarch.
	✦ The kings of Austria and Prussia announced their readiness to go to war to protect the French monarchs. The French Legislative Assembly responded, in April 1792, by declaring war on Austria.
	✦ The king and queen attempted to flee Paris but were captured; the attempt to escape the country convinced many that they were traitors. A Parisian crowd stormed the royal palace at the Tuileries in August 1792. When the king sought refuge at the nearby Legislative Assembly, they instead arrested and imprisoned him.
	✦ Radical clubs such as the Jacobins formed to advocate for the urban masses.

THE SECOND STAGE: "EGALITÉ"	
The Republic and the National Convention (1792–1795)	✦ The National Convention, dominated by Jacobins, declared France a republic in September 1792 and wrote a very liberal constitution that was never put into effect. Because of war abroad and disorder at home, a twelve-man Committee of Public Safety, led by Robespierre, was installed as the government in April 1793.
	✦ The Convention convicted the king of treason and executed him in January 1793.
	✦ Rebellions against the Paris government arose in 1793 in the Vendée region of western France and in Lyons in central France, mostly for royalist, Christian, and localist reasons.
	✦ The Committee of Public Safety established special courts to prosecute dissidents, rebels, and traitors; some 40,000 French citizens were executed or died in prison, and hundreds of thousands more were arrested. This was known as the Reign of Terror (1793–1794).
	✦ The French army managed to hold off the Prussians and Austrians, and the Convention declared war on Britain, Holland, and Spain. An all-out military mobilization, including a draft, led to success on the battlefield and made the efficacy of ideologically committed and nationalistic troops evident. The French army held on to Haiti against the Spanish and English and repressed rebellions at home.
	✦ As the political conflicts within France intensified, Robespierre ordered the execution of his critics, including long-standing collaborators like Georges Jacques Danton. Moderates in the Convention then arrested Robespierre, who was guillotined in July 1794. This so-called Thermidorian Reaction (named for Thermidor, the month of the revolutionary calendar in which it occurred) ended the radical stage of the Revolution.
The Directory (1795–1799)	✦ A five-man committee and an indirectly elected legislative assembly ran France but faced opposition from conservatives and had little popular support. It ruled dictatorially.
	✦ Napoleon Bonaparte—a Corsican noble and dedicated revolutionary who had risen rapidly as an artillery officer and as a general with glorious victories in Italy—was seen by opponents of the Directory as strong and charismatic. In November 1799, Napoleon and two others staged a coup d'état. Napoleon became first consul, a move approved by the majority of French voters in a subsequent plebiscite. Napoleon offered internal order and national glory.

THE THIRD STAGE: "FRATERNITÉ"	
The Consulate and the Empire (1799–1814)	✦ The codification of the civil and criminal laws was one of Napoleon's most important accomplishments. The Napoleonic Code established equality under the law for all French men and the sanctity of private property, but it also limited the rights of many and stripped away some of the gains in rights given women in earlier stages of the Revolution.
	✦ Napoleon streamlined the bureaucracy, created equality of opportunity, and granted amnesty to 100,000 nobles who had emigrated during the Revolution.
	✦ Napoleon's regime was repressive. Newspapers were censored or shut down, and a secret police was established to ferret out and detain political opponents.
	✦ Napoleon crowned himself emperor in 1804, which was also approved by plebiscite.
	✦ Napoleon's armies won Austria's Italian and German holdings in 1801, defeated Austria and Russia at the Battle of Austerlitz in 1805, and defeated Prussia at Jena in 1806. He then abolished the Holy Roman Empire and replaced it with the Confederation of the Rhine.
	✦ A planned invasion of England was thwarted by British victory at Trafalgar in 1805. Napoleon tried to restrict British trade with the rest of Europe. This "continental system" led to smuggling and a counter-blockade against France.
	✦ In the New World, Napoleon had less success. The Haitians had revolted in 1791, and their revolutionary leader Toussaint L'Ouverture was increasingly independent of France. Napoleon, who had re-established slavery in the colonies in 1799, had L'Ouverture arrested and brought to France, where he died. His followers routed the French forces, and Haiti became independent in 1804, marking the first successful revolution in Latin America and the only successful slave rebellion in history. In the wake of his failure to secure Haiti, Napoleon sold Louisiana to the United States in 1803.
	✦ Napoleon's Grand Empire reached its zenith in 1810. Only England stayed outside his orbit. Napoleon abolished feudalism in conquered states, but his imposition of French ideas and high taxes sparked nationalistic reaction, such as in Spain in 1808.
	✦ Napoleon was ultimately undone by his invasion of Russia in 1812. The Grand Army of more than half a million men was forced to retreat from Moscow in one of the greatest disasters in military history. Britain, Austria, Prussia, and Russia formed a coalition in the Treaty of Chaumont and defeated Napoleon in 1814.

The Restored Bourbon Monarchy (1814–1815)	✦ Napoleon abdicated in 1814 and went into exile on Elba, and the Bourbons were restored but as constitutional monarchs. Napoleon returned to power the following year for 100 days, but he was defeated on the battlefield of Waterloo by the combined European powers and sent into exile on a distant island, where he died in 1821.

Economy

+ Among the major causes of the French Revolution was the huge debt held by the monarchy because of its costly wars and its aid to the American colonies in their war against the British. France lacked a central bank and paper currency.

+ The harvests in 1788 were poor, which led to soaring bread prices and high urban unemployment as demand for manufactured goods dried up.

+ The National Assembly, following laissez-faire ideas, banned monopolies, guilds, and workers' associations, which served bourgeois interests but not those of the urban poor.

+ In 1790, new paper currency, *assignats,* was issued. It was backed by confiscated church lands.

+ The Committee of Public Safety created a type of socialistic economy, with nationalized workshops and maximum prices and rationing for key goods.

+ Napoleon established the Bank of France in 1800.

Religion

+ The National Assembly deprived the church of its right to tithe and confiscated its lands. In 1790, the Civil Constitution of the Clergy made priests state employees and put the church under the authority of the government, to whom clergymen had to swear allegiance. Only about half the clergy swore the loyalty oath.

+ The Convention attempted to de-Christianize France with a new calendar eliminating all religious elements, and by encouraging the Cult of Reason and creating civic holidays.

+ The Catholic Church and the government of France were reconciled through Napoleon's 1803 Concordat with the pope, in which Catholics were granted freedom of religion and Napoleon gained political power and influence over the church.

Society and Culture

+ Among the causes of the 1789 Revolution was the long-standing legal division of 25 million French people into one of three estates: the clergy, or first estate, which numbered about 100,000; the nobility, or second estate, which numbered about 400,000; and the third estate, made up of everyone else from the wealthy middle class to peasants, about 98 percent of the population. Both the first and second estates enjoyed tax exemptions and legal privileges. Many of the bourgeoisie and nobles were linked by marriage and business ties, and they shared Enlightenment ideas.

✦ Women were excluded from the 1789 *Declaration of the Rights of Man and of the Citizen,* and later the Convention banned women's political clubs. Olympe de Gouges published her own version of the Declaration in protest, and in 1792 Mary Wollstone-craft published *A Vindication of the Rights of Woman.* Napoleon restricted the rights of women and enhanced the authority of husbands over wives and children.

✦ The Committee of Public Safety abolished slavery in Haiti and all other French territories. Slavery was reinstated in the colonies by Napoleon.

✦ Napoleon set up elite schools for able young men of all classes to provide greater equality of opportunity. They still serve to create France's professional elite.

Ideas and Literature

✦ The widely popular pamphlet by Abbé de Sieyès, *What Is the Third Estate?,* defended the legitimacy of the demands of the bourgeoisie in 1789.

✦ Edmund Burke eloquently argued in his 1790 *Reflections on the Revolution in France* that rapid reform would lead only to tyranny and chaos.

✦ Napoleon spread Enlightenment ideas throughout Europe, but he repressed dissent, censored and banned newspapers, and persecuted intellectuals resisting him.

Arts

✦ Songs and political art were key ways people unified around the Revolution. Liberty was often personified as a woman.

✦ Napoleon favored Neoclassicism and had himself portrayed as a Roman emperor.

✦ Napoleon was seen by some as a romantic hero and painted as such by artists like Jacques-Louis David.

✦ Spanish artist Francisco Goya made powerful antiwar paintings and drawings during the French suppression of a Spanish revolt against their rule.

CHAPTER 20
The Revolution in Energy and Industry, ca. 1780–1850

Areas of focus: Great Britain, continental Europe

Main events: invention of the steam engine, the Industrial Revolution, the factory system, urbanization

---

The following is a thematic summary of the material covered in Chapter 20 of *A History of Western Society:*

Politics

✦ **AP Tip** The Industrial Revolution transformed Europe and had an equal or even greater impact on the entire world. Economic, social, political, and intellectual elements were intertwined in this process. Many AP essay questions focus on its social impact and political consequences. This is a good chapter to review heavily.

✦ The Industrial Revolution began in Britain, already a powerful nation with a stable political life, and made Britain the dominant world power for the next 100 years.

✦ Industrial workers emerged as a political force when they began to organize and advocate for political change. Unions were banned in Britain by the Combination Acts from 1799 to 1824. Anticapitalistic sentiments were expressed in newspapers, strikes, and protests. Over time they turned into political movements. In the 1830s, an attempt to create a national union failed. A few unions, like the machinists, won benefits.

✦ In the 1840s, many workers joined the Chartists, a reformist movement for political democracy whose greatest demand was universal manhood suffrage. Others became involved in political organizations to limit the workday and to lower bread prices by abolishing protectionist tariffs against foreign wheat (the Corn Laws; read more in *A History of Western Society,* Chapter 21).

✦ Parliament established commissions to investigate conditions in the mines and factories. It passed legislation to restrict abuses, such the Factory Act of 1833, which limited the hours of children, and the Mines Act of 1842, which banned women from working as miners.

✦ On the continent, industrialization developed with significant involvement of government, quite a different pattern than in Britain, where the government was little involved. By the outbreak of World War I in 1914, industrialization had progressed to a significant degree in Germany, Belgium, and France, but much less so in Italy, Russia, and Austria-Hungary. Governments used tariff protection to protect industries, to build roads and canals, and to fund the construction of railroads.

✦ By the mid-nineteenth century, Britain was moving toward free trade, with no import or export duties, and had repealed tariff protection laws; elsewhere economic nationalism dominated.

✦ In 1834 the *Zollverein,* a customs union of Germanic states, formed to remove trade barriers and forge common economic policies.

Economy

✦ Britain had a unique combination of factors that fostered industrialization as the solution to the economic needs of its rising population: a huge colonial empire that provided guaranteed markets as well as tax revenues and raw materials; wealth from trade in slaves and other goods; a well-developed shipbuilding industry; canals and plentiful rivers; highly productive agriculture; a national bank to provide credit; a mobile labor force; and substantial natural resources of coal and iron.

✦ The Industrial Revolution began in the textile industry, the most important sphere of manufacturing for centuries, when the cottage industry could not meet increasing consumer demand. Inventions increased production. The spinning jenny produced multiple threads from one spinning wheel, and the water frame—which used waterpower to operate spinning machines, threadmaking machines, and power looms—moved workers from the cottages to factories by the late eighteenth century.

✦ Early industrialists, coming from varied backgrounds, were often in precarious financial straits and cut production costs, including jobs and wages.

✦ Working conditions in early factories were terrible—regimented, unsafe, and brutal.

✦ Factories increased the demand for power provided by coal. The steam engine was invented in the 1760s to pump water out of coal mines, and it soon became the linchpin of the industrial economy.

✦ By 1850, Britain was covered with railroad tracks, which radically reduced the cost of shipping and opened previously inaccessible markets. As a result, Britain became the "workshop of the world," increasing British share of the world's industrial output tenfold.

✦ Continental states lacked British sources of capital for investment but had to compete with Britain. Capitalists imported British technology and workers, and numerous clever Englishmen went abroad to set up industrial enterprises. France, Belgium, and Germany implemented industrialization at the governmental level.

Religion

✦ Men and women working together, often unsupervised and in physically uncomfortable or dirty conditions, led to an easy intimacy, reducing adherence to strict religious rules about sexual behavior. This partially explains the explosion of illegitimate births in the late eighteenth century.

Society and Culture

✦ Urbanization, population growth, and significant changes in the social structure and family life accompanied industrialization.

✦ In the early years of industrialization, workers in factories and coal mines were often abandoned orphans—boys and girls as young as five or six—or women, who were paid very little for working long hours. They labored under strict and often brutal discipline.

✦ Many cottage workers were not willing to work in the new cotton mills because of the monotony of machine labor and the loss of the freedom to choose when to work. Those who made the switch continued their tradition of working as family units, with parents disciplining and working alongside their children. Parliament's Factory Act (1833) ended this pattern of the family working together.

✦ Overall, the living and working conditions of laborers were terrible until around 1850. Workers' purchasing power did not improve in the early years of industrialization. Statistical analysis shows that living conditions and wages declined until 1820. Many early factory workers lived in poorhouses, a type of industrial prison where they had to work to keep their lodging and food.

✦ By around 1840, real wages went up and the standard of living improved; poor people could afford cotton outer clothing and underwear, and they ate more varied food.

✦ Industrial workers typically worked some fifty days more a year in 1830 than farm laborers had worked in 1760. They worked about eleven hours per day.

✦ Population increased dramatically, more than doubling in eighty years, providing both more laborers and more consumers.

✦ Women had played an important role in many early enterprises but later were excluded and prohibited from certain industrial employment. Factory work became gendered, and the notion of "separate spheres" with a new ideal of domesticity emerged. Women were paid substantially less than men for the same work and given the poorer jobs. Over time, working-class women became less likely to work full-time, as that made it difficult to take care of babies and the household. Some workers resisted industrialization.

✦ Luddites, mostly artisans, protested vehemently against machine manufacturing by destroying machines.

✦ Even with industrialization under full sway, farming was still the primary occupation for the majority of British workers in 1850, and domestic service was the second-largest occupation.

✦ Robert Owen (1771–1858), a successful manufacturer who believed that workers would be more productive if treated well, formed cooperative, socialistic communities of workers.

✦ Class-consciousness in both middle and working classes rose as the industrial system created clearer demarcations in occupation and lifestyle.

Ideas and Literature

✦ Population growth was of much concern to observers at the time. Thomas Malthus argued in his famous 1798 *Essay on the Principle of Population* that population always grows faster than the food supply, meaning that poverty is inevitable unless there are "positive checks" to population growth (such as war or epidemics) or "prudential restraint" of young people (marrying late and limiting reproduction). Stockbroker and economist David Ricardo articulated the "iron law of wages," arguing that wages would always sink to subsistence level because of overpopulation.

✦ **AP Tip**   Thomas Malthus, David Ricardo, and Adam Smith are considered "classical liberals." The terms *liberal* and *conservative* had quite different meanings in the nineteenth century than they did in the twentieth. Liberals encouraged the passing of the Combination (anti–trade union) Acts (1799) and legislation freeing up the craft guilds on the basis that unions and guilds restricted the free operation of the market. Conservatives pushed for various factory and mine acts to protect workers and reduce the freedom of industrialists to operate without any regulation.

✦ Active government support for industrialization was encouraged by Friedrich List (1789–1846), a German journalist who argued in his influential *National System of Political Economy* (1841) that industrialization would lead to the reduction of poverty and would strengthen the defenses of the German nation.

✦ Romantic writers, such as the poets William Blake and William Wordsworth, lamented the loss of the rural lifestyle and protested the conditions of the urban poor.

✦ After visiting Manchester, Friedrich Engels (1820–1895), later a colleague of Karl Marx, wrote passionately about the horrific factory conditions in his *Conditions of the Working Class in England*. He bluntly blamed the middle classes for their exploitation and mistreatment of the workers. Engels and Marx argued that the poverty of urban workers was worse than rural poverty, because of relentless competition for jobs and demands on workers.

✦ Some contemporaries of Marx and Engels believed that conditions were improving for the workers. Andrew Ure described good conditions in cotton factories in 1835. Edwin Chadwick, a reformer and government official, asserted that the poor had more disposable income than they had had before.

Arts

✦ The Great Exhibition of 1851 at the Crystal Palace, so called because it was made of glass and iron, demonstrated Britain's industrial exuberance.

✦ A number of important artists—including J. M. W. Turner and Claude Monet—were fascinated by the steam power of trains and the majesty of train stations and railway bridges.

✦ Many artists portrayed factory life. Illustrations of young girls working in coal mines were instrumental in getting the Mines Act of 1842 passed.

CHAPTER 21
Ideologies and Upheavals, 1815–1850

> **Areas of focus:** Great Britain, France, Prussia, Austria, Greece
>
> **Main events:** the romantic movement, Metternich system, Great Reform Bill of 1832, the 1848 revolutions, Irish potato famine, *The Communist Manifesto*

The following is a thematic summary of the material covered in Chapter 21 of *A History of Western Society:*

Politics

+ The profoundly conservative Congress of Vienna restored the legitimate monarchs displaced by Napoleon's rule, and (with a few exceptions) undid the changes he had made. The four victorious powers (the Quadruple Alliance of Russia, Prussia, Austria, and Great Britain) gained some lands, not entirely at the expense of France, which lost relatively little territory.

+ After the Napoleonic wars (1803–1815; see *A History of Western Society,* Chapter 19), the major European powers (including France) formed a series of alliances and met periodically to enforce the peace settlement through military action, repressing liberal revolts in Spain and Sicily in the early 1820s. This system, enacted by Austrian foreign minister Klemens von Metternich, was generally successful until 1848, although Greece, Belgium, and the American colonies held by Spain gained independence in the intervening years.

+ Metternich imposed political repression in the German Confederation (Austria, Prussia, and thirty-seven other states) through the infamous Carlsbad Decrees (1819), which restricted freedom of assembly and the press and academic freedom in German universities. The Austrians feared liberalism and nationalism from two strong nationalities, the Hungarians (Magyars) and the Czechs (Bohemians), and dozens of other peoples in the empire.

+ **AP Tip** A good cross-period comparative topic might contrast the decisions and long-term consequences of the Congress of Vienna (1814–1815) with the Treaty of Versailles after World War I (1919; see *A History of Western Society,* Chapter 25, pp. 851–857). This chapter focuses on both political and intellectual history and their intersection in a revolutionary era. Be mindful of the big-picture changes taking place across the world stage during this period.

✦ Great Britain underwent significant political change in 1832 when the Great Reform Bill redistributed the seats in Parliament, expanded suffrage, and made the House of Commons more important than the House of Lords.

✦ Liberals in Parliament in the 1820s pushed through legislation providing civil rights for Catholics and Jews. In alliance with workers in the Anti–Corn Law League, they won repeal of these laws in 1846. Workers pushed for greater democracy in the Chartist movement, with 6 million people signing petitions that were soon rejected by the House of Commons.

✦ The British laissez-faire policies resulted in a slow, inadequate response to the Irish potato famine of the 1840s, which would later prompt Irish patriots to recall the tragedies of the famine when campaigning for home rule, land reforms, and independence from Great Britain.

✦ France became a constitutional monarchy when the Bourbons were restored in 1814. Charles X became king in 1824 and tried to restore unlimited monarchy. He repudiated the Constitutional Charter of 1814, censored the press, and reduced voting rights. In 1830, Parisian artisans, with many other groups, brought down the government. The new king, Louis Philippe (r. 1830–1848), restored the Constitutional Charter and called himself the "king of the French people." But many saw the "bourgeois monarchy" as corrupt, indifferent to the needs of the people, and resistant to electoral reform. These frustrations burst forth in Paris in the spring of 1848, sparking revolutions in most European states except England and Russia.

✦ **AP Tip**   The revolutions of 1848 are complex, multifaceted, and often confusing to students. Use the table on page 177 to clarify the chief events and issues in France, Austria, and Prussia. Get a clear sense of the conflicting ideologies involved so you can understand the shifting alliances of the revolutions.

✦ The year 1848 was an extraordinary and unprecedented one in which governments were toppled; kings and ministers fled; various promises were made to the people; and nationalism, liberalism, socialism, romanticism, and economic crises played various roles. Overall, the revolutions of 1848 achieved relatively little, as autocratic rulers successfully repressed nationalistic and socialistic forces. There were some permanent changes, however: the abolition of serfdom and slavery and the establishment of universal manhood suffrage in France, and some acknowledgement of the legitimacy of constitutionalism in most other states.

Economy

✦ **AP Tip**   The mutual relationship between economic and political changes that fused and reinforced each other after 1815 has been called a "dual revolution." Although they appear in two separate categories here, the economic and political happenings of this time are intricately related. Review the political changes in order to review the economic.

✦ The repeal of the Corn Laws in 1846 meant the victory of free trade in England.

✦ The House of Commons passed legislation to address the worst abuses of the factory system, limited the employment of children and women, and gave them a ten-hour workday.

Causes and Results of the 1848 Revolution

COUNTRY/ CHIEF MOVEMENTS	INITIAL SUCCESSES	PROBLEMS	END OF THE REVOLUTION
France: Liberalism and Socialism	Artisans and laborers barricaded the streets of Paris; Louis Philippe abdicated. The Provisional Government abolished slavery in the colonies and the death penalty. Parisian workers got a ten-hour workday. National workshops provided public works projects for the unemployed.	Divisions grew between workers wanting social and economic change and the middle classes wanting only political change. In May, moderates won in the first election with universal manhood suffrage. The new government canceled the national workshops.	A spontaneous uprising in Paris, the "June Days," ensued. Some 10,000 people died in its repression. In December, Louis Napoleon, the nephew of the late emperor, was elected with a huge majority and created an authoritarian regime.
The Austrian Empire: Nationalism and Liberalism	Subject nationalities such as the Hungarians sought both independence from Austrian rule and liberal constitutions. In Vienna, students and workers rebelled and Metternich fled. The Habsburg emperor Ferdinand I promised a constitution and abolished serfdom.	The peasants were content with their gains, but the middle classes feared the socialism demanded by workers. The Hungarian nationalists alienated the Slavic minorities in their part of the empire, and Czech nationalists fought German ones.	The emperor abdicated in favor of the eighteen-year-old Francis Joseph. The loyal army crushed radicals in Prague and Vienna. Russian troops ended the Hungarian republic. Nationalism re-surged throughout the empire in the second half of the nineteenth century.
Prussia: Liberalism and Nationalism	Prussian liberals were supported in March 1848 by artisans and factory workers; together they forced King Frederick William IV to make concessions.	Liberals wrote a constitution for a unified Germany at the Frankfurt assembly. They elected the king of Prussia as emperor.	Frederick William refused to take a "crown from the gutter." He took back control of Berlin, and he restored autocracy.

Religion

✦ Religious conflicts played little role in the post-Napoleonic period, except in Ireland.

✦ Catholics and Jews won some civil rights in Britain and in Prussia.

Society and Culture

✦ In Ireland in the 1840s, the potato crop failed because of blight. The Great Famine (1845–1851) and terrible diseases killed about one and a half million people and forced another one million Irish to flee the country. Ireland was the only area in Europe to lose population in the nineteenth century.

Ideas and Literature

✦ Powerful ideologies—conservatism, liberalism, nationalism, and socialism—developed in the early nineteenth century but were not mutually exclusive. Many nationalists were liberals; others were conservatives. Socialists were more isolated. Marxian socialism rejected nationalism, arguing that class, not nationality, determined identity.

✦ *Conservatism* insisted that traditional ruling elites and values would conserve stability, while liberalism, socialism, and nationalism would lead to revolution, violence, and less freedom.

✦ *Liberalism,* which stressed freedom, had two strands. *Political liberals* fought for constitutional government, equality before the law, the expansion of suffrage, and civil liberties. *Economic or classical liberals* opposed all hindrances to the free operation of the market. Businessmen enthusiastically joined in, frequently working with political liberals to secure their economic interests, but they often wanted to limit suffrage.

✦ *Nationalism* also had several strands. *Cultural nationalism* asserted that each nation (or people) has a distinct identity based on common language, food, music, and often, but not always, religion. Nationalists used emotionally laden symbols, folk legends, music, and (after 1850) mass education to create their "imagined communities." *Political nationalism* in already formed states meant love of country and efforts to enhance its prestige and power. In the multinational Austrian, Ottoman, and Russian empires, cultural nationalism grew into political demands for independence for subject nationalities.

✦ *Socialism* generally sought a just society to benefit the common people with a planned economy. Socialists wanted either the abolition or restriction of private property in favor of ownership by communes or by the state in the name of the people. Count Henri de Saint-Simon called for industrial development directed by a technocratic elite; fellow Frenchman Charles Fourier established small model communities with free choice in work and love. Louis Blanc, who played a key role in the 1848 revolution in France, demanded the government provide full employment. Pierre Proudhon was an anarchist who articulated a profoundly socialist idea in his 1840 pamphlet *What Is Property?* His answer, "Property is theft," denied the legitimacy of private property.

✦ Karl Marx and Friedrich Engels, in the *Communist Manifesto* (1848) called upon the workers to revolt. Marxism is both a theoretical analysis of history and society as well as an impassioned call for political action. It asserts that all profit is exploitative, that history is about class struggle between two classes in any society—the owners of the means of production (farms, factories, and so on) and those who work for them. *Marxian Socialism* argued that the victory of the urban industrial class, the proletariat, was inevitable and would create a just utopia.

✦ Romanticism was less an ideology than a movement with many threads, some romantics being conservative or even reactionary, others liberal or nationalistic. It appealed to many young artists, writers, and composers. Rejecting Enlightenment rationalism and classicism, romantics lamented the changes brought by the Industrial Revolution and sought to live free of social conventions and materialism amid the power of nature.

Arts

✦ In music and art, romanticism lasted for most of the nineteenth century. Painters (John Constable, Eugène Delacroix, Joseph M. W. Turner) used dramatic scenes, exotic subjects, and intense colors. Romantic composers expanded the size of the symphony orchestra and the range of musical forms, and they wrote with emotionality and sometimes with nationalistic intent. Great composer-pianists like Franz Liszt performed before huge, adoring crowds at new concert halls. Ludwig van Beethoven was the archetypal romantic artist, a genius with a tortured life whose music was deeply affective.

✦ Romanticism also flowered in English and French literature (e.g., William Wordsworth, Sir Walter Scott, Victor Hugo, George Sand).

CHAPTER 22
Life in the Emerging Urban Society, 1840–1914

Areas of focus: England, France, Austria

Main events: Darwinian evolution, rebuilding of Paris, urban planning, germ theory, Second Industrial Revolution

---

The following is a thematic summary of the material covered in Chapter 22 of *A History of Western Society:*

Politics

+ Urban planning was instituted all over Europe. Governments built or subsidized public transportation systems, theaters, office buildings, museums, and middle-class housing. They razed slums and improved sanitation and sewage systems.

+ In Britain, reformer Edwin Chadwick applied Jeremy Bentham's utilitarian ideas to report on the new Poor Law enacted in 1834. His findings, published in 1842, ignited a nationwide public health movement and resulted in Britain's first public health law in 1846.

Economy

+ Real wages, the purchasing power of earned income, were increasing for the working classes of Europe, especially in Britain, where they doubled between 1850 and 1906.

+ Public transportation systems were built by private companies in London and by city governments on the continent to help industries and cities expand and reduce congestion. Europeans adopted two American innovations—the horse-drawn streetcar in the 1870s and the electric streetcar in the 1890s. Public transport use grew phenomenally after 1886.

+ Domestic servants—mostly women—were the largest single group of unskilled workers, and their numbers grew during this era. Women frequently married and transitioned to working-class families, but those who did not often joined the sweated industries, which paid low wages by the piece for goods made in the home.

180

Religion

- ✦ There was a general decline in church attendance and donations throughout Europe in the late nineteenth century, more in working-class urban neighborhoods than in middle-class or rural ones. Most people continued to have their children baptized, but religion played a reduced role in their lives, except in areas where religion thrived as the core of ethnic identity, as with Irish Catholics in Protestant Britain and Jews in Russia.

- ✦ Protestant and Catholic churches were conservative and were seen as such by the working class, many of whom were dissatisfied with the social order and customs that conservatism upheld.

- ✦ Religious people were greatly offended by the Darwinian theory of natural selection, but it was relatively quickly accepted by the mass of the population and tolerated by most religious establishments.

Society and Culture

- ✦ The Industrial Revolution transformed Europe from a rural society based on agriculture and ruled by the aristocracy to an urban, industrial society dominated by the bourgeoisie.

- ✦ By 1851, more than half of the British population lived in cities. Urban life was awful in the early nineteenth century, with overcrowded housing, rampant diseases like cholera, widespread poverty, inadequate sewage systems and toilets, and no public transportation.

- ✦ As urbanization intensified, reformers sought to make cities safe and livable. Cheap iron pipes were installed underground to carry sewage away and to provide clean water. Overall, the public health movement saved millions of lives; death rates dramatically declined after about 1880 in what has been called a "great silent revolution."

- ✦ In France, Napoleon III (r. 1848–1870) undertook a massive rebuilding of Paris. Under the direction of Baron Georges Haussmann, the old Paris disappeared. It was replaced by broad boulevards, parks and squares, new sewage and water systems, and apartment buildings in new residential areas.

- ✦ Everywhere in Europe, but particularly in Britain, the gap between rich and poor grew more noticeable. The aristocrats, still wealthy and influential, divided their time between grand country estates and splendid townhouses. Many intermarried with the wealthy middle classes and engaged in capitalistic exploitation of their own resources.

- ✦ The two ever-more important social classes—the middle classes (about 20 percent of the urban population) and the working classes (about 80 percent)—were each subdivided into several subclasses.

- ✦ The middle classes: The upper-middle class, highly successful in commerce, banking, and industry, mimicked the aristocracy. The middle-middle class of small industrialists and professionals like lawyers and physicians was less wealthy but solidly comfortable. The lower-middle class—the small shopkeepers, tiny manufacturers, and low-level shop or office workers—often had incomes no higher than those of skilled workers. Still, they were firmly committed to their middle-class status, forever seeking to move up in society and to distinguish themselves from proletarians. Teachers, nurses, and dentists achieved respectable middle-class status in this period.

✦ The working classes: The working classes were divided by the level of skill required for their work. Highly skilled workers such as cabinetmakers, masters of technology like railroad engineers and machinists, and managers like factory foremen became the labor aristocracy. They adopted middle-class values. The middle working class, semi-skilled workers, felt superior to the huge numbers of unskilled workers, street vendors, and day laborers who performed, in desperate competition, menial tasks. Working-class women often worked at home on sewing machines producing garments in a new version of the domestic system.

✦ The middle classes lived puritanically but well, followed fashion, read novels, and went to concerts and the opera. For the working class, drinking, going to music halls, and participating in (and betting on) spectator sports were the most popular leisure activities. The need to read racing forms encouraged literacy.

✦ By the mid-nineteenth century, illegitimacy rates declined as contraceptives like condoms and the diaphragm became more available and affordable to the working class. Unplanned pregnancies led increasingly to marriage and the establishment of two-parent households, which reflected the increase in working-class respectability and economic standing. In most working-class families, kinship ties remained strong.

✦ Romantic love began to replace arranged marriage as the best way to achieve human happiness, although in middle-class families in France, economic concerns still took precedence.

✦ Prostitution was widespread, although it usually provided only temporary employment for poor women. Men of all classes patronized prostitutes, though the upper and middle classes supplied the majority of their earnings.

✦ Gender roles changed dramatically. Men and women were seen as inhabiting separate spheres: husbands were breadwinners, wives were household managers. Only poor women worked outside the home.

✦ Middle-class women began to agitate for equal legal rights and access to education and employment, as married women had few legal rights or work options. Feminists achieved some victories, but women were still barred from universities and most professions. Socialists argued that women's issues were a diversion from the goal of liberation for the entire working class.

✦ Child-rearing practices changed with the decline in the infant mortality rate. Women made greater emotional commitments to their children and increasingly breast-fed them rather than employing wet nurses. More parents limited the number of children they had, leading to a decline in the birthrate and the shrinking of family size to about six by the 1890s and to about four by the 1920s. Middle-class parents had fewer children but invested more in each of them. Working-class children, particularly boys, had easier times breaking free of strict household rules because they could leave home to work and earn bargaining power.

Ideas and Literature

✦ **AP Tip** It might seem that the various threads of this chapter—philosophical and scientific ideas, urban planning, and social history—have little to do with each other. In fact, intellectuals were responding to visible changes in urban life around them and proposing solutions to problems. Philosophy and social science was largely rooted in reality.

- There were major advances in scientific knowledge with the discovery of the fundamental laws of thermodynamics, the periodic table, and electromagnetism. The practical application of science, as in the new chemistry industry, increased its prestige. The Enlightenment's faith in progress seemed verified by improvements visible everywhere.

- Charles Darwin's (1809–1882) theory of evolution fundamentally altered conceptions about human origins and development. It was enormously influential. Darwinism was applied by thinkers such as Herbert Spencer (who came up with the phrase "survival of the fittest") to human society in a doctrine known as Social Darwinism, popular with the middle classes. It proposed that humans engage in a fierce struggle for survival, and that the poor are so because they are unfit.

- Late-nineteenth-century literary authors turned to realism, using prose more often than poetry, to report on contemporary social conditions and the daily life of the middle and working classes. They wrote about previously taboo topics including adultery, slums, strikes, violence, and alcoholism. Social determinists, they believed that heredity in conjunction with environment determined human behavior.

- The three great realistic authors in France were Honoré de Balzac, Gustave Flaubert, and Émile Zola. George Eliot and Thomas Hardy were two important British realists. In Russia, the masterful Leo Tolstoy wrote *War and Peace* about the French invasion of Russia in 1812.

- The table on page 184 highlights major scientists and theorists of the late nineteenth century.

Arts

- Artists too turned to realism, portraying urban life in its exciting variety, from elegant dinner parties to dance halls. French painters Gustave Courbet, Jean-François Millet, and Honoré Daumier painted scenes of laboring workers and peasants, using somber colors and simple composition.

- Illustrations in magazines and newspapers highlighted the plight of the urban poor.

FIELD OF STUDY	MAIN FIGURES AND WORKS	KEY IDEAS
Medicine	Edwin Chadwick, 1840s	Disease is spread by filth.
	Louis Pasteur, 1850s	Disease is spread by germs.
	Joseph Lister, 1860s	Antiseptic principle: surgical procedures must be clean.
	Robert Koch, 1870s	Specific bacteria cause specific diseases.
Biology	Charles Darwin *On the Origin of Species,* 1859; *The Descent of Man,* 1871	Species change through evolution, caused not as Lamarck suggested by inheritance of acquired characteristics, but by accidental mutations. These give certain members of a species advantages in their environment so that they survive, while others without these traits die out; the survivors reproduce, spreading their characteristics through populations; all life forms have evolved through the "struggle for survival."
Political Economy	Jeremy Bentham	Utilitarianism, the rational calculation of social problems to achieve "the greatest good for the greatest number."
Sociology	August Comte *System of Positive Philosophy,* 1830–1842; *A General View of Positivism,* 1856	The use of the scientific method (also called the positivist method) will lead social scientists to discover the laws of human relations.

The Age of Nationalism,
1850–1914

Areas of focus: Germany, Italy, England, France, United States, Austria, Russia, the Ottoman Empire

Main events: unifications of Italy and Germany, spread of Marxist socialism, 1905 revolution in Russia, revisionism

The following is a thematic summary of the material covered in Chapter 23 of *A History of Western Society:*

Politics

✦ **AP Tip**   This chapter offers a wealth of information for analysis of successful modernization (Germany, Italy, England, France) and incomplete efforts (the Russian, Ottoman, and Austrian Empires). These three empires collapsed at the end of World War I; understanding their weaknesses at the end of the nineteenth century is crucial to understanding why that happened.

✦ Although unsuccessful during the 1848 revolutions, nationalism became the dominant force in Europe in the second half of the nineteenth century and directly led to World War I. Appealing to people across class lines and political philosophies, the nation-state became the focus of strong nationalist sentiments that grew even deeper as suffrage increased.

✦ In France, Louis Napoleon Bonaparte was overwhelmingly elected president in December 1848. He staged a coup d'état in December 1851, and he declared himself Emperor Napoleon III the following year. He established an authoritarian government but won widespread approval by modernizing the economy, building railroads and housing, transforming Paris, and giving workers the right to form unions and to strike.

✦ The end of Louis III's regime, after its defeat by Germany in 1871, led to the last major Parisian revolution, the Commune, brutally repressed after two months. France became a republic permanently in 1871. About twenty-five years later, political divisions over the Dreyfus affair, when the first Jewish officer in the French army was falsely accused of treason, tore the Third Republic apart.

✦ The unifications of Italy and Germany fulfilled nationalist dreams and changed not only the face of Europe but also its balance of power. The weakest of the Great Powers in 1862, Prussia, became the most powerful state in Europe in less than a decade. The following table summarizes the unification processes in Italy and Germany under the

The Unifications of Italy and Germany

	ITALY (1859–1870)	GERMANY (1866–1871)
Dominant State and Leading Figures	Kingdom of Sardinia-Piedmont Count Cavour (prime minister) Victor Emmanuel (king) Giuseppe Garibaldi (militia leader)	Kingdom of Prussia Otto von Bismarck (chancellor) William I (king)
Problems Facing Unifiers	Resistance of Catholic Church; Sicily under Bourbon control; Lombardy and Venetia under Austrian control	"Small" Germany (without Austria) vs. "big" Germany (with it); reluctance of Catholic states to join largely Lutheran nation
Wars and Stages of Unification	1859—War with Austria: Lombardy awarded to Piedmont 1860—Other states vote to join; Turin, then Florence as capital 1866—Venice added 1870—Rome added	1864—War with Denmark over Schleswig-Holstein 1866—Victory in Austro-Prussian War eliminates Austria from the new state 1867—North German Confederation, with twenty-two states as members 1870–1871—Prussian victory in Franco-Prussian war; Germany gains Alsace-Lorraine
Outcomes	Constitutional monarchy Rome capital of unified Italy Papacy loses the Papal States, withdraws into the Vatican, and has hostile relationship to Italy Some lands still held by Austria Limited suffrage Conflicts between industrial north and the mostly agricultural and feudal south Socialist Party formed Christian Democrats dominate	Strongest European state Federal empire headed by a kaiser (emperor) Individual provinces under traditional rulers A parliament elected by universal male suffrage but its approval not required for military or foreign policy decisions Relationship with France contentious Bismarck goes after perceived domestic enemies: first Catholics (a process called *Kulturkampf*), then the socialists, instituting Europe's first social welfare legislation (social security, etc.) to co-opt them Social Democrats become the largest party

leadership of Sicilian count Camillo Benso di Cavour and revolutionary nationalist Guiseppe Garibaldi (1807–1882), and Prussian politician Otto von Bismarck (1815–1898), respectively.

✦ Most western European states developed into one form or another of parliamentary democracy, whereby the party that wins the majority of seats in the parliament forms the cabinet and the head of the party becomes prime minister. Mass politics led to a proliferation of parties except in England, where two main parties alternated in power.

✦ Socialist parties grew in size and importance, and over time became less radical. They formed the Socialist International in 1864.

✦ Conservatives were often able to manipulate the liberal- or socialist-leaning masses by using aggressive foreign policies to appeal to nationalism.

✦ Russia was a vast multinational state under absolutist rule. Russia's defeat in the Crimean War (1853–1856) and its rapid population growth revealed the need for industrialization.

✦ Tsar Alexander II liberated the serfs in 1861, with peasants collectively given land for which they had to pay. He also established new local elected assemblies (*zemstvos*) and equality before the law, liberalized education, reduced restrictions on Jews, and encouraged industrialization. Radical anarchists, using terrorism to try to bring down the government, assassinated him. His successors, Alexander III (1881–1894) and Nicholas II (1894–1917), rejected reform and repressed political dissent.

✦ Russia's regression became all too apparent in its humiliating defeat by Japan in 1905, which led to a revolution. Liberals sought to turn Russia into a constitutional monarchy, radical Marxists led a (still illegal) labor movement, non-Russian nationalities wanted autonomy, and peasants resented their continuing poverty. Nicholas II made concessions on civil rights and allowed a parliament (the Duma), but autocracy remained, with the apparatus but not the reality of limited monarchy.

✦ The Ottoman Empire continued to lose power and territory into the nineteenth century. Realizing that modernization of industry, technology, and military forces was needed, statesmen launched an era of reforms (the Tanzimat) in 1839. Reforms established equality before the law for Muslims, Christians, and Jews; liberalized commercial laws; and encouraged Western education and secularism. Nevertheless, nationalism among non-Turkish subjects grew. In 1908, the Young Turks, a group of patriotic officers and intellectuals, seized power and forced political reforms.

✦ Britain's two great parties had towering leaders: Benjamin Disraeli for the Conservatives and William Gladstone for the Liberals. Extensive social legislation (national health insurance, unemployment benefits, old-age pensions) was passed, and suffrage was extended, though not to women. Militant suffragettes such as Emmeline Pankhurst publicly protested. Gladstone hoped to pacify Catholic Irish nationalists with home rule or self-government, but the minority Irish Protestants, living mostly in Ulster, resisted any change, and the issue remained unresolved.

✦ The Austro-Hungarian Empire, created in 1867, contended with the nationalistic demands of its many subject nationalities. The dual monarchy — one king wore both crowns — gave Hungary virtual independence and rule over some of the minorities in the empire. In the Austrian half, ethnic Germans felt threatened by the Slavs, especially the Poles and the Czechs. In their part of the empire, the Hungarians insisted that their language be used in government and schools, creating huge resentment among ethnic minorities of the region.

Economy

✦ In most European countries, as industrialization deepened, national wealth increased and the industrial classes became more prominent. Unions became legal in most of western Europe; as their membership skyrocketed, they began to play important political roles, using less radical rhetoric and focusing on collective bargaining for better wages and benefits.

✦ In the United States, deep divisions arose between the industrialized, urban North and the agricultural South. Northern whites felt their labor system was economically and morally superior to the slave-based agriculture system of the South. Divisions led to the Civil War, which lasted from 1861 to 1865. The North won the war, preventing secession of the South and ending slavery.

✦ When the tsar emancipated the serfs, it freed up the labor force and capital in Russia, and industrialization fostered by the government produced rather quick and marked change.

✦ **AP Tip**   There is a useful parallel between Russia and the United States here. Both countries developed large plantation agriculture, both used forms of unpaid labor (serfdom in Russia, chattel slavery in the states), and both liberated that population in the 1860s, which freed up their economies and contributed to their rise as major world powers in the twentieth century.

Religion

✦ Pope Pius IX (pontificate 1846–1878) issued the *Syllabus of Errors* (1864), which denounced rationalism, liberalism, and socialism. In 1870, the papacy articulated the doctrine of papal infallibility.

✦ European Jews had long been under severe restrictions, but liberalism and revolutionary sentiment asserting the equality of all men argued against such discrimination. Jews were granted civil rights in France in 1791, and legal equality in newly unified Germany in 1871. Many Jews responded gladly to the opportunities to succeed in professions previously denied to them, such as medicine, journalism, academia, and the law.

✦ Most newly emancipated Jews in western and central Europe joined the middle classes and became fervent patriotic nationalists. But at the same time, anti-Semitism grew more virulent. Partially a reaction against liberalism and modernization—which had propelled the Jews forward, partially a response to economic competition, and partially drawing on long-standing anti-Judaism, modern anti-Semitism was distinguished from former versions in that the vilified group was the Jewish race, not the Jewish religion. Anti-Semitism was most virulent in Russia and eastern Europe. In Russia, Jews were the occasional victims of mass attacks called pogroms, which were encouraged by the tsarist government.

Society and Culture

✦ **AP Tip**   As the political, ideological, and economic landscapes of European nations diverged, so did the social and cultural particularities of their people. While this chapter focuses more on the political upheaval and modernization under way (as do most questions about this period of history), there are still several general social trends to keep in mind.

✦ The demand for representation (suffrage) followed in the wake of industrialization, as did improvements to education and standard of living.

✦ By 1914, nationalism had evolved into an almost universal faith in Europe and the United States, and it appealed to the broad masses of society. Nationalism generally reduced social tensions, and the responsive nation-state improved city life and brought social benefits to ordinary people.

Ideas and Literature

✦ Racism, of which political anti-Semitism is one form, flourished in Europe at the turn of the twentieth century, sometimes combined with Social Darwinism.

✦ In response to rising anti-Semitism, an Austrian Jewish journalist in Paris, Theodor Herzl, delineated a new idea, Zionism. He sought the creation of a Jewish homeland to provide Jews with the benefits and protection of the nation-state. Assimilation, Herzl argued, would ultimately not work. The First Zionist Congress met in 1897.

✦ As socialist parties became less radical and workers more moderate, some socialist intellectuals, such as Eduard Bernstein in Germany, turned away from radical revolution and espoused revisionism, hoping that socialism would be achieved through electoral politics and unions.

Arts

✦ Nationalism brought forth impressive buildings sponsored by governments—from memorials to statues to government centers to cultural institutions. Art promoted nationalism with portrayals of historic events, landscapes, and portraits.

CHAPTER 24
The West and the World,
1815–1914

> **Areas of focus:** Britain, France, Belgium, Germany, Italy, Asia, and Africa
>
> **Main events:** Berlin Conference, European takeovers of African and Asian states, South African (Boer) War, the opium trade, the Great Rebellion in India, Meiji restoration in Japan, the Boxer Rebellion in China, the great migration

The following is a thematic summary of the material covered in Chapter 24 of *A History of Western Society:*

Politics

+ The three decades before World War I (1914–1918) were the high point of European expansionism. European states—particularly France and Britain, but also Belgium, Italy, and Germany to a lesser extent—competed to take, either peacefully or forcefully, valuable colonies in Asia and Africa.

+ **AP Tip** The two major periods of European expansion had many similarities but important differences. The comparative chart on the next page highlights the chief differences. In studying the new imperialism of this period, be sure to consider its social impact at home as well as in the colonies and the political controversies.

+ Competition between the European states fostered imperialism. No nation, it was said by the German nationalist historian Heinrich von Treitschke, could be great without colonies. Political control of colonies served economic and nationalist interests. Aggressive imperialistic policies increased tensions among the Europeans, however, and led to wars or near-wars with non-Europeans. European superiority in weapons and medicine made the "new imperialism" possible.

+ The Scramble for Africa was the single most remarkable development in the new imperialism. In 1850, only a small part of Africa was colonized: Mozambique and Angola (by Portugal), Algeria (by France), and South Africa (by the Dutch). In the 1880s and 1890s, virtually the entire continent of Africa was carved up, mostly between the British (who aimed for a "Cape to Cairo" empire) and the French, with Italy, Belgium, and Germany also taking important colonies.

+ Prior to the 1880s, conservatives like Otto von Bismarck opposed imperialism as unnecessary, burdensome, and dangerous. But by 1900, most, including Bismarck himself, favored imperialism.

European Expansion, ca. 1400–1900		
	EUROPEAN COLONIZATION 15TH–18TH CENTURIES	**EUROPEAN IMPERIALISM 19TH CENTURY**
Dominant European States Competing with Each Other	Britain, France, Spain, Holland, Portugal	Britain and France (later Germany, Belgium, and Italy)
Areas Colonized	Coastal ports in Africa, Indian subcontinent, Indonesia; entire territories in the Americas	Coastal and interior regions in Africa and Asia
Chief Motivations	"Gold, God, Glory"	Strategic outposts for navies, exclusive control over resources, guaranteed markets for goods, national prestige
Goods Sought in Colonies	Gold, slaves, spices, rum, molasses, sugar	Rubber, minerals, diamonds, tea, coffee
Political Control	Native governments of colonies in Asia and Africa left intact; direct rule in New World	Direct European rule or indirect rule in spheres of influence or through protectorates
Relationship of Europeans and Natives	Respect for native rulers; disdain for cultural practices; Christianizing missions	Disdain for native rulers and "racially inferior" Asians and Africans; "White Man's Burden" to civilize the "half-savage and half-child" natives

✦ "Effective occupation" was the rule for takeover set by the 1884–1885 Berlin Conference, called by Jules Ferry and Otto von Bismarck to avoid conflicting claims among the Europeans that might lead to war—and to prevent any one power from dominating Africa. The British took South Africa from the Dutch in the brutal South African War (also known as the Boer War) of 1899–1902 and gave it nominal independence in 1910. They took control of the Suez Canal and ruled Egypt indirectly.

✦ No colony was as notorious for its brutality as the Congo, the personal colony of the king of Belgium, Leopold. Perhaps some 10 million Congolese were killed or maimed by the colonists who punished them severely (cutting off hands and feet) if they didn't meet their quotas for rubber. As outrage grew, Leopold was forced by an international conference in 1908 to give up his personal control and hand the Congo over to the Belgian government.

✦ Parts of Asia were also taken over by Europeans: Indochina by the French, Indonesia by the Dutch, and Central Asia by Russia. China was forcibly opened up to western trade by the British in the Opium Wars of the 1840s, as was Japan by the "gunboat diplomacy" of the United States a decade later. India was Britain's "Jewel in the Crown," under direct rule of Parliament after the 1857 Great Rebellion, called the

Sepoy Mutiny by the British. Direct rule by Britain would last there until 1947, when India and Pakistan gained independence.

✦ Responses to imperialism varied. Within Europe, socialists generally opposed imperialism while nationalists were enthusiastic. In the colonies, traditionalists sought to preserve native culture and sometimes organized violent resistance, while Westernizers espoused what they considered to be superior Western models and values. In India, a Western-educated native elite did most of the administrative and military work of imperial control but resented the racial discrimination of the British; in 1885, educated Indians came together to establish the Indian National Congress. In Japan, the feudal state was abolished, the emperor restored by Meiji reformers, and Western-style political, economic, and educational institutions were adopted. In China, native resentment over the European spheres of influence broke out in the violent Boxer Rebellion in 1900. The Qing Dynasty lost prestige when it was unable to prevent Western penetration and was overthrown in a revolution in 1912 that established a republic.

Economy

✦ Industrialization widened the gap between the industrialized states and the rest of the world. Areas that did not industrialize during the nineteenth century (namely Africa, Asia, and Latin America) came to be subject to political or economic imperialism.

✦ World trade expanded enormously before World War I, growing in value to about twenty-five times what it had been in 1800, sped up by new technologies like the steamship and transoceanic telegraphic cables.

✦ Britain's already far-flung empire provided the British basis for expansion when industrialization produced too many cheap goods for absorption by the domestic market. Once free trade became its policy, Britain turned quickly into the world's emporium, selling goods produced at home around the globe and stimulating the exploitation of colonial resources for export to Europe, such as jute, hemp, and rubber and popular foodstuffs like tea, coffee, and sugar.

✦ Technological innovations in the second half of the nineteenth century were crucial to Europe's success. Steamships easily traveled around the world and could go upriver, allowing Europeans to penetrate to the interior as never before. New ports and the newly constructed Suez Canal (between the Mediterranean and the Red Seas) and Panama Canal (connecting the Pacific and Atlantic in Central America) made trade faster, more efficient, and more profitable.

✦ The British, Germans, and French, flush with capital from their own industries, made enormous investments overseas, mostly to other industrial nations.

✦ Domestic problems seemed less important because of successful imperialistic ventures and nationalistic pride. Propagandists for imperialism argued that imperialism benefited not only capitalists but also ordinary workers in that it provided jobs and cheap raw materials that kept down the cost of manufactured goods for them to enjoy. Tabloid journalism promoted nationalism and imperialism, as did special-interest groups like shippers and shipbuilders, settlers, missionaries, humanitarians, military men, and colonial officials.

✦ Economic motives were prominent in the new imperialism. Great Britain was losing its industrial lead to Germany and the United States, which made it value its old colonies like India all the more and try to secure new colonies. Critics saw European wealth as stolen from exploited colonized peoples, but others saw Europe's expansion as a product of its scientific and technological advances, capitalistic business organization, and distinct worldview.

Religion

+ Most Europeans and Americans believed that they had a mission to civilize the "barbarian" peoples of the world, to bring the benefits of modern medicine, education, political democracy, and Christianity—the glories of Western civilization—to the primitive peoples of the world, and to end barbaric practices.

+ Christian missionary work was highly successful in Africa but much less so in India, China, and the Muslim world.

Society and Culture

+ European population doubled in the nineteenth century and by 1914 accounted for 38 percent of the world's population, but after 1900 it began to decline.

+ Sixty million Europeans emigrated between 1815 and 1932, mostly going (although not necessarily permanently) to areas of previous European settlement; this is one reason European expansion had such impact around the globe. Twenty million of the migrants came from the British Isles, and more than half of those emigrated in the decade before World War I. But national groups left Europe at different times: the British and Irish from the 1840s on, the Germans in the 1850s and 1880s, and the Italians around 1900.

+ The United States accepted the largest number of immigrants, but less than half of the total. Most of the migrants were young unmarried farmers and artisans, not usually the impoverished. White settlers in sparsely populated areas (such as the Argentine or American plains) benefited easily at the expense of natives.

+ Although not in numbers as large as Europeans, a significant number of Asians (mostly Chinese, Japanese, Indians, and Filipinos) left their homelands to work as indentured laborers in mines and on plantations in the United States, Africa, and Latin America. European migrants disliked the influx of Asian migrants, and by the 1880s the United States and Australia had enacted discriminatory laws designed to prevent Asians from settling permanently.

Ideas and Literature

+ Social Darwinism combined with racism postulated competition among the white peoples for survival and their (rightful, it argued) exploitation of "inferior" races like blacks and Asians.

+ Tabloid journalism promoted nationalism and imperialism.

+ As imperialism grew, so did criticisms of it. The British economist J. A. Hobson in his 1902 work *Imperialism* delineated the classic Marxist analysis that imperialism existed because the rich needed to invest their excess capital, and in fact damaged the home country whose taxpayers bore the brunt of the costs. Workers were manipulated by nationalism and diverted from the class struggle, which delayed domestic reform.

✦ Influential British writer Rudyard Kipling's poem "The White Man's Burden" eloquently conveyed the humanistic mandate of imperialism, while a satire of it by British member of Parliament Henry Labouchère called "The Brown Man's Burden" indicted imperialism as racist, exploitative, and brutal. Joseph Conrad's 1902 novel *The Heart of Darkness* showed the corrupting influence of imperialism. These European critics provided an ideological basis for independence and liberation movements.

Arts

✦ European imperialism had a great impact on the arts at home, as artists were fascinated by, and thus absorbed and incorporated, the artistic styles of Africa and the East, vastly different from traditional European styles.

✦ Songs of conquering armies became part of the popular musical lexicon.

✦ Artists often portrayed exotic elements of colonized peoples and conveyed the excitement of travel in posters and advertisements.

PRACTICE EXAM 3

EUROPEAN HISTORY
SECTION I

Multiple-Choice Questions
(Time—55 minutes)
Number of questions—80

Directions: Each of the questions or incomplete statements below is followed by five suggested answers or completions. For each question, select the best response.

1. Thomas Malthus in the early nineteenth century

    (A) predicted a better standard of living as a result of the Industrial Revolution
    (B) predicted that population would outgrow food sources as a result of the Industrial Revolution
    (C) influenced the Parliament in Britain to pass the Reform Bill of 1832
    (D) created railroad monopolies
    (E) stimulated inventions in the textile industry

2. When Captain Alfred Dreyfus was convicted of treason in 1894, he was denounced by all of the following groups EXCEPT

    (A) the Catholic Church
    (B) the French government
    (C) anti-Semites
    (D) civil libertarians
    (E) fellow French soldiers

3. The building of railroads had all of the following effects in the nineteenth century EXCEPT

    (A) the construction of new factories in more locations
    (B) the creation of new jobs and an increase in production
    (C) an increase in the demand for skilled laborers
    (D) the introduction of new expressions in language and new cultural heroes
    (E) the urbanization of workers

4. The largest group of female unskilled laborers in the late nineteenth century was employed in

    (A) factories
    (B) mines
    (C) domestic service
    (D) nursing
    (E) offices

GO ON TO THE NEXT PAGE.

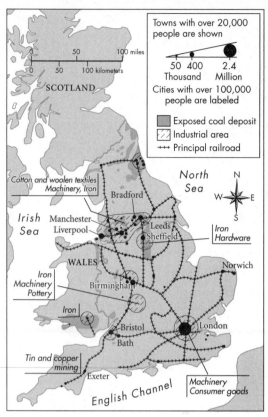

5. Which of the following statements is an accurate conclusion based on a comparison of these maps showing England (left) and the European continent in about 1850 (below)?

(A) England had more industrialized areas than the continent had emerging industrialized areas.

(B) England had a greater population than the German Confederation and France combined.

(C) The continent had more ironworks per capita than England.

(D) England had 50 percent more coalfields in terms of square miles than the continent did.

(E) England had a more efficient and interconnected railroad system than the continent did.

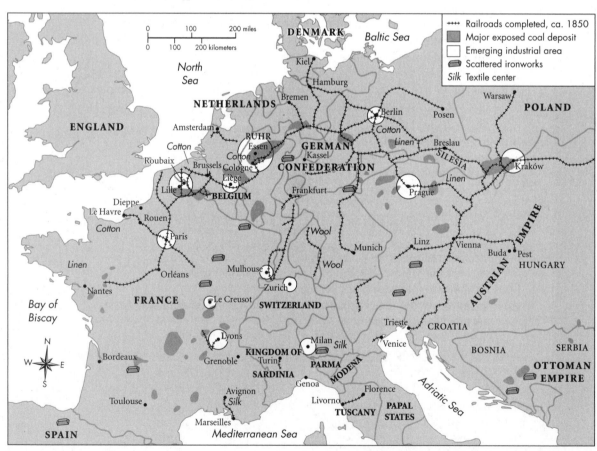

GO ON TO THE NEXT PAGE.

6. Romanticism in nineteenth-century art is best described as

   (A) an indirect protest against the inadequate social conditions
   (B) a school of painting that studied the effects of light and dark
   (C) very similar to Neoclassicism
   (D) secular in focus with careful and detailed portraiture
   (E) focusing on the dynamism of nature

Per Capita Levels of Industrialization, 1750–1913							
	1750	**1800**	**1830**	**1860**	**1880**	**1900**	**1913**
Great Britain	10	16	25	64	87	100	115
Belgium	9	10	14	28	43	56	88
United States	4	9	14	21	38	69	126
France	9	9	12	20	28	39	59
Germany	8	8	9	15	25	52	85
Austria-Hungary	7	7	8	11	15	23	32
Italy	8	8	8	10	12	17	26
Russia	6	6	7	8	10	15	20
China	8	6	6	4	4	3	3
India	7	6	6	3	2	1	2

Note: All entries are based on an index value of 100, equal to the per capita level of industrialization in Great Britain in 1900. Data for Great Britain includes Ireland, England, Wales, and Scotland.
Source: P. Bairoch, "International Industrialization Levels from 1750 to 1980," *Journal of European Economic History 1*1 (Spring 1982): 294, U.S. Journals at Cambridge University Press.

7. The table above illustrates

   (A) the gap between Great Britain's textile production and that of other countries
   (B) that Great Britain's per capita income increased four times by 1860
   (C) that the United States had the fastest rate of increase in per capita industrialization in the nineteenth century
   (D) that Germany was an industrial competitive force during the early nineteenth century
   (E) that East Asia was exhibiting its industrial potential in the nineteenth century

GO ON TO THE NEXT PAGE.

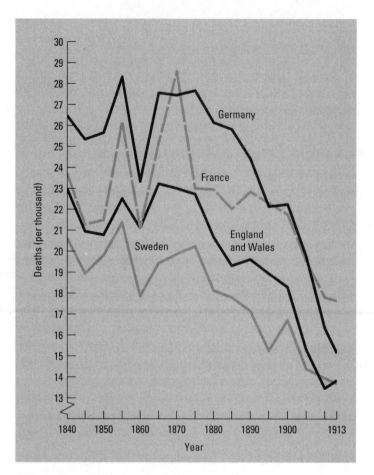

The Decline of Death Rates in England and Wales, Germany, France, and Sweden, 1840–1913

8. All of the following factors helped contribute to the trend exhibited by the chart above EXCEPT

   (A) a rising standard of living
   (B) improvements in public health
   (C) medical advances
   (D) the miasmatic theory of disease
   (E) the research of Louis Pasteur and Robert Koch

9. All of the following factors played a part in starting the French Revolution EXCEPT

   (A) religious struggles between Catholics and Huguenots
   (B) the success of the American Revolution
   (C) the rising debts of the French government
   (D) power struggles between the monarchy and the bourgeoisie
   (E) poor harvests and high bread prices

GO ON TO THE NEXT PAGE.

10. Why did the French so willingly submit themselves to Napoleon Bonaparte's rule?

   (A) Napoleon promised the French "peace, land, and bread."
   (B) French voters were charmed by his winning personality.
   (C) The French were no longer willing to submit themselves to absolute rulers.
   (D) Napoleon promised to continue the political reforms of the French Revolution.
   (E) The French were looking for stability and authority after years of turmoil.

11. One reason the Industrial Revolution began in Great Britain was that

   (A) inadequate farming methods made the British look for other sources of income
   (B) after years of political turmoil, the British were hoping industry would provide stability
   (C) the British never took part in cottage industry, so the country was waiting for something to fill this void
   (D) a multitude of waterways made shipping raw materials and finished goods relatively easy
   (E) the high tariffs imposed by the British government encouraged people to make their own manufactured goods

12. Which was a significant impact of industrialization on European society in the nineteenth century?

   (A) A dramatic decrease in agricultural output, as farmers abandoned their land to work in factories
   (B) Improved relations between the working classes and the middle classes
   (C) Growing socialist radicalism in industrially advanced countries
   (D) The growth of trade unions
   (E) Greater opportunities and rights for women

13. Which of the following best describes the Congress of Vienna?

   (A) It fomented a spirit of bitterness in defeated France.
   (B) The political leaders negotiated the settlement to further their national interests.
   (C) It disrupted the European balance of power.
   (D) Metternich refused to relinquish any conquered territory.
   (E) France was not represented in the negotiations.

14. Which of the following suffered the decimation of its population during the mid-nineteenth century?

   (A) England due to enclosures
   (B) Ireland due to famine
   (C) Germany due to war
   (D) Spain's colonies due to rebellion
   (E) Italy due to mass emigration

GO ON TO THE NEXT PAGE.

15. As ruler of France, Louis Napoleon's authority in the 1850s and early 1860s most closely resembled that of a(n)

    (A) enlightened despot
    (B) British prime minister
    (C) American president
    (D) British monarch
    (E) totalitarian dictator

16. Italy became an officially united nation in 1860 and created a(n)

    (A) autocratic monarchy with Count Camillo di Cavour as the king's prime minister
    (B) parliamentary monarchy led by Victor Emmanuel
    (C) republic led by Giuseppe Garibaldi
    (D) democracy led by Giuseppe Mazzini
    (E) dictatorship led by Vincenzo Gioberti

17. When Russian leaders decided to modernize, their most important social reform of the mid-nineteenth century was the

    (A) building of a transcontinental railway
    (B) formation of the zemstvos
    (C) creation of Russia's first parliament, the Duma
    (D) emancipation of the serfs
    (E) establishment of compulsory education for Russian peasants

18. The most typical European migrants in the latter half of the nineteenth century were

    (A) desperately impoverished landless peasants
    (B) small farmers and skilled artisans
    (C) urban proletarians
    (D) wealthy aristocrats
    (E) middle-class merchants and shopkeepers

19. At the Berlin Conference of 1885, the European powers

    (A) agreed on how to divide Africa among themselves
    (B) brought a halt to imperialism
    (C) opened China and Japan to imperialistic penetration
    (D) barred Asian migrants from entering European countries
    (E) agreed to establish a Jewish homeland

20. Motivations for the new imperialism included all of the following EXCEPT

    (A) nationalistic desires to demonstrate the virility of the European nation-states
    (B) the competition for foreign markets
    (C) the "white man's burden"
    (D) competition for economic dominance in the New World
    (E) spreading Christianity

GO ON TO THE NEXT PAGE.

21. Place the following events of the French Revolution in the correct chronological order.

      I.   The storming of the Bastille
      II.   The Tennis Court Oath
      III. The first meeting of the Estates General
      IV. The Reign of Terror
      V.   The execution of Louis XVI

    (A)   I, II, III, IV, and V
    (B)   III, II, I, V, and IV
    (C)   II, III, I, IV, and V
    (D)   III, I, II, IV, and V
    (E)   I, IV, V, II, and III

22. Women were involved in the French Revolution in all of the following ways EXCEPT

    (A)   marching on Versailles to accost the king and queen
    (B)   organizing political clubs advocating political rights for women
    (C)   as sans-culottes
    (D)   sewing tents and clothes for the war
    (E)   as delegates of the third estate in the National Assembly

23. Who of the following did NOT criticize the idea of large-scale industrialization?

    (A)   Luddites
    (B)   Romantics
    (C)   Marxists
    (D)   Malthusians
    (E)   Owenite Socialists

24. Most nineteenth-century liberals favored all of the following EXCEPT

    (A)   laissez-faire economics
    (B)   government-sponsored social welfare programs
    (C)   representative government
    (D)   equality before the law
    (E)   freedom of press and speech

GO ON TO THE NEXT PAGE.

25. What conclusion can be drawn from the map above, which shows the number of European cities of 100,000 or more in 1800 and 1900?

   (A) There were more large cities in Great Britain in 1900 than in all of Europe in 1800.
   (B) Cities demonstrated slower growth at the end of the nineteenth century.
   (C) Many cities grew due to migration among European countries.
   (D) Most populous areas grew due to immigration from the state's colonies.
   (E) The largest cities emerged along sixteenth-century trade routes.

26. In reference to income distribution in Britain, by the end of the nineteenth century

   (A) the gap between rich and poor grew significantly smaller as a result of the Industrial Revolution
   (B) there were few subclasses between the rich and the poor, just as Marx predicted
   (C) the wealthy paid high taxes
   (D) real wages for workers went up but income distribution barely changed
   (E) the middle classes had become about half of the population

GO ON TO THE NEXT PAGE.

27. Which of the following was NOT a common strategy of both Germany and Italy in their unification efforts?

    (A)   Strong political leadership

    (B)   Utilizing inspiration from nationalist movements

    (C)   Making the dominant state militarily and economically strong

    (D)   Machiavellian tactics that enabled progress toward the goal

    (E)   Defeating their common enemies, Austria and France

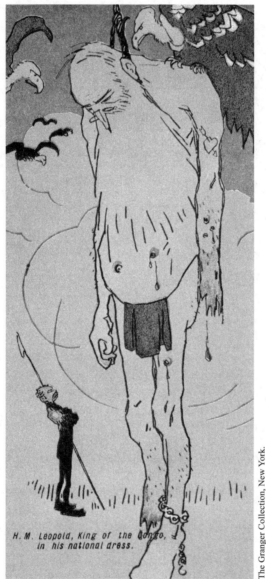

H. M. Leopold, King of the Congo, in his national dress.

The Granger Collection, New York.

28. The 1908 cartoon above, "Leopold, King of the Congo, in his national dress," depicts

    (A)   the end of colonial rule in the Congo

    (B)   the end of King Leopold's rule in the Congo

    (C)   growing scrutiny of imperialism by the United States

    (D)   the bitterness of African nobles toward Western colonists

    (E)   the brutality of native Africans toward whites

GO ON TO THE NEXT PAGE.

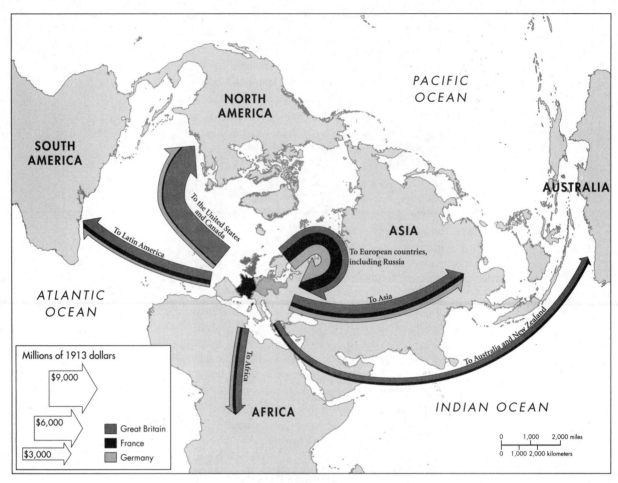

European Investment to 1914

29. This map indicates that the largest part of financial investment

    (A) from both Britain and France went to colonies in Asia
    (B) from both Britain and France went to colonies in Africa
    (C) from both Britain and France went to North America
    (D) from Britain went to North America, and from France went elsewhere in Europe
    (E) from Britain went elsewhere in Europe, and from France went to North America

30. The chief problem facing the French monarchy before 1789 was

    (A) constant, nearly yearly, peasant revolts
    (B) near bankruptcy
    (C) the refusal of the Estates General to pass tax reform
    (D) lack of an heir
    (E) hostile relations with the church

GO ON TO THE NEXT PAGE.

31. Choose the correct chronological order for the following events.

   I.   American Revolution
   II. France becomes a republic
   III. France becomes a constitutional monarchy
   IV. Haitian independence
   V.   Napoleon becomes first consul

   (A) I, III, II, IV, and V
   (B) I, III, II, V, and IV
   (C) III, I, II, IV, and V
   (D) I, II, III, IV, and V
   (E) I, III, V, II, and IV

32. J. A. Hobson criticized imperialism in his important 1902 book mostly

   (A) for its contradiction of Christian principles
   (B) for its obvious racism
   (C) because imperialism in fact brought virtually no benefits to the peoples of the colonies
   (D) because the great benefits to English workers came at the expense of non-Western workers
   (E) for diverting attention from the need for domestic reform

33. The constitution of the constitutional monarchy created in the first French Revolution

   (A) allowed for universal suffrage
   (B) allowed for universal male suffrage
   (C) was accepted by the king only with great reluctance
   (D) led to the attempted coup d'état by Napoleon
   (E) did very little to limit royal or noble power

34. Which was NOT an attempt to change French culture made during the second or radical stage of the French Revolution?

   (A) Metric system of measurement for all of France
   (B) A new calendar
   (C) Promotion of deism with celebrations of the Supreme Being
   (D) Dress codes for citizens
   (E) Restrictions on the production of consumer goods

35. The Civil Constitution of the Clergy and Napoleon's Concordat with the pope both

   (A) placed the clergy under direct supervision of the papacy
   (B) alienated the mostly religious peasants
   (C) restored expropriated lands to the church
   (D) effectively put the French church under national authority
   (E) allowed priests to marry

36. The Reign of Terror and Napoleon's regime shared which political practice?

   (A) Repression of nobles
   (B) Repression of political dissidents
   (C) Use of the plebiscite to mask dictatorship
   (D) Dictatorship by one individual that ended only after foreign intervention
   (E) Reliance on political support from labor unions

GO ON TO THE NEXT PAGE.

37. Which statement about the war against Austria during the second French revolution and the Reign of Terror is most accurate?

    (A) France survived militarily only because the Reign of Terror ended.
    (B) The government relied on volunteers to man its army.
    (C) Many soldiers refused to fight because of their opposition to the Terror.
    (D) Robespierre proved to be a surprisingly effective general.
    (E) Robespierre's planned economy worked well enough to supply the army effectively.

38. Napoleon's Civil Code

    (A) gave women full equality including the vote
    (B) gave women equality before the law but not the vote
    (C) made women legally subservient to their husbands or fathers
    (D) allowed women economic rights, like the signing of contracts, but not political rights
    (E) gave legal equality to noble women but not to bourgeois women

39. How did Napoleon act regarding slavery in the French colonies?

    (A) He abolished slavery in his Civil Code.
    (B) He effectively canceled earlier abolition policies of the Convention.
    (C) He did nothing.
    (D) He continued the policies of the Convention.
    (E) He temporarily restored slavery to Haiti, promising to abolish it in twenty years.

40. Napoleon's blockade of British goods

    (A) was undermined by a successful counter-blockade
    (B) led Britain to make a treaty with Napoleon in 1810
    (C) devastated the British economy
    (D) was hugely popular in France because it promoted the sale of French goods
    (E) effectively prevented the smuggling of British goods into Europe

41. The government that replaced Napoleon in 1814 was a(n)

    (A) absolute monarchy under Louis XVIII
    (B) constitutional monarchy under Louis XVIII
    (C) provisional government that was to write a new constitution for France
    (D) monarchy under Charles X, a puppet of the coalition that defeated Napoleon
    (E) republic with Napoleon's nephew as president

42. The chief effect of Napoleon's rule on the territories he conquered in Europe was

    (A) the stimulation of nationalistic resistance
    (B) a series of unsuccessful revolutions against their monarchs
    (C) little, in that he did not impose any major reforms
    (D) the stimulation of local industries
    (E) permanent change in the ruling families in Spain and Italy

43. In the first factories in England, workers were most likely to be

    (A) women displaced from the cottage industry
    (B) skilled weavers
    (C) unemployed agricultural day laborers
    (D) young boys but not girls
    (E) foundling apprentices

GO ON TO THE NEXT PAGE.

44. Economic nationalists like Friedrich List in nineteenth-century Germany

    (A) supported industrialization as the best way to reduce poverty
    (B) rejected the idea of a Zollverein as a hindrance to economic progress
    (C) warned against the dangers of Prussian industrialization
    (D) claimed that free trade was the best path to prosperity
    (E) agreed with Thomas Malthus and David Ricardo that poverty was inevitable

45. One significant difference in the process of industrialization in England and on the continent was

    (A) banks were less important on the continent
    (B) support for free trade was strong in Germany
    (C) the English focused on production of luxury goods
    (D) many governments actively promoted industrialization on the continent
    (E) there was reluctance to use skilled workers from Britain on the continent because of nationalistic sentiments

46. The industries that first propelled industrialization forward in Britain, Germany, and Belgium were

    (A) textiles in all countries
    (B) textiles in Britain and railroads in Germany and Belgium
    (C) iron production in Britain and textiles in Germany and Belgium
    (D) textiles in Britain and armaments in Germany and Belgium
    (E) shipbuilding in Britain and iron production in Germany and Belgium

47. By the mid-nineteenth century, industrial workers in Great Britain

    (A) were working fewer days than they had as agricultural laborers
    (B) typically worked eight- to nine-hour days
    (C) saw a rise in real wages
    (D) had organized a powerful national union
    (E) were the majority of the employed

48. Women were forbidden from working in mines in legislation passed in 1842 because

    (A) it was believed that the conditions of the mines encouraged debauchery
    (B) women went on strike in the mines
    (C) they were seen as too physically weak to do such work
    (D) it was such well-paid work that men argued it should be given to the breadwinners in the families
    (E) women had to be paid for the days they took off to give birth

49. By the early nineteenth century, artisans in craft workshops

    (A) had disappeared because of competition from factory-produced goods
    (B) developed a sense of solidarity with workers as the guilds became more competitive
    (C) continued working in some fields like baking but not in others like ironmongering
    (D) refused to join unions or labor groups
    (E) opened up their leadership to women to infuse new blood

GO ON TO THE NEXT PAGE.

50. The gendering of work and the idea of separate spheres

    (A) affected working-class women but not the middle classes
    (B) affected middle-class women but not the working classes
    (C) affected women in domestic service but not other female workers
    (D) affected both working- and middle-class women
    (E) was restricted mostly to aristocratic women

51. In the early days of the Industrial Revolution, child labor was

    (A) banned completely by legislation
    (B) considered desirable by parents because it kept families together
    (C) opposed by working-class parents who were, however, powerless to prevent it
    (D) considered unnecessary and undesirable by most industrialists
    (E) limited to abandoned or orphaned children

52. The testimony of mine workers in the 1840s showed that

    (A) female workers were generally illiterate
    (B) the coal owners were well aware of conditions in the mines
    (C) girls were rarely used as hurriers, workers who move coal wagons underground
    (D) girls usually did not start working in the mines until they were in their teens
    (E) Sunday schools provided good religious instruction

53. The Greeks were able to win their independence from the Ottoman Empire because

    (A) Austria supported their cause to weaken an old enemy
    (B) Britain, Russia, and France put pressure on the Ottoman Empire on behalf of the Greeks
    (C) Russia agreed to stay neutral in the Greek-Ottoman conflict
    (D) Prussia helped them in order to maintain the balance of power in the Balkans
    (E) Romania, which was already independent, supported them

54. The restored Bourbon king Louis XVIII

    (A) executed the revolutionaries who had executed Louis XVI
    (B) tried to restore absolute monarchy
    (C) helped preserve constitutional monarchy for France
    (D) was overthrown in the revolution of 1830
    (E) modified the constitution to give all adult men the vote

55. The repeal of the Corn Laws in Britain in 1846

    (A) was enacted by the Tories to help the landowning class
    (B) reflected the changes in Parliament since the Great Reform Bill
    (C) ended free trade
    (D) was opposed by the working classes
    (E) caused the famine in Ireland

56. The Frankfurt Assembly failed because the delegates

    (A) could not agree on what to do about Schleswig-Holstein
    (B) offered the crown to the king of Bavaria
    (C) were not supported by the middle classes
    (D) tried to write a constitution for Prussia
    (E) failed to convince the king of Prussia to accept the crown

GO ON TO THE NEXT PAGE.

57. The "June Days" in France in 1848 refers to

   (A) the election of Louis Napoleon

   (B) fighting between workers and the army in Paris when the national workshops were canceled

   (C) riots that took place when Louis Blanc was given a position in the provisional government

   (D) fighting between liberals and monarchists in Paris

   (E) the period when Louis Philippe abdicated

58. The revolutions of 1848 in Berlin and Vienna were similar because

   (A) in both, the chief issue was nationalistic agitation by minorities wanting autonomy

   (B) both were crushed within two weeks

   (C) both were led by socialists seeking economic reforms

   (D) the rulers of both countries promised liberal constitutions but then reneged on their promises

   (E) the Russians helped defeat the revolutionaries in both cities

59. Which is NOT a key point of Marxism?

   (A) Workers are inevitably exploited by their employers.

   (B) History is fundamentally about class struggle.

   (C) The proletariat can only win over the bourgeoisie by appointing leaders from outside of its class.

   (D) The value of any object is determined by the labor that went into making it.

   (E) The bourgeoisie has been a revolutionary class.

60. The Great Reform Bill of 1832

   (A) gave greater representation in the House of Commons to industrial cities

   (B) made the House of Lords and the House of Commons equal

   (C) expanded the suffrage to about the same percentage of adult men that had the vote in France

   (D) was a victory for the Chartist movement

   (E) eliminated aristocrats from any significant political role

61. Which of the following were typical middle-class child-rearing practices in the late nineteenth century?

      I. Mothers breast-fed their children themselves.

      II. Children were given a great deal of personal freedom so they could learn responsibility.

      III. Children were educated and trained for success.

      IV. Illegitimate children were typically abandoned to foundling hospitals.

   (A) II, III, and IV

   (B) I and III

   (C) III and IV

   (D) I, II, and III

   (E) I, III, and IV

GO ON TO THE NEXT PAGE.

62. The women's movement in the nineteenth century focused mostly on obtaining for women

    (A) legal rights such as the right to own property
    (B) the vote
    (C) the right to divorce
    (D) equal pay for equal work
    (E) the right to a medical abortion to end an unwanted pregnancy

63. Which was NOT a reason for Baron Haussmann's building of broad and straight boulevards in the city of Paris?

    (A) To justify the razing of old buildings and slums
    (B) To allow for the building of the subway
    (C) To encourage the smoother and faster flow of traffic
    (D) To prevent revolutionaries from being able to barricade the streets
    (E) To provide impressive vistas for Parisians and visitors alike

64. Religious donations and church attendance

    (A) stayed about the same throughout the nineteenth century
    (B) declined in the late nineteenth century, particularly among the working classes
    (C) noticeably declined in the nineteenth century in the middle classes but not in the working classes
    (D) increased in general as a response to the stresses of urbanization
    (E) increased in the working classes but not in the middle classes

65. Nineteenth-century prostitutes in London and Paris

    (A) were usually women who became prostitutes when they were young and remained so for their whole lives
    (B) generally had working-class men as their clientele, as the middle classes were very moralistic
    (C) were relatively few in number because of the easy availability of premarital sex
    (D) generally married and had children after some years on the streets
    (E) mostly worked in government-supervised brothels

66. Charles Darwin's chief contribution to science was

    (A) proving the old age of earth
    (B) describing the mechanisms of evolution through accidental mutation
    (C) being the first to suggest the role of the environment in the changes of species
    (D) his successful challenge to Malthusian ideas that there is always a struggle for existence
    (E) providing the basis for Social Darwinism

67. Early sociologists like Emile Durkheim, Ferdinand Tönnies, and Gustav Le Bon all took a critical view of

    (A) nineteenth-century middle-class family life
    (B) modern industrialized society
    (C) societies dominated by tradition
    (D) religion, which Durkheim called "the opiate of the masses"
    (E) imperialism

GO ON TO THE NEXT PAGE.

68. One major change in the world of science in the later nineteenth century was
    (A) science became so complex and abstract that the ordinary person had little interest in it
    (B) scientists came to be seen as less important than poets and philosophers
    (C) most scientific work involved applying already existing scientific knowledge rather than seeking general theories
    (D) important philosophers like Darwin argued that science was an unreliable path to truth
    (E) many scientists were employed by various industries in research and development

69. Bismarck made his "blood and iron" speech as chancellor of Prussia in response to
    (A) the rise of socialism
    (B) parliamentary resistance to his military budgets
    (C) Austria's aggressive statements provoking the Seven Weeks' War
    (D) efforts to form the North German Federation
    (E) the resistance of Bavaria to joining a unified Germany

70. In terms of their political systems, Sardinia-Piedmont and Prussia in the 1860s
    (A) were both constitutional monarchies
    (B) were not constitutional monarchies
    (C) were both ruled by incompetent kings
    (D) differed in that Sardinia-Piedmont was a constitutional monarchy but Prussia was not
    (E) differed in that Prussia was a constitutional monarchy but Sardinia-Piedmont was not

71. Bismarck's attacks on the socialist movement and the ban on the Social Democratic Party
    (A) weakened the socialist movement in Germany permanently
    (B) proved to be counterproductive
    (C) were much more successful than Kulturkampf (his attack on the Catholic Church)
    (D) spawned anti-Semitism in Germany
    (E) led him to reject workers' demands for social welfare legislation

72. The creation of the dual monarchy of Austro-Hungary in 1867 meant that
    (A) there were smoother relationships with all of the subject nationalities in the empire
    (B) the German language and culture were taught everywhere in the schools
    (C) a weakened Habsburg dynasty retained its most important ethnic minority
    (D) the king of Hungary replaced the Habsburgs as the Austro-Hungarian emperor
    (E) Hungary ceased to have its own parliament but joined the one in Vienna

GO ON TO THE NEXT PAGE.

73. Which of the states listed below faced nationalistic or independence movements of ethnic groups within their borders at the end of the nineteenth century and in the early twentieth century?

> I. Britain   II. Germany   III. Russia   IV. The Ottoman Empire   V. France

- (A) All of them
- (B) None of them
- (C) I, III, IV, and V
- (D) III, IV, and V
- (E) I, III, and IV

74. The Tanzimat reforms in the Ottoman Empire sought to

- (A) increase the power of the sultans
- (B) reorganize the janissaries and make them the army officer corps
- (C) westernize the government and army
- (D) give legal privileges to Muslims over Christians and Jews
- (E) turn the Ottoman Empire into a republic

75. Political anti-Semitism, which developed at the end of the nineteenth century, was different from previous forms of anti-Semitism in that it

- (A) called for the murder of all Jews
- (B) was strongest in Germany
- (C) called for all Jews to assimilate to the majority culture
- (D) defined Jewishness as a race rather than a religion
- (E) was highly unpopular

76. In the period after the assassination of Alexander II in 1881 up to the 1905 revolution, Russia

- (A) was a constitutional monarchy
- (B) strongly discouraged anti-Semitism and liberalized laws relating to Jews
- (C) promoted industrialization with Western investment
- (D) ended the redemption payments former serfs had to pay for the land they got on emancipation
- (E) focused on internal development and avoided foreign entanglements

GO ON TO THE NEXT PAGE.

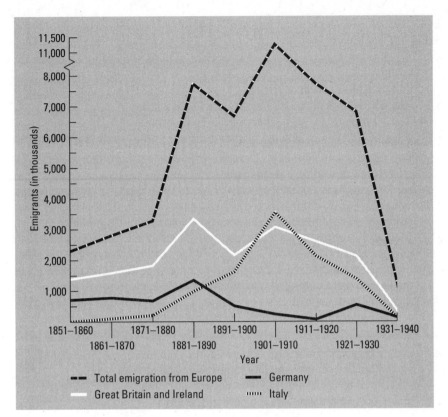

Emigration from Europe by Decades, 1851–1940

77. Which pattern of migration is described accurately by this chart?

(A) Italians mostly left in the 1860s, just before unification was completed.

(B) Australia welcomed Chinese immigrants more than the United States did.

(C) The United States received more than half of all immigrants from Europe in the nineteenth century.

(D) Germans emigrated in large numbers in the 1850s and again in the 1880s.

(E) Many Irish considered themselves swallows, who were only temporarily abroad.

GO ON TO THE NEXT PAGE.

78. The economic expansion of Europe abroad had which of the following consequences in the nineteenth century?

    (A) Significant improvements in the standard of living throughout the non-European world
    (B) The industrialization of Africa
    (C) The takeover of oil-producing Middle Eastern states
    (D) The creation of a world economy for the first time
    (E) A significant gap in average income between Europeans and non-Europeans

79. The battle of Omdurman in the Sudan showed that

    (A) the Portuguese would defend their colonies from takeover by other European states
    (B) Britain would go to any lengths to secure control of oil supplies
    (C) Europeans' technology was the decisive factor in their ability to take control over Africa
    (D) the principles established at the Berlin Conference ended up meaning very little
    (E) the French were willing to withdraw to avoid war with the British

80. Before 1914, economic benefits of the new imperialism were

    (A) quite limited
    (B) enormous profits in the investments in the colonies
    (C) so meager that several small colonies were abandoned
    (D) substantial for investors and workers at home alike
    (E) much more important than the political benefits

STOP

END OF SECTION I

EUROPEAN HISTORY
SECTION II

Part A
(Suggested writing time—45 minutes)
Percent of Section II score—45

Directions: The following question is based on the accompanying Documents 1–13. The documents have been edited for the purpose of this exercise.

This question is designed to test your ability to work with and understand historical documents. Write an essay that:

✦ Provides an appropriate, explicitly stated thesis that directly addresses all parts of the question and does NOT simply restate the question.

✦ Discusses a majority of the documents individually and specifically.

✦ Demonstrates understanding of the basic meaning of a majority of the documents.

✦ Supports the thesis with appropriate interpretation of a majority of the documents.

✦ Analyzes the documents by explicitly grouping them in at least three appropriate ways.

✦ Takes into account both the sources of the documents and the authors' point of view.

You may refer to relevant historical information not mentioned in the documents.

1. Analyze the various views of British leaders about the Eastern Question and the Russo-Turkish War of 1877–1878.

Historical background: Britain, then under the leadership of Prime Minister Benjamin Disraeli, was divided over how best to respond to growing tensions in the Balkans in the 1870s. British concerns about the Middle East intensified after the purchase of the Suez Canal in 1875. There was unrest in most areas of the Balkans still under Ottoman rule. In 1877, the Russians invaded the Ottoman Empire to defend their fellow Orthodox Slavs and fulfill long-standing Russian territorial ambition. The Russian advance was temporarily stopped by the Turks in September 1877, but when it continued, Turkey asked Britain to mediate. In 1878, Britain sent a fleet to Constantinople. In March 1878, the Russo-Turkish War ended with the signing of the Treaty of San Stefano by Turkey and Russia, in which the Ottoman Empire granted independence to Serbia, Montenegro, and Romania and parts of Bulgaria were put under Russian protection. This settlement was unsatisfactory to the other great powers of Europe, who met at the Congress of Berlin and arrived at a new settlement putting Bosnia and Herzegovina under Austrian occupation and checking Russian expansion.

GO ON TO THE NEXT PAGE.

Document 1

Source: Sir Edwin Pears, British lawyer and resident of Constantinople. From *Forty Years in Constantinople, 1873–1915,* published 1916.

Mr. Disraeli was then Prime Minister, and treated the matter very lightly. He declared, in reply to a statement that persons had been tortured as well as killed, that he doubted whether torture was practiced among a people "who generally terminated their connection with culprits in a more expeditious manner." . . . His light manner of speaking on the subject irritated Members on both sides of the House, who recognized that if my statements were true they constituted a damning charge against Turkish methods of government in Bulgaria, and demanded at least serious examination. . . . It should be understood that at this time there was no revolt in Bulgaria, though there had been considerable expression of discontent. The idea of the Turks was to crush out the spirit of the Bulgarian people, and thus prevent revolt. . . . The London Daily News sent Mr. MacGahan, an Irish-American of great experience and fine character, to Bulgaria to report more fully than I had been able to do. . . . [He] had been in Central Asia and knew something of Russia, and could not be charged with having any prejudice against the Turks.

One of the first places they visited was Batak, . . . a thriving town, rich and prosperous in comparison with neighboring Moslem villages. . . . Its prosperity had excited the envy and jealousy of its Moslem neighbors. . . . In all the Moslem atrocities, Chiot, Bulgarian, and Armenian, the principal incentive has been the larger prosperity of the Christian population; for, in spite of centuries of oppression and plunder, Christian industry and Christian morality everywhere make for national wealth and intelligence.

Document 2

Source: W. T. Stead, British educator, social reformer, and journalist, articles in *The Northern Echo,* published June 24, 1876, and July 5, 1876.

A War of extermination is being carried on against the Christians in Bulgaria. . . . England is Turkey's friend. The Mussulmans [sic] are going about saying that England will not see the Empire broken up—that, if necessary, it will help to put down insurrections. . . . Serbia and Montenegro are at war with Turkey . . . Much as war is to be detested, in cases like the present, war is the only solution which has yet been devised . . . it is a war of Liberation. . . . The Premier [Prime Minister] . . . is quite capable of plunging the country into a disastrous war in order to perpetuate the dying agonies of the Turkish Empire by opposing the liberators of Bosnia. Our duty is to stand aloof, extending merely such as moral support to the insurgents. . . . Woe be unto that man, be he Premier or be he Earl, who in the name of England . . . [or] from jealousy of Russia . . . dares to oppose the brave men who are struggling for liberty among the Bosnian hills.

GO ON TO THE NEXT PAGE.

Document 3

Source: J. A. MacGahan, American journalist, war correspondent, dispatch to *The London Daily News,* August 22, 1876.

Since . . . yesterday, I have supped full of horrors. Nothing has as yet been said of the Turks that I do not now believe; nothing could be said of them that I should not think probable and likely. . . . Let me tell you what we saw at Batak. . . . As we ascended, bones, skulls, and skeletons became more frequent . . . fragments of half dry, half putrid flesh attached to them. . . . We drew reign with an exclamation of horror, for right before us, almost beneath our horses' feet, was a sight that made us shudder. It was a heap of skulls . . . it emitted a sickening odor, and it was here that the dogs had been seeking a hasty repast. . . . We looked again at the heap of skulls and skeletons before us, and we observed that they were all small and that the articles of clothing intermingled with them and laying about were all women's apparel. These then, were all women and girls. . . . These women had all been beheaded. . . . The Turkish authorities did not even pretend that there was any Turk killed here or that the inhabitants offered any resistance. . . . Of the 8,000 to 9,000 people who made up the population of the place only 1200 to 1500 are left, and they have neither tools to dig graves with, nor strength to use spades if they had them.

Document 4

Source: Benjamin Disraeli, Conservative Party leader and prime minister of England, letter to Lady Bradford, September 2, 1876.

All the papers are arguing whether the great victory of the Serbians may not retard peace. Fortunately, we now have a military attaché, a General officer of our own, at Turkish Headquarters, and he informs us that there has been no victory, no battle, scarcely any fighting; things remain the same.

Document 5

Source: William Gladstone, Liberal Party statesmen and four-time prime minister of England, *Bulgarian Horrors and The Question of the East* pamphlet, September 6, 1876.

The Turkish race . . . were, upon the whole, from the black day when they first entered Europe, the one great anti-human specimen of humanity. Wherever they went a broad line of blood marked the track behind them, and as far as their dominion reached, civilization disappeared from view. They represented everywhere government by force as opposed to government by law . . . that which has been done, which has too late been examined but which remains unavenged, which has left behind all the foul and all the fierce passion which produced it and which may again spring up in another murderous harvest from the soil soaked and reeking with blood and in the air tainted with every imaginable deed of crime and shame. That such things should be done once is a damning disgrace to the portion of our race which did them; that the door should be left open to their ever so barely possibly repetition would spread that shame over the world.

GO ON TO THE NEXT PAGE.

Document 6

Source: Lord Salisbury, British foreign minister, Conservative Party leader, and three-time prime minister, letter to Benjamin Disraeli, September 23, 1876.

We have not the power, even if we have the wish, to give back any of the protected districts to the . . . government of the Porte.* . . . We must have something more than promises . . . let there be an Officer of state established at Constantinople who shall be in fact if not in name Protector of Christians . . . nominated in concert with the Powers and for a term of year. He should always have access to the Sultan, and it should be his duty to call the attention of the Turkish Government to any breach of the decrees which have been issued in protection of the Christians. . . . It should further be his duty to submit to the Turkish government a list of persons fit to hold office as Governors of Bosnia, Herzegovina, and Bulgaria, and the Porte should be forced to choose the governors from that list. . . . The problem is solved, if you can get good governors for these oppressed provinces, men who will be just for the Christians but not disloyal to the Porte and who cannot be driven or dismissed by the corrupted intrigues of the seraglio.†

*The Turkish Government.
†The harem at the Sultan's palace.

Document 7

Source: *The Pall Mall Gazette,* Conservative newspaper until 1880, London, March 22, 1877.

That Lord Derby was thoroughly justified—more than justified—in his determination that a clear undertaking on Russia's part to recall her armies from the frontier is an indispensable condition of accepting any such engagement as the protocol implies, will be the universal opinion in England, and it may be taken for certain by all whom it concerns that the Government will abide by its decision.

A special dispatch from Paris to the *Times* says: "when Russian demobilization is once ordered, Europeans will be surprised with the speed with which it will be effected. Numerous regiments are already encamped away from the frontier, and the protocol once signed the Czar will address a proclamation ordering demobilization to an almost empty camp."

GO ON TO THE NEXT PAGE.

Document 8

Source: "An Ugly Outlook for the Czar," special dispatch by cable to the *New York Times,* September 15, 1877.

London: September 15. A week of bloodier work than even that terrible one when Suleiman Pasha encountered such heavy losses in the Schipka Pass, closes with 10,000 dead and wounded Russian and Rumanian soldiers lying around Plevna. The sacrifice of life has been immense in the efforts made to dislodge the troops of Osman Pasha, but the Turkish flag still floats victorious and defiant over as brave an Army as ever defended an entrenched position. American rifles, Krupp guns, and the stubborn resistance and endurance so characteristic of the Ottoman soldiers has completed frustrated the supreme effort of the Muscovites. . . . Only another month of weather fit for fighting remains, and the army of invasion is further off than ever from their attempted conquest of Turkey. . . . Serbia now appears upon the scene as an armed ally of the Defender so called of the Christian faith. She makes most arrogant demands in return for proffered aid and meanwhile poses as the champion of the Slavonic race.

Document 9

Source: Lord Derby, foreign secretary in Disraeli's Cabinet, later a member of the Liberal Party and Gladstone's cabinet, secretary of state for the Colonies, in a letter to Benjamin Disraeli, January 23, 1878.

After our . . . discussions in Cabinet on the question of sending up the fleet to Constantinople and the decision which was come to this afternoon, you will feel as I do that the only one result is possible as far as I am concerned.

The question of which we were unable to agree is obviously one of grave importance; it is certain to be eagerly and frequently discussed both in and out of Parliament. The Foreign Secretary more than any other minister would in the ordinary course of things be charged with the duty of defending the decision taken. And as I cannot think it, or say that I think it, a safe or wise one, it is clear that no alternative is left me except to ask you to allow me to retire from the post I hold.

GO ON TO THE NEXT PAGE.

Document 10

Source: Queen Victoria, letters to Benjamin Disraeli, January/February 1878.

The Queen is feeling terribly anxious lest delay should cause us to be too late and lose our prestige for ever! It worries her night and day. . . . And the language, the insulting language—used by the Russians against us! It makes the Queen's blood boil. . . . Oh, if the Queen were a man, she would like to go and give those Russians, whose word one cannot believe, such a beating! We shall never be friends again till we have it out. This the Queen feels sure of. This delay, this uncertainty by which abroad, we are losing our prestige and our position while Russia is advancing and will be before Constantinople in no time! Then the Government will be fearfully blamed and the Queen so humiliated that she thinks she would abdicate at once. Be Bold! . . . She feels, she cannot remain the sovereign of a country that is letting itself down to kiss the feet of the great barbarians, the retarders of all liberty and civilization that exists.

Document 11

Source: Popular song sung January 1878 in streets of London.

We don't want to fight, but, by Jingo! if we do,

We've got the ships, we've got the men, we've got the money too!

We've fought the Bear before, and while we're Britons true

The Russians shall not have Constantinople.

GO ON TO THE NEXT PAGE.

Document 12

Source: "A 'Happy Family' at Berlin" cartoon by Sir John Tenniel, British illustrator, 1878. The male figure depicted is Benjamin Disraeli.

A "HAPPY FAMILY" AT BERLIN.

The caption reads: *Showman: "The British Lion and the Russian Bear will now embrace! (Aside.) It's all right, ladies and gentlemen, this effect has been WELL REHEARSED!"*

www.CartoonStock.com.

Document 13

Source: Terms of the Cyprus Convention of Defensive Alliance between Great Britain and Turkey, with respect to the Asiatic Provinces of Turkey, signed at Constantinople, June 4, 1878.

Article 1: . . . If any attempt shall be made at any future time by Russia to take possession of any further territories of His Imperial Majesty the Sultan in Asia. . . . England engaged to join His Imperial Majesty the Sultan in defending them by force of arms.

In return, His Imperial Majesty the Sultan promises to England to introduce necessary Reforms . . . for the protection of Christen and other subjects of the Porte in these territories. . . .

And in order to enable England to make necessary provision for executing her engagement, His Imperial Majesty the Sultan further consents to assign the Island of Cyprus to be occupied and administrated by England.

GO ON TO THE NEXT PAGE.

EUROPEAN HISTORY
SECTION II

Part B
(Suggested planning and writing time—35 minutes)
Percent of Section II score—27.5

Directions: You are to answer ONE question from the three questions below. Make your selection carefully, choosing the question that you are best prepared to answer thoroughly in the time permitted. You should spend 5 minutes organizing or outlining your answer.

Write an essay that:

+ Has a relevant thesis.

+ Addresses all parts of the question.

+ Supports the thesis with specific evidence.

+ Is well organized.

2. To what degree and in what ways did Napoleon betray the ideals of the French Revolution?

3. Describe and explain the changes in family life in the late nineteenth century in the middle and working classes of Europe.

4. Analyze the development of socialism as a movement in the nineteenth century.

GO ON TO THE NEXT PAGE.

EUROPEAN HISTORY
SECTION II

Part C
(Suggested planning and writing time—35 minutes)
Percent of Section II score—27.5

Directions: You are to answer ONE question from the three questions below. Make your selection carefully, choosing the question that you are best prepared to answer thoroughly in the time permitted. You should spend 5 minutes organizing or outlining your answer.

Write an essay that:

✦ Has a relevant thesis.

✦ Addresses all parts of the question.

✦ Supports the thesis with specific evidence.

✦ Is well organized.

5. Compare and contrast the processes of industrialization in England and on the European continent.

6. Compare and contrast European imperialism of the late nineteenth century and European colonialism in the early modern period.

7. Compare and contrast the problems facing proponents of Italian and German unification from 1848 to1870 and the processes by which they achieved their goals.

STOP

END OF EXAM

Answer Key for Practice Exam

Answers for Section I: Multiple-Choice Questions

1. B	21. B	41. B	61. B
2. D	22. E	42. A	62. A
3. C	23. C	43. E	63. B
4. C	24. B	44. A	64. B
5. E	25. A	45. D	65. D
6. E	26. D	46. B	66. B
7. C	27. E	47. C	67. B
8. D	28. B	48. A	68. E
9. A	29. D	49. B	69. B
10. E	30. B	50. D	70. D
11. D	31. B	51. B	71. B
12. D	32. E	52. A	72. C
13. B	33. C	53. B	73. E
14. B	34. E	54. C	74. C
15. A	35. D	55. B	75. D
16. B	36. B	56. E	76. C
17. D	37. E	57. B	77. D
18. B	38. C	58. D	78. E
19. A	39. B	59. C	79. C
20. D	40. A	60. A	80. A

Scoring the Multiple-Choice Section

Use the following formula to calculate your raw score on the multiple-choice section of the exam:

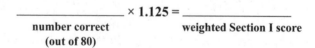

$$\underline{\hspace{3cm}} \times 1.125 = \underline{\hspace{3cm}}$$

number correct
(out of 80)

weighted Section I score

Rationales

1. **Answer: (B)** The dramatic growth of the population caused some economists to analyze the problem. Malthus predicted that population would continue to grow exponentially, surpassing the available food supply, which could only grow linearly, and

creating widespread poverty and famine unless constraints were placed on population growth. (McKay, *A History of Western Society*, Eleventh Edition, pp. 660–661)

2. **Answer: (D)** While the French army and government conspired to convict Captain Alfred Dreyfus of treason, and the Catholic Church stood behind them, civil libertarians and radical republicans like novelist Émile Zola came to Dreyfus's defense, accusing France's General Staff of falsifying evidence to keep him in prison and letting the guilty person go. The Dreyfus Affair divided France into two bitter camps at the end of the nineteenth century and resulted in severed ties between the Catholic Church and the state. (McKay, *A History of Western Society*, Eleventh Edition, p. 773)

3. **Answer: (C)** Many new jobs emerged. Millions of workers were involved in the construction of the railroads (miners, iron workers, those who built the railroads, and those who ran them) and in the growth of industry they produced. Most of these workers moved to the cities. Demand for unskilled labor for construction was huge. (McKay, *A History of Western Society*, Eleventh Edition, pp. 657–660)

4. **Answer: (C)** Domestic service took a large percentage, about 14 percent of all British workers in 1911, of the workforce in the nineteenth century, particularly of young women, of whom about one-third were household servants. (McKay, *A History of Western Society*, Eleventh Edition, p. 732)

5. **Answer: (E)** According to these maps, England had a more developed railroad system than the continent did. The railroad connected major industrialized areas to key cities and ports; this allowed for the rapid industrialization of Britain before the rest of Europe. (McKay, *A History of Western Society*, Eleventh Edition, pp. 657–660, 663–665)

6. **Answer: (E)** Romantics were fascinated by images of dynamism. They were much taken by images of nature, such as stormy seas, and those made by humans, such as locomotives. (McKay, *A History of Western Society*, Eleventh Edition, pp. 695–699)

7. **Answer: (C)** Although Great Britain was in the forefront, all countries profited from the Industrial Revolution. From 1800 to 1900, Britain's per capita industrialization went up more than six times, while that of the United States went up more than seven times. (McKay, *A History of Western Society*, Eleventh Edition, pp. 662–663)

8. **Answer: (D)** The decline of death rates in many European countries throughout the latter half of the nineteenth century can be attributed to a rising standard of living, public health improvements, better medicine, and an understanding of how diseases are spread (the germ theory). The miasmatic theory, that disease was caused by filth (rather than caused by germs and spread by filth) limited the success of public health reformers. (McKay, *A History of Western Society*, Eleventh Edition, pp. 721–724)

9. **Answer: (A)** The French Revolution was fueled by desires for liberty and equality within society, inspired in part by the success of the American Revolution. The extreme poverty of the lowest classes made them all the more willing to revolt against the monarchy. The bourgeoisie also clashed with the monarchy, when the monarchy tried to find ways to pay the government's debts. Religious differences in France were not an important factor in starting the French Revolution. (McKay, *A History of Western Society*, Eleventh Edition, pp. 619–623)

10. **Answer: (E)** The French were willing to give up some of their liberty in exchange for stability within their country, so they willingly allowed Napoleon Bonaparte to lead them as an absolute ruler. Napoleon came to power after the years of turmoil due to the French Revolution and the ensuing Directory. By taking power in a coup d'état, he revealed that he was not a republican. (McKay, *A History of Western Society*, Eleventh Edition, pp. 634–635)

11. **Answer: (D)** Surrounded by water, with many rivers and canals inland, Great Britain was able to ship goods quickly and efficiently. This fact, along with their stable government and bountiful harvests, was one of the main reasons that Britain was ready for the Industrial Revolution before other European nations. (McKay, *A History of Western Society*, Eleventh Edition, pp. 650–651)

12. **Answer: (D)** Working-class solidarity gave rise to trade unions. Though these were outlawed in many countries, the labor movement could not be so easily suppressed, and it continued to grow from the time of the Industrial Revolution. Radical socialists were giving way to revisionist reformers by the end of the nineteenth century. Law and new social values like "the separate spheres" increasingly restricted opportunities for women. (McKay, *A History of Western Society*, Eleventh Edition, pp. 677–678, 737–739, 781–784)

13. **Answer: (B)** In 1814, European powers at the Congress of Vienna established a balance of power following the defeat of Napoleon. This would prevent any state from seeking hegemony and it would restore stability, which all agreed were in their national interests. Metternich did relinquish Belgium and southern Germany. France was very much involved in the negotiations. (McKay, A History of Western Society, Eleventh Edition, pp. 684–685)

14. **Answer: (B)** The potato blight wiped out nearly all the potatoes in Ireland in the mid-nineteenth century. Without this staple crop, the Irish experienced a famine that devastated the country. The famine also caused emigration from Ireland in significant numbers. Everywhere else in Europe in the nineteenth century population grew. (McKay, *A History of Western Society*, Eleventh Edition, pp. 704–705)

15. **Answer: (A)** Louis Napoleon declared himself emperor of France in 1852. He had nearly absolute control over the government, though he did maintain the elected assembly. He was like an enlightened despot in that he was an authoritarian ruler, yet he exhibited some progressive principles, was concerned about the betterment of his people, and made many improvements. (McKay, *A History of Western Society*, Eleventh Edition, pp. 754–756)

16. **Answer: (B)** All of these men played a role in uniting Italy, but it was Victor Emmanuel who became the first king of the parliamentary monarchy. Mazzini inspired nationalism, Garibaldi's Red Shirts conquered southern Italy, and Cavour brokered *realpolitik* diplomacy. The parliamentary (or constitutional) monarchy meant neither autocracy nor republicanism had a place in the new state. (McKay, *A History of Western Society*, Eleventh Edition, pp. 756–758)

17. **Answer: (D)** Russian leaders realized that they could not hope to modernize their country with the institution of serfdom holding them back. In 1861, Tsar Alexander II freed the serfs in the first of many great reforms in Russia. The Duma was not created until after the 1905 revolution. (McKay, *A History of Western Society*, Eleventh Edition, pp. 764–769)

18. **Answer: (B)** There was too little land in Europe to accommodate all the small farmers, so many of them moved to countries where land was bountiful and cheap. Also, skilled artisans were competing against the cheap manufactured goods of the Industrial Revolution, so they were also seeking a new way to make a living. (McKay, *A History of Western Society*, Eleventh Edition, p. 798)

19. **Answer: (A)** In 1884 and 1885, European powers met at the Berlin Conference to discuss their claims on African territories. They established the principle that in order to claim a colony as their own, they had to have effective occupation of that land. (McKay, *A History of Western Society*, Eleventh Edition, p. 805)

20. **Answer: (D)** The new imperialism took place around the turn of the twentieth century, when most of South America had already become independent states. Many missionaries went to Asia and Africa to convert the natives. Nationalists like Treitschke emphasized the importance of proving national strength and virility. (McKay, *A History of Western Society*, Eleventh Edition, pp. 807–810)

21. **Answer: (B)** The Estates General convened on May 5, 1789. On June 20 of that year, the Oath of the Tennis Court was sworn. Then on July 14, French citizens stormed the Bastille. Later in the Revolution, Louis XVI was executed (January 1793), and the Reign of Terror began shortly thereafter. (McKay, *A History of Western Society*, Eleventh Edition, pp. 620–621, 623, 627–628)

22. **Answer: (E)** Women were not allowed to be delegates to the Estates General, the National Assembly, or on any other legislative body during the French Revolution. (McKay, *A History of Western Society*, Eleventh Edition, pp. 624–625, 627–629, 631)

23. **Answer: (C)** Malthus did not criticize the Industrial Revolution per se, but he despaired that it would end poverty and saw that industrialization loosened sexual morality. Luddites tried to destroy machines. Romantics lamented the loss of a more natural society. Owenite socialists tried to create model communities as an alternative to large-scale industries. Marxists applauded the industrializing idea, but they condemned the way it was done under capitalism. (McKay, *A History of Western Society*, Eleventh Edition, pp. 660–661, 676–678, 692–699)

24. **Answer: (B)** Nineteenth-century liberals opposed government social welfare programs; this changed by the early twentieth century. (McKay, *A History of Western Society*, Eleventh Edition, pp. 690–691)

25. **Answer: (A)** Great Britain was in the forefront of industrialization during the early nineteenth century; this resulted in rapid urbanization. (McKay, *A History of Western Society*, Eleventh Edition, p. 718)

26. **Answer: (D)** Although the Industrial Revolution raised the overall standard of living and Britain was in the forefront, the large gap between rich and poor was little changed. The middle classes were about 20 percent of the population. The rich paid rather low taxes. Marx was wrong in his prediction that industrialization would reduce the number of subclasses. (McKay, *A History of Western Society*, Eleventh Edition, pp. 725–732)

27. **Answer: (E)** Prussia did defeat both Austria and France, and Sardinia-Piedmont went to war with Austria but with France as an ally. Both Cavour and Bismarck built up their states, used nationalistic sentiments, and cleverly manipulated the unification process. (McKay, *A History of Western Society*, Eleventh Edition, pp. 756–762)

28. **Answer: (B)** In 1908 an international human rights campaign forced the Belgian king, Leopold, to cede his personal right to the Congo due to the brutal practices he had enforced there, including cutting off hands of Africans who did not gather enough rubber. (McKay, *A History of Western Society*, Eleventh Edition, p. 805)

29. **Answer: (D)** Britain heavily invested in North America in the nineteenth century, while most of France's external investment went to other European countries, especially Russia. Relatively little went to their colonies. (McKay, *A History of Western Society*, Eleventh Edition, pp. 791–792)

30. **Answer: (B)** It was the financial crisis and the threat of bankruptcy that forced the king to call the Estates General into session in 1789 for the first time in 175 years. Although there had been occasional peasants' revolts, they were not annual or all that

disturbing to the king. (McKay, *A History of Western Society*, Eleventh Edition, pp. 619–623)

31. **Answer: (B)** The outbreak of the Haitian uprising was in 1791, after the first French Revolution; Haiti won independence in 1804 under Napoleon, who had become first consul in 1799. (McKay, *A History of Western Society*, Eleventh Edition, pp. 615–616, 624, 627, 634, 641–643)

32. **Answer: (E)** Hobson denied that British workers or Britain as a whole benefited from imperialism; only special interests, and particularly the capitalist class, benefited. His arguments were largely economic, since he himself was an economist. (McKay, *A History of Western Society*, Eleventh Edition, pp. 811–812)

33. **Answer: (C)** Louis reluctantly became a constitutional monarch. Only about half of the men had the vote. The nobility lost their legal distinction. Napoleon's coup was not until nearly a decade later. (McKay, *A History of Western Society*, Eleventh Edition, p. 624)

34. **Answer: (E)** The Committee of Public Safety attempted to revolutionize French society. Although there were price controls on important goods like bread, the government did not regulate the production of consumer goods. There was a plethora of them, particularly those with revolutionary themes. (McKay, *A History of Western Society*, Eleventh Edition, p. 632)

35. **Answer: (D)** Both documents put the church under state authority. The latter pleased the peasants, while they were alienated by the first. No changes were made in religious doctrine or practice in either case. (McKay, *A History of Western Society*, Eleventh Edition, pp. 625, 636)

36. **Answer: (B)** Both the Reign of Terror and Napoleon ruthlessly suppressed political dissent. Labor unions were banned by Napoleon; the Reign of Terror did not use plebiscites. While Robespierre dominated, he did not rule alone; he was part of a twelve-man Committee of Public Safety empowered by the Convention to rule. (McKay, *A History of Western Society*, Eleventh Edition, pp. 628–630, 634)

37. **Answer: (E)** In spite of domestic turmoil, the French did well militarily and occupied the Rhineland and the Austrian Netherlands by 1794. They instituted the draft in 1793. Robespierre was not a general. The planned economy—with rationing, nationalization of workshops, requisitioning of raw materials and grain—worked to provision the troops. (McKay, *A History of Western Society*, Eleventh Edition, pp. 627–628)

38. **Answer: (C)** Women lost rights under Napoleon and could no longer sign contracts or open bank accounts in their own names. They certainly were not given the vote or legal equality. They were under the authority of fathers or husbands. (McKay, *A History of Western Society*, Eleventh Edition, pp. 635–636)

39. **Answer: (B)** The convention had abolished slavery in 1794, and that abolition was confirmed in the Constitution of 1795, but Napoleon announced that French laws would not apply in the colonies. This meant that slavery would be restored, and it prompted fierce resistance in Haiti, which ultimately led to the defeat of the French army and to Haitian independence. (McKay, *A History of Western Society*, Eleventh Edition, pp. 640–643)

40. **Answer: (A)** The demand for British manufactured goods was so great that Napoleon's blockade could not be enforced. Many goods were smuggled in through Helgoland. Alexander repudiated the blockade; this prompted the invasion of Russia. The British imposed a counter-blockade, which hurt the French economy. (McKay, *A History of Western Society*, Eleventh Edition, p. 637)

41. **Answer: (B)** Louis XVII died in prison and never ruled. Louis XVIII ruled as a constitutional monarch from 1814 to 1824, replaced by Charles X. Napoleon's nephew became president in 1848. (McKay, *A History of Western Society*, Eleventh Edition, p. 639)

42. **Answer: (A)** Nationalism was sparked in the conquered peoples because Napoleon typically imposed a ruler he chose—usually someone from his own family, and because he demanded men and taxes to pay for his wars. The attempt to blockade British goods also brought resentment among people dependent on imports from Britain. (McKay, *A History of Western Society*, Eleventh Edition, p. 637)

43. **Answer: (E)** Foundlings were apprenticed to factory owners and worked under harsh conditions. Because working conditions in the first factories were so terrible, few people were willing to work in them. (McKay, *A History of Western Society*, Eleventh Edition, p. 654)

44. **Answer: (A)** List was an economic nationalist, supporting industrialization to make the Germanic states stronger and reduce poverty, which he believed—unlike Malthus and Ricardo—could be eradicated. He supported the Zollverein. Only the British—and only some of them—were free traders in the nineteenth century. (McKay, *A History of Western Society*, Eleventh Edition, pp. 665–666)

45. **Answer: (D)** The role of the government was a significant difference in industrialization, in that it stayed out of the picture in Britain by and large, but governments were actively involved on the continent, protecting investments and building infrastructure. (McKay, *A History of Western Society*, Eleventh Edition, pp. 663–665)

46. **Answer: (B)** The Industrial Revolution began in the textile industry in Britain. But for Belgium and Germany, it was the building of the railroads that prompted industrial growth in other sections, particularly iron. The industrial armaments industry was relatively small at this time. (McKay, *A History of Western Society*, Eleventh Edition, p. 663)

47. **Answer: (C)** Industrial workers were still a minority of the workforce in 1800; agriculture and domestic service were the dominant areas for work. They worked more days than before and usually eleven hours a day, but real wages began to rise. (McKay, *A History of Western Society*, Eleventh Edition, p. 725)

48. **Answer: (A)** Because of the heat, men and women often worked nearly naked, and this, some observers argued, led to immorality. (McKay, *A History of Western Society*, Eleventh Edition, pp. 671–673)

49. **Answer: (B)** When the legislation protecting apprentices and wages in the guilds was repealed, craft workers found themselves unprotected and facing competition that drove down their wages. This led them to greater class-consciousness. They continued to be active until the mid- to late nineteenth century, still making iron goods, although with machine-made iron. (McKay, *A History of Western Society*, Eleventh Edition, pp. 677–678)

50. **Answer: (D)** Middle- and working-class women were both affected by the gendering of work. Middle-class women were pushed out of managerial roles, and working-class women were restricted by law from certain types of labor. (McKay, *A History of Western Society*, Eleventh Edition, pp. 670–673)

51. **Answer: (B)** As families had worked together on the farm and in the cottage, parents continued that pattern in the early days of factory work until child labor was limited by legislation in 1833; it was not banned completely until much later. (McKay, *A History of Western Society*, Eleventh Edition, pp. 667–670)

52. **Answer: (A)** Two girls whose testimony is reproduced in Chapter 20 said they did not know how to read or write. They all started working in the mines before they were ten, and all had been hurriers. One girl said she had never heard of Jesus. The testimony of the coal master showed he had little idea of the real conditions in the mines. (McKay, *A History of Western Society*, Eleventh Edition, pp. 672–673)

53. **Answer: (B)** It was chiefly the British and French whose support helped the Greeks, though Russia also sent a navy. Austria did nothing, Romania was not yet independent, and Prussia was hardly involved. (McKay, *A History of Western Society*, Eleventh Edition, pp. 701–702)

54. **Answer: (C)** Louis XVIII appointed moderates as ministers and resisted the demands of the nobility to restore absolutism. As the suffrage was extremely limited, the king retained substantial power. It was Charles X, his successor, who was overthrown in 1830, precisely because he tried to restore absolutism. (McKay, *A History of Western Society*, Eleventh Edition, pp. 705–706)

55. **Answer: (B)** The Great Reform Bill gave the liberal bourgeoisie much greater representation in the House of Commons, and it was they who enacted the repeal of the Corn Laws, much to the distress of the aristocracy. The working classes supported the repeal since it would lower bread prices. It was passed in part to relieve conditions in Ireland. The repeal of the Corn Laws began a period of free trade. (McKay, *A History of Western Society*, Eleventh Edition, pp. 702–703)

56. **Answer: (E)** The mostly middle-class Frankfurt Assembly dealt effectively with the Schleswig-Holstein issue but failed to convince Frederick William IV to accept the constitution they wrote. (McKay, A History of Western Society, Eleventh Edition, pp. 712–713)

57. **Answer: (B)** During the "June Days," Parisian workers battled the French army and lost. This incident remains famous because of the intensity of violence, the large numbers of workers' lives lost, and the hostility between the classes it represented. (McKay, *A History of Western Society*, Eleventh Edition, p. 709)

58. **Answer: (D)** Only in France was a specific socialist issue crucial—the national workshops. In Prussia and Austria, workers took to the streets to support demands for liberal constitutions. The chief issue was political reform, not nationalism or socialism. Both kings at first felt forced to grant the constitutions because of widespread popular protests, but they both reneged on those promises once they had regained control of their capital cities. It was the Hungarian revolt that was crushed by Russian troops aiding the Austrian emperor. (McKay, *A History of Western Society*, Eleventh Edition, pp. 709–713)

59. **Answer: (C)** Marxists accept the labor theory of value and argue that all history is about class struggle. However, they believe that some individuals can rise above their own class backgrounds to play important roles in the revolution. (McKay, *A History of Western Society*, Eleventh Edition, pp. 693–695)

60. **Answer: (A)** The Great Reform Bill still limited the suffrage, although more British had the votes than the French. Its chief importance was it gave the industrial cities representation in the House of Commons. It was passed by the House of Lords only reluctantly, and it meant that they lost significant power. Aristocrats remained important in both the Whig and Tory parties. (McKay, *A History of Western Society*, Eleventh Edition, pp. 702–703)

61. **Answer: (B)**   Children were carefully supervised by their parents or guardians. Fewer illegitimate children were born, and typically they were not abandoned to foundling hospitals. (McKay, *A History of Western Society*, Eleventh Edition, pp. 739–740)

62. **Answer: (A)**   Women had significantly fewer legal rights than men; for example, they could not own property in their own name or keep their earnings. Abortion, divorce, equal pay, and the vote all were the focus of women's movements in the twentieth century. (McKay, *A History of Western Society*, Eleventh Edition, pp. 740–741)

63. **Answer: (B)**   The Paris subway would not be built until the turn of the century. (McKay, *A History of Western Society*, Eleventh Edition, pp. 724–725)

64. **Answer: (B)**   Decline was particularly acute in the working classes. (McKay, *A History of Western Society*, Eleventh Edition, p. 733)

65. **Answer: (D)**   Most prostitutes saw their work, like domestic service, as temporary and necessary because of the lack of other opportunities. (McKay, *A History of Western Society*, Eleventh Edition, p. 735)

66. **Answer: (B)**   Lamarck suggested the role of the environment in evolution but had the process wrong. Darwin's explanation was verifiable scientifically. It was Lyell who proved the age of earth. Darwin accepted Malthusian principles about scarcity. Social Darwinists tried to transfer Darwin's sound scientific reasoning to society. (McKay, *A History of Western Society*, Eleventh Edition, pp. 744–745)

67. **Answer: (B)**   Durkheim, in his *Suicide*, concluded that rising suicide rates resulted from a feeling of "anomie," or rootlessness, brought on by modern industrialized society. Tönnies contrasted the sense of community felt by those who lived in traditional societies to the more isolated life in contemporary society; he seemed to prefer social connectedness in traditional society. Le Bon wrote of the dangers of groups forming mobs in modern society. Durkheim wrote about religion, but not critically; it was Marx who called it "the opiate of the masses." J. A. Hobson, not these writers, critiqued imperialism. None of them focused on modern middle-class marriage. (McKay, *A History of Western Society*, Eleventh Edition, pp. 745–747)

68. **Answer: (E)**   Particularly in the chemical industries, many scientists found good employment in new research and development labs. (McKay, *A History of Western Society*, Eleventh Edition, pp. 743–744)

69. **Answer: (B)**   The major issue confronting Bismarck as chancellor of Prussia was the power of the purse held by the Prussian parliament, which he effectively removed. (McKay, *A History of Western Society*, Eleventh Edition, pp. 760–761)

70. **Answer: (D)**   Although Prussia had a parliament, it had little real power, and Bismarck was able to collect taxes without its consent. Sardinia-Piedmont became a constitutional monarchy during the 1848 revolution. (McKay, *A History of Western Society*, Eleventh Edition, pp. 756, 760–761)

71. **Answer: (B)**   The ban only made the movement stronger. Bismarck put in Europe's first broad social welfare legislation in an effort to reduce the appeal of socialism. The Kulturkampf was unsuccessful, as Catholics stayed loyal to their party, and was abandoned by Bismarck. (McKay, *A History of Western Society*, Eleventh Edition, pp. 771–772, 781)

72. **Answer: (C)**   Austria felt compelled to appease Hungarian Magyar nationalists when its military weakness was revealed in the Seven Weeks' War and agreed to let each half of the empire deal with its own ethnic minorities. Hungary had its own parliament and imposed its language on the subject nationalities within its jurisdiction, thereby

infuriating them. The Habsburg emperor became king of Hungary as well. (McKay, *A History of Western Society*, Eleventh Edition, pp. 774–775)

73. **Answer: (E)** Britain had the Irish problem, the Ottoman Empire was challenged by its subject peoples in North Africa and the Balkans, and there were uprisings among the subject nationalities in the 1905 revolution in Russia. Germany and France faced no such problems. (McKay, *A History of Western Society*, Eleventh Edition, pp. 765, 769–770, 773–774)

74. **Answer: (C)** The Tanzimat sought to revitalize the Ottoman Empire by adopting many Western ideas. (McKay, *A History of Western Society*, Eleventh Edition, p. 769)

75. **Answer: (D)** It was the racial definition of Jews and its electoral success that marked nineteenth-century anti-Semitism, which was particularly strong in Austria but not in Germany at that time. People like Lueger called for the elimination of the Jews from public life but not their extermination. Herzl was disillusioned by the Dreyfus Affair and Lueger's election. This led him to despair about assimilation. He became convinced that Jews would never be fully accepted unless they had a state of their own. (McKay, *A History of Western Society*, Eleventh Edition, pp. 777, 779–781)

76. **Answer: (C)** Redemption payments ended only after the 1905 revolution. Russia never really became a constitutional monarchy. Anti-Semitic pogroms were fostered by the government to deflect popular resentment. Under the finance minister, Witte, industrialization intensified with investments from abroad. (McKay, *A History of Western Society*, Eleventh Edition, pp. 765–769)

77. **Answer: (D)** Germans left Europe in the 1850s and 1880s. It was the Italians who considered themselves swallows; they left mostly around 1900, not before 1860. Immigration tended to drop in the early twentieth century. Australia as well as the United States passed laws to limit Chinese immigration. The United States received the greatest number of immigrants, but not more than half. (McKay, *A History of Western Society*, Eleventh Edition, pp. 797–801)

78. **Answer: (E)** While in 1750 the income gap between Europeans and non-Europeans was narrow, it had grown enormously by 1900. The standard of living in most non-European countries would only improve after independence in the twentieth century. A world economy had already come into being in the Age of Exploration. Africa was exploited for its natural resources, rather than factory labor. (McKay, *A History of Western Society*, Eleventh Edition, pp. 790–792)

79. **Answer: (C)** The British won at Omdurman with the use of the machine gun. The Portuguese held onto their old colonies but were little involved in the Scramble for Africa. Oil reserves were not involved in this battle. Omdurman did not violate the principles of the Berlin conference, only the rights of native Africans. The French did withdraw in the face of the British to avoid war, but that was at Fashoda, not Omdurman. (McKay, *A History of Western Society*, Eleventh Edition, p. 807)

80. **Answer: (A)** Although there were several economic motives for the new imperialism, its benefits were relatively limited before 1914, both in terms of return on investment and in terms of selling European goods, as the people in the colonies were still too poor to be consumers. (McKay, *A History of Western Society*, Eleventh Edition, pp. 807–808)

Answers for Section II: Part A

Remember that the two parts of the exam—Section I (multiple-choice) and Section II (three essays) are equally weighted at 50 percent each in determining the final score. Of the three essays, the document-based question counts for 45 percent of the Section II score, and the thematic question essays together count for 55 percent of the Section II score.

As these are not official AP Exam questions, we don't have official AP scoring standards for them. But you can use the following general guidelines to score your own essays.

AP European History DBQ essays are scored using the core-scoring method. Each specific instruction before the DBQ question itself refers to a core point. Once you earn all core points, you can earn additional points for doing those tasks well or for effectively bringing in outside information.

Include a thesis. To earn a point for your thesis, it must be specific, refer to documents, and not just repeat the question. If you don't earn a point for the thesis, you can't earn the point for supporting the thesis with an appropriate number of documents.

The following examples are of thesis statements that would *not* earn a point:

There were many views on the issue of what to do about unrest in the Balkans, and people were very emotional about that.

Why is this not acceptable? It doesn't refer to the documents in any specific way, nor does it address the specific terms of the questions. Here's another poor example:

The Russo-Turkish War of 1877–1878 was very controversial, and the political leaders of Britain were divided about how best to respond to the crisis in the Balkans.

This is better, but it doesn't show you've done much more than read the question and the historical background. Here is an example of a thesis statement and introductory paragraph that would earn a point:

British leaders were sharply divided in their attitudes toward the Ottoman Empire and the question of how to protect the Christian subjects under Turkish rule and also how to maintain the balance of power in the region. While many were appalled by atrocities reported in 1876 against the Bulgarians and called for British military intervention on behalf of the Christians, or called for a hands-off policy to allow those fighting the Turks to win, others were afraid that such a course would bring disastrous war and undermine the security of the Ottoman Empire and the stability of the region in which Britain had many important investments, including the Suez Canal. Still others were more concerned about the danger of Russian expansion there should the Turks prove vulnerable. This issue was so divisive that at least one Cabinet member resigned over the issue and even changed political parties.

This thesis refers to both positive and negative views about the intervention of the British in this war and gives a specific basis for those views, therefore addressing the question. Without those specifics, the thesis statement adds nothing to the question itself and could have been written without reading the documents.

Use a majority of the documents.   You must use at least half of the documents to earn this point. In the case of this practice exam, that means seven documents. Using a document means discussing something in the box specifically. You can still earn this point even if you make mistakes on one or two documents.

Interpret documents correctly.   You are allowed to make only one major error, which is defined as an interpretation that leads you to an erroneous conclusion or to an erroneous grouping. A major error, for example, would be if you described Lord Salisbury (Document 6) as a noninterventionist in this war.

Group the documents.   You must have three groups of documents. A group must have at least two documents in it, discussed specifically and together. Be specific when describing each group; that is, don't merely list documents together by number (for example, Documents 4, 5, and 7) but explain what the documents in a group have in common. Typical ways of making groups include: by opinion of author, by identity of author (nationality, political party or orientation, gender, age, position, etc.), by type of document (speeches, government documents, artworks, and so on), or by time period.
Possible groups in this DBQ include:

Social reformers/Liberals: [2] Stead, [5] Gladstone

Describing Turks as oppressors of Christians: [2] Stead, [5] Gladstone, [6] Salisbury

Outraged by atrocities: [1] Pears, [3] MacGahan

Conservatives: [4] Disraeli, [6] Salisbury, [7] *Gazette*, [9] Derby

Opposing war: [2] Stead, [6] Salisbury, [7] *Gazette*, [9] Derby

Opposing Russian expansion: [8] *Times*, [10] Queen Victoria, [11] Song, [12] Cartoon, [13] Cyprus Convention

Analyze point of view.   This is a crucial core point, one that some students don't do or do poorly. POV analysis shows that you understand that a particular person wrote a document at a particular time and place for a particular purpose, and that it may not present the whole truth. It's important to think about the reliability of the document. For example, if a painting is painted thirty years after the event it shows took place, can we rely upon it to provide an accurate depiction? Another way to do POV analysis is to connect the source's position in society—or anything given in the source identification—with the views the source expresses. The document summaries that follow show examples of the POV analysis you might make for each document.

Analyze individual documents.

Document 1   Sir Edwin Pears condemned Disraeli for his casual response to reports of atrocities in Bulgaria against Christians, which he said was part of intentional plans. He reported that a knowledgeable and objective reporter, the Irish-American MacGahan, was sent to the area to investigate. He also gave a reason for Turkish hostility to the Christians in Bulgaria, namely economic competition. POV: Having lived in Constantinople for forty years, Pears could be judged to be a reliable witness. He had a clear bias toward Christians, seeing them as more industrious, moral, and intelligent than the Turks or Muslims in the Balkans; this may be because he, most likely, was a Christian himself. He said that economic competition was at the heart of Christian-Muslim tensions; this may be because he lived in Constantinople for forty years (presumably safely) as a Christian and therefore did not see religion as the key factor in and of itself.

Document 2   W. T. Stead argued forcefully against British intervention on behalf of the Turks, whom he vilified for what he described as a campaign against the Christians, whom he labeled freedom fighters. POV: Stead was a social reformer who saw the Ottoman Empire as oppressive as well as decaying and was opposed to the Conservatives like Disraeli. As someone who saw war as terrible, he was opposed to what he saw as an unnecessary war to prop up an oppressive regime.

Document 3   MacGahan describes Turkish atrocities he witnessed in Batak, including the murder of children and the beheading of women. Batak's population was mostly gone. He said that he now could believe any accusation against the Turks. POV: MacGahan was the reporter described by Pears in Document 1 as not prejudiced against the Turks, but in this document he certainly vilified them. His views may have been changed as a result of what he witnessed.

Document 4   Disraeli said in a private letter that Britain now had a general in Turkish headquarters who challenged the view that the Serbs had won an important victory. POV: Disraeli was probably expressing his true views because they were expressed in a private letter. He was writing to an aristocrat who may have been a Conservative like himself. As prime minister, he may have sent the general to Turkish headquarters. As he had been instrumental in the acquisition of the Suez Canal, he was concerned that the Middle East remain stable. A Serbian victory would destabilize the region. Disraeli might have underestimated the strength of the Serbs for this reason.

Document 5   William Gladstone described the Turks as brutal, uncivilized, and inherently opposed to European values. The title of his pamphlet referred to the horrors in Bulgaria. He warned that atrocities might be committed again. POV: Gladstone and Disraeli were perpetual rivals, and when Gladstone wrote that pamphlet about Bulgaria, it might have been an attempt to win popular support for the next election. Gladstone was the leader of the Liberal Party and would oppose the Ottoman regime because it lacked democracy and social reforms.

Document 6   Lord Salisbury suggested in a letter to Disraeli a solution to the problem of Christians within the Ottoman Empire that would avoid direct British involvement by creating a new position to protect the Christians. He warns against the idea that any liberated territories could be returned to the Turkish government. POV: As a British foreign minister, Lord Salisbury was trying to find a solution to the problem that would appease those like Gladstone anxious to protect Christians in the Ottoman Empire. As Salisbury wrote this in a letter, it may have been only for Disraeli's private consideration and may have expressed his true views.

Document 7   The newspaper praised Lord Derby for his support of the protocol that was signed by Russia and Serbia. Russian demobilization was praised. POV: *The Pall Mall*

Gazette was a Conservative newspaper when this article was published, so it spoke in praise of the Conservative foreign secretary Lord Derby. Although Russian withdrawal was promised, the Russians invaded a few months after this article appeared.

Document 8   The *New York Times* reported from London that the Russian advance was stopped by the brave and heroic Turks. Serbs were described as arrogant aggressors claiming to defend Christians. POV: Although the source of the news from London was not identified, the views represent those of the Conservatives, who praised the victory of the Serbs and doubted the claims of the Serbs to be protectors of Christians.

Document 9   Lord Derby resigned from the Cabinet in 1878 because he disagreed with Disraeli's decision to send the fleet to protect Constantinople. POV: Lord Derby's disillusionment with Conservative policies in the Balkans is reflected by the fact that he switched parties and served under Prime Minister Gladstone. He may have been influenced by Gladstone's pamphlet (Document 5) in his views on the matter.

Document 10   Queen Victoria expressed her rage at the Russians and her concern for Britain's reputation. She urged in a letter to Disraeli that he take military action to prevent the Russian conquest of Constantinople. She threatened to abdicate if no action was taken. POV: The Queen expressed herself emotionally because she was writing a letter to Disraeli. She was anxious to defend the British Empire.

Document 11   This song represented "jingoism" or willingness to fight for nationalistic reasons. It was popular on the streets of London in early 1878. POV: The popularity of the song indicates that there was popular support, perhaps stirred by Gladstone's pamphlet two years earlier, for British intervention against Russia.

Document 12   This cartoon shows the British Lion and the Russian Bear about to embrace. The ringmaster (Disraeli) gives an aside that this will be explained and the crowd need not worry. POV: This is clearly a nationalistic cartoon that can be seen as satirical and opposing Britain's compromise with Russia at the Conference of Berlin. Disraeli is displayed in Roman military dress and as the ringmaster of a circus; his Jewish ancestry is also portrayed, rather negatively, in the cartoon.

Document 13   The treaty convention showed that Britain gained a strategic territory from the Ottoman Empire, Cyprus, before the Berlin Conference, in exchange for promises of military support to preserve its territorial integrity. At the same time, the Ottoman Empire promised reforms and protection of Christians. POV: Cyprus strengthened Britain's military presence in the eastern Mediterranean and allowed it to check further Russian advances; this is clearly a victory for the Conservative position as well as the Turks. This convention was a way to show the British people that Conservative policies would benefit them.

Answers for Section II: Parts B and C

General AP Scoring Standards for Thematic Essay Questions

The essays are scored on a scale of 0 to 9, with 0 being a real score. A response that is completely off task does not even earn a zero. Here are generic scoring guidelines for the essays in Parts B and C.

9–8
Has a clear, well-developed thesis
Is well organized
Addresses the terms of the question
Supports the thesis with substantial specific evidence
Has sophisticated analysis
May contain minor errors; even a 9 need not be flawless

7–6
Has a clear thesis
Addresses all parts of the question but discussion is uneven
Has competent analysis, but it may be superficial
Supports the thesis with some specific evidence

5–4
Contains a thesis, perhaps superficial or simplistic
Has uneven responses to the question's terms
May contain errors, factual or interpretative
Addresses the question with generally accurate discussion but without specific evidence; analysis is implicit or superficial
May contain major errors within a generally accurate and appropriate discussion
Is descriptive rather than analytical

3–2
Has weak or muddled thesis, perhaps suggesting false or inappropriate dichotomies or connections
Contains significant errors of chronology or fact
Has minimal discussion
Offers limited evidence

1–0
Has confused or absent thesis or merely restates the question
Misconstrues the question or omits major tasks
May contain major errors or irrelevant historical information
Addresses only one part of the question
Offers minimal or no evidence

Reread your essay and ask yourself the following questions—or if you can work with a fellow student in AP European History (APEH), read each other's essays and ask these questions:

1. How well organized is the essay? Is it clearly divided into distinct paragraphs? Is there an introduction and a conclusion?

2. How clear is the thesis? Is the thesis statement at the beginning of the essay or in the conclusion?

3. How many arguments support the thesis?

4. How much evidence is used to support the thesis? How specific was it?

5. Were all parts of the question addressed? Was the discussion of the different parts more or less balanced?

6. How many of the points noted in the explanations of the answer were made in the essay?

7. Were there major factual, chronological, or interpretative errors? Or minor errors?

8. Was the analysis explicit or implicit? Was it sophisticated or minimal?

Now reread the Scoring Guidelines and give yourself a score.

In general, the scores on the document-based questions average higher than those of the thematic essay questions, because the DBQ is a skill-based question that uses evidence, while the thematic essays are content-based and require recall of information. The median score on the DBQ is 5 (usually because of lack of POV), while the median scores on the thematic essays are typically 4 to 5 on the first and approximately 3 to 4 on the second, often because students run out of time.

Part B Responses

2. To what degree and in what ways did Napoleon betray the ideals of the French Revolution?

To answer this question well, you must first define the ideals of the French Revolution. This is not a yes-or-no question, but one where you are asked to make an evaluation. A simple organizational structure, as below, is to use the three-part slogan of the Revolution—liberty, equality, fraternity. Because Napoleon's regime was ambivalent on these issues, you can make very different but strong theses, supported by many different arguments, some of which are below.

Liberty: There was no political freedom in Napoleon's France, with a secret police, arrests of dissenters, and censorship of the press. There were no real elections, only yes-or-no plebiscites. Napoleon took power in a coup d'état and later crowned himself emperor, and put members of his family on the thrones of many conquered states rather than giving the conquered people a choice. Economic policies guaranteed property rights and encouraged opportunity and economic development, however, promoting economic liberty even if individual political liberty was discouraged.

Equality: Legal equality before the law was established for men. Women lost some rights, but it can be argued that because the revolutionary government did not extend the vote or equality to women either (although they did gain the right to financial support for their illegitimate children and then lost it under Napoleon), he was continuing the pattern established in the Revolution. Army commanders came from common as well as noble origins, continuing the practice begun in the Revolution. Feudalism and serfdom was abolished and the Napoleonic Code was enforced in countries conquered by Napoleon. Napoleon also opened new educational institutions, the lycée system, for young men of talent from all social classes. But Napoleon reinstated slavery in the colonies, which had been abolished by the Convention.

Fraternity: There was a huge stimulus to French nationalism and great pride taken in Napoleon's string of victories and conquests. Napoleon sought to reunify France after its divisive revolutionary years; he instituted new honors for service to the state, and he signed the Concordat of 1801 with the pope, which reconciled the religious Catholics. He welcomed the émigré nobles back and gave them roles to play in his government. French influence spread throughout Europe in the wake of his armies.

3. **Describe and explain the changes in family life in the late nineteenth century in the middle and working classes of Europe.**

Population growth was accomplished by a decline in death rates. Because fewer children died young, parents limited the number of their offspring through the use of various contraceptive methods now available. Parents of all classes were more devoted to their children and invested more in preparing them for future success. Fewer illegitimate children were born and fewer of these were abandoned.

Gender roles in the family changed as "separate spheres" became the ideal and in many case the practice, especially when real wages rose after 1850. This meant that the family was no longer an economically productive unit, except in working-class families where the husband could not support the family, and also in the retail business. Women were limited to household roles—such as supervision of servants—and had few legal rights.

Religion became less important in working-class families, although they continued to baptize their children.

Most working-class families continued to live close to kinship groups. Public transportation systems made it possible for many families to move into better housing and to have weekend excursions.

The ideal of romantic love emerged as the motivation for marriage, rather than finances or status that might be accrued through marriage. This was generally more the case of working-class than middle-class families. Married and unmarried couples went out together to pubs or music halls or concerts.

4. **Analyze the development of socialism as a movement in the nineteenth century.**

To fully explore nineteenth-century socialism, the response must analyze both the utopian socialists who wrote early in the century and the more militant socialists of midcentury and after. As suggested by the question itself, socialism was a broad and varied movement. An effective answer will describe the ideas of a number of different prominent socialists and not focus exclusively on Marxist socialism.

Possible thesis: Early utopian socialists, influenced by Enlightenment ideals and the French Revolution, established the fundamental ideas of socialism: the creation of a just society based on common ownership of property, equality, and central planning. Later socialists, having witnessed the sharp social and economic divisions brought about by developing industrialization, took a more militant stand against capitalism, some even promoting revolution as the only—and inevitable—solution to what they saw as the exploitation of the working class.

Utopian socialists: Utopian socialism emerged primarily in France and was shaped by the ideas of the Enlightenment and the experience of the French Revolution. Optimistic Enlightenment belief in the perfectibility of society shaped socialists' confidence in the potential for social transformation, and the principle of equality forcefully advanced by French revolutionaries shaped their values. The central planning instituted by Robespierre and the Committee of Public Safety amid the crisis of war and internal division demonstrated to these thinkers the effectiveness of government direction of the economy and society. The aristocrat Count Henri de Saint-Simon was the first to formulate utopian socialism. His vision of a just society rested on faith in a new elite of scientists, engineers, and industrialists who would take over from the old order of aristocrats and clergy and engineer a new order that would improve conditions for the poor. Charles Fourier envisioned a rigidly structured society, with people ordered into communities called "phalanxes" of equal size. Robert Owen, a British utopian socialist, took a similar approach, advocating—and even attempting—the creation of ideal communities that mixed agriculture and manufacturing. While Owen's ideal communities ultimately failed, as did those founded on the basis of Saint-Simon's and Fourier's ideas, the visions offered by these utopian socialists continued to influence socialism and inspire followers.

Militant socialists: By around 1840, industrialization was well under way on the continent, and social and economic differences between the middle and working classes sharpened. Industrialists—on whom Saint-Simon counted to take part in leading the new planned society—came under increasing criticism from socialists. More militant socialists came to embrace the interests of the working class specifically. While they still promised a more just, more equitable society, it was with the laboring class—not the capitalists—in control. Pierre Joseph Proudhon reflects this view. His *What Is Property?* (1840) saw property as nothing but the theft of the working class's productive labor. Proudhon did not wish to abolish all private property, however, only that which arose from the exploitation of another's labor. Louis Blanc, in *The Organization of Work* (1839), believed the working class only needed to gain suffrage to become the dominant political force in society and, once in control of the government, to institute state-run workshops that would guarantee full employment. The militant critique of capitalism culminated in the radical socialism of Karl Marx, who saw the capitalist bourgeoisie and working-class proletariat as fundamentally at odds with one another, the former thriving by the exploitation of the latter. Unlike Blanc, Marx did not have faith in curing this social ill through democratic means. Only by revolution, by the seizure of power from the bourgeoisie, could the proletariat achieve this ideal society.

Part C Responses

5. **Compare and contrast the processes of industrialization in England and on the European continent.**

This is a comparison question, so it's important to show similarities and differences. Your thesis can focus on one or more of these, such as the role of governments.

Similarities: Industrialization was accompanied by urbanization and by deplorable working and housing conditions that slowly ameliorated. Labor unions and political parties representing the interests of workers became important. Labor legislation was initiated by conservative political leaders. Mercantilism was adopted to protect local industries. Per capita productivity and income increased within a half century.

Differences: British industrialization began in the eighteenth century, while on the continent industrialization began first in Belgium in 1830s, and even later elsewhere. British industrialization was almost completely a result of private initiative, with little government involvement, but on the continent governments played a greater role, particularly in Prussia and later in Russia. British industrialization began in the textile industries, but because it was hard for other nations to compete with British goods, other industries became dominant on the continent, especially steel and iron. In Britain there were transformative inventions like the steam engine; continental technological advancements increased productivity but were less revolutionary. Britain abandoned protectionism and adopted free trade with the repeal of the Corn Laws in 1846, while most states on the continent retained protectionist tariffs. In Britain, industrialization was thorough and deep and maintained its momentum over time, but it was much more gradual and more inconsistent on the continent, often accompanied by economic dislocation and inflation. Industrialization was less widespread in France and Russia.

Continental countries had disadvantages and advantages over Britain. Advantages included well-established artisanal and commercial communities that could build on already developed technologies. They also had strong governments interested in promoting industry, issuing bonds or guaranteeing investments, and establishing corporate banks. Disadvantages included the difficulties of competing with British manufactured goods and of mastering the complicated British machines. Britain had decades of economic superiority over the continental industrial states; it continued to produce its goods so cheaply that they couldn't easily compete.

6. **Compare and contrast European imperialism of the late nineteenth century with European colonialism in the early modern period.**

To answer this question well, you should discuss several similarities and differences.

Similarities: In both periods, Europeans were motivated partially by economic aims, religious missionary zeal, and national glory. In both periods, colonies were seen as crucial for national prestige as well as necessary for naval reasons.

Differences: In the early period, Europeans rarely penetrated into the interior of colonized lands, building mostly coastal settlements, except in the Americas. In Asia and Africa during this early period, they showed some respect for native rulers. Their impact there tended to be limited to those with whom they came into contact, though in the New World, the European conquest thoroughly transformed those societies. Economically, Europeans were mostly interested in raw materials, slaves, and agricultural produce. By the nineteenth century, Europeans had lost most of their colonies in the New World but colonized virtually all of Africa and most of Asia. They penetrated to the interior because of medical and shipping technological advances, and they had vast military superiority that allowed them to take over politically through either direct or indirect rule. They built infrastructure and imposed European educational and value systems. Economically, rubber, oil, and other products needed for industrial economy were important resources.

7. **Compare and contrast the problems facing proponents of Italian and German unification from 1848 to 1870 and the processes by which they achieved their goals.**

To answer this question well, you should discuss several similarities and differences.

Similarities: In 1848, proponents of unification in both Germany and Italy faced opposition from rulers of individual states, and both states saw democratic attempts to forge a unified state in the 1848 revolutions. Mazzini established a republic in Rome, and the Frankfurt

Assembly offered the crown of a unified constitutional monarchy to the King of Prussia. Both of these attempts failed, and unification in each was engineered by strong, modernized, and industrialized states (Sardinia-Piedmont, Prussia) under the exceptional leadership of royal appointees (Cavour and Bismarck). Both Sardinia-Piedmont and Prussia went to war with Austria (in 1859 and 1866, respectively). Both states used France to achieve unification (Cavour's alliance with France in 1859, Rome joining the rest of Italy when the French withdrew their troops in 1870, and Bismarck fighting the Franco-Prussian War of 1870). Both states had to contend with Catholic reluctance to join the new nation-states but were able to generate sufficient nationalistic sentiments to overcome that resistance.

Differences: In 1848, Germany faced the problem of who should be in the united Germany—if it were to include all Germans, then that would mean the Austrians and Bohemians. If Austria were to join, then it would bring the many non-Germans in its empire into unified Germany, or it would have to give up the areas where they lived. The Catholic Germanic states were reluctant to be part of a state dominated by Protestants. Some of the Italian states were under the rule of various external powers—Austria held Lombardy and Venetia, the Kingdom of Two Sicilies was under Bourbon rule, and the Papal States and Rome were under the pope. The two states that forged unification also had different governments. Sardinia-Piedmont was a constitutional monarchy, and Prussia was an autocratic state where the Reichstag had limited power. Republican ideals and republicans, represented by Garibaldi, played an important role in bringing Naples, Sicily, and Rome into unified Italy; there was no role for republicans in Germany. Germany was unified as an empire in which individual states kept their princely rulers; Italy was a unified state under a single monarch. The German empire was declared at Versailles, accentuating the importance of military victory; Italian capitals were first Florence and then Rome, each of which had been republics, however briefly. Italy had limited suffrage; Germany had universal manhood suffrage. Cavour died before final unification was achieved; Bismarck was chancellor of unified Germany for another two decades.

PART 4
The Twentieth Century to the Present

This part covers the following chapters in *A History of Western Society,* Eleventh Edition:

Chapter 25   War and Revolution, 1914–1919

Chapter 26   The Age of Anxiety, 1880–1940

Chapter 27   Dictatorships and the Second World War, 1919–1945

Chapter 28   Cold War Conflict and Consensus, 1945–1965

Chapter 29   Challenging the Postwar Order, 1960–1991

Chapter 30   Life in an Age of Globalization, 1990 to the Present

Europeans began the twentieth century proud of their high standard of living, their scientific and technological mastery, and their domination on the world stage. Fifty years later, Europe lay in shambles, economically, politically, and socially devastated by two world wars and the knowledge of the violent offenses its factions were all too capable of committing against one another. For most of the next half century, Europe was overshadowed by two superpowers, the United States and U.S.S.R., that had blossomed in the wake of their victory in World War II and faced each other in fierce competition during the Cold War. But by the end of the twentieth century, Europe transformed itself from a continent of bickering nation-states to a more or less unified economic unit, the European Union, able to compete effectively in the world economy and take an increasingly active role in world politics.

The First World War that shattered the self-satisfied and comfortable world of Europeans was caused by the forces that had built over the long nineteenth century. Industrialization led to competition for control over natural resources and markets around the globe in the late nineteenth century and provided the means for imperialism with modern weapons. This in turn led to an arms race among the Great Powers—the United Kingdom, France, Germany, Austria, and Russia. Tensions over colonial aspirations and within Europe encouraged the creation of alliances and ententes ("understandings") that drew nations into war whether they wanted it or not.

Nationalism, unleashed as a modern force during the French Revolution, rocked the stability of early twentieth-century Europe. Newly unified Germany underestimated its need to protect itself from France, which strove to take back Alsace-Lorraine (lost to Germany in 1870) in its own nationalistic fervor. In the Balkans, Austria grabbed territories as the Ottoman Empire weakened; Serbian nationalistic frustrations over Austrian occupation sparked World War I in 1914. After nearly a century of general peace, there was widespread enthusiasm for war. Most thought a war would, like those of the late nineteenth century, be short, decisive, and glorious. That was not the reality.

Also known as the Great War, World War I grew into a battle on the world stage between the Allies (members of the Triple Entente: the United Kingdom, France, and Russia)

and the Central Powers (members of the Triple Alliance: the German, Austro-Hungarian, and Ottoman Empires, along with Bulgaria). The machine gun gave the advantage to the Allies' defense, and once the German invasion of France was stopped at the Marne, neither side could score a decisive victory. Instead, the western front was a thousand miles of well-dug trenches that remained more or less the same for four years despite huge battles that cost hundreds of thousands of lives but yielded little territorial gain. On the eastern front, there was more movement, but no clear winner emerged. The war ended in 1918 with armistice, not surrender or victory, with some 10 million dead and 20 million wounded.

The war was rife with technological advances, new weapons designed to break the stalemate — the submarine, the tank, the airplane, and chemical warfare. It also inspired wonderful poetry written on both sides of the trenches. It changed the roles of women in society for good. With so many men at the front, women took positions previously closed to them, adopted new fashions and behaviors, and asserted independent decision making, so much so that after the war, women finally won their long fight for the right to vote. Unions gained new respectability for not striking during the war. Class tensions eased as nationalism and grief brought people together. During the war, governments abandoned laissez-faire capitalism and intervened directly in the economy, planning industrial production and rationing foods and goods. They also restricted civil liberties and engaged in vigorous propaganda to keep spirits up.

After the First World War, Europe experienced a crisis of confidence in its traditional values. Democracy lost out to authoritarianism or totalitarianism in most places. Artists and scholars rejected their nineteenth-century predecessors. They adopted atonality in music; free verse in poetry; abstractionism, expressionism, and cubism in painting; functionalism in architecture; Freudian psychoanalysis; and existentialism and logical positivism in philosophy. The Russian Revolution, which unfolded during World War I, profoundly influenced the postwar period and the Cold War that grew out of it. The tsar's refusal to become a constitutional monarch in 1905 was a fatal mistake. In 1917, after three years of poor military leadership, he was turned away by his own troops during popular demonstrations and forced to abdicate his throne. When the government that replaced him continued participation in World War I, a new leader emerged. Vladimir Ilyich Lenin generated much popular support and organized the November 1917 coup d'état that created the world's first Communist state. His Bolshevik brand of Marxism asserted that revolution could occur only violently and only if led by committed revolutionaries. The peasant class, if large enough, was capable of replacing the bourgeoisie. Lenin's success in 1917 — and later Joseph Stalin's rapid industrialization and achievement of Great Power status — provided a model for colonized peoples around the globe.

During the first decade after the revolution, the Soviet Union saw extraordinary change and violent civil war. Joseph Stalin, who took over after Lenin's death, imposed a strict order, persecuting millions of people who opposed his policies; many millions (the exact number is unknown) died in his labor camps. He imposed Russian interests over those of the other nationalities, as was evident by the regime's allowing 6 million Ukrainians to die in a famine. Under Stalin's rule, artistic and intellectual freedom disappeared. He forcibly industrialized the country and collectivized agriculture. Ordinary people saw tangible benefits like guaranteed jobs as well as free education and medical care. Their adherence to the system was revealed by their fierce self-defense during the Second World War.

Fascism, too, was born of World War I and the Treaty of Versailles. The treaties that ended the war were negotiated by the victors — the United States, France, and the United Kingdom — without the participation of those who had sued for peace, unlike the Congress of Vienna in 1814. U.S. president Woodrow Wilson had promised a just, not a punitive, peace in his Fourteen Points, which also called for self-determination of subject peoples. He compromised most of his principles to achieve the fourteenth point, the creation of the League of Nations. France and Britain assigned blame for the war to Germany and saddled the Germans with a huge bill for reparations. While some of its territorial losses were predictable (its colonies in Africa and Alsace-Lorraine), Germany lost its territorial integrity when the Polish corridor was created to give newly reconstituted Poland access to the sea. And it lost its ability to defend itself by a vast reduction in the size of its army and navy. Other states were disappointed by the treaties as well. Italy was not given back all of its land held by Austria, and Arabs and other colonized peoples were not allowed self-determination, seeding long-lasting problems in the Middle East.

Many Italian nationalists, frustrated over Italy's treatment at Versailles, were attracted to a new movement: fascism, the brainchild of a former socialist, Benito Mussolini. Fascism rejected the Enlightenment rationalist vision, stating that passion, not reason, is man's driving force. Fascists thought that war and violence bring out the best in a society, the individual counts for nothing except insofar as he serves the state, and the leader acts like the brain in the body that is the people. Mussolini's Fascists denounced democracy and Marxist class warfare equally. Fascism appealed to nationalists, the disaffected, the young, veterans yearning for the excitement and comradeship of war, and the middle class fearing a proletarian revolution during postwar labor unrest.

Mussolini was appointed prime minister by the king and within a few years had established a repressive, authoritarian, one-party state that was more conservative than totalitarian. The Fascists sought to end class warfare by creating the corporate state and to restore Italy's greatness with an invasion of Ethiopia in 1935. While the left and many intellectuals were opponents, the Fascist government was generally popular for its restoration of law and order and for making Italy seem important once again. The fate of the Italian Fascists became tied to that of the Germans after they established the Rome-Berlin Axis in 1936.

German fascism also drew on fear and dissatisfaction, which had grown in Germany after the Treaty of Versailles. After the armistice forced the kaiser to abdicate, the newly formed Weimar Republic inherited a troublesome birthright. The republic, whose first president was a Social Democrat, survived attempted revolutions by the Communist left and the Fascist right and devastating hyperinflation, but over time the government restored Germany to prosperity and slowly won solid support. These gains fell apart when the Great Depression hit Germany hard.

German fascism, like the Italian version, was intensely nationalistic and disparaging of democracy, individualism, and Marxism. A small extremist group called the National Socialist Germany Workers' Party, or Nazis, under the leadership of Adolf Hitler, called for a unique brand of German national socialism that would create a mighty "people's community." Nazism declared the German *volk* (people) superior not only culturally but biologically. Jews in particular, but also Communists, Roma and Sinti (Gypsies), and other "undesirables," were the targets of Hitler's virulent racist views. By articulating a single enemy, the Nazi movement and its charismatic leader Adolf Hitler garnished wide support during the depression. The party won the plurality in 1933, in the last free election before Hitler's takeover.

The Nazi state, the Third Reich, lasted twelve years (to 1945). It quickly established a totalitarian society, eliminating all political opposition and remaking Germany on every front. Hitler fulfilled many of his campaign promises: he eliminated Jews from public life first and "Aryanized" their businesses. In violation of the Treaty of Versailles, he restored Germany to military strength and provided jobs by rearmament. And he achieved *lebensraum* (living space) by creating a "Greater Germany" in 1938 through the annexation of Austria and the Sudetenland, a part of Czechoslovakia inhabited by ethnic Germans. World War II began in September 1939 with the German invasion of Poland, following which Britain and France abandoned their policies of appeasement and declared war. German *blitzkrieg* (lightning war) tactics were amazingly effective, defeating France in only a few weeks and taking over virtually all of western Europe. Britain stood alone against Germany for one year, until the Soviet Union (which had signed a nonaggression treaty with Germany in 1939) and the United States entered the war in 1941. The Soviets were brought into the war by the German invasion of their land, the United States by an attack by Japan (a German ally) on its naval base at Pearl Harbor. The tide of war changed in 1942 with decisive Allied victories, although it would take another three years for Germany and Japan to surrender.

During the war, the Nazis abused millions of Slavs and other "inferior" races with brutal work in slave-labor camps. They systematically killed half of Europe's Jews (some 6 million of them) in extermination camps alongside a high percentage of the Roma and Sinti populations. These mass murders, collectively known as the Holocaust, haunt Europe to this day.

The two superpowers who came into the war in 1941 and were largely responsible for German defeat almost immediately faced each other as enemies ideologically, politically, and economically in the fifty-year Cold War. The Stalinist Soviet Union imposed Communist regimes on Eastern Europe, which it had liberated from the Germans, and held onto them tightly until the 1980s. Western Europe was rebuilt economically with American aid in the Marshall Plan (1947) and militarily with NATO, the North Atlantic Treaty Organization (1949). In 1949, heated confrontations in Berlin led to a more permanent East/West divide: West Germany became a democratic, capitalistic state welcomed into NATO, and East Germany, a Communist dictatorship firmly in the Soviet bloc. Both sides built up nuclear weapons and engaged in proxy wars in Asia (Korea, Vietnam), Latin America (El Salvador, Nicaragua), the Middle East (Israel), and Africa (Congo, Angola, and elsewhere). In the decades after World War II, European empires ended as they lost their colonies either through voluntary relinquishment (as in India and Ghana) or war (as in Algeria and Vietnam).

The first two decades after the war were generally ones of consensus. Western European governments were mostly run by democratic socialists who created or expanded the welfare state in the wake of economic resurgence. When that "economic miracle" began to wane in the 1970s, western Europeans turned to conservative leaders. At the same time, the Soviet Union, which had ended the worst abuses of Stalinism in the 1950s, experienced economic and political stagnation. In the eastern European satellites, various popular movements demanded greater democracy, independence from Russian control, and consumer goods. In the 1950s and 1960s, the U.S.S.R. crushed such reform efforts; by the late 1980s, however, it had lost its will and its capacity to do so. Soviet leader Mikhail Gorbachev opened up the system with *glasnost* and *perestroika*. In 1989, a year of great surprises, a democratic election was held in the Soviet Union, and very quickly, the symbol of Communist repression, the Berlin Wall, was torn down. One satellite after another threw off the Communist yoke, the U.S.S.R. disappeared, and Germany reunited. The transition to capitalism and democracy proved difficult for many eastern Europeans, and Russia returned to authoritarian rule under Vladimir Putin in 2000.

The great story of the last fifty years in Europe was the slow but steady movement toward unification in Europe. Beginning with the European Coal and Steel Community in the 1950s, France, Germany, and other states abandoned their long-standing nationalistic hostilities and forged an economic union that slowly morphed into the European Union, with free movement of goods and people and a Europe-wide bureaucracy, military force, and parliament. While this gradual unification process was occurring, some European states had broken into smaller nations (Yugoslavia, Czechoslovakia), and the U.S.S.R. had disappeared. Europe has positioned itself as a major force in the world economy and in world politics, defending democratic principles, resurgent from the ashes of World War II and totalitarianism.

Areas of focus: Britain, Germany, Austria-Hungary, Ottoman Empire, Russia

Main events: the outbreak of World War I, trench warfare, the Russian Revolution, armistice, the Versailles/Paris Peace Conference

---

The following is a thematic summary of the material covered in Chapter 25 of *A History of Western Society:*

Politics

+ After nearly one hundred years of general peace, rising prosperity, and international power, Europeans began a four-year war that destroyed millions of lives and brought down four European empires—the Russian, Ottoman, Austro-Hungarian, and German.

✦ **AP Tip**   World War I, the Versailles treaties, and the Russian Revolution were world historical events and are absolutely crucial for an understanding of modern history. Virtually every AP Exam asks for an essay about causes or consequences of the war, the peace treaties, or the revolution.

+ What might have been a localized conflict between Serbia and Austria became a world war due to a complicated alliance system (the Triple Alliance of Austria, Germany, and Italy versus the Triple Entente of Britain, Russia, and France) that drew states into war. Xenophobia, nationalism, imperialistic competition, and militarism pitted peoples against each other, encouraged an arms race, and weakened internationalism. In this hostile atmosphere, the assassination of the heir to the Austro-Hungarian throne, Archduke Francis Ferdinand, by a Serb in Bosnia easily provided the spark for war.

+ When war broke out in August 1914, crowds enthusiastically rallied and young men lined up to volunteer thinking the war would be brief and decisive. Instead, it lasted over four years and had no simple resolution, as victory eluded each of the two sides—the Central Powers (Germany, Austria-Hungary, the Ottoman Empire, and Bulgaria) and the Allies (France, Britain, Russia, and some thirty other states including the United States after 1917).

+ The thousand-mile-long western front became a series of trenches with high death tolls due largely to the introduction of the machine gun. Attempts to end the stalemate by force of new weapons and heavy machinery (the tank, airplane bombing, the submarine, mustard gas, and other forms of chemical warfare) and by widening the fighting to other arenas outside of Europe (the Middle East) were largely ineffective. Major battles—such as the Marne (near Paris), Gallipoli, Tannenberg, Verdun, and the Somme—had death tolls of hundreds of thousands on each side for little real result.

✦ On the eastern front, death tolls were even higher, with huge losses for both Germany and Russia. Fighting was more mobile there, but definitive victories were just as elusive as in the west.

✦ In order to maintain such a long and damaging war effort, governments permanently increased the scope of their authority to ensure continued popular support and sufficient men and materials for war. Governments on both sides manipulated public opinion through censorship of the press and propaganda, and severely limited civil liberties.

✦ Initially, virtually everyone supported the war, but by 1916, antiwar sentiment grew. Britain faced, but quickly crushed, a rebellion by Irish nationalists on Easter Sunday in 1916. At the front, too, disillusionment was evident. In May 1917, there was a mutiny in the French forces; Russian soldiers frequently deserted in droves; and the Italian army also collapsed.

✦ The war saw mass killings on the basis of ethnicity, including the Armenian genocide—the Turkish massacre of perhaps a million and a half Armenians in 1915.

✦ In Russia, the war intensified the discontent long felt about the tsarist regime. Russia's early defeats by the German army, the tsar's direct leadership of a poorly managed war effort, and the lack of democracy led to a spontaneous uprising of the people in March 1917, also known as the February Revolution. Tsar Nicholas II abdicated, and a provisional government was formed. In spring 1917, many Russian soldiers walked away from the front, inspired by the promises of "Peace, Land, and Bread" made by Vladimir Lenin, head of the Bolshevik wing of the Social Democratic Party.

✦ In November 1917, the Bolsheviks took power in a coup d'état and founded the first Communist regime in the world. Lenin was the head of a new government in which councils (or "soviets") of workers, peasants, and soldiers were to have all the power. Lenin immediately sued for peace, giving in to tough demands from the Germans for territory in the Treaty of Brest-Litovsk of March 1918. Russia was quickly embroiled in a bloody, two-year civil war between the Whites, who opposed communism and the terms of the peace treaty, and the Communist Reds. The Reds won because of the effective leadership of Leon Trotsky, an energetic secret police, and "War Communism," or control of the economy and food supplies. They established the Union of Soviet Socialist Republics, ruled by the Communist Party as the "dictatorship of the proletariat," that lasted more than seventy years.

✦ **AP Tip** The Russian Revolution is the last of the three great successful European revolutions, along with the English in the seventeenth century and the French in the eighteenth. While the issues in each varied widely, a certain pattern of revolution can be discerned—reform, radicalization, civil war, dictatorship, and reaction or restoration of some elements of the prerevolutionary state.

✦ World War I ended on November 11, 1918, after the Germans failed in their last offensive and a revolution forced Emperor William II to abdicate. The Social Democratic Party in Germany established the Weimar Republic, and the Austro-Hungarian Empire was split into the independent states of Austria, Hungary, Czechoslovakia, and Romania.

✦ The peace settlement of 1919, commonly known as the Treaty of Versailles, was a compromise between French and British desires for revenge on a weak Germany and U.S. president Woodrow Wilson's negotiations for an international organization to prevent further war. Although not defeated on the battlefield, Germany was not invited to the peace conference. The treaty it was forced to accept was punitive. Although it lost relatively little territory (its African colonies to France, Japan, and Britain; Alsace-Lorraine to France; and East Prussia to newly reconstituted Poland), Germany was forced to pay huge reparations, to accept blame for the war, and to limit its army to 100,000 men. Austria lost most of its territory as Poland, Hungary, Czechoslovakia, and Yugoslavia came into being. The Ottoman Empire was dismembered.

✦ Although Wilson had articulated a war aim of self-determination of subject nationalities, a mandate system for the former German and Ottoman colonies was established. Many people around the globe were disappointed: Arabs had been promised independence if they joined the war against the Ottoman Empire but were instead put under the indirect rule of Britain and France; Zionist Jews were frustrated that the Balfour Declaration was ignored and they were not given their promised homeland; Vietnamese hopes for independence from the French were dashed as well.

✦ The League of Nations was created, with a weak executive and no army, to negotiate disputes, act collectively against aggression, and supervise the mandates of the Treaty of Versailles.

✦ The U.S. Senate refused to ratify the terms of the treaty, and the United States effectively turned its back on Europe, beginning a new age of American isolationism. Great Britain followed suit, leaving France effectively without allies.

✦ Arab nations were generally unable to attain the freedom vaguely promised to them by the treaty terms. But the Turks rebounded from the near deathblow of the war with a strong leader, Mustafa Kemal, who organized a Turkish military force and defeated British and French forces. He created an authoritarian, westernized Turkish republic, separated church and state, established a secular educational system, and granted more rights to women.

✦ Almost everyone was disappointed in the treaties, and those frustrations directly led to the rise of fascism and World War II. In the Middle East, the broken promises of self-determination after the war led to resentment. They were a huge cause of the violence and disorder there, and are to this day.

Economy

✦ To manage the long war, governments abandoned laissez-faire capitalism in favor of the planned economy (where governments decide what is to be produced, who produces it, and how), instituted rationing, set wage and price controls, and limited workers' rights. This was total war, with every aspect of life engaged.

✦ Successful state management of the wartime economy gave credibility to socialism.

✦ Germany encouraged the making of synthetic goods like rubber to aid in war material production. With inflation, black markets, food shortages due to the British blockade, and deficit spending, times were difficult in Germany toward the end of the war, with many near starvation.

✦ Britain was economically better off than Germany because of its empire and imports from the United States.

Religion

✦ Religious issues played no role in causing the war, but the experience of the war both at the front and at home encouraged secularism and made religion irrelevant to some.

✦ In Russia, the close affiliation of the Russian Orthodox Church with the tsarist regime meant that the new Communist government was extremely hostile to it.

✦ Both the provisional government formed in Russia after the February Revolution and the Turkish government under Mustafa Kemal established freedom of religion, which had previously been absent in these areas.

Society and Culture

✦ Class distinctions lessened both at the front and at home. Labor unions and workers grew in importance and prestige because of their loyalty and cooperation with the war effort.

✦ Women took jobs in industry, transportation, and public service at home, and at the front as nurses and ambulance drivers, becoming visible in the public sphere as never before. Postwar disillusionment led to looser sexual morality, which led some women to bob their hair, shorten their skirts, and smoke cigarettes in public. Women were given the vote immediately after the war in Britain, Germany, Poland, and the United States.

Ideas and Literature

✦ Vladimir Lenin (1870–1924) modified Marxian ideology by insisting that socialism could be achieved only through revolution. This could occur in countries only partially industrialized and partially feudal like Russia, if led by a small, tightly disciplined revolutionary vanguard. Marxist-Leninists took the name Bolsheviks to distinguish themselves from the more democratic Marxists in Russia, the Mensheviks, and later called themselves Communists.

✦ **AP Tip**   Perhaps in no other war has there been such an outpouring of wonderful literature. Poets stationed on the western front wrote stirring, sometimes grim, poems of their experiences, and after the war, that experience informed virtually every art form. Such literature or artwork could easily appear in a document-based question section relating to World War I.

Arts

✦ The war and the Russian Revolution sparked the use of striking propaganda posters.

The Age of Anxiety, 1880–1940

> **Areas of focus:** Germany, England, France, the United States
>
> **Main events:** the Great Depression; the New Deal; consumer society; Modernism in art, architecture, and music; the rise of existentialism, surrealism, and Dadaism

The following is a thematic summary of the material covered in Chapter 26 of *A History of Western Society:*

Politics

+ Most Germans hated the 1919 Treaty of Versailles, especially the bill for reparations, set for $33 billion, which they had to pay or face occupation. The first postwar international crisis occurred when the Germans couldn't meet a reparations payment in 1922; the French occupied the Ruhr, an industrial area of western Germany. Moderates won out in both countries, and the crisis was resolved. The reorganization of reparations under the American Dawes Plan (1924) reduced Germany's annual payments but created a dangerous financial system in which, effectively, Germany received private loans from the United States in order to pay reparations to France and Britain, which they then used to repay the large war debts they owed the United States.

+ In 1925, Germany, France, and other states signed the Treaty of Locarno, accepting the borders created by the Treaty of Versailles. Germany made similar agreements with Czechoslovakia and Poland and joined the League of Nations. Fifteen nations (including the United States) signed the Kellogg-Briand Pact in 1928, agreeing to avoid war and solve international disputes peacefully. The pact fostered optimism at the time of its signing but did little to halt World War II eleven years later.

+ The new German republic survived an attempted coup d'état in Bavaria in 1923 by a small, extremely nationalist, anti-Semitic party: the National Socialists, or Nazis. Its leader, Adolf Hitler, came to national attention during his trial and with the subsequent 1924 publication of *Mein Kampf,* outlining his racist views and plans for the expansion of Germany.

+ France rebuilt quickly after the war, and the Great Depression arrived later there than in more heavily industrialized countries. There were frequent changes of government and a growing Fascist movement in France when the Great Depression hit in 1929. Communists, socialists, and others allied in the Popular Front in order to combat the growth in fascism at home and abroad. They won the election of 1936.

✦ In Britain, the postwar period saw high unemployment. The moderately socialist Labour Party helped to maintain the greater social equality achieved during the war and to ensure social harmony.

✦ In 1922, the Irish Republic was created, although the northern province remained part of the United Kingdom.

Economy

✦ When the French sent troops into the Ruhr (1923–1925), the German economy was paralyzed. The situation was saved when a new chancellor, Gustav Stresemann, agreed to pay reparations if France agreed to compromise on the amount. Germany returned to prosperity with remarkable speed and was able to pay a good part of its reparation bills by 1928.

✦ The Great Depression (1929–1939), which began in the United States mostly because of speculation in the stock market, hit Europe hard, causing high unemployment, spiraling deflation, and loss of productivity. Governments were not very effective in dealing with the crisis, and in many cases made it worse by imposing protectionist tariffs and cutting spending instead of increasing it to stimulate the economies. Britain went off the gold standard to drop the value of its currency.

✦ Franklin Delano Roosevelt's (U.S. president, 1933–1945) New Deal was only partly successful as a response to the Great Depression. While certain projects such as the Works Progress Administration (WPA) and the national Social Security system, both established in 1935, were popular and enduring legacies of the New Deal, it wasn't until World War II that the United States was fully catapulted out of the depression.

✦ The Scandinavian response was the most successful of the industrialized nations. Sweden increased spending on social welfare programs and used large deficits to fund public works to keep people employed.

Religion

✦ The decades after World War I saw a revival of fundamental Christian thought. Søren Kierkegaard, a rediscovered nineteenth-century Danish philosopher, called for a "leap of faith." He believed that even if God is unknowable and his existence cannot be proven, faith in God's power and majesty can remain. Karl Barth similarly called for an emotional and trusting acceptance of God's grace, regardless of reason and logic.

✦ Catholic existentialists argued that the Catholic Church offered a way out of the conundrums of the modern world. Many prominent English poets and novelists turned toward Catholicism.

Society and Culture

✦ During the 1920s, mass culture deeply penetrated ordinary life. Inexpensive manufactured goods sold in department stores and energetically advertised created mass consumerism.

✦ The somewhat stereotyped image of the "new woman" emerged during the 1920s. Women had gained economic independence and voting rights, and the emergence of a consumer society allowed them greater personal freedom. The "new woman" image was used as a marketing tool in this consumer society.

✦ Radio and the cinema provided inexpensive entertainment and transformed cultural life on a mass scale never hitherto seen. Radio and film stars became celebrated figures, often on an international scale.

✦ During the 1930s, Britain and Germany saw unemployment skyrocket, with poverty, ill health, and hopelessness in millions of homes and a dramatic decline in birthrates.

Ideas and Literature

✦ **AP Tip**   Europe in the 1920s and 1930s was a fountain of new ideas in literature, philosophy, and the arts, which came to play an important role in the profound struggle between a new political idea (fascism) and the older ideas of constitutionalism and Marxism. This made the period phenomenally fertile but also very destabilizing. You will probably have looked at some of these artworks or read some of the poetry or novels; use what you are learning in history to contextualize your experience of the arts, and vice versa. It is a good idea to bring such insights into an AP essay, particularly if modernist primary sources appear in a document-based question.

✦ New ideas in philosophy, physics, and psychology developed before the Great War had significant impact afterwards. Many abandoned or revised the rational worldview and the belief in progress created by the Scientific Revolution, the Enlightenment, and the Industrial Revolution. The table on pages 254–256 summarizes some of the major ideas to influence science and philosophy during this period.

Arts

✦ Modernism, a general term for experimentation and new modes of expression, dominated the arts. Artists created new genres to convey the complex desires, memories, and ideas of the inner person.

✦ An international artistic culture came into being. Picasso was the model of the modern artist—famous, innovative, prolific, and politically engaged.

✦ Atonal and twelve-tone music found little popularity with concertgoers.

✦ The movies, at first silent and short, were created in the 1890s. The United States dominated the film industry as Hollywood stars became hugely popular. By the 1930s, movies were part of the weekly life of most Europeans and Americans.

✦ In 1920, the first radio broadcast was heard all over Europe, and national broadcasting networks were quickly established, mostly under state ownership. Radio rapidly became popular as entertainment, but also as a powerful tool for propaganda for both dictators and democratic leaders.

✦ Movies, too, served as propaganda. Lenin and Hitler promoted the film industry and encouraged great directors like Sergei Eisenstein in Russia (*Potemkin*) and Leni Riefenstahl (*Triumph of the Will*) in Germany.

✦ The new artistic, literary, and musical movements were fiercely denounced by Fascists and Nazis, who defined them as degenerate. Many of the modernist artists, architects, filmmakers, and writers were forced into exile during the Nazi period. The following table summarizes the major art forms and leading figures within each form, as well as their major works and the ideas found in these works.

Ideas and Literature			
FIELD	**LEADING FIGURES**	**SELECT MAJOR WORKS**	**KEY IDEAS**
Philosophy	Friedrich Neitzsche (German)	*On the Genealogy of Morals* (1877)	Christianity embodies a "slave morality" that glorifies weakness. Individuals rise above meaninglessness by breaking free of the masses.
	Henri Bergson (French)		Immediate experience and intuition are as important to explaining reality as reason and science.
	Ludwig Wittgenstein (Austrian)	*Tractatus Logico-Philosophicus* (1922)	Logical positivism—Everything humans can know must be based on rational facts and direct observations. Nothing that cannot be studied scientifically is worth studying at all.
	Jean-Paul Sartre (French)	*Being and Nothingness* (1943)	Existentialism—Life is inherently meaningless, so humans must find and create their own meaning. There is no God who gives truth, so humans must define truth for themselves.
Physics	Marie Curie (Polish-French)		Radium emits subatomic particles and has no constant weight.
	Max Planck (German)		Subatomic energy occurs in small bursts or "quanta," rather than a steady stream. Matter and energy are closely related, and unstable.
	Albert Einstein (German)		Theory of special relativity—Time and space are relative to the viewpoint of the observer; only the speed of light is a constant. Each particle of matter contains enormous energy potential.
	Ernest Rutherford (British)		Atoms can be split into subatomic particles.
	Werner Heisenberg (German)		Uncertainty principle—Nature is entirely unpredictable; the universe lacks objective reality and everything depends on the observer's frame of reference.

Ideas and Literature

FIELD	LEADING FIGURES	SELECT MAJOR WORKS	KEY IDEAS
Psychology	Sigmund Freud (Austrian)	*Civilization and Its Discontents* (1930)	Concept of self is divided into id (unconscious desires), ego (rational self), and superego (conscience), which are constantly at odds. Denying the id makes living in communities possible, but ultimately leads to unhappiness and dissatisfaction.
Literature	Virginia Woolf (British)	*Jacob's Room* (1922)	Stream of consciousness, captures inner voice.
	James Joyce (Irish)	*Ulysses* (1922)	Stream of consciousness, abandons traditional plot and language to mirror the riddle of modern life.
	Franz Kafka (Czech)	*The Metamorphosis* (1915), *The Trial* (1925)	Existential angst of ordinary people.
	T. S. Eliot (American)	*The Waste Land* (1922)	Widespread desolation and despair after WWI.
	George Orwell (British)	*The Road to Wigan Pier* (1937)	Socialism, well implemented, could end unemployment crises.
Visual Arts	Claude Monet (French)	*Water Lilies series* (early 20th cent.)	Impressionism—Conveying fleeting moments of light and color.
	Vincent Van Gogh (Dutch)	*The Starry Night* (1889)	Expressionism—Use of vivid colors and new techniques to illuminate inner feelings.
	Pablo Picasso (Spanish)		Cubism—Subjects broken into overlapping planes and geometric shapes.
	Salvador Dali (Spanish)	*Metamorphosis of Narcissus* (1937)	Surrealism—Portrays inner world of dreams, symbols, fantasies.
	Hugo Ball (German)	"Karawane" (1916)	Dadaism—Attacks all conventional art forms and delights in the outrageous and absurd.

Ideas and Literature			
FIELD	**LEADING FIGURES**	**SELECT MAJOR WORKS**	**KEY IDEAS**
Architecture	Le Corbusier (Swiss)	Towards New Architecture (1923)	Functionalism—Form follows function, eliminate unnecessary ornamentation.
	Walter Gropius (German)	Bauhaus School in Dessau Germany (1925)	Bauhaus—German school of art and architecture, valued sleek, functional design.
	Ludwig Mies van der Rohe (German)	Lake Shore Apartments, Chicago (1948)	Epitome of modern, international architecture style.
Music	Igor Stravinski (Russian)	*The Rite of Spring* (1913)	Expressionism—Rejection of nineteenth-century romanticism, using intense rhythms and dissonance.
	Alban Berg (Austrian)	*Wozzeck* (1925)	Atonality—Half spoken, half sung, often harsh and unmelodic.
	Arnold Schönberg (Austrian)		Twelve-tone scale—No musical key; notes seemed unrelated, but had mathematical patterns called "tone rows."

CHAPTER 27
Dictatorships and the Second World War, 1919–1945

> **Areas of focus:** Italy, Germany, the U.S.S.R., the Pacific
>
> **Main events:** fascism, Nazism, Stalinism, World War II

The following is a thematic summary of the material covered in Chapter 27 of *A History of Western Society:*

Politics

+ The 1920s and 1930s saw the waning of European democracy, replaced in one country after another by authoritarian or Fascist dictatorships. Democracy survived only in Britain, France, Scandinavia, the Netherlands, Czechoslovakia, and Switzerland. Both authoritarian and totalitarian regimes rejected the entire liberal agenda of democracy, parliamentary governments, and individual liberties. Authoritarian governments in eastern and central Europe were conservative and relied on traditional sources of authority like the military.

+ A new form of dictatorship was created in Germany, Russia, and Italy to a lesser degree—the totalitarian state—which aimed to control all economic, social, intellectual, and cultural aspects of society. Totalitarian dictators ruled with particular brutality but also with remarkable effectiveness.

+ After Lenin's death in 1924, Stalin, whose program was "socialism in one country," defeated Trotsky and his ideas of "permanent revolution." He rose to power with cunning, skill, and charisma. By 1927 he had effectively become a dictator who was ready to revolutionize Russia from above. He built the new socialist Soviet Union by terrorizing the masses and executing dissenters like the "Old Bolsheviks."

+ Italian leader Benito Mussolini's fascism was a combination of revolutionary nationalism, anti-Marxism, and conservatism. In 1920, Mussolini and a few fellow veterans formed the Black Shirts, a Fascist militia that raided and threatened Socialist Party headquarters, newspaper offices, and union halls, finally pushing the Socialists out of northern Italy. After their March on Rome in 1922 to threaten the king, Mussolini was appointed prime minister. The Fascist Party won a parliamentary majority in 1924 and created a one-party state with government by decree, strict censorship, abolition of independent labor unions, propaganda to win over the masses, and repression of opposition. Italian fascism was never fully totalitarian or a very thorough police state. The old power structure was not replaced, and the king, albeit weak, remained on the throne throughout.

257

✦ **AP Tip** Although there were many similarities between Fascist and Communist states in practice—their intrusions into private life, their masterful use of propaganda, their brutal suppression of dissidents, and in the case of Nazi Germany and Stalinist Russia, the murder of millions—there were important differences that you should understand. Communists saw war and violence as *a means to an end,* whereas Fascists saw them as ends themselves; Communists believed that when socialism was fully established, the state would wither away, while Fascists believed that the state was the essential element of any nation and must remain all-powerful; Communists were generally internationalists (Stalin may have been an exception), while Fascists were nationalists; Communists sought a just society that provided real freedom, but Fascists sought to create powerful nations and rejected freedom completely.

✦ Nazism shared some of the characteristics of fascism, but it was more radical and interventionist. It was distinguished by a complete control of all aspects of society; virulent, vicious anti-Semitism; and aggressive expansionism. Its political success was because of three main factors: the dynamic leadership of Adolf Hitler, an Austrian war veteran and charismatic speaker who blamed both communism and large-scale capitalism on the Jews; its promises of comradeship and change; and the crisis of the Great Depression. In 1932, when businesses went bankrupt and many Germans were unemployed, the Nazis became the largest party in the Reichstag.

✦ Hitler and his National Socialists, or Nazis, quickly established a totalitarian dictatorship. Shortly after his appointment as chancellor in January 1933, Hitler was granted emergency dictatorial powers in the Enabling Act. He immediately banned all independent organizations including unions and other political parties. Nazi party members took over government bureaucracies and transformed every aspect of public life. The Gestapo (Hitler's secret state police) and the elite SS (Hitler's personal guards) ferreted out and interned in concentration camps tens of thousands of political enemies. Jews lost their government jobs in 1933, their citizenship with the Nuremburg Laws in 1935, and then their private businesses. Other victims of Hitler's ethnic cleansing plan were Gypsies (Roma and Sinti), Jehovah's Witnesses, and homosexuals.

✦ A major Nazi goal was territorial expansion for living space (*lebensraum*) in the east for the racially superior Germans. Voiding provisions of the Treaty of Versailles, Germany withdrew from the League of Nations, established a military draft, rearmed, and remilitarized the Rhineland. All the while France and Britain practiced appeasement policies to avoid war. In 1936, Italy and Germany formed the Rome-Berlin Axis, soon joined by Japan. Hitler achieved his goal of a Greater Germany in 1938 by invading and annexing Austria unopposed (the Anschluss), and as the result of an act of appeasement when France and Britain granted Germany control of the Sudetenland (a German part of Czechoslovakia) at the Munich Conference.

✦ In March 1939, Hitler invaded and occupied the rest of Czechoslovakia. The U.S.S.R. and Germany signed a nonaggression pact in August 1939, with secret protocols to divide up Poland and Baltic states. Hitler then ordered the invasion of Poland on September 1, 1939. In response Britain and France declared war. World War II, which would ultimately claim more than 50 million lives, had begun.

✦ The German *blitzkrieg,* or "lightning war," was hugely successful. By 1940, virtually every European country had been defeated or was a German ally. Spain, Switzerland, Turkey, and Sweden were officially neutral. For one year, Britain stood alone against Germany and survived the attempt to subdue it by air. Then in 1941 the United States and the U.S.S.R. were both attacked (by Japan and Germany respectively) and joined the war.

- Britain, Russia, and the United States were allies but didn't share ideologies. They agreed to accept only unconditional surrender from the Axis powers.

- Effective mobilization for war, nationalism, and the sacrifices of the people made possible Allied victory in World War II. The United States had exceptional industrial might, outproducing its enemies and indeed the rest of the world by 1943. Britain played a crucial role as the strategic center for the Allied war on the continent. The U.S.S.R. moved its industrial plant and a large percentage of its population east of the Urals.

- The turning point in the war in Europe came in 1943. The Germans met with catastrophic defeat at Stalingrad in the Soviet Union, which took the offensive; the United States and Britain, having ousted German troops from North Africa, invaded Sicily. The Italians deposed Mussolini and surrendered. On June 6, 1944, in history's greatest naval invasion, 2 million Allied soldiers landed on the beaches of Normandy, France. British and American forces marching eastward from France met Soviet troops liberating Eastern Europe on the Elbe in April, 1945. Hitler committed suicide on May 8, 1945, and Germany quickly surrendered, leaving the Allies to focus the remainder of their energies on the war in the Pacific.

- As in Nazi Germany and Fascist Italy, the Japanese government was highly nationalistic, militaristic, and committed to expansion based on racial theories of Asian superiority. Propagandists promoted a "Greater East Asia Co-Prosperity Sphere," but in reality power remained in the hands of Japan's military. By 1942 Japan had conquered a vast empire in the Pacific and threatened Australia. The outcome of the war in the Pacific was determined by great naval battles such as the Coral Sea, Midway, and Leyte Gulf. The Allied tactic of island-hopping to defeat Japan by retaking its colonial holdings was expensive in terms of lives.

- On August 6, 1945, the United States dropped its newly developed atomic bomb on Hiroshima and three days later on Nagasaki, killing and maiming a few hundred thousand people in a single moment. The Japanese surrendered a few days later. The war was over.

Economy

- In the U.S.S.R, Lenin's New Economic Policy (NEP) allowed some capitalistic profit making but kept major industries, banks, and utilities nationalized. Stalin's five-year plans set high targets for heavy industry and agriculture, to spectacular result, restoring production to prewar levels. Collectivization created large farms more efficient in the use of machinery, animals, and labor, but it was resisted by peasants.

- In 1932 the Soviet government forced the Ukraine collectives to deliver grain at excessively high levels, resulting in starvation of the peasants; 6 million Ukrainians died.

- The Italian Fascists allowed big business to regulate itself, compromised with the elites who controlled the economy, and did not implement land reform.

- The depression hit Germany hard, and was a major factor behind Nazi ascension to power. It had little impact in Russia.

- The Nazi government initiated huge public works projects and in 1936 began to rearm, which reduced unemployment and modestly improved the standard of living, fulfilling Hitler's promise of "work and bread."

Religion

✦ The papacy signed the Lateran Agreement with Mussolini's government in 1929, which made the Vatican independent of Italy and restored relations between church and state.

✦ Russian communism was ideologically opposed to the Orthodox Church and actively repressed it. Churches were converted to "museums of atheism."

✦ Some members of the Protestant and Catholic churches in Nazi Germany were active in opposing the Nazi state, but these efforts were aimed mainly at preserving religious life, not overthrowing Hitler.

Society and Culture

✦ Under the Communists in Russia, a new class system privileged the industrial and political managerial elite; contrary to the egalitarian ideals of socialism, this elite earned significantly higher wages than unskilled workers and farmers. Women's lives were radically transformed with full equal rights, including divorce and abortion. Some women did hard physical work, and others pursued higher education and became doctors and engineers. Although women did make significant advances, they often earned less than their male counterparts.

✦ In Fascist Italy and Nazi Germany, women lost rights and were returned to traditional roles.

✦ In Germany, the mentally ill, handicapped, and other "undesirables" were euthanized or sterilized to purify the race. The Nazi regime justified this purification process by using the pseudoscience of eugenics.

✦ In all three totalitarian states, youth groups were created to inculcate loyalty to the cause.

✦ In the German-controlled areas of conquered Europe, Nordic peoples, deemed racially close to the Germans, received preferential treatment, while Slavic peoples were considered subhuman slave laborers to serve the "master race." Slavs, Gypsies, and Jews were put to work for Germans under the harsh supervision of the SS.

✦ The Nazis wanted to make Germany free of Jews. Dehumanizing treatment led about half of the German Jews to flee Germany, especially after the pogrom called *Kristallnacht* in November 1938. Jews in German-controlled lands, and especially in occupied eastern Europe, were moved into ghettoes or slave labor camps and millions were murdered, first by shooting by *Einsatzgruppen*, then in extermination camps run by the SS. Some 6 million Jews were killed by the end of the war in 1945.

✦ Civilians in Europe and Japan were the victims of unprecedented bombing raids that destroyed entire cities, killed millions, and rendered many more homeless. Notable raids include the 1940 German air raid attacks on Britain (Battle of Britain); the Allied destruction of Dresden, Hamburg, and Berlin; and the atomic bombing of Hiroshima and Nagasaki, Japan.

Ideas and Literature

✦ Fascist ideology rejected democracy and the validity of the individual in favor of the state. Its slogan was "everything in the state, nothing outside the state, nothing against the state."

✦ For Nazism, the fundamental basis of ideology was race rather than state. The image of an ideal German was deeply infused with Aryan (German) mythology, anti-Semitism, and contempt for other "inferior" races.

✦ The Nazis burned books written by Jews, socialists, and democrats, rewrote school and university curricula to teach Nazi "science," and prohibited Modernism in the arts.

✦ Both authoritarian and totalitarian states censored the press and repressed intellectuals and artists; many went into exile. Totalitarian regimes also used the media for propaganda.

Arts

✦ The arts became ideological tools of the totalitarian states. Under Stalin, socialist realism glorified the workers, Russia, and the Communist Party, while in Nazi Germany, the arts glorified Hitler, German heroes like Siegfried, and the idealized Aryan.

✦ In the U.S.S.R. and Germany, approved artists were invited into the ruling elites, while the dissidents were persecuted. Both states made particularly effective use of the radio. The images of the dictators were everywhere.

CHAPTER 28
Cold War Conflict and Consensus, 1945–1965

Areas of focus: Germany, Russia, France, eastern Europe

Main events: division of Germany, de-Stalinization in Russia, western European economic miracle, decolonization, the consumer revolution

---

The following is a thematic summary of the material covered in Chapter 28 of *A History of Western Society:*

Politics

+ The defeated Axis powers of World War II were occupied by the victors. At conferences in Teheran (1943), Yalta (1945), and Potsdam (1945), the Allies decided the shape of postwar Europe. They divided Germany, its capital city of Berlin, and Austria into four zones of occupation.

+ Thousands of Nazis were tried and convicted, and many others "denazified." The Allies jointly put the Nazi leaders that had not fled or committed suicide on trial at Nuremberg for war crimes and crimes against humanity; twelve were given the death penalty.

+ With Europe weakened by war, the two dominant world powers, the United States and the U.S.S.R, each with a string of allies, engaged in a fierce ideological, economic, political, and cultural struggle called the Cold War. During World War II, eastern Europe was liberated by the U.S.S.R., which insisted on control of these states after the war as a buffer zone. In 1946 former British prime minister Winston Churchill lamented the "iron curtain" dividing Europe.

+ Europe was the focal point of Soviet-American tensions. The popularity of Communist parties in France and Italy and the civil wars in Greece and China raised fears of the spread of communism. These fears led the United States to issue the Truman Doctrine in 1947, promising American military and economic aid to groups resisting communism.

+ U.S. foreign policy was containment (the Truman Doctrine), preventing the further spread of communism but accepting existing Communist states. Most western European countries joined the United States in a military alliance, the North Atlantic Treaty Organization (NATO), in 1949; those under Soviet control joined the Warsaw Pact (1955). The United Nations replaced the League of Nations and was often the venue for the display of Cold War tensions.

✦ **AP Tip**   If you are answering an essay question on the AP European History Exam about the Cold War or the postwar period of the 1950s and 1960s, be sure to focus your essay on Europe, rather than on American developments and attitudes.

✦ In occupied Germany, cooperation among the four powers quickly diminished. When England, France, and the United States announced a common currency for their zones in 1948, the U.S.S.R. cut off traffic through its zone to West Berlin. A yearlong Allied airlift forced the Soviets to relent. The next year, the occupation ended as East and West Germany became independent states. In 1961, the East Germans built a wall to divide East from West Berlin.

✦ In western Europe, constitutional governments replaced wartime regimes, with republics created in France, Italy, Austria, and West Germany. Governments, whether of the left (the Labour Party in England) or the center (Christian Democrats in France, West Germany, and Italy) expanded social welfare programs. The Christian Democrats, anticommunist and moderate, dominated western European politics for some twenty years.

✦ Eastern European states became one-party dictatorships after Stalin purged noncommunists from coalition governments. Only Yugoslavia, free of Soviet troops, remained outside the Soviet orbit. Its war hero, Josip Broz Tito, successfully stood up to Stalin in 1948; until its dissolution in the 1980s, Yugoslavia was unique—a European Communist state independent of the U.S.S.R.

✦ Decolonization began shortly after the end of the war. In India, long-standing opposition to British rule, energized by the pacifist leadership of Mahatma Gandhi, led Britain to partition Muslim and Hindu India and grant independence in 1947. A similar solution was used to resolve the tensions between Zionist Jews and Arabs in Palestine; a UN partition plan created Israel in 1948 and was immediately followed by a war from which Israel emerged victorious and enlarged.

✦ The French lost Indochina (now Vietnam, Laos, and Cambodia) in 1954 after military defeat led by the forces of Communist nationalist Ho Chi Minh, and Algeria in 1962 after a fierce civil war.

✦ Elsewhere in Africa and Asia, most French and English colonies became independent without much violence and retained substantial economic and cultural ties with their colonial overlords. Two notably violent exceptions were in Indonesia and the Congo.

✦ Asia was where the Cold War heated up. In China, the Nationalists led by Chiang Kai-shek were defeated in 1949 by the Communists, who quickly established a one-party state and created radical programs empowering the peasants.

✦ In Korea, three years of indecisive warfare between the North Koreans (backed by Communist China) and the South Koreans (supported by U.S. troops) ended in 1953, resulting in a negotiated division of Korea that continues to this day.

✦ Newly independent states were wooed by the superpowers, and most allied with one or the other. Each side used covert actions to undermine governments on the other side. Some states, India most noticeably, formed a nonaligned bloc.

✦ Within the U.S.S.R., World War II had created a strong nationalistic bond between government and people. After the war, dissidents and Jews were targeted, rigid political authoritarianism returned, and the five-year plans that emphasized heavy industry at the expense of consumer goods were reinstituted. In 1953, a workers' rebellion in East Germany was crushed by force.

✦ After Stalin's death in 1953, his successors, realizing reforms would be necessary, restricted the secret police and closed many of the labor camps. Premier Nikita

Khrushchev revealed Stalin's crimes to the Party Congress in 1956, initiating a de-Stalinization or liberalization process.

✦ Khrushchev initially moved Soviet foreign policy toward "peaceful coexistence" with the West, but not liberalization in the Soviet satellites. He toppled reforming governments in Poland and Hungary in 1956. The crushing of the Hungarian revolution by Soviet tanks led to widespread disillusionment with communism. In 1962, Khrushchev tried to place nuclear missiles in newly Communist Cuba, but he was forced to withdraw them.

Economy

✦ Western Europe recovered remarkably quickly from the devastation of World War II. This "economic miracle" involved government focus on economic growth, the adoption of Keynesian economics, help from the Marshall Plan (1947), and a mixture of government intervention and free-market capitalism. Extensive welfare programs such as Britain's "cradle to grave" model became the norm in western Europe.

✦ Eastern Europe stagnated economically in spite of COMECON, the Soviet economic program for its satellites. East Germany, Romania, and Hungary, which fought the U.S.S.R. in the war, paid it reparations in the form of factories and machines. The Soviet satellite states nationalized industries and instituted collectivization of agriculture and Soviet-style five-year plans.

✦ West Germany and other countries instituted guest worker programs to supplement their labor forces in boom times, attracting millions of people from poorer countries. Many thousands of Turks settled in West Germany.

✦ European federalists began to imagine economic cooperation as the way to restore Europe's leadership in world affairs and prevent another war. In 1951, six states—France, Belgium, West Germany, Italy, Luxembourg, and the Netherlands—created the European Steel and Coal Community, a single market with no tariffs or quotas. They expanded it in 1957 into the European Economic Community, or Common Market, an economic union with free movement of peoples and goods. The Common Market was a huge success and added other member countries over the years, rivaling the United States as an economic power.

✦ Virtually full employment and rising wages bolstered the growth of the consumer economy in western Europe in the 1950s and 1960s. The number of cars in western Europe grew ninefold by 1965. The ready availability of inexpensive consumer goods in the West became part of Cold War ideological competition.

✦ In the Eastern bloc, leaders were critical of the Western-style consumer culture, and the availability of goods lagged, leading to complaints and disillusionment.

Religion

✦ In Eastern Europe and the U.S.S.R., the Communists attempted to eradicate all religious practices. Religiosity became a form of anticommunism.

✦ Many Jewish survivors of World War II immigrated to Palestine. The state of Israel was founded as a Jewish homeland in 1948.

Society and Culture

✦ Europe was devastated by World War II. Cities from London to Dresden to Leningrad were in ruins. Some 50 million people died, including large numbers of civilians, and a similar number were left homeless. Many of these lived in displaced persons camps run by the United Nations.

✦ During the 1950s and 1960s, social mobility increased and traditional class barriers blurred. Family connections and inherited property became less important. Many industrial workers became better educated and moved into white-collar (service or office) jobs. As the standard of living rose, poorer people could afford what had been luxuries for the rich, such as cars and household gadgets, month-long vacations, and travel. The middle class became dominated by corporate and government managers.

✦ National identities also became more fluid. Millions of people from former colonies moved to the colonizing power, forming significant minority populations.

✦ The emancipation of women in the twentieth century is one of its most important developments. The strong demand for labor in the postwar economic boom, the shortage of men due to war death tolls, and the decline in birthrates allowed women to enter the workforce in momentous numbers, many in white-collar jobs, especially in the Communist Soviet Union and eastern Europe.

✦ The high birthrate in the decade after World War II led to an unusually high proportion of the population that was young. With economic prosperity and a more open class structure, a distinct youth culture and rebellious "counterculture" emerged with its own consumer goods marketed specifically to the new youth culture. This culture had its own idols and its own music, rock 'n' roll, all of which worried the older generations and led to a "generation gap."

Ideas and Literature

✦ During the war, inventions like radar and the nuclear bomb were crucial. Afterwards, "Big Science" came to be organized in public and private large bureaucracies employed in the Cold War arms and space races. The U.S.S.R. was the first to put a satellite (*Sputnik*) into orbit in 1957 and a man into orbit four years later. The United States was the first to put a human on the moon in 1969. Big science also benefited ordinary people, with transistors invented for computers, creating the consumer electronics industry, and research providing the means for the green revolution that increased agricultural yield. The discovery of the double helix, the mechanism for genetic transmission, transformed science, psychology, and medicine.

✦ In the Soviet Union, intellectuals such as the novelists Boris Pasternak (*Doctor Zhivago*) and Alexander Solzhenitsyn (*One Day in the Life of Ivan Denisovich*) indicted Stalinism.

Arts

✦ Soviet and eastern European artists and writers were required to conform to socialist realism and represent the ideals of their party. The U.S.S.R. and its satellites were dappled with idealized paintings and monumental sculptures trying to build a consensus for communism.

✦ American jazz and rock 'n' roll found a ready audience among European youth, aided by the invention of the long-playing record album (LP) and 45 rpm singles.

CHAPTER 29
Challenging the Postwar Order, 1960–1991

Areas of focus: eastern Europe, Russia, western Europe, the United States

Main events: Vietnam War, German unification, 1989 revolutions, fall of the Communist system, end of the U.S.S.R., radical youth groups and counterculture movement, feminist movement

---

The following is a thematic summary of the material covered in Chapter 29 of *A History of Western Society:*

Politics

+ During the 1960s and early 1970s, the left, such as the Labour Party in Britain and the Social Democrats in Germany, generally dominated European politics.

+ Willy Brandt, the chancellor of West Germany, initiated détente, a compromise with the Communist east. He signed a treaty of reconciliation with Poland in 1970, apologized for German crimes during World War II, and opened direct negotiations with East Germany. This *Ostpolitik* policy eased tensions and allowed greater contact between the two Germanies.

+ In eastern Europe in the 1960s and 1970s, continuing economic shortages prompted changes — decentralization, provision of consumer goods, and cultural freedom — with mixed success. The most important movement for change was "socialism with a human face" in Czechoslovakia, seen in the "Prague Spring" of 1968. Led by Alexander Dubček, this period of political and cultural freedom was ended by Warsaw Pact forces, after which Soviet leader Leonid Brezhnev announced the Brezhnev Doctrine, asserting the right of the Soviet Union to intervene in the internal affairs of the satellite states. The U.S.S.R. also invaded Afghanistan in 1979 to support its local Communist regime, embroiling it in a long and costly war.

+ In the late 1960s and 1970s, environmentalists formed Green parties and later had some electoral success, particularly in Germany. At the same time, far-right parties opposing increased immigration, such as the French National Front, led by Le Pen, and the Austrian Freedom Party, grew in size and importance during the 1970s and 1980s.

+ When Vietnamese nationalists and Communists forced the French out in 1954, Vietnam was divided into two states, which led to civil war and American military involvement on behalf of the anticommunist South Vietnamese government. By the mid-1960s the war had escalated to a half million U.S. soldiers fighting abroad. Costly in lives as well as money, the long Vietnam War alienated many U.S. allies, sparked fierce protests at home and abroad, and ended in U.S. withdrawal in 1973 and Vietnam's subsequent unification as a Communist state.

✦ The tumultuous year 1968 saw significant left-wing and student protests against the Vietnam War throughout the world. Local issues also fed into the discontent. In May 1968, students infused with New Left ideals, and supported by workers on strike, fought with police in a short-lived Paris insurrection, bringing the French economy to a standstill. President Charles de Gaulle surrounded Paris with troops, made promises to the workers that ended the strike, and brought the conservatives to victory in the next election. The student movement declined in the 1970s.

✦ Radical youth groups from West Germany (the Red Army Faction) and Italy (the Red Brigades) tried to achieve change through sabotage, kidnapping, and murder. Most of these terrorists were incarcerated and their goals unachieved. Separatist movements in Spain (Basque ETA) and Northern Ireland (IRA) also used violent tactics.

✦ Conservatives dominated in western Europe (except in France) in the late 1970s and 1980s. They followed neoliberal policies like cutting spending, privatizing industries, and modifying the welfare state.

✦ In 1975, the Helsinki Accords—aimed at reducing Cold War tensions and guaranteeing human and political rights—were signed by thirty-five nations, including all of the states in Europe, the Soviet Union, and the United States.

✦ The first successful challenge to Communist rule in eastern Europe was won by striking dockworkers at Gdansk in Poland, who organized a national labor union demanding political and labor rights, which then grew into a political party led by Lech Walesa. With the support of the first Polish pope, John Paul II, Solidarity won concessions from the government, was legalized in 1988, and won an overwhelming victory in an open election. It quickly destroyed the Communist economy with neoliberal "shock therapy" policies.

✦ Within the U.S.S.R. there was significant apathy and growing frustration over the stagnant economy, the privileged Communist elite, and the lack of freedom. Growing demands for reform led in 1985 to the premiership of Mikhail Gorbachev, who instituted glasnost (a policy of government openness) and perestroika (economic reconstruction). Glasnost brought open criticism of the state-directed (command) economy, a floodgate of public discussion, and demands for democracy. Free elections were held in the U.S.S.R. in 1989, the first since 1917. Gorbachev also renounced the Brezhnev Doctrine, withdrew Russian troops from Afghanistan, and sought arms limitations treaties with the United States.

✦ At the same time, within the Soviet bloc, larger and larger peaceful demonstrations demanded greater freedom. When Hungary opened its borders to Germans wishing to flee to the West, the response was so great that the East German government opened the Berlin Wall in November 1989. It was torn down by jubilant Berliners on both sides, a moment of liberation celebrated around the globe. Similarly, popular demonstrations led to the end of communism in other satellite states. In Czechoslovakia, this process was so smooth it was called the Velvet Revolution. Only in Romania did the toppling of the Communist system involve violent revolution; there the Communist dictator Nicolae Ceaușescu was executed.

✦ In October 1990, Germany was reunified under West German leadership, disappointing those who sought a "third way" between oppressive communism and ruthless capitalism. Germany once again became the dominant continental state.

✦ In 1990, the delegates of twenty-two European nations, the United States, and the Soviet Union signed the Paris Accord agreeing to scale down their armed forces and affirming all existing borders.

✦ Political instability followed the fall of communism in Russia. The Communist Party lost the election in 1990 and Gorbachev was replaced by Boris Yeltsin, the leader of the Russian Federation Parliament, who won widespread popular support by stopping an attempted coup by hardliners. The Communist Party was outlawed in Russia, and the Soviet Union dissolved in 1991. The Baltic republics and Ukraine became independent states, although other former Soviet republics joined a new Commonwealth of Independent States.

✦ **AP Tip** There's a certain American triumphalism that ought to be avoided in discussing the end of the Communist system in Russia and Eastern Europe. While Americans often credit U.S. president Ronald Reagan for its collapse, it was a much more complex phenomenon with deep roots in local histories and the limitations of the command economy.

Economy

✦ By the 1970s, the eastern European economic successes brought about under Communist leadership—collectivized agriculture, nationalized industry and business, increased class mobility, and welfare benefits—became known as "real existing socialism."

✦ After some twenty years of prosperity, the European economy experienced simultaneous inflation and stagnation (stagflation) in the 1970s, sparked by the sudden, sharp increase in the cost of oil and uncertainty in the international monetary system. Unemployment rose to its highest level since the Great Depression, and living standards declined.

✦ In the late 1970s, conservatives won office and enacted neoliberal policies. Margaret Thatcher, prime minister of Great Britain for eleven years, replaced much of the welfare system, privatized industries, and reduced taxes. The results were high unemployment, widening gaps between rich and poor, and riots, but also the creation of new groups of property owners. In Germany, similar cuts in taxes and government spending prompted economic growth.

✦ Heavy industry lost economic ground to high-tech industries like computing and biotechnology, and to service industries like medicine, banking, and finance. This shift brought about what scholars now refer to as the postindustrial society or "information age."

✦ The Common Market became the European Economic Community (EEC), with twelve member states.

✦ The standard of living and quality of life in the former Communist states severely declined as industries were privatized and unemployment and prices soared.

Religion

✦ The Second Vatican Council in the early 1960s aimed to democratize and open the church. The Latin mass was replaced by the vernacular in an attempt to broaden church appeal.

✦ The council's efforts did little to counteract secularization. Church attendance fell virtually everywhere in western and central Europe, though it was less pronounced in Catholic areas such as Poland.

Society and Culture

✦ The plethora of household gadgets and easy shopping in supermarkets increased rather than lessened the domestic duties of women. Feminist movements grew stronger and better organized. Women in Catholic countries fought for divorce and abortion rights; elsewhere feminists focused on legal and employment equity.

✦ Family ties lessened as prosperity and the ease of movement offered by the European Community made it easier for young people to move away from their native areas. More people lived alone, the divorce rate was high, and family size shrank.

✦ The youth subculture, in addition to its political activism, fought for individual freedom on personal and sexual matters, stating that "the personal is the political." Their rock 'n' roll music, their highly spirited consumerism, their publicly acknowledged use of illegal drugs, and the sexual revolution, fueled by the safe, reliable, and inexpensive oral contraceptive ("the pill") that made it easier to separate sex from procreation, upset traditionalists.

Ideas and Literature

✦ The feminist movement was sparked by *The Second Sex* (1949) by Simone de Beauvoir. This book inspired feminists like Betty Friedan, author of *The Feminine Mystique* (1963) and cofounder of the National Organization for Women in the United States.

✦ American biologist Rachel Carson's 1962 book *Silent Spring* was read widely across Europe and helped to spark the early environmental movement.

✦ *Samizdat*, underground literature critical of communism, blossomed in East Bloc countries during the 1960s. Distribution of this literature helped to build support for the growing countercultural movement in the East Bloc.

✦ Intellectuals challenged the conformity, Americanization, and vulgarity of the new consumer society, and many lamented the loss of traditional foods, values, and lifestyles.

✦ Intellectuals on the right and left sought new ideologies to replace those of the Cold War. The "New Left" criticized both Stalinism and corporate capitalism, exploring how to create socialism without oppression. Neoliberals argued for a modern form of laissez-faire capitalism to free up economic life, reduce and regulate taxes, and increase private profits, their means to achieve economic growth.

Arts

✦ The counterculture rejected the artistic canon and advocated pop and performance art.

✦ Rock music became international, with English bands like the Rolling Stones and the Beatles wildly adored around the globe, bringing east and west Europe closer.

Life in an Age of Globalization, 1990 to the Present

Areas of focus: European Union, eastern Europe, Russia, United States, Iraq and Afghanistan

Main events: Maastricht Treaty (formation of the EU), Russian revival, Bosnian War, globalization

---

The following is a thematic summary of the material covered in Chapter 30 of *A History of Western Society:*

Politics

+ Europe moved toward political unity with the Maastricht Treaty of 1991, which created a multinational currency, defense, and foreign policy. The European Community became the European Union (EU), with twenty-seven members by 2010. Free movement of peoples, services, capital, and goods, and common standards made the EU powerful though all members did not accept the new currency.

+ Nationalism and ethnic tensions flared up in the former Eastern bloc countries after the fall of communism, particularly in Yugoslavia. When Croatia became independent in 1991, Serbian president Slobodan Milosevic invaded to take back as much territory as he could. Bosnia-Herzegovina broke away the next year, leading to a brutal civil war between Bosnian Serbs and Bosniaks (Muslims). Some 300,000 Bosniaks were slaughtered in "ethnic cleansing," the first mass killings in Europe since the Holocaust.

+ The United States, the UN, the EU, and NATO at various points intervened in Bosnia; ultimately a complicated accord ended the violence. When Serbia used force to prevent Kosovo from gaining independence, NATO bombed Serbia to force it to withdraw. In 2001, Slobodan Milosevic was turned over to the war crimes tribunal in the Netherlands for his role in the "ethnic cleansing." Kosovo declared its independence from Serbia in 2008 after ten years of civil war, but tensions remain.

+ In Russia, Yeltsin applied neoliberal shock therapy in 1992 and privatized industries. Instead of prompting rapid economic growth and spreading prosperity, the elite of the old Communist system turned previous state monopolies into private ones, and high inflation, huge decline in production, and hardship on ordinary citizens lasted nearly a decade.

+ Criminal elements took control over Russia's valuable oil and natural resources. Democracy seemed to many to be a hollow cover for corruption and decline. The next president, Vladimir Putin, a former secret police officer, restored order by re-instituting authoritarian rule and repressing independent media and political opposition. He asserted Russia's role on the international stage, increased military spending, and challenged the United States. Putin also engaged in a long brutal war against the tiny state of Chechnya that had declared its independence and intervened in Georgia. Under Putin, high prices for oil and expansion of Russia's energy market share led to sustained economic growth. Putin stepped down as president after his term ended in 2008, but became prime minister.

✦ The close foreign policy relationship of western Europeans and the United States began to break down in the 1990s, as the EU asserted its independence and NATO expanded to become a virtually Europe-wide alliance. Europeans, except for the British, generally took dim views of the U.S. wars in Iraq and Afghanistan that began in 2003 in response to the al-Qaeda attacks in New York and Washington of September 11, 2001. Although initially enthusiastic over the toppling of Iraqi president Saddam Hussein, most EU states doubted the legitimacy of the "war on terror" and worried that the United States had violated international law and tolerated human rights abuses.

✦ By the 1990s, immigration had become a hot political issue and had given rise to new parties and movements, particularly successful in France and Austria. The issue became more complicated when Islamic terrorism came to haunt Europe with bombings in Madrid in 2004 and London in 2005 committed by Muslim residents.

✦ The expansion of the EU to include the former Soviet satellites slowed the pace of political unification and led to a new EU constitution in the Treaty of Lisbon (2009). A continuing issue is the much-resisted application of Turkey, a large Muslim state, to EU membership.

✦ As the EU expanded, conservatives and nationalists chafed at times over "Eurocrats" in EU headquarters dictating policies. The unpopularity of the EU structure had led to defeat of a draft constitution in 2004. In the 2010s, British Conservative prime minister David Cameron pledged an "in or out" vote on EU membership. An economic crisis that threatened the common currency in the 2010s added to renewed uncertainty over the EU's future.

✦ **AP Tip**   In a way, Europe is returning full circle to where it was at the start of this AP course—many small states unified by a central structure. In the Middle Ages, the structure was the Holy Roman Empire, and now it is the EU. Both versions of Europe wrestled with two sets of identities at the same time: strong local bonds but also participation in an international culture. But as the EU is slowly creating an effective government, what is happening now is quite unlike the Holy Roman Empire: there is a remarkable willingness to abandon old hostilities and fears, bringing west, north, east, and south Europe together for the first time. However, economic troubles and political restiveness in the 2010s suggest that some tensions between local and European interests remain.

Economy

✦ The transition from the Communist command economy to market capitalism proved easier in Hungary, the Czech Republic, and Poland—all of which had made economic reforms before 1989 and had stronger entrepreneurial traditions than Romania and Bulgaria did.

- Virtually everywhere in the former Communist states, ordinary people suffered from high inflation that devalued pensions and savings, unemployment, and uncertainty as the guaranteed employment and social benefits of the Communist states disappeared. The young and the elite thrived, and capital cities catered to the wealthy, while provincial cities declined and gangsterism grew, particularly in Russia.

- In 2002, the euro, the common currency adopted by most EU members, transformed European trade and travel.

- A recession that began in the United States in 2008 spread across the world, a sign of the interconnectedness of the global economy. First Ireland and then other countries were severely hit. By 2010, Spain, Portugal, and Greece were on the verge of bankruptcy. Austerity measures imposed by wealthy EU states as a condition for needed financial aid proved highly unpopular at home, and by 2013, several countries in southern Europe debated the question of pulling out of the euro.

- The process of globalization—brought about by factors like the ever-increasing speed of communication resulting from the Internet and the easy availability of personal computers, the ability to hire technically proficient people from anywhere in the world (outsourcing), and the growth of the multinational corporations—transformed the world economy and Europe's role in it starting in the 1990s.

- Globalization revealed the underdevelopment of Mediterranean Europe and the dangers of overreliance on industry but helped London transition to a global center. Conglomerates like the German firm Siemens have vast holdings in many economic arenas. Because of globalization, global recessions were triggered by local events, like the Asian banking crisis of 1997, the collapse of Iceland's currency and banking in 2008, and the U.S. housing market collapse in 2008. Recovery from this global recession was slow and weak.

- Outsourcing of jobs to the still-industrializing world accelerated the decline of the industrial sector of employment in Europe. Many previously employed in well-paying industry jobs faced unemployment and had to take service jobs, some of which were poorly paid.

- Dependency on fossil fuels was an important factor in the U.S. wars in the Middle East and Russian interventions in Georgia and Chechnya. Europe's dependency on Russian natural gas made it possible for Russia to assert its international power.

- Climate change and environmental concerns became ever more important as globalization of the economy increased the use of energy and coal emissions in expanding economies like China. The EU is at the forefront of efforts to contain climate change, develop alternative sources of energy, protect water resources, and to take preventive measures against future rises in sea levels.

Religion

- The integration of the more than 15 million Muslims within the EU became a fraught issue in many countries as Europeans debated the degree to which these immigrants would embrace European values. Muslim youths born in France but with little hope of good employment, decent housing, and cultural acceptance, rioted on the outskirts of Paris in 2005 and 2009.

- Some Europeans had difficulties accepting the religiosity of many resident Muslims and were disturbed by women wearing the traditional veil. At the same time, some devout Muslims had difficulty accepting secular Western culture. Some commentators have emphasized that Islam is not new to Europe but has been a vital part of European society for many centuries.

Society and Culture

✦ Economic hardship in postcommunist Russia devalued the working classes and had a huge impact on health. Life expectancy of males sharply declined.

✦ The digital revolution—the easy availability of ever more sophisticated, compact, and affordable systems of entertainment and communication, and the remarkable speed of information gathering on the Internet—transformed every aspect of life. The spread of the Internet and of social media created new ways for people to access information, communicate, and connect to one another.

✦ The deindustrialization of Europe changed its social structure. While the managerial and technical elite did well, the standard of living of the middle class declined. A poorly paid underclass of unskilled laborers was made up of recent immigrants, often nonwhites.

✦ European birthrates continued to decline, prompting general concern over declining and aging national populations. Immigration from poorer nations in Asia, Africa, and the Middle East sharply increased the percentage of Europe's population that was non-white. Illegal immigration became easier when the EU abolished border controls between member states. The rapid rise in the percentage of foreign-born residents, evident in ethnically and racially mixed national sports teams and multicultural foods, has created a crisis of identity for some Europeans and led to some tensions as well as celebrations of a new multicultural Europe.

Ideas and Literature

✦ Some, often conservative, intellectuals urged Europe to assert its identity in fear of Euro-Islam, which was going to increase in size and undermine European values of individualism, secularism, and tolerance, because Muslim immigrants would never assimilate.

✦ Others, however, argued that Europe needs immigrant labor and that multiculturalism will invigorate European culture. Muslim immigrants will acculturate as previous groups had and ought to be integrated in order to prevent radicalization and alienation.

✦ **AP Tip** Europe had been virtually all white and mostly Christian until the late twentieth century. This new immigration is forcing Europeans to wrestle with issues of race and identity, complicated by threats to ethnic identities from the "wired" global culture and the slow development of a Europe-wide identity. The question "What does it mean to be a European?" is a difficult one to answer.

✦ Intellectuals and ordinary Europeans often expressed anti-Americanism. Others delineated a new global role for Europe as standard-bearer of human rights.

✦ Multicultural authors, mostly immigrants or first-generation Europeans, explored their engagement with European culture and their transitions in the second generation.

Arts

✦ New forms of popular music like rai developed from the multicultural mix and created new international superstars such as the Algerian Cheb Khaled.

✦ Film has also been an important venue for exploring European multiculturalism. Films such as the British *Bend It Like Beckham* (2002) and French *The Class* (2008) portray the challenges caused by cross-cultural interaction in the new European society.

PRACTICE EXAM 4

EUROPEAN HISTORY
SECTION I

Multiple-Choice Questions
(Time—55 minutes)
Number of questions—80

Directions: Each of the questions or incomplete statements below is followed by five suggested answers or completions. For each question, select the best response.

Imagebroker.net/SuperStock.

1. The Bauhaus, represented by the photograph above,

    (A)   represents the type of architecture commissioned by the Nazi government in Germany

    (B)   was an elite institution separating out art from traditional crafts

    (C)   promoted the idea that form should follow function

    (D)   was an important concert hall in Weimar Germany

    (E)   was the most important museum of new art in Vienna in the 1930s

GO ON TO THE NEXT PAGE.

2. The Treaty of Brest-Litovsk between Germany and Russia represented

    (A) the provisional government's withdrawal from the war in 1917
    (B) German defeat on the eastern front due to severe food shortages
    (C) the end of the German siege of Leningrad
    (D) their nonaggression pact before World War I
    (E) Lenin's fulfillment of his political promises made before the Bolshevik Revolution

Georgios Makkas/Alamy.

3. This reproduction of a relief sculpture illustrates the artistic style of

    (A) expressionism
    (B) surrealism
    (C) Dadaism
    (D) socialist realism
    (E) romanticism

4. The most compelling cause of European decolonization after World War II was that

    (A) European states were too weak to resist Asian and African peoples' demands for national self-determination
    (B) Europeans were losing money from their colonies
    (C) Europeans had already taken all the natural resources from the colonies, so they no longer had need for them
    (D) the Treaty of Versailles called for self-determination
    (E) the colonies were turning to communism

GO ON TO THE NEXT PAGE.

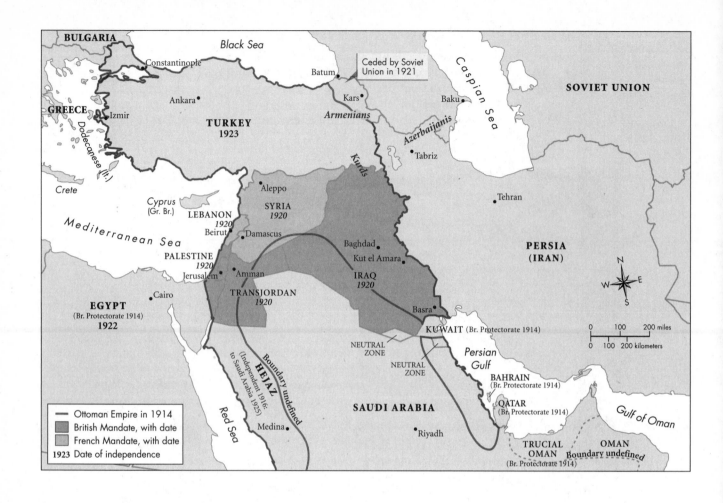

5. The map above illustrates the fulfillment of

(A) promises made to Arab nationalists during World War I

(B) the Balfour Declaration of 1917

(C) the Sykes-Picot Agreement of 1916

(D) the idea of self-determination expressed in Wilson's Fourteen Points

(E) Turkey's acceptance of the peace settlement made after World War I

6. Which is true about the rise of the Nazis to political power in Germany?

(A) Hitler won popular support for his refusal to cooperate with conservative leaders.

(B) The Nazi Party grew in strength little by little but continuously in the 1920s and 1930s.

(C) Voters abandoned moderate parties in the elections of the early 1930s.

(D) Nazism appealed to the youth and working class.

(E) Even working together, the Communists and Social Democrats could not overcome the Nazis.

GO ON TO THE NEXT PAGE.

Solo Syndication/Associated Newspapers Ltd.

7. The cartoon above illustrates the idea that Hitler

    (A) overcame the resistance of the peasants
    (B) succeeded due to weak leadership by the European powers
    (C) gained power over the silent majority
    (D) used various organizations as the foundation of his rise to success
    (E) created an image that prompted the public to bow before him

8. The "baby bust" in Europe in the 1980s and 1990s was a reflection of all of the following EXCEPT

    (A) high unemployment
    (B) the rejection of motherhood by some women
    (C) the late age of women at first pregnancies
    (D) increasing participation of women in the workforce
    (E) similar attitudes toward family size of women across class lines

9. German reunification in 1989 was swift due to all of the following EXCEPT

    (A) Chancellor Kohl promised the East Germans an even exchange for their weak currency
    (B) Chancellor Kohl accommodated those East Germans who sought to keep some elements of the socialist system
    (C) the Soviet Union allowed reunification if Germany agreed to prohibit the development of nuclear weapons
    (D) half of the East German population poured into West Germany when it occurred
    (E) the Paris Accord affirmed the new borders, solidifying reunification

GO ON TO THE NEXT PAGE.

10. The impact of World War I on the home front included all of the following EXCEPT
    (A) labor unions were seen as unpatriotic because they organized strikes during wartime
    (B) greater visibility of women in the public sphere
    (C) free enterprise capitalism was abandoned for the planned economy
    (D) civil liberties were restricted in most countries
    (E) some women bobbed their hair, shortened their skirts, and smoked

11. The Treaty of Versailles
    (A) ensured peace in Europe through the League of Nations
    (B) allowed Germany and Russia to participate as a conciliatory measure
    (C) gave Germany fewer territorial losses than its wartime allies, Austria, and the Ottoman Empire
    (D) created a French buffer state to protect against Germany
    (E) gave Germany's colonies their independence as promised in the Fourteen Points

12. Which of the following Soviet policies was the greatest compromise of Communist ideals with capitalism?
    (A) New Economic Policy
    (B) Collectivization
    (C) Five-year plans
    (D) Stalin's purges
    (E) Building of housing blocks on the outskirts of cities

13. After World War II, western European demographic trends could be described as
    (A) a baby boom followed by a decline in birthrates after the mid-1960s
    (B) a baby boom with an average of four children per family until the 1980s
    (C) population staying about the same, neither growing or declining very much
    (D) fewer marriages due to high unemployment
    (E) women continuing to work in heavy industry and thus postponing marriage

14. Which of the following are most closely associated with the twentieth-century feminist movement?
    (A) Leni Riefenstahl and Margaret Cavendish
    (B) Simone de Beauvoir and Betty Friedan
    (C) Germaine de Stael and Marie Thérèse Geoffrin
    (D) Mary Wollstonecraft and John Stuart Mill
    (E) Elizabeth Cady Stanton and Lucretia Mott

15. The revolutions of 1989 resulted in all of the following EXCEPT
    (A) the breakup of Yugoslavia
    (B) the breakup of Czechoslovakia
    (C) the reunification of East and West Germany
    (D) a rapid rise in the standard of living for citizens of former Communist states
    (E) the rise to power of Solidarity in Poland

GO ON TO THE NEXT PAGE.

16. Alliances among the Great Powers before World War I changed when

    (A) Britain dropped its uncommitted position
    (B) Russia refused to renew its nonaggression treaty with Germany
    (C) Italy began to negotiate with France and Britain
    (D) Serbia signed a treaty with France after the first Balkan War
    (E) France and Britain nearly went to war with each other over Morocco

17. World War I was considered a total war because

    (A) widespread bombing of civilians became acceptable
    (B) every country in the world became involved
    (C) European women were recruited for military service for the first time
    (D) newspapers reported all the most gruesome aspects of the war
    (E) governments controlled social and economic policies on the home front

18. Which of the following was NOT a reason for Bolshevik success in the civil war after the Russian Revolution?

    (A) The establishment of War Communism
    (B) Intimidation by the Cheka of political opponents
    (C) Foreign military intervention on behalf of the Whites
    (D) Trotsky forming a disciplined army
    (E) Socialist volunteers from Europe and the United States who joined the Communist forces

19. In the decades before World War I, modern philosophers like Henri Bergson and Friedrich Nietzsche

    (A) expressed optimism in Europe's ability to improve the world
    (B) turned back to the ancient Greek philosophers for answers to life's questions
    (C) relied heavily on scientific principles as the basis for their ideas
    (D) challenged the Enlightenment belief in rationalism
    (E) turned to traditional Christianity

20. Which of the following was NOT true of Mussolini's Italy and Hitler's Germany?

    (A) Both leaders signed pacts with the Vatican.
    (B) Both leaders replaced traditional sources of power and authority.
    (C) Both governments created Fascist youth movements.
    (D) Both countries were fiercely nationalistic.
    (E) Both societies emphasized the woman's role in the home.

21. The tensions in the Balkans were intensified just before 1914 when Albania

    (A) was given to Serbia
    (B) became part of Bosnia and Herzegovina
    (C) was taken back by the Ottoman Empire in the second Balkan War
    (D) was given to Bulgaria
    (E) became independent because of Austrian insistence

GO ON TO THE NEXT PAGE.

22. Germany is often blamed for starting the First World War because it
    (A) mobilized first
    (B) promised unconditional support to Austria-Hungary
    (C) invaded Belgium even before Serbia responded to Austria's ultimatum
    (D) declared war on Britain first
    (E) sent its troops with the Austrian army into Serbia

23. The initial response to the outbreak of war in 1914 was
    (A) votes against funding for the war by socialists in France and Britain
    (B) enthusiasm in Germany, Austria, and Russia, but less so in Britain and France
    (C) widespread enthusiasm that goaded politicians into further confrontation
    (D) pacifists staged many demonstrations
    (E) British women like Vera Brittain tried to convince their countrymen not to enlist

24. Which battle was a victory for the Central Powers in World War I?
    (A) The first battle of the Marne in 1914
    (B) Verdun in 1915
    (C) Gallipoli in 1915
    (D) The Somme in 1916
    (E) The second battle of the Marne in 1918

25. The death tolls from World War I were
    (A) some 20 million people, half soldiers, half civilians
    (B) more than the death tolls of World War II
    (C) high on the battlefield but low on the civilian front
    (D) about 5 million soldiers and 2 million civilians
    (E) significantly less than the death tolls in the worldwide influenza epidemic of 1918

26. The United States entered World War I mostly because of
    (A) the sinking of the Lusitania
    (B) the invasion of Belgium
    (C) German resumption of submarine warfare
    (D) the Treaty of Brest-Litovsk giving the Germans too many advantages
    (E) Wilson's Fourteen Points

27. Which best explains Lenin's role in creating successful Communist movements?
    (A) His insistence on strict adherence to traditional Marxist doctrine
    (B) His strong leadership of the Menshevik faction
    (C) His rejection of Stalin's "socialism in one country" policy
    (D) His acceptance of bourgeois democracy as a step toward socialism
    (E) His organization of a tightly controlled small revolutionary vanguard party

GO ON TO THE NEXT PAGE.

28. Which is NOT true about the new media of the radio and the cinema?

    (A) They provided inexpensive entertainment for the common people.
    (B) In Europe, governments fostered their development.
    (C) They were used for political purposes by both totalitarian and democratic leaders in the 1930s.
    (D) Until the 1940s, people were too poor to go to the movies but could afford radios.
    (E) Germany and Russia developed innovative filmmaking industries in the 1920s.

29. Collectivization of agriculture in the Soviet Union

    (A) equalized the landholdings of the peasants
    (B) removed peasants from land with substantial mineral resources needed by the state
    (C) was supported by peasants in most areas except the Ukraine
    (D) met with widespread opposition but was achieved within a decade
    (E) greatly increased the efficiency of agricultural production

30. The Armenian genocide began when

    (A) the Muslims in Turkey went on an anti-Christian rampage
    (B) some Armenians welcomed Russian armies in 1915
    (C) Armenians started an armed revolt against the Sultan's government
    (D) some Armenians joined the Russian army when war broke out in 1914
    (E) the Turks were losing the battle of Gallipoli

31. The best description for the two Russian revolutions in 1917 is

    (A) both were coup d'états
    (B) neither was a coup d'état
    (C) the first was a coup d'état, the second a mass insurrection
    (D) the first was a mass insurrection, the second a coup d'état
    (E) both were mass insurrections

32. Which contradicted the principle of self-determination in the Versailles treaties?

    (A) The re-creation of Poland
    (B) Making Danzig into an international city under the League of Nations
    (C) Giving Britain control of Ottoman territory
    (D) The creation of Yugoslavia
    (E) The return of Alsace and Lorraine to France

33. Germany and Austria, as a result of World War I, were similar in that both

    (A) lost about half their former landmass
    (B) became constitutional monarchies
    (C) nearly had their own Bolshevik revolutions
    (D) had revolutions that turned them into democratic republics
    (E) faced war crimes trials

34. The Allies reacted as they had said they would in the Treaty of Versailles

    (A) when Germany suspended reparations payments in 1922
    (B) when Nazi Germany incorporated Austria in 1938
    (C) when Hitler remilitarized the Rhineland in 1936
    (D) when Germany rearmed in the 1930s
    (E) when Germany revalued its currency in the 1920s

GO ON TO THE NEXT PAGE.

35. Which artist is most closely associated with the development of Cubism?
    (A) Vincent Van Gogh
    (B) Wassily Kandinsky
    (C) Pablo Picasso
    (D) Henri Matisse
    (E) Paul Gauguin

36. Before the Great Depression, Britain, France, and Germany had all
    (A) suppressed attempted revolutions from either the right or the left
    (B) achieved political and economic stability
    (C) placed real power in the hands of a single individual
    (D) reduced the influence of Communists
    (E) suffered from the lack of competent leadership

37. Atonal or twelve-tone music was often hard to listen to because it
    (A) was not sung but only spoken
    (B) used new instruments unfamiliar to most concertgoers
    (C) was played usually without a conductor, as musicians rejected the traditional hierarchy
    (D) lacked a dominant key to organize the musical notes
    (E) was randomized so much that a listener could never hear the same piece twice

38. Freudian theory postulates that the unconscious mind is a battleground between
    (A) rationality and irrationality
    (B) sexuality and aggression
    (C) instinctual drives and internalized societal rules
    (D) self and the internalized other
    (E) the mother principle and the father principle

39. The impact of logical positivism on philosophy was to make it
    (A) very optimistic about human progress
    (B) more mathematical
    (C) more focused on religion than it had been in the nineteenth century
    (D) more metaphysical, exploring the major questions of human existence
    (E) smaller in the scope of its inquiry

40. The 1929 stock market crash in the United States caused the Great Depression in Europe because
    (A) Europeans had heavily invested in the U.S. stock market
    (B) inflation in the United States caused a rapid rise in prices in Europe
    (C) U.S. banks demanded repayment of their postwar loans to Europeans to pay off their own debts
    (D) U.S. banks demanded full repayment of their World War I loans to European states
    (E) the U.S. government immediately set up protectionist tariffs to keep out European goods

GO ON TO THE NEXT PAGE.

41. Which best characterizes the response of European governments to the Great Depression in Europe?

   (A) The heads of state called a conference to coordinate Europe-wide recovery.
   (B) Each country tried to solve its problems alone but most adopted similar policies.
   (C) Germany and France, in the spirit of Locarno, worked closely together.
   (D) The Popular Front government in France coordinated with the Labour government in Britain.
   (E) The finance ministers in Europe agreed it was important to stay on the gold standard.

42. Generally speaking, which was the most effective program in dealing with the depression?

   (A) Deficit spending to finance public works
   (B) Protectionist tariffs
   (C) Cutting social welfare benefits to balance the budget
   (D) Adherence to orthodox economic theory
   (E) Abandoning the gold standard

43. The Locarno Pact was important in the 1920s because it

   (A) outlawed war
   (B) provided the French with a secure alliance with the Little Entente
   (C) ended the possibility of a French-German war over their borders
   (D) renegotiated the German reparations payment schedule
   (E) ended the French occupation of the Ruhr

44. Which physicist is correctly matched with his contributions to science?

   (A) Max Planck—demonstrated that energy is emitted in quanta, or uneven spurts
   (B) Albert Einstein—demonstrated that the atom could be split
   (C) Ernest Rutherford—formulated the uncertainty principle
   (D) Marie Curie—showed that matter and energy are interchangeable
   (E) Werner Heisenberg—discovered that radium emits subatomic particles

45. What was the primary difference between conservative authoritarian and radical totalitarian states?

   (A) Antiliberalism
   (B) Importance given to the military
   (C) Absence of parliamentary democracy
   (D) Control over private and family life
   (E) Strength of centralized government

46. The ideal Fascist and the ideal Communist state would both achieve, albeit in different ways,

   (A) national glory
   (B) racial purity
   (C) the end of the necessity for central government
   (D) equality between men and women
   (E) the end of class warfare

GO ON TO THE NEXT PAGE.

47. Italian fascism as an ideology

   (A) rejected socialism outright and completely
   (B) argued for the superiority of the state over the individual
   (C) was profoundly racist
   (D) incorporated Enlightenment ideals
   (E) claimed that fascism would bring true social equality

48. In both Germany and Italy, Fascists came to power because

   (A) they threatened to use violence if they were not given power
   (B) they won parliamentary majorities
   (C) they had won parliamentary pluralities
   (D) their leaders had won elections to become president
   (E) their leaders were appointed to high office by legitimate authorities

49. Joseph Stalin's general industrial goals in the five-year plans were

   (A) never met
   (B) about as successful as collectivized agriculture
   (C) remarkably successful
   (D) successful but only marginally so
   (E) undermined by the depression in Europe

50. Nazi economic policies

   (A) were no more successful than the Weimar government's policies in dealing with the depression
   (B) were hardly different from those of the British and French governments of the early 1930s
   (C) relied on private initiatives to restore production and employment
   (D) were successful because they managed to win over the labor union leadership
   (E) successfully reduced unemployment

51. The tide of World War II definitively turned against the Germans when

   (A) Hitler refused to let his army retreat from Stalingrad in 1942
   (B) D-day began in 1944
   (C) the Allied armies met at the Elbe in 1945
   (D) the Holocaust took too much of German army personnel to carry out
   (E) Italy surrendered to the Allies in 1943

52. The Truman Doctrine and Brezhnev Doctrine both

   (A) promised that superpowers would support the civil rights of all Europeans
   (B) promised that superpowers would act militarily only in cooperation with their allies
   (C) claimed that superpowers have the right to intervene in the domestic affairs of smaller countries
   (D) focused on the rights of superpowers in occupied Germany and Austria
   (E) were enunciated initially in relationship to civil war in Turkey and Greece

GO ON TO THE NEXT PAGE.

53. Britain differed from other western European states in the early years after World War II in that
    (A) it rejected the welfare state
    (B) it established an independent nuclear force
    (C) it was the only monarchy left
    (D) the governing party was socialist leaning
    (E) it refused at first to join NATO

54. The Christian Democrats in western Europe in the 1950s
    (A) resisted adopting social welfare programs
    (B) initiated the Common Market
    (C) uniformly rejected the idea of a mixed economy
    (D) reduced the size of government
    (E) supported the Hungarian revolution

55. Détente between eastern and western Europe was initiated by the
    (A) West German chancellor Willy Brandt
    (B) British prime minister Margaret Thatcher
    (C) U.S. president Ronald Reagan
    (D) Soviet premier Nikita Khrushchev
    (E) French president Charles de Gaulle

56. When the United States announced the Marshall Plan,
    (A) it offered aid only to noncommunist states
    (B) only NATO members were allowed to get aid
    (C) the Soviet Union refused to allow its satellites to get aid
    (D) the Communist Party had become the largest party in Italy
    (E) the civil wars in Greece and Turkey had already ended

57. The origins of the Cold War are most directly found in
    (A) the long-standing hostility between the United States and the Soviet Union
    (B) the decision to defeat Germany by a direct attack on the Balkans
    (C) Churchill's "iron curtain" speech
    (D) the lack of planning for postwar Europe
    (E) the military strategy adopted by the United States and the Soviet Union at Teheran

GO ON TO THE NEXT PAGE.

Bruno Barbey/Magnum Photos.

58. The chief issue prompting these French student protests in the 1960s was

   (A) the government's acceptance of Algerian independence
   (B) lack of jobs
   (C) discrimination against women
   (D) the need for reforms in the university system
   (E) French military involvement in the Vietnam War

59. Most western European nations responded to the "stagflation" crisis of the 1970s and 1980s

   (A) with increased deficit spending
   (B) with an arms buildup to provide employment
   (C) by returning to the gold standard
   (D) by cutting government spending
   (E) by maintaining social welfare programs to help the unemployed

60. By the 1950s, the middle classes

   (A) tended to be owners of family businesses in western Europe but party members in eastern Europe
   (B) were dominated by managers and experts in both western and eastern Europe
   (C) were dominated by professionals like doctors in both western and eastern Europe
   (D) shrank in size as the working classes grew in both western and eastern Europe
   (E) benefited from the greater social inequality of the postwar period in both western and eastern Europe

GO ON TO THE NEXT PAGE.

61. Decolonization in Indochina and Indonesia was different from that in India because
    (A) the United Nations supervised their transition to independence
    (B) they had to fight militarily against their European overlords to achieve independence
    (C) they got military aid from newly communist China
    (D) their independence was granted more than a decade after India's
    (E) the United States aided their independence movements

62. European unity in the 1950s and 1960s
    (A) was successful first politically, then economically
    (B) was enthusiastically endorsed by Charles de Gaulle
    (C) began with Belgium and Holland over the objections of Germany
    (D) involved creating an independent nuclear force under European control
    (E) developed without the participation of Britain

63. Alexander Dubček's establishment of "socialism with a human face" in Czechoslovakia
    (A) was militarily and economically supported by the United States as part of the Truman Doctrine
    (B) received the same treatment as the Hungarian revolution by the Soviet Union
    (C) proved to be a sham in that little change was really made
    (D) sparked a similar movement in Poland
    (E) led to the building of the Berlin Wall

64. In which eastern Europe state was the challenge to the Communist system successful first?
    (A) Romania
    (B) Poland
    (C) Hungary
    (D) Czechoslovakia
    (E) Chechnya

65. In which state was the end of Communist rule accompanied by the execution of its former leader?
    (A) Poland
    (B) Hungary
    (C) Yugoslavia
    (D) Romania
    (E) Czechoslovakia

66. Mikhail Gorbachev's goal in initiating perestroika and glasnost was to
    (A) introduce capitalism but prevent political democracy
    (B) enforce the Brezhnev Doctrine on the Soviet satellites
    (C) outmaneuver his rival, Boris Yeltsin
    (D) reform the Soviet system in order to maintain it
    (E) respond to criticisms from U.S. president Ronald Reagan

GO ON TO THE NEXT PAGE.

67. The disintegration of the Soviet Union began when

    (A) Lithuania declared its independence
    (B) Yeltsin announced Russian independence
    (C) East Germany reunified with West Germany
    (D) Gorbachev became president of the Russian Federation
    (E) Poland broke free of Soviet control

68. Hungary's opening of its borders with East Germany

    (A) resulted in the opening of the Berlin Wall
    (B) led to the re-election of the reformist Communist leadership in Hungary
    (C) was strongly protested by West Germany
    (D) led to a mass exodus from Hungary
    (E) had few consequences beyond the symbolic

69. Which was NOT an early result of the collapse of Soviet communism in Russia?

    (A) A decline in life expectancy
    (B) A growing gap between rich and poor
    (C) Many new businesses, mostly created by ordinary Russians
    (D) Inflation and the erosion of savings
    (E) A decline in production

70. Since the 1990s, most western European countries have experienced

    (A) a decline in the number of Muslim immigrants after a high point reached in 1990
    (B) the expansion of immigrant slums within big cities like Paris and London
    (C) rising religiosity among all groups
    (D) the development of multiculturalism
    (E) a brain drain to the United States

71. The Maastricht Treaty of 1991

    (A) ended World War II by accepting national borders
    (B) replaced NATO once the Cold War was over
    (C) promised European intervention to prevent human rights abuses
    (D) accepted eastern European countries into the European Union
    (E) established a common currency for most European Union members

72. The violence accompanying the breakup of Yugoslavia can best be explained by

    (A) the conflicting nationalisms of its former members
    (B) differing experiences in postcommunist economic life
    (C) Slav hatred of non-Slavs
    (D) interference from outside powers
    (E) conflicts between Communists and anticommunists

GO ON TO THE NEXT PAGE.

73. Post-9/11 terrorist attacks by militant Muslims were particularly disturbing to Europeans because

   (A) they showed that the EU had made it easy for terrorists to live in Europe
   (B) the terrorists came from Turkey, which was applying for membership in the EU
   (C) it revealed a fissure in the unity of Europe, as only Great Britain was attacked
   (D) most of the terrorists were citizens or long-standing residents of the countries they attacked
   (E) the United States criticized the countries that were attacked for not supporting its war on terror

74. Illegal immigrants into western and central Europe in the 1990s

   (A) came mostly from Turkey and the Middle East
   (B) were mostly Muslim
   (C) tended to come from eastern Europe and Africa
   (D) formed their own political parties
   (E) were generally welcomed

75. Optimism that liberal capitalism would be permanently triumphant after the fall of communism was contradicted most clearly by

   (A) the EU's indifference to human rights
   (B) globalization's encouragement of small business enterprises around the globe
   (C) resurgent nationalism in Europe
   (D) the entry of Turkey and its 60 million Muslims into the EU
   (E) a growing trend toward dictatorship in central and eastern Europe

76. What most clearly distinguishes the Holocaust from other twentieth-century genocides?

   (A) Its victims included many children.
   (B) Women were brutalized and murdered.
   (C) Virtually all victims were of one ethnicity or religion.
   (D) Advanced technology was created for the purpose.
   (E) There was an international trial of some of those responsible.

77. European responses to the U.S. wars in Vietnam in the 1960s and in Iraq in 2003 were similar in that

   (A) generally, most western European governments supported them enthusiastically
   (B) both western and eastern European states sent small numbers of troops to support the United States
   (C) they created a rift between western Europe and the United States
   (D) they voted against the United States in the United Nations Security Council
   (E) students protested but they were in the distinct minority in Europe

78. The European Union in the late twentieth century was on its way toward

   (A) dissolution because of nationalistic tensions
   (B) economic integration but not political integration
   (C) political and military integration but economic nationalism
   (D) rivaling the United States as an economic power
   (E) becoming a "United States of western Europe"

GO ON TO THE NEXT PAGE.

79. World War I and World War II were similar in that the main cause of each was

(A) arms races
(B) alliances
(C) colonial competition in Africa and the Middle East
(D) Russian mobilization
(E) aggression of strong powers against smaller states

80. The best title for this map would be

(A) Battle Sites of the Napoleonic Wars
(B) The Revolutions of 1848
(C) World War I Battles
(D) Sites of Nazi Concentration Camps During World War II
(E) Democratic Movements in 1989

STOP

END OF SECTION I

EUROPEAN HISTORY
SECTION II

Part A
(Suggested writing time—45 minutes)
Percent of Section II score—45

Directions: The following question is based on the accompanying Documents 1–12. The documents have been edited for the purpose of this exercise.

This question is designed to test your ability to work with and understand historical documents. Write an essay that:

+ Provides an appropriate, explicitly stated thesis that directly addresses all parts of the question and does NOT simply restate the question.

+ Discusses a majority of the documents individually and specifically.

+ Demonstrates understanding of the basic meaning of a majority of the documents.

+ Supports the thesis with appropriate interpretation of a majority of the documents.

+ Analyzes the documents by explicitly grouping them in at least three appropriate ways.

+ Takes into account both the sources of the documents and the authors' point of view.

You may refer to relevant historical information not mentioned in the documents.

1. Analyze the changing views held by women about the nature of women and their place in society between 1500 and the early twentieth century.

Historical background: Most European women were granted the right to vote in the early twentieth century, generally after World War I. Before that, women were by and large severely restricted in their rights and opportunities for education or employment, both by law and by custom. While poor women always did productive labor, whether in the fields or in towns, middle- and upper-class women lived more comfortable lives but were barred from the educational, intellectual, and employment opportunities available to the men of their station in life. Even so, a number of women played important political roles, such as Queens Elizabeth I of England and Isabella of Spain. Numerous women wrote about women's issues over the centuries.

GO ON TO THE NEXT PAGE.

Document 1

Source: Christine de Pizan, French writer, *The Book of the City of Ladies: Advice for a "Wise Princess,"* 1404.

The sixth teaching: how the wise princess will keep the women of her court in good order. The women should restrain themselves with seemly conduct among knights and squires and all men. They should speak demurely and sweetly and, whether in dances or other amusements, divert and enjoy themselves decorously and without wantonness. They must not be frolicsome, forward, or boisterous in speech, expression, bearing or laughter. They must not go about with their heads raised like wild deer. This kind of behavior would be very unseemly and greatly derisory in a woman of the court, in whom there should be more modesty, good manners and courteous behavior than in any others, for where there is most honor there ought to be the most perfect manners and behavior.

Document 2

Source: Laura Cereta, Italian humanist, *Epistolae familiares,* from a letter to Bibulus Sempronius, January 13, 1488.

You [Bibulus] brashly and publicly not merely wonder but indeed lament that I am said to possess as fine a mind as nature ever bestowed upon the most learned man. You seem to think so learned a woman has scarcely before been seen in the world. You are wrong. . . . The explanation is clear: women have been able by nature to be exceptional, but have chosen lesser goals. For some women are concerned with parting their hair correctly, adorning themselves with lovely dresses . . . or standing at mirrors to smear their lovely faces. But those in whom a deeper integrity yearns for virtue, restrain from the start their youthful souls, reflect on higher things, harden the body with sobriety and trials, and curb their tongues, open their ears, compose their thoughts in wakeful hours, their minds in contemplation to letters bonded to righteousness. For knowledge is not given as a gift, but [is gained] with diligence. Nature has generously lavished its gifts upon all people, opening to all the doors of choice through which reason sends envoys to the will. . . . You pretend that I alone am admirable because of the good fortune of my intellect. But I, compared to other women who have won splendid renown, am but a little mousling.

Document 3

Source: St. Teresa of Ávila, sixteenth-century Spanish nun and Catholic saint, *The Life of St. Teresa of Jesus, of The Order of Our Lady of Carmel,* ca. 1565.

I will relate what I saw, by way of warning to men to be on their guard against women who will do things of this kind. . . . Women—for they are more bound to purity than men—if once they have lost all shame before God, are in nothing whatever to be trusted; and that in exchange for the gratification of their will, and of that affection which the devil suggests, they will hesitate at nothing. . . . All men must have a greater affection for those women whom they see disposed to be good; and even for the attainment of earthly ends, women must have more power over men because they are good. . . . For the rest, it is enough that I am a woman to make my sails droop: how much more, then, when I am a woman, and a wicked one?

Document 4

Source: Louise Labé, French Renaissance poet, letter to a friend, ca. 1555.

Since a time has come, Mademoiselle, when the severe laws of men no longer prevent women from applying themselves to the sciences and other disciplines, it seems to me that those of us who can, should use this long-craved freedom to study and to let men see how greatly they wronged us when depriving us of its honor and advantages. And if any woman becomes so proficient as to be able to write down her thoughts, let her do so and not despise the honor but rather flaunt it instead of fine clothes, necklaces, and rings. For these may be considered ours only by use, whereas the honor of being educated is ours entirely.

Document 5

Source: Mary Cary, member of the millenarian Fifth Monarchy sect during the English Civil War, which believed they were living in the "end of days," *The New Jerusalem's Glory,* 1656.

And if there be very few men that are thus furnished with the gift of the Spirit; how few are the women! Not but that there are many godly women, many who have indeed received the Spirit: but in how small a measure is it? How weak are they? And how unable to prophesie? For it is that that I am speaking of, which this text says they shall do; which yet we see not fulfilled. . . . But the time is coming when this promise shall be fulfilled, and the Saints shall be abundantly filled with the spirit; and not only men, but women shall prophesie; not only aged men, but young men; not only superiours, but inferiours; not only those that have University learning, but those that have it not; even servants and handmaids.

GO ON TO THE NEXT PAGE.

Document 6

Source: Mary Astell, unmarried English writer, *Some Reflections Upon Marriage,* 1700.

But how can a Woman scruple entire Subjection, how can she forbear to affirm the Worth and Excellency of the Superior Sex, if she at all considers it! Have not all the great Actions that have been performed in the World been done by Men? Have they not founded Empires and over-turned them? Do they not make Laws and continually repeal and amend them? Their vast Minds lay Kingdoms waste, no Bounds or Measures can be prescribed to their Desires. War and Peace depend on them; they . . . have the Wisdom and Courage to get over all . . . the petty Restraints which Honor and Conscience may lay in the way of their desired Grandeur. What is it they cannot do? They make Worlds and ruin them, form Systems of universal Nature, and dispute eternally about them; their Pen gives Worth to the most trifling Controversy. . . . It is a Woman's Happiness to hear, admire and praise them, especially if a little Ill nature keeps them at any time from bestowing the Applauses to each other! And if she aspires no further, she is thought to be in her proper Sphere of Action, she is as wise and as good as can be expected from her!

Document 7

Source: Marianne Loir (1715–1769), French artist, portrait of Madame du Châtelet, translator of Newton's *Principia Mathematica,* companion of Voltaire.

GO ON TO THE NEXT PAGE.

Document 8

Source: Lady Mary Wortley Montagu, author and wife of a Whig member of British Parliament, *in a paper called The Nonsense of Common-Sense,* January 24, 1738.

Among the most universal errors, I reckon that of treating the weaker sex with a contempt which has a very bad influence on their conduct. How many of them think it excuse enough to say they are women, to indulge any folly that comes into their heads! This renders them useless members of the commonwealth, and only burdensome to their own families. . . . What reason nature has given them is thrown away. . . .

A woman really virtuous, in the utmost extent of this expression, has virtue of a purer kind than any philosopher has ever shown. I have some thoughts of exhibiting a set of pictures of such meritorious ladies, where I shall say nothing of the fire of their eyes, or the pureness of their complexions, but give them such praises as befit a rational sensible being: virtues of choice, and not beauties of accident. . . . I would not have them place so much value on a quality that can be only useful to one, as to neglect that which may be of benefit to thousands, by precept or by example. There will be no occasion of amusing themselves with trifles, when they consider themselves capable of not only making the most amiable, but the most estimable, figures in life. Begin, then, ladies, by paying those authors with scorn and contempt who, with a sneer of affected admiration, would throw you below the dignity of the human species.

Document 9

Source: Mary Wollstonecraft, English writer, translator, governess, *A Vindication of the Rights of Women,* 1792.

My own sex, I hope, will excuse me, if I treat them like rational creatures, instead of flattering their fascinating graces, and viewing them as if they were in a state of perpetual childhood, unable to stand alone. I earnestly wish to point out in what true dignity and human happiness consists—I wish to persuade women to endeavor to acquire strength, both of mind and body, and to convince them that the soft phrases, susceptibility of heart, delicacy of sentiment, and refinement of taste, are almost synonymous with epithets of weakness, and that those beings who are only the objects of pity will soon become objects of contempt.

Dismissing those soft pretty feminine phrases, which the men condescendingly use to soften our slavish dependence, and despising that weak elegancy of mind, exquisite sensibility, and sweet docility of manners, supposed to be the sexual characteristics of the weaker vessel, I wish to shew that elegance is inferior to virtue, that the first object of laudable ambition is to obtain a character as a human being, regardless of the distinction of sex. . . . Why must the female mind be tainted by coquettish arts to gratify the sensualist and prevent love from subsiding into friendship, or compassionate tenderness, when there are not qualities on which friendship can be built? Let the honest heart shew itself, and reason teach passion to submit to necessity; or, let the dignified pursuit of virtue and knowledge raise the mind above those emotions.

GO ON TO THE NEXT PAGE.

Document 10

Source: Clara Zetkin, German socialist and suffragist who died in exile from Nazi Germany, *A Socialist Solution to the Question of Women's Rights,* 1887.

Given the fact that many thousands of female workers are active in industry, it is vital for the trade unions to incorporate them into their movement. In individual industries where female labor plays an important role, any movement advocating better wages, shorter working hours, etc., would be doomed from the start because of the attitude of those women workers who are not organized. Battles which begin propitiously enough, ended up in failure because the employers were able to play off non-union female workers against those that are organized in unions. These non-union workers continued to work (or took up work) under any conditions, which transformed them from competitors in dirty work to scabs.

Certainly one of the reasons for these poor wages for women is the circumstances that female workers are practically unorganized. They lack the strength which comes with unity. They lack the courage, the feeling of power, the spirit of resistance, and the ability to resist which is produced by the strength of an organization in which the individual fights for everybody and everybody fights for the individual. Furthermore, they lack the enlightenment and the training which an organization provides.

Document 11

Source: Adelheid Popp, Viennese socialist and founder of the proletarian women's movement, *The Autobiography of a Working Woman,* 1913.

From the women of this factory one can judge how sad and full of deprivation is the lot of a factory worker. In none of the neighboring factories were the wages so high; we were envied everywhere. Parents considered themselves fortunate if they could get their daughters of fourteen in there on leaving school . . . and even, here in this paradise, all were badly nourished. All humbled themselves and suffered the worst injustice from the foreman not to risk losing this good work, not to be without food. . . .

[When I became a Social Democrat], in the factory I became another woman. . . . I told my [female] comrades all that I had read of the workers' movement. Formerly I had often told stories when they had begged me for them. But instead of narrating . . . the fate of some queen, I now held forth on oppression and exploitation. . . . It often happened that one of the clerks passing by shook his head and said to another clerk "that girl speaks like a man."

GO ON TO THE NEXT PAGE.

Document 12

Source: Annie Steel, best-selling author of books about India, education, and women's issues, *The Complete Indian Housekeeper and Cook,* London, 1902.

It is not necessary, or in the least degree desirable, that an educated woman should waste the best years of her life in scolding and petty supervision. Life holds higher duties, and it is indubitable that friction and over-zeal is a sure sign of a bad housekeeper. . . .

The personal attention of the mistress is quite as much needed here as at home. . . . The first duty of a mistress is, of course, to be able to give intelligible orders to her servants, therefore it is necessary she should learn to speak Hindustani. . . .The next duty is obviously to insist on her orders being carried out. . . . The secret lies in making rules and keeping to them. The Indian servant is a child in everything save age, and should be treated as a child, that is to say, kindly but with the greatest firmness. . . . A good mistress in India will try to set a good example to her servants, in routine, method and tidiness. . . . An untidy mistress invariably has untidy, a weak one, idle servants.

GO ON TO THE NEXT PAGE.

EUROPEAN HISTORY
SECTION II

Part B
(Suggested planning and writing time—35 minutes)
Percent of Section II score—27.5

Directions: You are to answer ONE question from the three questions below. Make your selection carefully, choosing the question that you are best prepared to answer thoroughly in the time permitted. You should spend 5 minutes organizing or outlining your answer.

Write an essay that:

+ Has a relevant thesis.

+ Addresses all parts of the question.

+ Supports the thesis with specific evidence.

+ Is well organized.

2. Analyze how the causes and the course of World War I affected the negotiations at the Versailles Peace Conference.

3. Analyze the reasons for the rise of a successful Fascist movement in Italy, and describe how it implemented its ideology when it took power in 1922 up to when Italy joined the Rome-Berlin Axis in 1936.

4. Describe how Leninism revised Marxism, and analyze how that helped the Bolsheviks to take power in Russia.

GO ON TO THE NEXT PAGE.

EUROPEAN HISTORY
SECTION II

Part C
(Suggested planning and writing time—35 minutes)
Percent of Section II score—27.5

Directions: You are to answer ONE question from the three questions below. Make your selection carefully, choosing the question that you are best prepared to answer thoroughly in the time permitted. You should spend 5 minutes organizing or outlining your answer.

Write an essay that:

✦ Has a relevant thesis.

✦ Addresses all parts of the question.

✦ Supports the thesis with specific evidence.

✦ Is well organized.

5. Discuss the economic problems faced by western Europeans from the end of the Second World War until 1985, and analyze the success or failure of governments in dealing with those problems.

6. Compare and contrast the goals and practices of Nazi Germany and Stalinist Russia in the 1930s, and explain how these helped prepare for war.

7. Describe three eastern European resistance movements to Soviet domination from 1946 to 1985 and analyze the reasons for their success or failure.

STOP

END OF EXAM

Answer Key for Practice Exam 4

Answers for Section I: Multiple-Choice Questions

1. C	21. E	41. B	61. B
2. E	22. B	42. A	62. E
3. D	23. C	43. C	63. B
4. A	24. C	44. A	64. B
5. C	25. A	45. D	65. D
6. C	26. C	46. E	66. D
7. B	27. E	47. B	67. A
8. E	28. D	48. E	68. A
9. B	29. D	49. C	69. C
10. A	30. B	50. E	70. D
11. C	31. D	51. A	71. E
12. A	32. C	52. C	72. A
13. A	33. D	53. D	73. D
14. B	34. A	54. B	74. C
15. D	35. C	55. A	75. C
16. A	36. B	56. C	76. D
17. E	37. D	57. E	77. C
18. E	38. C	58. D	78. D
19. D	39. E	59. D	79. E
20. B	40. C	60. B	80. E

Scoring the Multiple-Choice Section

Use the following formula to calculate your raw score on the multiple-choice section of the exam:

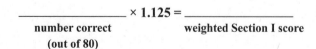

$$\underset{\substack{\textbf{number correct}\\ \textbf{(out of 80)}}}{\underline{\hspace{3cm}}} \times \textbf{1.125} = \underset{\textbf{weighted Section I score}}{\underline{\hspace{3cm}}}$$

Rationales

1. **Answer: (C)** The Bauhaus advocated functionalism—the idea that form follows functions. It was a school of architecture and design that also included weavers, printers, and other craftspeople unlike most of the other movements. The Nazis closed the Bauhaus. (McKay, *A History of Western Society,* Eleventh Edition, pp. 870–871)

2. **Answer: (E)**   Lenin had promised "Peace, Land, and Bread" in 1917 before the Bolshevik seizure of power. By signing this treaty, Russia ended its participation in World War I, which the provisional government had not done. (McKay, *A History of Western Society,* Eleventh Edition, pp. 844–845, 847)

3. **Answer: (D)**   Socialist realism glorified the common working people and was the typical art form of the Soviet Union. (McKay, *A History of Western Society,* Eleventh Edition, p. 935)

4. **Answer: (A)**   With the African and Asian peoples calling for freedom from European rule and in some places, starting to revolt, the Europeans began to think more seriously about relinquishing them. After World War II, the clamor for independence increased, and the European countries, devastated by war, eventually gave in (or lost) to these demands. (McKay, *A History of Western Society,* Eleventh Edition, pp. 956–957)

5. **Answer: (C)**   The map shows that most of the former Ottoman territories were placed under British and French controls as mandates of the League of Nations. This contradicted promises made to both Arabs and Jews during the war and the principle of self-determination. The division of territory follows the Sykes-Picot agreements of 1916. (McKay, *A History of Western Society,* Eleventh Edition, pp. 853–855)

6. **Answer: (C)**   Hitler had formed a political alliance with conservative leaders in 1932. He appealed to the young but not the working class. The Nazi Party stayed small from 1924 to 1928 and only won many seats in the Reichstag after the depression and voters abandoned the moderate parties. (McKay, *A History of Western Society,* Eleventh Edition, pp. 911–913)

7. **Answer: (B)**   The European powers adopted a policy of appeasement in the wake of economic woes and then regretted that they had allowed Hitler to expand as he did. The caption on the cartoon says, "Spineless leaders of democracy." (McKay, *A History of Western Society,* Eleventh Edition, pp. 916–917)

8. **Answer: (E)**   The higher the social class of a woman, the more professional and educated, the greater the likelihood of having fewer or no children. (McKay, *A History of Western Society,* Eleventh Edition, p. 1024)

9. **Answer: (B)**   Kohl ably outmaneuvered those who sought a "third way" between socialism and capitalism. Kohl negotiated carefully with East Germans, promising them economic bonanzas, and with the international community. Kohl and Gorbachev signed an agreement to allow unification. (McKay, *A History of Western Society,* Eleventh Edition, pp. 1001–1002)

10. **Answer: (A)**   Although women's role in the home continued, it was also necessary for women to take the jobs of men who were fighting in the war. They became more and more visible in the public sphere. Labor unions won increasing respect for their cooperation and avoidance of strikes during the war. (McKay, *A History of Western Society,* Eleventh Edition, pp. 838–840)

11. **Answer: (C)**   Although the causes of World War I were complex, Germany was judged the aggressor and was not invited to the Paris Peace Conference. Germany lost about 10 percent of her territory, but Austria and the Ottoman Empire were decimated in size, with many new states carved out of their former territories. (McKay, *A History of Western Society,* Eleventh Edition, pp. 851–855)

12. **Answer: (A)**   Lenin's New Economic Policy compromised socialist ideals because it allowed some capitalistic practices, such as private profit. (McKay, *A History of Western Society,* Eleventh Edition, pp. 900–901)

13. **Answer: (A)** Although there was a slight increase in family size after World War II, in general the birthrate has declined in Europe since the mid-1960s. (McKay, *A History of Western Society,* Eleventh Edition, pp. 965–966, 975)

14. **Answer: (B)** Simone de Beauvoir wrote *The Second Sex* (1949) and Betty Friedan wrote *The Feminine Mystique* (1963), raising consciousness about women's rights. Riefenstahl was a filmmaker in Nazi Germany; the others all lived before the twentieth century. (McKay, *A History of Western Society,* Eleventh Edition, pp. 989–990)

15. **Answer: (D)** When communism ended in eastern Europe, underlying ethnic tensions escalated and both Yugoslavia and Czechoslovakia broke apart. Germany reunified quickly, but the standard of living for most people in the former Communist states declined in the transition to capitalism. (McKay, *A History of Western Society,* Eleventh Edition, pp. 998–1002, 1013–1015)

16. **Answer: (A)** After defeating France in the Franco-Prussian War, Bismarck wanted to ensure that France remained politically isolated. With this in mind, he signed a non-aggression treaty with Russia, but Kaiser Wilhelm II refused to renew it. Britain, in the wake of increased economic competition and the German naval buildup, abandoned its role as an uncommitted power and began to form alliances. (McKay, *A History of Western Society,* Eleventh Edition, pp. 824–825)

17. **Answer: (E)** World War I was a total war in that every aspect of life was affected in some way. Governments had control over all the resources of their countries to use for the good of their militaries. Governments could ration food, draft soldiers, force people to work in factories, or do anything else that might further their cause in the war. (McKay, *A History of Western Society,* Eleventh Edition, p. 830)

18. **Answer: (E)** The White Army, which fought the Bolshevik Red Army, was on the fringes of Russia and was very disunited. This made it easier for the Bolsheviks to defeat them. Foreign intervention on behalf of the Whites tainted them with unpatriotic associations. Socialist volunteers from other countries were few in number and insignificant for victory. (McKay, *A History of Western Society,* Eleventh Edition, pp. 845–849)

19. **Answer: (D)** Modern philosophers attacked the idea that humanity was progressing and that rational thought could be relied on. Both Nietzsche and Bergson stressed the importance of individual passion and intuition. Nietzsche famously said, "God is dead." (McKay, *A History of Western Society,* Eleventh Edition, pp. 864–865)

20. **Answer: (B)** Though Germany and Italy shared many characteristics under Hitler and Mussolini regimes, respectively, the king remained on the throne in Italy and other traditional sources of authority kept their positions and influence, including the church. (McKay, *A History of Western Society,* Eleventh Edition, pp. 908–910, 912–916)

21. **Answer: (E)** Serbia desperately wanted to expand, and Bosnia and Herzegovina had already been annexed by Austria. Serbia thought it had the right to Albania because of its victories in the Balkan wars, but Austria demanded that Serbia give up Albania. (McKay, *A History of Western Society,* Eleventh Edition, p. 827)

22. **Answer: (B)** Russia mobilized first. Britain declared war on Germany after it invaded Belgium, which occurred a few days after the outbreak of war between Austria and Serbia. Some commentators feel that Austria-Hungary would not have been so bold with Serbia without Germany's promise of unconditional support. (McKay, *A History of Western Society,* Eleventh Edition, pp. 828–829)

23. **Answer: (C)** There was enthusiasm for the war everywhere. Vera Brittain was enthusiastic for war in the beginning but then became deeply disillusioned. (McKay, *A History of Western Society,* Eleventh Edition, pp. 829–830, 839)

24. **Answer: (C)** The two battles of the Marne stopped the first German advance in August–September 1914 and the last German offensive in 1918. The Somme was an extremely costly British victory in 1916, Verdun effectively a draw. At Gallipoli, the Turks defeated the British forces in a clear if costly victory. (McKay, *A History of Western Society,* Eleventh Edition, pp. 830–832, 835, 849)

25. **Answer: (A)** The death tolls in World War I were huge, about 20 million dead, about half of them civilians, plus 10 million more wounded. A similar number died in the worldwide flu epidemic right as the war ended. (McKay, *A History of Western Society,* Eleventh Edition, pp. 855, 857–858)

26. **Answer: (C)** The Fourteen Points were enunciated some eight months after U.S. entry into the war when Germany resumed unrestricted submarine warfare. The Lusitania was sunk in 1915, two years before U.S. entry. (McKay, *A History of Western Society,* Eleventh Edition, pp. 836–837, 851)

27. **Answer: (E)** Lenin revised traditional Marxism in a number of ways. His formation of a tightly controlled, small party of committed revolutionaries made it possible for the Bolsheviks to seize power in November 1917 and created a model for a way to achieve radical political change adopted in many countries around the globe. (McKay, *A History of Western Society,* Eleventh Edition, pp. 843–845)

28. **Answer: (D)** Although ordinary people struggled financially in the 1930s, they went to the movies frequently, with many going once or twice a week. Democratic leaders like FDR or Stanley Baldwin in the United Kingdom were masters at using the radio. In Europe, unlike in the United States, the governments actively promoted the new media and established national radio networks such as the BBC. (McKay, *A History of Western Society,* Eleventh Edition, pp. 878–880)

29. **Answer: (D)** Collectivization, announced in 1929, was achieved by 1938. It met great opposition from kulaks, and millions of peasants died in the process. The collectivized lands were by and large used for agriculture, not for mineral resources. Productivity remained stagnant. (McKay, *A History of Western Society,* Eleventh Edition, pp. 903–905)

30. **Answer: (B)** The Armenian genocide was the first of the twentieth century. It was caused when some Armenians welcomed Russian forces into the Ottoman Empire's eastern areas. The Ottoman government forced Armenians away from the area, and more than a million Armenians died. (McKay, *A History of Western Society,* p. 835)

31. **Answer: (D)** The first revolution in March 1917 resulted from widespread protests and created the provisional government; the Bolshevik Revolution in November 1917 was a coup d'état of that government executed by the Petrograd Soviet under the Bolsheviks. (McKay, *A History of Western Society,* Eleventh Edition, pp. 842–845)

32. **Answer: (C)** In the mandate system, former colonies were given to European powers and not allowed a choice, as they expected based on Wilson's Fourteen Points. (McKay, *A History of Western Society,* Eleventh Edition, p. 853)

33. **Answer: (D)** Both the kaiser and the Habsburg emperor were forced to abdicate by revolutionary outbursts. Both states became republics for the first time. (McKay, *A History of Western Society,* Eleventh Edition, pp. 849–851)

34. **Answer: (A)** German rearmament, the Anschluss (unification with Austria), and the remilitarization of the Rhineland were all expressly forbidden in the Treaty of Versailles, but England and France did nothing. France sent troops to the Ruhr when Germany suspended reparations payments in 1922. The German revaluation of its currency did not violate the Versailles Treaty. (McKay, *A History of Western Society,* Eleventh Edition, pp. 881–883, 916–918)

35. **Answer: (C)** Picasso is generally considered to be the originator of Cubism. (McKay, *A History of Western Society,* Eleventh Edition, p. 872)

36. **Answer: (B)** All three countries faced severe economic dislocations after the war and experienced political turmoil in the early to mid-1920s, but they had achieved relative stability by the end of the decade. Only Germany faced attempted revolutions. There were effective leaders like Gustav Stresemann in Germany. Communists remained important and powerful throughout the decade in France and Germany and played a role in England at least up to 1926. (McKay, *A History of Western Society,* Eleventh Edition, pp. 883–885)

37. **Answer: (D)** Atonality was difficult because it lacked a key, so it sounded dissonant to most people. Wozzeck was a half-sung, half-spoken, atonal opera. Most orchestras retained their conductors and used traditional instruments. (McKay, *A History of Western Society,* Eleventh Edition, pp. 876–877)

38. **Answer: (C)** Freud delineated three parts of the unconscious mind, the instinctual drives (the id), the internalized rules and values of society (the superego), and the self (ego), which mediates between the two. (McKay, *A History of Western Society,* Eleventh Edition, pp. 869–870)

39. **Answer: (E)** Logical empiricism argued that language was the only meaningful subject for discourse and analysis in philosophy, not religion or metaphysics, thus sharply reducing the scope of inquiry. (McKay, *A History of Western Society,* Eleventh Edition, p. 865)

40. **Answer: (C)** The depression led to deflation, not inflation. U.S. investors pulled their money out of Europe, and U.S. banks insisted on repayment of the loans they had made to Europeans in the heady days of the 1920s in order to pay off their debts. The United States did establish protectionist tariffs, but it was the flow of gold reserves out of Europe to the United States that damaged the European economies initially. (McKay, *A History of Western Society,* Eleventh Edition, p. 886)

41. **Answer: (B)** There was very little coordination among the states, each trying to solve the problem alone. Most states went off the gold standard and imposed protectionist tariffs. (McKay, *A History of Western Society,* Eleventh Edition, p. 886)

42. **Answer: (A)** The Scandinavians did better than any other states in Europe because they used deficit spending to finance public works and increased social welfare spending. (McKay, *A History of Western Society,* Eleventh Edition, pp. 890–892)

43. **Answer: (C)** In the Locarno Pact, France and Germany accepted their borders as established by the Versailles Treaty. The Ruhr crisis had been over for two years when it was negotiated. The Dawes and Young Plans reorganized German reparations payments. France was tied to the Little Entente but not by formal treaty. (McKay, *A History of Western Society,* Eleventh Edition, p. 883)

44. **Answer: (A)** Max Planck founded quantum mechanics, Curie discovered radium, Heisenberg formulated the uncertainty principle, and Rutherford first split the atom. Einstein showed matter and energy are interchangeable. (McKay, *A History of Western Society,* Eleventh Edition, pp. 867–869)

45. **Answer: (D)** Totalitarian states intruded into private and family life while authoritarian states didn't bother to. The latter were mostly interested in maintaining the status quo, while the former sought to entirely remake society. (McKay, *A History of Western Society,* Eleventh Edition, p. 898)

46. **Answer: (E)** Both Communists and Fascists sought to end class warfare, Communists by eliminating all exploiting classes and Fascists by turning people's energies

toward the nation or the race and to its leader. Only Nazis had racism as a key element of their ideology; Communists opposed racism, while the Italians were more nationalistic than racist. (McKay, *A History of Western Society,* Eleventh Edition, pp. 898–900)

47. **Answer: (B)**   Fascism was profoundly anticommunist and anti-union and sought to replace existing socialism with a different type of socialism that would provide benefits for workers and replace unions with state-run workers' organizations. It was a profound rejection of the Enlightenment and rejected the concept of equality. One of Mussolini's slogans was "Everything in the state, nothing outside the state, nothing against the state." (McKay, *A History of Western Society,* Eleventh Edition, pp. 908–910)

48. **Answer: (E)**   Both Hitler and Mussolini were appointed to their positions by high-ranking authorities, Hitler by President Hindenburg and Mussolini by the king of Italy. In both cases, their parties did not have a majority, but their appointments were fully constitutional. (McKay, *A History of Western Society,* Eleventh Edition, pp. 908–909, 912–913)

49. **Answer: (C)**   Unlike in agriculture, industrial development was stupendous under the five-year plan. (McKay, *A History of Western Society,* Eleventh Edition, pp. 905–906)

50. **Answer: (E)**   The Nazi government generated jobs with large-scale public works projects and later with rearmament. There were no trade unions in Nazi Germany. (McKay, *A History of Western Society,* Eleventh Edition, p. 914)

51. **Answer: (A)**   By not allowing his army to retreat, Hitler lost some 300,000 German soldiers and the Soviets gained the advantage. (McKay, *A History of Western Society,* Eleventh Edition, pp. 929–930)

52. **Answer: (C)**   While on opposing sides, both doctrines allowed the two states to send military aid, even troops, to states where movements to destabilize the regime, either Communist or liberal, occurred. (McKay, *A History of Western Society,* Eleventh Edition, pp. 941, 983)

53. **Answer: (D)**   In Germany, Italy, and France, Christian Democrats dominated the political scene, while in Britain, the Labour Party defeated the Conservatives in 1945. Holland, Belgium, and Norway were monarchies; Italy became a republic. (McKay, *A History of Western Society,* Eleventh Edition, pp. 944–945)

54. **Answer: (B)**   France and Germany under their Christian Democratic leaders forged European economic cooperation. France created a mixed economy, and all adopted social welfare programs. (McKay, *A History of Western Society,* Eleventh Edition, pp. 944–947)

55. **Answer: (A)**   Brandt made a trip to Poland in 1970 and opened relations with East Germany. (McKay, *A History of Western Society,* Eleventh Edition, pp. 972–973)

56. **Answer: (C)**   The Communists were never the largest party in Italy, nor were the conflicts in Turkey and Greece over when the Marshall Plan was announced. The United States offered aid to all European nations, but Stalin refused it for eastern Europe. (McKay, *A History of Western Society,* Eleventh Edition, pp. 941–942)

57. **Answer: (E)**   At Teheran, they decided to defeat Germany through a direct attack on German forces in France, which meant that only the Soviet Union would liberate eastern Europe. The basic shape of western versus eastern postwar Europe had its origins here. There were several important conferences planning for postwar Europe. (McKay, *A History of Western Society,* Eleventh Edition, p. 939)

58. **Answer: (D)** It was the sudden expansion of unprepared universities that infuriated the students already upset over the U.S. war. They demanded educational reforms. Most belonged to the New Left and supported Algerian independence. The French were not militarily involved in the U.S. war in Vietnam. (McKay, *A History of Western Society,* Eleventh Edition, pp. 979–981)

59. **Answer: (D)** Inflation, as well as stagnation and high unemployment and energy costs, marked this economic downturn. England, Germany, and France, after trying another approach initially, cut their budgets by reducing social welfare spending and other expenses. (McKay, *A History of Western Society,* Eleventh Edition, pp. 983–987)

60. **Answer: (B)** The middle classes in both the capitalistic West and the Communist East were more and more dominated by managers or technocrats, experts in their respective fields. Most family-owned businesses disappeared, and while professionals were important members of the middle classes, they didn't dominate. There was greater equality in the early postwar period. (McKay, *A History of Western Society,* Eleventh Edition, p. 963)

61. **Answer: (B)** Indonesia had to fight the Dutch, Indochina the French. They achieved independence without help from either China or the United States within a decade of India's independence in the mid-1950s. (McKay, *A History of Western Society,* Eleventh Edition, pp. 958–960)

62. **Answer: (E)** The Common Market, later the European Economic Community, was a huge success economically. Germany and France were key players right from the beginning. Britain only joined in 1973. Britain limited the initial efforts at political unification. It still uses the pound, not the euro, as its currency. (McKay, *A History of Western Society,* Eleventh Edition, pp. 945–946)

63. **Answer: (B)** Both the 1956 Hungarian revolution and the 1968 "Prague Spring" were crushed by the invasion of Soviet and Warsaw Pact forces in order to prevent the spread of liberal reform movements. (McKay, *A History of Western Society,* Eleventh Edition, pp. 954–955, 982–983)

64. **Answer: (B)** It was the Solidarity movement in Poland that led to revolution in eastern Europe. (McKay, *A History of Western Society,* Eleventh Edition, pp. 994–996, 998–1000)

65. **Answer: (D)** Only in Romania was the Communist ruler executed. Ceauşescu was executed by military court in 1989. (McKay, *A History of Western Society,* Eleventh Edition, pp. 1000–1001)

66. **Answer: (D)** Gorbachev sought to reform the Soviet Union in order to save it. Yeltsin came on the scene after the reforms were already in place. Gorbachev renounced the Brezhnev Doctrine. (McKay, *A History of Western Society,* Eleventh Edition, pp. 997–998)

67. **Answer: (A)** Lithuania was the first to declare independence. Yeltsin, not Gorbachev, was president of the Russian Federation and announced his intentions to declare Russia independent of the Soviet Union a few months after Lithuania's bold move. (McKay, *A History of Western Society,* Eleventh Edition, pp. 1002–1003)

68. **Answer: (A)** When Hungary opened its borders, large numbers of East Germans fled through its gates; this led the East German government to open the Berlin Wall a few months later. (McKay, *A History of Western Society,* p. 1000)

69. **Answer: (C)** The transfer of ownership from the Soviet government to its former managers and the intrusion of criminal elements limited opportunities for ordinary

citizens to successfully enter the new economy. Privatization resulted in the concentration of wealth and large-scale enterprises that sought to eliminate competition. (McKay, *A History of Western Society,* Eleventh Edition, pp. 1008–1009)

70. **Answer: (D)** Western European countries have become multicultural with the development of new art, music, and literature fusing different cultural traditions. Muslim populations in several cities constitute well over 10 percent. Immigration from Muslim countries has continued to climb. In France, immigrants live in suburbs on the outskirts of Paris; in England, they congregate in smaller cities. There had been a brain drain to the United States in the early postwar period, but that diminished with Europe's development of its own scientific and research institutions. (McKay, *A History of Western Society,* Eleventh Edition, pp. 1025–1029)

71. **Answer: (E)** Maastricht established a monetary union. The treaty accepting borders was the Paris Accord. NATO remains in force. (McKay, *A History of Western Society,* Eleventh Edition, pp. 1002, 1016–1017)

72. **Answer: (A)** Croatian, Kosovan, and Bosnian nationalist goals of independence conflicted with Serbian nationalist goals for Greater Serbia. All these peoples are Slavs. The violence occurred after the Communists lost power and played little further role. (McKay, *A History of Western Society,* Eleventh Edition, pp. 1013–1015)

73. **Answer: (D)** Britain and Spain both suffered lethal terrorist attacks in 2004 and 2005 made by residents or citizens in those counties. (McKay, *A History of Western Society,* Eleventh Edition, pp. 1026–1027)

74. **Answer: (C)** Immigrants from eastern Europe and Africa fled poverty and civil war. Illegal immigrants had a hard time getting to western Europe and often were smuggled in, but once they landed, they had an easy time traveling in Europe because of the EU's open borders. Anti-immigration political movements developed in most European countries in response to the growing immigrant, legal as well as illegal, population. (McKay, *A History of Western Society,* Eleventh Edition, pp. 1024–1025)

75. **Answer: (C)** Turkey has not been admitted to the EU, which has committed itself to protecting human rights. Global capitalism tends toward encouragement of large corporate structures. In many former Communist states, authoritarian leaders like Putin in Russia have taken charge, but they are not dictators. Nationalistic tensions have flared up all over the region. (McKay, *A History of Western Society,* Eleventh Edition, pp. 1011–1013)

76. **Answer: (D)** By definition, the victims of genocide belong to one ethnicity. Most other genocides (in Armenia, in Bosnia in Europe, in Rwanda in Africa, in Cambodia in Asia) have been low-tech operations in which children and women were murdered. The Nazis, however, employed the latest technology to implement their "final solution." (McKay, *A History of Western Society,* Eleventh Edition, pp. 923–927)

77. **Answer: (C)** Both wars were unpopular with Europeans. In the long run, though ties with the United States remained solid, European states increasingly responded independently to global affairs. (McKay, *A History of Western Society,* Eleventh Edition, pp. 978–979, 1032)

78. **Answer: (D)** The EU with nearly half a billion people proved to be an economic powerhouse. By admitting as members former Communist states in eastern Europe, it was becoming, perhaps, a United States of Europe. (McKay, *A History of Western Society,* Eleventh Edition, pp. 1016–1019)

79. **Answer: (E)** World War I began when Austria attacked Serbia, World War II when Germany attacked Poland. In neither case could the smaller states have defended

themselves on their own. (McKay, *A History of Western Society,* Eleventh Edition, pp. 827–828, 919)

80. **Answer: (E)** The fact that Hungary and Czechoslovakia are on the map means it could not be in the nineteenth century (options A, B) or before World War I; they came into being afterward. Because there is an East Germany, that means the map represents time after World War II. These states are all former satellites of the U.S.S.R. (McKay, *A History of Western Society,* Eleventh Edition, p. 999)

Answers for Section II: Part A

Remember that the two parts of the exam—Section I (multiple-choice) and Section II (three essays)—are equally weighted at 50 percent each in determining the final score. Of the three essays, the document-based question counts for 45 percent of the Section II score, and the thematic question essays together count for 55 percent of the Section II score.

As these are not official AP Exam questions, we don't have official AP scoring standards for them. But you can use the following general guidelines to score your own essays.

AP European History DBQ essays are scored using the core-scoring method. Each specific instruction before the DBQ question itself refers to a core point. Once you earn all core points, you can earn additional points for doing those tasks well or for effectively bringing in outside information.

Include a thesis.   To earn a point for your thesis, it must be specific, refer to documents, and not just repeat the question. If you don't earn a point for the thesis, you can't earn the point for supporting the thesis with an appropriate number of documents.

The following examples are of thesis statements that would not earn a point:

Women had many views about their roles over the centuries.

Or

Women have always been opposed to and unhappy about the roles they were given by society.

Why are these not acceptable? They don't refer to the documents in any specific way, nor do they address the specific terms of the questions. Here is an example of a stronger, more acceptable thesis, though it still needs some work:

Women had many views about their roles in society. Some argued that women had to serve as examples to others, while others argued that women were rational beings who should devote themselves to their intellect.

Here is an example of a strong thesis statement that would earn a point:

Women writers reflected their historical times in asserting the roles women should play. During the Renaissance, women sought to be educated and to play a role in literary and intellectual circles. In the seventeenth and eighteenth centuries, women writers focused on the importance of education for women and their rejection of superficial roles. In the nineteenth and twentieth centuries, women socialists saw the solution to women's rights in the labor movement.

Use a majority of the documents.   You must use at least half of the documents to earn this point. In the case of this practice exam, that means seven (six would be half; seven constitutes a "majority"). Using a document means discussing something in the box specifically. You can still earn this point even if you make mistakes on one or two documents.

Interpret documents correctly. You are allowed to make only one major error, which is defined as an interpretation that leads you to an erroneous conclusion or to an erroneous grouping. A major error, for example, would be if you described Christine de Pizan as a radical feminist.

Group the documents. You must have three groups of documents. A group must have at least two documents in it, discussed specifically and together. Be specific when describing each group; that is, don't merely list documents together by number (for example, Documents 4, 5, and 7). Typical ways of making groups include: by opinion of author, by identity of author (nationality, political party or orientation, gender, age, position, and so on), by type of document (speeches, government documents, artworks, etc.), or by time period.
Possible groups in this DBQ include:

French: Christine de Pizan [1], Labé [4], Loir [7]
English: Cary [5], Astell [6], Montagu [8], Wollstonecraft [9], Steel [12]
15th century: Christine de Pizan [1], Cereta [2]
16th century: Teresa of Ávila [3], Labé [4]
18th century: Astell [6], Loir [7], Montagu [8], Wollstonecraft [9]
19th/20th century: Zetkin [10], Popp [11], Steel [12]
Condemns women for being frivolous: Labé [4], Montagu [8], Wollstonecraft [9]
Asks women to be good examples: Christine de Pizan [1], Steel [12]
Is concerned about virtue: Cereta [2], Teresa of Ávila [3], Montagu [8],
    Wollstonecraft [9]
Asks women to contribute to society: Montagu [8], Zetkin [10], Popp [11]
Claims women are rational: Cereta [2], Labé [4], Montagu [8], Wollstonecraft [9]
Religious orientation: Teresa of Ávila [3], Cary [5]
Humanistic training: Cereta [2], Labé [4]
Socialists: Zetkin [10], Popp [11]

Analyze point of view. This is a crucial core point, one that some students don't do or do poorly. POV analysis shows that you understand that a particular person wrote a document at a particular time and place for a particular purpose, and that it may not present the whole truth. It's important to think about the reliability of the document. For example, the events recorded in a letter may be presented in a way meant to influence the opinion of the letter's recipient. They may not be entirely truthful. Another way to do POV analysis is to connect the source's position in society or anything given in the source identification with the views the source expresses. The document summaries that follow show examples of the POV analysis you might make for each document.

Analyze individual documents.

Document 1   Christine de Pizan exhorts women at court to be demure, modest, and well behaved and emphasizes the role of the princess in maintaining such behavior. POV: Although seeking to enhance the prestige of women, the author is careful not to do so at the expense of their modesty. She might be seeking the patronage of a princess and therefore wants to emphasize the importance of the leadership of the princess at court. She had to take care to preserve her own reputation and therefore stressed the importance of modest behavior.

Document 2   Laura Cereta criticizes a male correspondent for praising her intellect, saying that all women are born with such possibilities but only some choose to pursue them. She connects intellectual pursuit with virtue, and she implicitly criticizes women who spend their energies adorning themselves. POV: As a woman humanist, Cereta sought acceptance from male humanists, which was not easily achieved. The sense of the human capabilities she expresses reflects Renaissance Neoplatonism; it's an insult to that sense if she is seen as unique among women. She also wants to show that she has worked as hard as any male humanist to acquire classical skills and knowledge; this is why she emphasizes the importance of diligence. Renaissance women adorned themselves with beautiful fabrics and jewels to express the wealth of their families, but Cereta is rejecting this as the most useful activity for women.

Document 3 Teresa of Ávila complains about the loose immorality of women and the dangers such women pose to men. She argues that such women have turned away from God. Women, she says, are naturally pure and inclined to the good and deserve respect from men for that reason. POV: As a religious figure, Teresa of Ávila is little concerned with women's scholarship or prestige; she's concerned about morality and goodness. She also is very modest, and she sees that being a woman is itself enough to lower her self-esteem; this reflects a Christian sense of the moral weakness of women beginning with Eve. As an author, she is also trying to avoid the sin of pride. She also argues that good women must be given respect and power; religious women, nuns like herself, belong in this category.

Document 4 Louise Labé criticizes women for superficial preoccupations when it's now possible for women to become educated in science and humanities. She applauds those women who take advantage of these new freedoms, and comments that education and culture truly belong to the women who acquire them, unlike jewels, which they can use but not own. POV: Labé is writing during the French Renaissance in the sixteenth century and reflects the increasing possibilities for women of that period. Because she is a well-known poet, she wants to be respected for that rather than typical womanly traits. As this is a private letter to a woman, her intent is to encourage her friend to engage in letters, and it probably reflects her true feelings.

Document 5 Mary Cary laments how few men and even fewer women are ready for the highest spiritual level and are ready to act like prophets. She expects that soon not only will men be able to prophesize but women will, too. A time will come in which there will be greater equality all around. POV: Cary reflects the equalitarian spirit of the radical millenarian group she was a member of during the English Revolution. Radicals could imagine not only social equality, but also gender equality, which for her, a religious person, meant the equal ability and opportunity to prophesize. Her writing a book about the New Jerusalem indicates her belief that she was already able to do so.

Document 6 Mary Astell condemns marriage in a passage that is highly ironical in tone. She lambastes men for depriving women of their equality, doing harm to people, and spinning their wheels in their search for power. She defines marriage as subjugation, as little more than slavery, and laments that women with few aspirations are the ones who are considered praiseworthy. POV: As Astell never married, her views on marriage are theoretical and not based on experience.

Document 7 Marianne Loir portrays Madame du Châtelet in a beguilingly feminine way. POV: Although a woman artist, Loir focuses on Madame du Châtelet's feminine attractions rather than her scholarship. There are no notebooks or any symbols of scholarship in the portrait, even though Madame du Châtelet was widely admired for her intellectual gifts.

Document 8 Lady Montagu condemns women for being frivolous and rejecting the use of reason, which she says makes them useless in society and even in their own families. She calls upon women to reject those authors who disparage women and to give up being amiable in order to become estimable. POV: Lady Montagu defined her social role as much greater than limited to aristocratic elegance. Although she herself is an aristocrat, she condemns the typical virtues associated with women of her class.

Document 9 Mary Wollstonecraft condemns the frivolities of women and exhorts them to live up to their rational potential. Such frivolities make women weak and sensuous and are encouraged by men. POV: Written during the French Revolution, *A Vindication of the Rights of Women* was a crucial feminist tract that sought to extend the rights won by French men in 1789 to women. Recognizing that these rights were unlikely to be given to women by men, she focuses on getting women to change themselves, as she herself has done by becoming educated and a serious writer.

Document 10 Clara Zetkin condemns women for being easily swayed into becoming scabs and weakening the labor movement. Women need the strength and training that will come with being members of a labor union. POV: As a socialist, Zetkin is concerned about proletarian women specifically and believes that only membership in labor unions can save them. For her, enlightenment for women comes from participation in the socialist movement, not by study and use of reason on their own. That she is German reflects the great importance of the socialist movement there.

Document 11 Adelheid Popp describes the sorry conditions for working women in Vienna, even in a good factory, and she reveals how empowering it was for her to become a socialist and discuss politics rather than inconsequential stories. POV: Popp's statement seems to verify Zetkin's exhortation that participation in the socialist movement is empowering. As a woman who took on roles that typically were men's, she makes the point to say that speaking as a socialist made her sound like a man, that is, someone with authority. As a socialist, she also shows that even improvements in the factory system will not be enough, as workers will still be beholden to the foremen.

Document 12 Annie Steel reflects two aspects of English attitudes in India. On the one hand, she urges women to learn Hindustani and to not waste their time on overzealousness in housework. On the other hand, she articulates the main role of educated women is to run an efficient and orderly household by being efficient and orderly themselves. She describes the Indians as childlike. POV: Steel's portrayal of the Indians as inferior and childlike is similar to Kipling's in "White Man's Burden," and it reflects the typical attitude of the British colonists. Her definition of women's role is limited to the household, so although she calls for education and learning the native language, it is not so that women can make contributions to society but so that they can better manage their households. Her book is clearly written for the housekeeping market, so perhaps she tailored her views to homemakers, contradicting her own activities as a writer in the public sphere.

Answers for Section II: Parts B and C

General AP Scoring Standards for Thematic Essay Questions

The thematic essays are scored on a scale of 0 to 9, with 0 being a real score. A response that is completely off topic does not even earn a zero. Here are generic scoring guidelines for the essays in Parts B and C.

9–8

Has a clear, well-developed thesis
Is well organized
Addresses the terms of the question
Supports the thesis with substantial specific evidence
Has sophisticated analysis
May contain minor errors; even a 9 need not be flawless

7–6

Has a clear thesis
Addresses all parts of the question but discussion is uneven
Has competent analysis, but it may be superficial
Supports the thesis with some specific evidence

5–4

Contains a thesis, perhaps superficial or simplistic
Has uneven responses to the question's terms
May contain errors, factual or interpretative
Addresses the question with generally accurate discussion but without specific
    evidence; analysis is implicit or superficial
May contain major errors within a generally accurate and appropriate discussion
Is descriptive rather than analytical

3–2

Has weak or muddled thesis, perhaps suggesting false or inappropriate dichotomies
    or connections
Contains significant errors of chronology or fact
Has minimal discussion
Offers limited evidence

1–0

Has confused or absent thesis or merely restates the question
Misconstrues the question or omits major tasks
May contain major errors or irrelevant historical information
Addresses only one part of the question
Offers minimal or no evidence

Reread your essay and ask yourself the following questions—or if you can work with a fellow student in AP European History (APEH), read each other's essays and ask these questions:

1. How well-organized is the essay? Is it clearly divided into distinct paragraphs? Is there an introduction and a conclusion?

2. How clear is the thesis? Is the thesis statement at the beginning of the essay or in the conclusion?

3. How many arguments support the thesis?

4. How much evidence is used to support the thesis? How specific was it?

5. Were all parts of the question addressed? Was the discussion of the different parts more or less balanced?

6. How many of the points noted in the explanations of the answer were made in the essay?

7. Were there major factual, chronological, or interpretative errors? Or minor errors?

8. Was the analysis explicit or implicit? Was it sophisticated or minimal?

Now reread the Scoring Guidelines and give yourself a score.

In general, the scores on the document-based questions average higher than those of the thematic essay questions, because the DBQ is a skill-based question that uses evidence, while the thematic essays are content-based and require recall of information. The median score on the DBQ is 5 (usually because of lack of POV), while the median scores on the thematic essays are typically 4 to 5 on the first and approximately 3 to 4 on the second group, often because students run out of time.

Part B Responses

2. **Analyze how the causes and the course of World War I affected the negotiations at the Versailles Peace Conference.**

For this essay, you must connect the causes of the war and developments during the war to the peace settlement. Don't simply discuss the causes of the war or the peace settlement without drawing connections between the two.

One cause of the war was tensions and competition over colonial claims, particularly in Africa. The Moroccan crisis of 1905 was an incident between Germany and France that spurred hostilities. Another source of tension in Europe before the war was the competition between Austria and Russia over Ottoman territories in the Balkans. France and Britain coveted its Arab lands; for Britain it was a way to secure control over the Suez Canal, and both states were interested in trade in the eastern Mediterranean as well as in oil. During negotiations at Versailles, Britain and France made sure that they took the territories they wanted, in spite of promises made during the war and the principle of self-determination. Britain took East and West Africa and France got Cameroon from Germany. They also divided the former Ottoman Arab areas, with France getting Syria and Lebanon, and Britain getting Palestine, Iraq, and Jordan. At the conference, Britain and France created the mandate system, where their rule over colonies was officially authorized by the League of Nations and was theoretically temporary.

Germany's invasion of Belgium, in violation of the 1839 neutrality treaty, as well as its alliance with and support of Austria in its conflict with Serbia, was sufficient reason for Britain and France to assign the blame to Germany for starting the war. Once that responsibility was assigned, it was logical to them that Germany had to pay for the costs of the war. Therefore, war reparations were put into the treaty. This was an important issue particularly for Britain, as the length of the war had meant skyrocketing financial costs. Lloyd George had won the election in 1916 with the promise that Germany would pay for the war.

The terrible loss of human lives had a direct impact on peace negotiations. Because of its smaller population, France felt vulnerable to Germany. Because most of the war on the western front was fought in France and Belgium, France came into the negotiations wanting revenge and a permanently weakened Germany, as well as a buffer state between them. U.S. president Woodrow Wilson and Lloyd George were able to reduce these demands to a smaller Germany with a small army, a few battleships, and no air force; a demilitarized Rhineland; and the return of Alsace and Lorraine to France. A buffer state between Germany and Russia was made with the re-creation of Poland.

Wilson had articulated war aims for the United States in January 1918, and these were the focus of American interests in the peace negotiations. Among these Fourteen Points was creation of a League of Nations, an international body to prevent future wars. In order to gain the agreement of the doubting Georges Clemenceau and Lloyd George for the League, Wilson did not insist on the application of some of his other points, particularly self-determination.

3. **Analyze the reasons for the rise of a successful Fascist movement in Italy, and describe how it implemented its ideology when it took power in 1922 up to when Italy joined the Rome-Berlin Axis in 1936.**

This is another common question; the key element is your ability to analyze fascist ideology in comparison with Fascist practice.

Possible thesis: In spite of their ideology, Italian Fascists took power legally and were cautious and limited in their implementation of fascism.

The ideology of Italian fascism, as articulated by its leader, Benito Mussolini, was a fundamental rejection of constitutionalism, liberalism, democracy, and pacifism. Instead, Fascists promoted action and the use of violence as legitimate political tools, and they demanded a state that would end the class rivalries impeding Italian unity—one led by a single leader who represented the soul of Italy and who would return it to greatness. Political parties, labor unions, representative government—all would be abolished. Fascist bands attacked socialists and destroyed their newspaper, offices, and union halls.

Nevertheless, the Fascists took power legally, after the March on Rome when the king asked Mussolini to become prime minister. Although it considered itself a revolutionary party, the Fascists never abolished the monarchy or challenged the church, a major political power in Italy. Instead, they negotiated a settlement with the papacy, which had rejected the new Italian state since its formation in 1870. The Lateran Agreement returned to the church important rights, such as a role in the education of children. Therefore, the Italian Fascists left in place two important traditional authorities, the monarchy and the church.

Because they were a minority party in the Chamber of Deputies, it was several years before the Fascists could eliminate the other parties and restrict civil liberties. The first cabinet under Mussolini included ministers from other parties. The electoral law reform of 1923 ended up giving them an absolute majority after the election that year. The leader of the Socialist Party in the Chamber of Deputies, Giacomo Matteotti, was assassinated by the Fascists. The Fascists soon thereafter arrested political opponents, abolished civil liberties, and ended freedom of the press; by 1926 Italy became a one-party state. But elections were held, even if they were fixed, and the Fascists collaborated with the old conservative classes, taking little radical action on social and economic issues. Relatively few people were executed for political reasons under Mussolini.

But parts of fascist ideology were enacted. Fascists created a youth movement to indoctrinate the young, and they restricted the rights of women in the workforce and at home when they abolished divorce. The Fascist regime abolished labor unions, and big business was free to regulate itself. The end result was that workers lost benefits and political power.

Thus, Italian fascism was more authoritarian and conservative than radical in practice, though its ideology and accompanying rhetoric remained revolutionary.

4. **Describe how Leninism revised Marxism, and analyze how that helped the Bolsheviks to take power in Russia.**

Lenin revised Marxism in three ways. Firstly, while Marxist doctrine argued that revolution could only occur when industrialization had created a large enough proletariat to take power, Lenin argued that revolution could occur in a state that was still largely agricultural and feudal and the proletariat was small. Peasants could join the proletariat to make a revolutionary mass. Therefore, society could skip the bourgeois, industrial stage. Secondly, Marxists had come to believe that socialism could happen in an evolutionary process, rather than revolutionary. Lenin insisted that sudden, violent revolution was necessary, that evolutionary socialism would lead to compromise and trade union piecemeal negotiations, not socialism. Thirdly, revolution could succeed only if it was led by a small group of full-time Communist revolutionaries, completely committed to the cause. Communists should not forge a broad-based party with nonrevolutionary groups.

These ideas helped the Bolsheviks take power. The idea that revolution was possible in backward Russia was rejected by the other Marxist party, the Mensheviks, because it contradicted Marxist theory. The Bolsheviks, however, understood that the enraged peasants together with small numbers of well-organized workers could make the revolution. The Bolshevik Order Number 1 fomented revolution because it allowed the peasants to walk away from the front, thus depriving the tsarist regime of its military base; the peasants in the summer of 1917 were grabbing whatever land they could in anticipation that the Bolsheviks would redistribute the land. The Bolsheviks had already formed a small party while in exile in Switzerland; when Lenin returned to Russia in April 1917, they rejected compromise with the provisional government. Allowing a bourgeois state to take hold, according to Leninist theory, would unnecessarily delay the revolution and therefore the easing of the suffering of peasants and workers. Once they had won a majority in the Petrograd Soviet, they were easily able to stage a coup d'état and with relatively few people take power in November 1917.

During the civil war, Lenin's model of top-down control (in contrast to Menshevik democratic principles) made the Bolsheviks effective. Lenin's willingness to use violence for political purposes was demonstrated when he used Bolshevik troops to disband the Constituent Assembly that had a Social Revolutionary, not a Bolshevik, majority.

Part C Responses

5. **Discuss the economic problems faced by western Europeans from the end of the Second World War until 1985, and analyze the success or failure of governments in dealing with those problems.**

In the early postwar period, western European states were faced with a number of serious economic problems: the need to rebuild infrastructure and factories, transitioning from wartime to peacetime production, inflation, and production shortages and resulting black marketeering. These states were helped by the enormous infusion of funds from the United States as part of its Marshall Plan to rebuild Europe quickly.

Western European states expanded already existing social welfare programs in the postwar period. The Labour Government of England, elected shortly after the end of the war, nationalized major industries and banks. France, now in its Fourth Republic, established a mixed economy, with elements of both socialism and capitalism. France and West

Germany elected their first postwar governments in 1949—both were run by Christian Democrats. Germany retained its extensive social welfare system while reintroducing free-market capitalism.

Western European states recovered quickly and reached prosperity within a few years after the end of the war. Germany, France, Italy, and three small states organized the Common Market. This arrangement ended tariffs among the members—first on steel and coal, and later on other commodities, and it helped create a European economic revival to compete with the United States. Overall, economic policies in the three major states of western Europe were highly successful.

In the 1970s and 1980s, western European states suffered economic decline, with high energy costs, stagnation, and unemployment figures reaching as high as they had been during the Great Depression. Britain and Germany instituted austerity measures. Britain, under Prime Minister Margaret Thatcher, elected in 1979, privatized previously nationalized industries, reduced the influence of trade unions, shrank the welfare state, and reinvigorated the economy by encouraging unbridled free-market capitalism. France initially attempted to address the crisis with a socialist program under President Mitterrand, but a few years later adapted austerity measures too. By 1985, all these policies were only marginally effective; the western European economy remained troubled by high unemployment and stagnation.

6. **Compare and contrast the goals and practices of Nazi Germany and Stalinist Russia in the 1930s, and explain how these helped prepare for war.**

Similarities: Both totalitarian regimes were one-party states with the goal of thorough societal transformation. No civil liberties or freedom of the press were allowed; the governments relied on constant propaganda to mobilize the populations, and they arrested and persecuted political enemies. Millions of civilians were imprisoned or murdered in both states. Each government's economic goals—in both cases to expand industry—were to be achieved by state intervention. In both states, the leaders were treated as godlike figures.

Differences: Ideological goals were profoundly different. The proponents of communism believed they were achieving equality and social justice that would be models for international change, while the proponents of Nazism sought an unequal order with privileges for the racially pure elite at the expense of peoples judged inferior (e.g., Slavs, Jews). Nazi ideology called for German expansion into the east, and it glorified violence; communist ideology under Stalin focused on "socialism in one country." German ideology particularly targeted Jews, while Russia promised equal treatment of peoples of all ethnic backgrounds. Although the German government intervened in the economy, it relied on capitalism and was allied with the middle and upper classes. Its economic policies successfully pulled Germany out of the depression. In Russia, the Communists crushed those classes and expropriated their property; there was virtually no private economy in the U.S.S.R. Stalin pursued rapid and extensive industrialization with five-year plans and forced collectivization of agriculture.

Preparations for war: Through their economic policies during the 1930s, both states were prepared for war, with strong industries and effective government planning. Both states had built effective propaganda machines and achieved notable successes that stirred the patriotism of their peoples. Germany was planning for war and instituted rearmament and conscription, while the U.S.S.R. did little to plan for war. But when Germany invaded Russia in 1941, the mechanisms were in place for rapid transformation of the economy for war.

7. **Describe three eastern European resistance movements to Soviet domination from 1946 to 1985 and analyze the reasons for their success or failure.**

Possible theses:

(1) Resistance movements in the Soviet bloc had no chance of achieving the reforms they demanded if Soviet troops were present or easily available.

(2) Poland, more than any other eastern European state except Yugoslavia, successfully resisted Soviet domination by cautiously avoiding direct challenges to the U.S.S.R.
This essay asks you to address several decades of eastern European history focusing on attempts to overthrow or resist Soviet rule or Soviet-dominated regimes and evaluating the reasons for their success and failure. You can easily trace resistance movements by decade.

1940s: In 1948, Tito broke away from Soviet control and established an independent Communist state in Yugoslavia. He succeeded because there were no Russian troops there or nearby. Yugoslavia, a multiethnic state, became more prosperous and modernized than the states under Soviet domination and pursued an independent foreign policy, while remaining Communist.

1950s: Poles and Hungarians both revolted in 1956 for nationalistic reasons and for greater political and economic democracy. Widespread rioting in Poland brought about a change of government with a greater degree of autonomy. But when a liberal Communist regime took power in Hungary in October 1956, which promised free elections and other reforms, the Soviet troops that had been forced to leave returned with Warsaw Pact troops and tanks. The Hungarians, hoping in vain for help from the United States, fought back against the tanks but were crushed. The disappointment of the Hungarian reform movement led most eastern Europeans to believe that they had to accommodate Soviet demands.

1960s: In 1968, a liberal reform movement successfully took the reins of power in Czechoslovakia. Alexander Dubček, the leader of the reformers in the Czech Communist Party, was elected in January and initiated a series of reforms known as the "Prague Spring." These included the reduction of censorship and bureaucratic planning, greater political and artistic freedom, and substantial democracy within the party as well as in industry. In August 1968, Warsaw Pact troops invaded and occupied Czechoslovakia, ended the reform program, and replaced the leadership. The U.S.S.R. announced the Brezhnev Doctrine that claimed the right to intervene in the internal affairs of members of the Warsaw Pact.

1980s: In Poland in 1980, a strike of thousands of workers in the Gdansk shipyards developed into a movement called Solidarity, which demanded not only redress of economic grievances but also free trade unions, civil liberties, and economic reforms. They occupied the shipyards until the government gave in to Solidarity's demands. The support of a new pope of Polish origin helped fuel the resistance. Led by Lech Walesa, Solidarity drew millions of members, but it did not try to take power directly, settling for some concessions. Nevertheless, the Communist leader of Poland crushed the movement, arresting its leaders and outlawing it in December 1981. But as the government was unwilling to impose full-scale repression, Solidarity continued to be an important voice for reform. There was greater political and artistic freedom in Poland in the 1980s than elsewhere in the Soviet Bloc. Solidarity would emerge later in the decade as the fulcrum around which the end of Communist rule in Poland was achieved.